T0344538

Network Security Attacks and Countermeasures

Dileep Kumar G.
Adama Science and Technology University, Ethiopia

Manoj Kumar Singh
Adama Science and Technology University, Ethiopia

M.K. Jayanthi
King Khalid University, Saudi Arabia

A volume in the Advances in Information Security,
Privacy, and Ethics (AISPE) Book Series

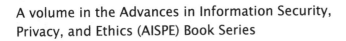

An Imprint of IGI Global

Published in the United States of America by
Information Science Reference (an imprint of IGI Global)
701 E. Chocolate Avenue
Hershey PA, USA 17033
Tel: 717-533-8845
Fax: 717-533-8661
E-mail: cust@igi-global.com
Web site: http://www.igi-global.com

Library of Congress Cataloging-in-Publication Data

Network security attacks and countermeasures / Dileep Kumar G., Manoj Kumar Singh, and M.K. Jayanthi, editors.
    pages cm
  Includes bibliographical references and index.
  ISBN 978-1-4666-8761-5 (hardcover) -- ISBN 978-1-4666-8762-2 (ebook) 1. Computer networks--Security measures. 2.
Computer crimes--Prevention. I. Kumar G., Dileep, 1982- II. Singh, Manoj Kumar, 1972- III. Jayanthi, M. K., 1976-
  TK5105.59.N3377 2016
  005.8--dc23
                              2015019967

This book is published in the IGI Global book series Advances in Information Security, Privacy, and Ethics (AISPE) (ISSN: 1948-9730; eISSN: 1948-9749)

British Cataloguing in Publication Data
A Cataloguing in Publication record for this book is available from the British Library.

All work contributed to this book is new, previously-unpublished material. The views expressed in this book are those of the authors, but not necessarily of the publisher.

For electronic access to this publication, please contact: eresources@igi-global.com.

Advances in Information Security, Privacy, and Ethics (AISPE) Book Series

ISSN: 1948-9730
EISSN: 1948-9749

Mission

As digital technologies become more pervasive in everyday life and the Internet is utilized in ever increasing ways by both private and public entities, concern over digital threats becomes more prevalent.

The **Advances in Information Security, Privacy, & Ethics (AISPE) Book Series** provides cutting-edge research on the protection and misuse of information and technology across various industries and settings. Comprised of scholarly research on topics such as identity management, cryptography, system security, authentication, and data protection, this book series is ideal for reference by IT professionals, academicians, and upper-level students.

Coverage

- Electronic Mail Security
- CIA Triad of Information Security
- Privacy-Enhancing Technologies
- Data Storage of Minors
- Risk Management
- Cyberethics
- Security Classifications
- Security Information Management
- Tracking Cookies
- Technoethics

IGI Global is currently accepting manuscripts for publication within this series. To submit a proposal for a volume in this series, please contact our Acquisition Editors at Acquisitions@igi-global.com or visit: http://www.igi-global.com/publish/.

Titles in this Series

For a list of additional titles in this series, please visit: www.igi-global.com

Network Security Attacks and Countermeasures
Dileep Kumar G. (Adama Science and Technology University, Ethiopia) Manoj Kumar Singh (Adama Science and Technology University, Ethiopia) and M.K. Jayanthi (King Khalid University, Saudi Arabia)
Information Science Reference • copyright 2016 • 311pp • H/C (ISBN: 9781466687615) • US $205.00 (our price)

Next Generation Wireless Network Security and Privacy
Kamaljit I. Lakhtaria (Gujarat University, India)
Information Science Reference • copyright 2015 • 372pp • H/C (ISBN: 9781466686878) • US $205.00 (our price)

Improving Information Security Practices through Computational Intelligence
Wasan Shaker Awad (Ahlia University, Bahrain) El Sayed M. El-Alfy (King Fahd University of Petroleum and Minerals, Saudi Arabia) and Yousif Al-Bastaki (University of Bahrain, Bahrain)
Information Science Reference • copyright 2016 • 327pp • H/C (ISBN: 9781466694262) • US $210.00 (our price)

Handbook of Research on Security Considerations in Cloud Computing
Kashif Munir (King Fahd University of Petroleum & Minerals, Saudi Arabia) Mubarak S. Al-Mutairi (King Fahd University of Petroleum & Minerals, Saudi Arabia) and Lawan A. Mohammed (King Fahd University of Petroleum & Minerals, Saudi Arabia)
Information Science Reference • copyright 2015 • 408pp • H/C (ISBN: 9781466683877) • US $325.00 (our price)

Emerging Security Solutions Using Public and Private Key Cryptography Mathematical Concepts
Addepalli VN Krishna (Stanley College of Engineering and Technology for Women, India)
Information Science Reference • copyright 2015 • 302pp • H/C (ISBN: 9781466684843) • US $225.00 (our price)

Handbook of Research on Emerging Developments in Data Privacy
Manish Gupta (State University of New York at Buffalo, USA)
Information Science Reference • copyright 2015 • 507pp • H/C (ISBN: 9781466673816) • US $325.00 (our price)

Handbook of Research on Securing Cloud-Based Databases with Biometric Applications
Ganesh Chandra Deka (Ministry of Labour and Employment, India) and Sambit Bakshi (National Institute of Technology Rourkela, India)
Information Science Reference • copyright 2015 • 530pp • H/C (ISBN: 9781466665590) • US $335.00 (our price)

Handbook of Research on Threat Detection and Countermeasures in Network Security
Alaa Hussein Al-Hamami (Amman Arab University, Jordan) and Ghossoon M. Waleed al-Saadoon (Applied Sciences University, Bahrain)
Information Science Reference • copyright 2015 • 426pp • H/C (ISBN: 9781466665835) • US $325.00 (our price)

www.igi-global.com

701 E. Chocolate Ave., Hershey, PA 17033
Order online at www.igi-global.com or call 717-533-8845 x100
To place a standing order for titles released in this series, contact: cust@igi-global.com
Mon-Fri 8:00 am - 5:00 pm (est) or fax 24 hours a day 717-533-8661

Editorial Advisory Board

Table of Contents

Detailed Table of Contents

Chapter 1

C. V. Anchugam, Government Arts College (Autonomous), India
K. Thangadurai, Government Arts College (Autonomous), India

Writing a chapter on network security is something like writing a brief introduction to flying a commercial airliner. Dissimilar, data communications of the past, today's networks incorporate varied devices that handle the data because it passes from the sender to the receiver. The first question to address is what we mean "network security". Network security consists of the provisions and policies adopted by a network administrator to prevent and monitor unauthorized access, misuse, modification, or denial of a computer network and network-accessible resources. A generic definition of security is "freedom from risk or danger and safety". However it is not only human errors that can cause problem to network security, problems can also be caused by natural forces like fire breakouts, earthquakes, floods lightning etc. The ways network administrators think about securing networks has been changed by an increasingly dynamic and technically challenging risk environment. Security is an assessment of risk. Secure environments are designed and developed through an intentional effort.

Chapter 2

Arif Sari, Girne American University, Cyprus

The varieties of studies in literature have been addressed by the researchers to solve security problems of Mobile Wireless Ad Hoc Networks (MANET) against denial of service (DoS) and distributed denial of service (DDoS) attacks. Attackers have proposed variety of methods and techniques by considering weaknesses of the wireless nature of the channels and specific characteristics of mobile wireless networks. This chapter evaluates variety of attacks proposed in the literature against MANET by classifying variety of security strategies and mechanisms proposed by the researchers. The algorithms are discussed and explained separately. All these attacks are classified in different categories and security strategies proposed by the researchers have been explained.

Virtual Private Network, Its 'Virtual', Its 'Private' and it's a 'Network'. A virtual private network (VPN) provides a secure connection between a sender and a receiver over a public non-secure network such as the Internet. A secure connection is generally associated with private networks. (A private network is a network that is owned, or at least controlled via leased lines, by an organization.). We can define a VPN by the following relationship: VPN = Tunneling + Security + QoS Parameters. This Chapter deals with Advantages of VPNs, Types of VPNs, VPN Architectures, VPN Models, VPN Devices, Technologies and Protocols Used to Enable Remote Access VPNs.

Network security has become more important and the growing rate of network attacks together with hacker, cracker, and criminal enterprises are increasing, that impact to the availability, confidentiality, and integrity of vital information data. In order to understand and defend against network attacks, it is necessary to understand the kind of attack. This chapter focuses on the provisioning of a method for the analysis and categorization of both computer and network attacks, thus providing assistance in combating new attacks, improving computer and network security as well as providing consistency in language when describing attacks. Attacks are thus attempts by unauthorized individuals to access or modify information, to deceive the system so that an unauthorized individual can take over an authorized session, or to disrupt service to authorized users. During this chapter we tend to area unit providing the elucidation against black hole attack that relies on fuzzy rule in case study section.

Wireless Sensor Networks (WSN) consists of large number of low-cost, resource-constrained sensor nodes. The constraints of the WSN which make it to be vulnerable to attacks are based on their characteristics which include: low memory, low computation power, they are deployed in hostile area and left unattended, small range of communication capability and low energy capabilities. Examples of attacks which can occur in a WSN are sinkhole attack, selective forwarding attack and wormhole attack. One of the impacts of these attacks is that, one attack can be used to launch other attacks. This book chapter presents an exploration of the analysis of the existing solutions which are used to detect and identify passive and active attack in WSN. The analysis is based on advantages and limitations of the proposed solutions.

Chapter 6

Mamta Bachani, Mehran University of Engineering and Technology, Pakistan
Ahsan Memon, Mehran University of Engineering and Technology, Pakistan
Faisal Karim Shaikh, Mehran University of Engineering and Technology, Pakistan & Umm
*   Al-Qura University, Saudi Arabia*

This chapter aims to develop an understanding of sensor networks and the security threats posed to them, owing to the inherently insecure wireless nature. It also highlights the current security issues associated with the exchange of information and presents respective countermeasures that can be used to secure the network of malevolent behavior. It builds the reader's understanding of security threats by presenting an idealistic security mechanism and comparing it to currently practiced security mechanisms. Doing so, it identifies the security flaws in each mechanism, henceforth, enumerating a list of well-known security attacks that are connected to the respective security flaws. To provide a better understanding of security threats, the security attacks, in general, are discussed in the perspective of a network administrator, and an adversary. Their impact is also considered from the side of a network administrator and its respective benefits to the adversary. The chapter is later concluded along with future directives and an insight on requirements of forthcoming technologies.

Chapter 7

Dileep Kumar, Adama Science and Technology University, Ethiopia

Billions of people rely on internet to discover and share ideas with the world. However, the websites are vulnerable to deliver the attacks, preventing people to access them. The recent study of global surveys showed that DDoS Attacks evolved in strategy and tactics. A Distributed Denial of Service (DDoS) attack is a new emerging bigger threat that target organization's business critical services such as e-commerce transactions, financial trading, email or web site access. A DDoS attack is a large-scale, coordinated attack on the availability of services of a victim system or network resource, launched indirectly through many compromised computers on the Internet. To create attacks, attackers first discover vulnerable sites or hosts on the network. Then vulnerable hosts are exploited by attackers who use their vulnerability to gain access to these hosts. This chapter deals with the introduction, architecture and classification of DDoS Attacks.

Chapter 8

Mohammad Jabed Morshed Chowdhury, Daffodil International University, Bangladesh
Dileep Kumar G, Adama Science and Technology University, Ethiopia

Distributed Denial of Service (DDoS) attack is considered one of the major security threats in the current Internet. Although many solutions have been suggested for the DDoS defense, real progress in fighting those attacks is still missing. In this chapter, the authors analyze and experiment with cluster-based filtering for DDoS defense. In cluster-based filtering, unsupervised learning is used to create profile of the network traffic. Then the profiled traffic is passed through the filters of different capacity to the servers. After applying this mechanism, the legitimate traffic will get better bandwidth capacity than the malicious traffic. Thus the effect of bad or malicious traffic will be lesser in the network. Before describing the proposed solutions, a detail survey of the different DDoS countermeasures have been presented in the chapter.

Chapter 9

Manoranjan Pradhan, GITA, India

Chinmaya Kumar Nayak, GITA, India

Sateesh Kumar Pradhan, Utkal University, India

Over the last two decades, computer and network security has become a main issue, especially with the increase number of intruders and hackers, therefore systems were designed to detect and prevent intruders. This chapter per the authors investigated the most important design approaches, by mainly focusing on their collecting, analysis, responding capabilities and types of current IDS products. For the collecting capability, there were two main approaches, namely host- and network-based IDSs. Therefore, a combination of the two approaches in a hybrid implementation is ideal, as it will offer the highest level of protection at all levels of system functions. The analysis capability of an IDS can be characterised by the misuse and anomaly detection approaches. Therefore, a combination of the two approaches should improve the analysis capability of an IDS i.e. hybrid of misuse and anomaly detection.

Chapter 10

Bijaya Kumar Panda, GITA, India

Manoranjan Pradhan, GITA, India

Sateesh Kumar Pradhan, Utkal University, India

In the last decade, there is a rapid growth in the use of Internet by the organization for information sharing. As information is very vital to the organizations, it should be preserved and insulated from any unauthorized access or alternation. In last few years, attacks on the computer infrastructures have increased exponentially. Several information security techniques are available now a days like firewalls, anti-virus software and Intrusion prevention systems (IPSs), which are important tools for protecting an organization from intrusions. Now most attacks are impossible to defend with firewalls and anti-virus software alone. Without an IPS, such attacks are difficult to detect and prevent. This chapter presents different definitions of intrusion prevention system with meaningful explanation; compare network IPS with Host IPS, common and the advanced detection methods, common IPS components, coverage of attacks by IPS and criteria to select right IPS. Finally, this chapter concludes with an analysis of the challenges that still remain to be resolved.

Chapter 11

P. Natesan, Kongu Engineering College, India

P. Balasubramanie, Kongu Engineering College, India

G. Gowrison, Institute of Road and Transport Technology, India

Recently machine learning based intrusion detection system developments have been subjected to extensive researches because they can detect both misuse detection and anomaly detection. In this paper, we propose an AdaBoost based algorithm for network intrusion detection system with single weak classifier. In this algorithm, the classifiers such as Bayes Net, Naïve Bayes and Decision tree are used as weak classifiers. KDDCup99 dataset is used in these experiments to demonstrate that boosting algorithm can greatly improve the classification accuracy of weak classification algorithms. Our approach achieves higher detection rate with low false alarm rates and is scalable for large datasets, resulting in an effective intrusion detection system.

Behnam Rahnama, ScaleDB Inc., USA
Arif Sari, Girne American University, Cyprus
Marwan Yassin Ghafour, Sulaimani Polytechnic University, Iraq

Security is utilized to keep the information safe. Online resources, e-commerce, internet banking and a
lot of similar services are protected by use of well-known protocols such as Secure Socket Layer (SSL).
This protocol makes use of the RSA key exchange protocol for authentication. New innovations and
boost ups in the computational power of supercomputers today makes it quite easier than before to break
through RSA and consequently decrypt the payload transferred over SSL. In this research demonstrates
the use of SSL; how to utilize it in the best shape? We also discuss reasons of why we need to improve
its strength. The proposed solution is to replace the RSA key exchange mechanism utilized in SSL with
Elliptic Curve Cryptography (ECC).

Alok Vishwakarma, Sysbiz Technologies, India
Wafa Waheeda S, Qatar University, Qatar

With increasing number of users on the internet, risk of security and probability of vulnerable attacks are
increasing day by day. For every user connected to network, security attacks like hacking and cracking
are very frequent which leaves enormous amounts of sensitive data at the risk of being altered, lost or
misused. This apparently leads to the need for security measures on ports and protocols also search for
application security, VPN, IPS, and a firewall support. The hacking and cracking threats and attacks in
a network are no longer in control with the existing methods and standard firewalls. The introduction
of Next Generation Firewalls leads to improved security over network. This chapter deals with hacking
and cracking attacks over network and their countermeasures, also focusing on the changing dynamics
of network security with next generation firewalls.

Preface

With the phenomenal growth in the Internet, network security has become an integral part of computer and information security. In order to come up with measures that make networks more secure, it is important to learn about the vulnerabilities that could exist in a computer network and then have an understanding of the typical attacks that have been carried out in such networks. This book to provide a framework for Network Attacks and emphasizes on issues related to Network Security Attacks.

There are many reasons why network security is hard, ranging from the fact that networks are increasingly sophisticated and complex to the fact that economic incentives can work against proper security. Network security is essentially asymmetric warfare where adversaries can probe anywhere but defend must be everywhere. This creates a technological bias in favor of the attackers.

As networks grow and incorporate more sophisticated technologies, it can become difficult to maintain the necessary situational awareness. However, the world of network security is evolving very rapidly. It is more important, then, to understand the principles on which the attacks and exploits are based in order to properly plan either a network attack or a network defense. The attacks are deadly because they exploit principles, assumptions, and practices that are true today and that we believe are likely to remain true for the foreseeable future.

The prospective audience for this book will be researchers, academics, Network administrators and practitioners from the fields of Network security. The book will also be of value to a wider audience of readers who are interested in monitoring the networks.

This book aims to increase evolutionary computation awareness in network security by providing a clear direction for the monitoring, analyzing and detection of network attacks that would improve the network security industry. In this sense, the intended audience will include all researchers who are trying to find effective solutions for the network attacks.

Security system designers and developers would benefit from reading such a book, as they would gain an understanding of network-based attacks that are needed for developing effective and efficient intrusion detection systems (IDS).

This book provides the information on security issues that exist in the network, illustration on various types of attacks, focusing on DDoS attacks, various countermeasures for the network security attacks etc.

Moreover, it will encourage the security industry to take a proactive attitude toward evolutionary defense mechanisms for the attacks, thus resulting in improved design of the network.

FEATURES

A computer network or just a network could be an assortment of connected computers. Two or a lot of computer systems are thought about as connected, if they will send and receive information from one another through a shared access medium. The communication entities in a computer network are typically called *principles, subjects or entities*. These principals will be additional divided into users, hosts and processes.

- A user could be a human entity, to blame for its actions in a computer network.
- A host is associate degree available entity inside a computer network. Every host incorporates a distinctive address inside a network.
- A method is associate degree instance of associate degree viable program. It's employed in client / server model, so as to tell apart between the consumer and also the server processes.
- A client method could be a method that creates requests of a network services.
- A server method could be a method that gives a network services.

In order to formalize the method that networking is performed, network reference models are developed, that cluster similar functions into abstractions called layers. Every layer's functions will communicate with a similar layer's functions of another network host. On a similar host, the functions of a selected layer have interfaces to speak with the layers bellow and on top of it. This abstraction simplifies and properly defines the mandatory actions for networking.

This book discusses the following features of Network Security,

- Introduction to Network Security,
- IP Spoofing and Issues related to Network Security Attacks,
- Virtual Private Networks
- Classification of Network Attacks and Countermeasures,
- Attacks in Wireless Sensor Networks,
- Sensor Networks in regard with security aspects and countermeasures
- AdaBoost Algorithm with Single weak classifier in Network Intrusion Detection
- Solving SSL Security Vulnerability by Applying ECC Authentication
- Intrusion Detection System and their Types,
- Intrusion Prevention System,
- Cluster based countermeasure for DDoS Attacks
- Security Issues in Mobile Wireless Networks and Virtual Private Networks

ORGANIZATION

The Chapters 1–3 give foundation while describing basic network security concepts- Introduction to Network Security, Security issues in mobile wireless networks, IP Spoofing and Virtual Private Network.

Chapters 4–6 cover Classification of Network Attacks and countermeasures, Attacks in Wireless Sensor Networks, Sensor Networks in regard with security aspects and countermeasures concepts.

Chapters 7–10 give description on Distributed Denial of Service Attacks and their types, Cluster based countermeasure for DDOS Attacks, Intrusion Detection and Intrusion Prevention Systems.

AdaBoost Algorithm with Single weak classifier in Network Intrusion Detection, Countering RSA Vulnerabilities and Its Replacement by ECC, Changing Dynamics of Network Security involving Hacking/Cracking with Next Generation Firewalls, and Privacy-Preserving Public Auditing and Data Integrity for Secured Cloud Storage are discussed in Chapters 11–13.

Chapter 1
Introduction to Network Security

C. V. Anchugam
Government Arts College (Autonomous), India

K. Thangadurai
Government Arts College (Autonomous), India

ABSTRACT

Writing a chapter on network security is something like writing a brief introduction to flying a commercial airliner. Dissimilar, data communications of the past, today's networks incorporate varied devices that handle the data because it passes from the sender to the receiver. The first question to address is what we mean "network security". Network security consists of the provisions and policies adopted by a network administrator to prevent and monitor unauthorized access, misuse, modification, or denial of a computer network and network-accessible resources. A generic definition of security is "freedom from risk or danger and safety". However it is not only human errors that can cause problem to network security, problems can also be caused by natural forces like fire breakouts, earthquakes, floods lightning etc. The ways network administrators think about securing networks has been changed by an increasingly dynamic and technically challenging risk environment. Security is an assessment of risk. Secure environments are designed and developed through an intentional effort.

INTRODUCTION

A computer network or just a network could be an assortment of connected computers. Two or a lot of computer systems are thought about as connected, if they will send and receive information from one another through a shared access medium. The communication entities in a computer network are typically called *principles, subjects or entities*. These principals will be additional divided into users, hosts and processes.

DOI: 10.4018/978-1-4666-8761-5.ch001

- A user could be a human entity, to blame for its actions in a computer network.
- A host is associate degree available entity inside a computer network. Every host incorporates a distinctive address inside a network.
- A method is associate degree instance of associate degree viable program. It's employed in client / server model, so as to tell apart between the consumer and also the server processes.
- A client method could be a method that creates requests of a network services.
- A server method could be a method that gives a network services.

In order to formalize the method that networking is performed, network reference models are developed, that cluster similar functions into abstractions called layers. Every layer's functions will communicate with a similar layer's functions of another network host. On a similar host, the functions of a selected layer have interfaces to speak with the layers bellow and on top of it. This abstraction simplifies and properly defines the mandatory actions for networking.

The *International Standards Organization (ISO)* and *Open Systems Interconnection (OSI)* reference models outline seven network layers, further as their interfaces. Every layer depends on the services provided by its intermediate lower layer all the method all the way down to the physical network interface card and also the wiring. Then, it provides its services to its immediate higher layer, all the far to the running application. The network layers within the *ISO/OSI reference model* are the subsequent (from all-time low to highest): 1) The Physical Layer 2) the info Link Layer 3) The Network Layer 4) The Transport Layer 5) The Session Layer 6) The Presentation Layer 7) the applying Layer. A lot of details on network reference model will be found in Models and stratified Protocol Organization.

Each reference model wants a collection of network protocol so as to implement the functions of every layer. Generally, a network protocol could be a well-defined specification that permits network hosts to speak in a very explicit and predefined ways that. From a degree of read, protocols outline the "syntax" of the communication. By properly combining protocols in protocol stacks, the layers of network reference models will be enforced and permit network communication. It must be noted that not all protocol suites embrace all the seven layers of the ISO/OSI model. The foremost standard protocol suite, the *Transmission Call Protocol / Internet Protocol (TCP/IP)*, has 5 layers. There are not any presentation and session layers; the functions of those layers are incorporated within the layers on top of and below. Though elaborated description of the TCP/IP is given elsewhere, it's vital to grasp however it works, so as to grasp network security.

A network is taken into account as a wired or mounted network if the access medium is a few reasonably physical cable affiliations between the computers, like a copper or a fiber optic cable. On the opposite hand, a network is taken into account as a wireless network, if the access medium depends on some reasonably sign through the air, like RF communication. A network can even be divided in keeping with its geographical coverage. Looking on its size, a network will be a private space Network (PAN), an area space Network (LAN), a Metropolitan space Network (MAN), or a large space Network (WAN).

It appears that each different day there's a story within the newspapers a couple of electronic network being compromised by hackers. In fact, not too earlier the *Department of Defense (DoD)* was the victim of a prosperous hacker raid; hackers were able to penetrate DoD computers throughout a two-week amount before they were detected. Fortuitously, the computers contained solely non-classified personnel and payroll data, therefore national security wasn't vulnerable.

More recently, Yahoo, Amazon.com, eBay, and a few different standard *World Wide Web (WWW)* sites were targets of what seems to possess been a coordinated "denial-of-service" attack. Throughout a three- or four-day amount, the sites were overcome with large bombardments of false traffic from multiple sites. As a result, the sites were close up for hours at a time. These attacks illustrate however pervasive the threat from outside hackers has become. At a similar time, each organization that uses computers faces the threat of hacking from people inside the organization. Employees or former employees with malicious intent or who wish to get data like worker salaries or read different employee's files are a threat to associate degree organization's computers and networks.

Computerworld recently ran a story a couple of technologist worker of a corporation WHO allegedly launched a denial-of-service attack against his own company, a supplier of on-line stock commerce services. Apparently, this technologist was in negotiations with the corporate for a lot of compensation. He became pissed off with the progress of the negotiations associate degreed determined to demonstrate to the corporate its vulnerability by launching an attack on its systems from the net. He was intimately at home with the company's systems and computer code, and his within information enabled him to hit the firm in a very manner that shut it down. In fact, the attack noncontiguous stock commerce services at the corporate for 3 days. The U.S. United States Secret Service was eventually utilized, and also the attack was derived to the worker, who was afterwards inactive.

Every organization ought to monitor its systems for potential unauthorized intrusion and different attacks. This must be a part of the daily routine of each organization's IT unit, because it is crucial to safeguarding a company's data assets. The most reliable thanks to make sure the safety of a company's computers is to refrain from golf shot them on a network and to stay them behind fastened doors. Sadly, however, that's not a awfully sensible answer. Today, computers are most helpful if they're networked along to share data and resources, and that place their computers on a network got to take some easy precautions to cut back the danger of unauthorized access.

Every year, corporations, governments, and different organizations pay billions of greenbacks on expenditures associated with network security. The speed at that these organizations are outlay a fund appears to be increasing. However, once firms got to realize areas within which they will decrease defrayal, operating cost like security and business commencement coming up with have traditionally been a number of the primary to be cut.

What Is Security?

In general, security is "the quality or state of being secure to be free from danger."[11] In different words, protection against adversaries from people who would do damage, advisedly or otherwise is the target. National security, for instance, could be a multilayered system that protects the sovereignty of a state, its assets, its resources, and its individuals. Achieving the acceptable level of security for a corporation additionally needs a multifarious system. A prosperous organization ought to have the subsequent multiple layers of security in situ to guard its operations:

- **Physical Security:** To guard physical things, objects, or areas from unauthorized access and misuse.
- **Personnel Security:** To guard the individual or cluster of people who are licensed to access the organization and its operations.
- **Operations Security:** To guard the main points of a selected operation or series of activities.
- **Communications Security:** To guard communications media, technology, and content.
- **Network Security:** To guard networking elements, connections, and contents.

- **Information Security:** To guard the confidentiality, integrity and accessibility of data assets, whether or not in storage, processing, or transmission. It's achieved via the applying of policy, education, coaching and awareness, and technology.

What Is Computer Security?

A Definition of computer Security, the *National Institute of Standards and Technology* computer security enchiridion [NIST95] defines the term computer security as follows: "The protection afforded to an automatic data system so as to achieve the applicable objectives of protective the integrity, accessibility, and confidentiality of data system resources (includes hardware, software, firmware, data / information, and telecommunications)". This definition introduces three key objectives that are at the center of computer security:

- **Confidentiality:** This term covers two connected concepts:
  - **Data Confidentiality:** Assures that non-public or wind isn't created on the market or disclosed to unauthorized people.
  - **Privacy:** Assures that people management or influence what data associated with them is also collected and keep and by whom and to whom that data is also disclosed.
- **Integrity:** This term covers two connected concepts:
  - **Data Integrity:** Assures that data and programs are modified solely in a very such and licensed manner.
  - **System Integrity:** Assures that a system performs its supposed perform in associate degree undamaged manner, free from deliberate or unintended unauthorized manipulation of the system.
- **Availability:** Assures that systems work promptly and repair isn't denied to authorize users.

The *Committee on National Security Systems (CNSS)* defines data security because the protection of data and its essential parts, together with the systems and hardware that use, store, and transmit that data.[12] Figure 1 shows that data security includes the broad areas of data security management, computer and information security, and network security. The CNSS model of data security evolved from an idea developed by the computer security business known as the C.I.A. triangle. The C.I.A. triangle has been the business commonplace for computer security since the event of the mainframe. It's supported the three characteristics of data that provides it price to organizations: confidentiality, integrity, and accessibility. The protection of those three characteristics of data is as vital nowadays because it has perpetually been, but the C.I.A. triangle model now not adequately addresses the perpetually everchanging atmosphere. The threats to the confidentiality, integrity, and accessibility of data have evolved into an enormous assortment of events, together with accidental or intentional harm, destruction, theft, unintentional or unauthorized modification, or different misuse from human or inhuman threats. This new atmosphere of the many perpetually evolving threats has prompted the event of and a lot of sturdy model that addresses the complexities of the present data security atmosphere.

The three ideas embody the basic security objectives for each information and for data and computing services. For instance, the NIST standard FIPS 199 (Standards for Security Categorization of Federal

Figure 1. The security requirements triad

data and knowledge Systems) lists confidentiality, integrity, and accessibility because the three security objectives for data and for data systems.

FIPS 199 provides a helpful characterization of those three objectives in terms of necessities and therefore the definition of a loss of security in every category:

- **Confidentiality:** Conserving approved restrictions on data access and revealing, together with means that for safeguarding personal privacy and proprietary data. A loss of confidentiality is that the unauthorized revealing of knowledge.
- **Integrity:** Guarding against improper data modification or destruction, together with guaranteeing data nonrepudiation and credibility. A loss of integrity is that the unauthorized modification or destruction of knowledge.
- **Availability:** Guaranteeing timely and reliable access to and use of knowledge. A loss of convenience is that the disruption of access to or use of knowledge or Associate in Nursing system.

Although the employment of the *Central Intelligence Agency* triad to outline security objectives is well established, some within the security field feel that extra ideas are required to gift an entire image. Two of the foremost usually mentioned as follows:

- **Authenticity:** The property of being real and having the ability to be verified and trusted; confidence within the validity of a transmission, a message, or message creator. This implies validating that user's are World Health Organization they are saying they're which every input incoming at the system came from a sure supply.
- **Accountability:** The safety goal that generates the need for actions of an entity to be copied unambiguously to that entity. This supports nonrepudiation, deterrence, fault isolation, intrusion detection and hindrance, and after-action recovery and proceeding. As a result of actually secure systems aren't nonetheless in realizable goal, we tend to should be able to trace a security breach to an accountable party. Systems should keep records of their activities to allow later rhetorical analysis to trace security breaches or to assist in group action disputes.

That means of the term *computer security* has evolved in recent years. Before the matter of knowledge security became wide advertised within the media, most people's plan of computer security targeted on the physical machine. Historically, computer facilities are physically protected for three reasons:

- To stop thievery of or harm to the hardware
- To stop thievery of or harm to the data
- To stop disruption of service

Strict procedures for access to the machine space are utilized by most organizations; these procedures are typically an organization's solely obvious computer security measures. Today, however, with pervasive remote station access, communications, and networking, physical measures seldom give meaningful protection for either the data or the service; solely the hardware is secure. Even so, most computer facilities still shield their physical machine much better than they are doing their knowledge, even once the worth of the info is many times larger than the worth of the hardware. You probably aren't reading this book to be told a way to padlock your computer. Data security is that the subject of this book. Moreover, we tend to limit our study to the corporate executive problem: the safety violations perpetrated (perhaps inadvertently) by legitimate users whom padlocks and passwords cannot deter. Most computer crimes are if truth be told committed by insiders and most of the analysis in computer security since 1970 has been directed at the corporate executive downside.

The Challenges of Computer Security

Computer and network security is each fascinating and sophisticated. A number of the explanations follow:

1. Security isn't as easy because it may first seem to the novice. The necessities appear to be straight-forward; so, most of the main necessities for security services are often given obvious, one-word labels: confidentiality, authentication, nonrepudiation, or integrity. However the mechanisms ac-customed meet those necessities are often quite advanced, and understanding them might involve rather delicate reasoning.
2. In developing a selected security mechanism or algorithmic rule, one should always take into ac-count potential attacks on those safety features. In several cases, winning attacks are designed by observing the matter in a very fully completely different means, so exploiting sudden weakness within the mechanism.
3. Because of point 2, the procedures accustomed give explicit services are typically unreasonable. Typically, a security mechanism is advanced, and it's not obvious from the statement of a selected demand that such elaborate measures are required. It's only the varied aspects of the threat are thought-about that elaborate security mechanisms be.
4. Having designed numerous security mechanisms, it's necessary to choose wherever to use them. this is often true each in terms of physical placement (e.g., at what points in a very network are sure security mechanisms needed) and in a very logical sense [e.g., at what layer or layers of Associate in Nursing design like TCP/IP (Transmission management Protocol/Internet Protocol) ought to mechanisms be placed].
5. Security mechanisms usually involve over a selected algorithmic rule or protocol. They addition-ally need that participants be in possession of some secret data (e.g., Associate in Nursing coding

key), that raises questions on the creation, distribution, and protection of that secret data. There additionally is also a reliance on communications protocols whose behavior might complicate the task of developing the safety mechanism. as an example, if the correct functioning of the safety mechanism needs setting limits on the transit time of a message from sender to receiver, then any protocol or network that introduces variable, unpredictable delays might render such limits nonsense.

6. Computer and network security is actually a battle of wits between culprits World Health Organization tries to search out holes and therefore the designer and administrator World Health Organization tries to shut them. The nice advantage that the assailant has is that he or she want solely notice one weakness, whereas the designer should notice and eliminate all weaknesses to attain excellent security.

7. There's a natural tendency on the part of users and system managers to understand very little get pleasure from security investment till a security failure happens.

8. Security needs regular, even constant, monitoring, and this is often tough in today's short, over-loaded setting.

9. Security remains too typically Associate in Nursing when thought to be incorporated into a system after the look is complete instead of being Associate in Nursing integral a part of the look method.

10. Several users and even security directors read robust security as an impediment to economical and easy operation of a system or use of knowledge.

Why Systems aren't Secure?

Despite vital advances within the state of the art of computer security in recent years, data in computers is additional vulnerable than ever. Every major technological advance in computing raises new security threats that need new security solutions, and technology moves quicker than the speed at that such solution are often developed. We'd be fighting a losing battle, except that security needn't be an isolated effort: there's no reason why a replacement technology can't be in the middle of an integrated security strategy, wherever the trouble to safeguard against new threats solely needs filling in a very logical piece of a well-defined design. We tend to most likely cannot modification the means the globe works, however understanding why it works the means it will facilitate America avoid the standard pitfalls and select acceptable security solutions. This chapter explores a number of the classic reasons why the implementation of security lags behind its theory.

Security is Fundamentally Difficult

Why are computer systems thus unhealthy at protective information? In spite of everything, if it's attainable to make a system containing innumerable lines of package (as proved by today's massive operational systems), why is it thus onerous to create that package operate securely? The task of keeping one user from going to another user's files appears easy enough especially once the system is already able to keep track of every user and every file.

In fact, it's way easier to make a secure system than to make an accurate system. However what number massive operational systems are correct and bug-free? For all massive systems, vendors should sporadically issue new releases, every containing thousands of lines of revised code, abundant of that are bug fix. No major software has ever worked utterly, and no merchandiser of software has dared provide a guaranty against malfunctions. The trade appears resigned to the actual fact that systems can perpetually have bugs. Nonetheless most systems are fairly dependable, and most of them adequately (but not perfectly) do the work that they were designed.

What is adequate for many functions, however, isn't sufficient for security. If you discover an isolated bug in one perform of software, you'll be able to sometimes circumvent it, and therefore the bug can have very little impact on the opposite functions of the system: few bugs are fatal. However one security "hole" will render all of the system's security controls valueless, particularly if the bug is discovered by a determined intruder. You would possibly be able to sleep in a house with a couple of holes within the walls; however you'll not be able to keep burglars out.

As a result, securing a system has historically been a battle of wits: the intruder tries to search out holes, and therefore the designer tries to shut them. The designer will ne'er be assured of getting found all the holes, and therefore the intruder needn't reveal any discoveries. Data to outsized software or to a computer on a network has reason to agonize regarding the privacy of that data. If the data is effective enough to an intruder to warrant the trouble, there's very little reason to assume that the intruder won't succeed.

But in fact there's hope: with acceptable techniques, a system are often designed that has fairly high assurance of the effectiveness of its security controls a level of assurance abundant on top of that of the system's overall correctness. The necessary issue isn't the chance of a flaw (which is high), however the chance that an intruder can notice one (which we tend to hope is incredibly low). Whereas we tend to ne'er will understand whether or not a system is utterly secure, we will build a system in a very means that may create the penetrator's job thus tough, risky, and expensive that the worth to the intruder of winning penetration won't be definitely worth the effort. The key to achieving an appropriate degree of security is that the systematic use of correct techniques. Accidental security measures give, at best, insignificantly inflated protection that seldom justifies their expense. At worst, they supply a false sense of security that renders the users additional prone than ever to the important threats.

Security is an After Thought

Despite the packaging regarding computer security within the press, computer and code vendors have seldom taken the difficulty to include purposeful security measures into their systems. Security, if thought-about in any respect, typically comes at the lowest of an inventory that appears one thing like this:

- **Functions:** *What will it do?*
- **Price:** *What will it cost?*
- **Performance:** *How briskly will it run?*
- **Compatibility:** *Will it work with earlier products?*
- **Reliability:** *Can it perform its supposed function?*
- **Human Interface:** *However straightforward is it to use?*
- **Availability:** *However typically can it break?*
- **Security Functions:** *What protection options will it provide?*
- **Security Assurance:** *However foolproof are the protection features?*

Based on past and current observe, you would possibly say that this complete book is regarding two of the smallest amount vital factors within the style of computer systems. It's unfair to fault vendors entirely for this lack of attention to security. Whereas customers might want improved security, they sometimes have second thoughts once safety features adversely have an effect on different, "more important" options. Since few customers are willing to pay further for security, vendors have had very little incentive to take a position in intensive security enhancements.

A few vendors have taken steps to assist the few security-conscious customers UN agency are willing to take a position in extra protection. These customers embody not solely the govt. however some banks, makers, and universities. Many add-on security packages for major operative systems are on the marketplace for a while. The foremost notable of those are CGA code merchandise Group's prime SECRET, Uccel Corporation's ACF2, and IBM's RACF, all for IBM's MVS package. Stronger obligatory controls (a subject of chapter 6) designed to be integrated into the package seem in SES/VMS, associate degree improvement to VMS offered by Digital instrumentality (Blotcky, Lynch, and Lipner 1986), and are beneath development within the applied scientist (now Unisys) 1100 package (Ashland 1985). These packages and enhancements are commercially viable despite their important purchase and body prices. Many vendors have created a substantial investment in internal security enhancements to their operative systems while not value add-ons. These systems embody DEC's VMS and Honeywell's Multics (Organick 1972; Whitmore et al. 1973). Management information has conjointly incorporated security enhancements into its NOS package. Honeywell was the primary to supply commercially a extremely secure digital computer, the SCOMP (Fraim 1983), supported a security kernel, (a subject of chapter 10). Gemini Computers offers the GEMSOS package, conjointly supported a security kernel (Schell, Tao, and Heckman 1985). These and several other examples show that there has invariably been a definite demand for safety features within the user community. However the examples conjointly show that demand is fairly weak and may simply evaporate if the options ought to have associate degree adverse impact on value or the other functions.

Security is an Impediment

A common perception among users is that security could be a nuisance. Security measures are alleged to thwart somebody UN agency tries to interrupt the rules; however attributable to poorly integrated unexpected solutions, security measures typically interfere with associate degree honest user's traditional job. Vendors typically implement security enhancements in response to specific client demands. Such enhancements, created to existing systems at minimal value, typically lead to reduced convenience or poor performance. Vendors usually adopt the angle that a client UN agency desires security badly enough ought to be willing to measure with the inconvenience.

Many customers take it upon themselves to mend security issues at their own sites. attributable to inherent limitations within the system, fixing security issues typically needs restrictive procedural controls: restricted access from remote terminals; restricted physical access to native terminals; and printers; multiple paroles or logins; frequent password changes; automatic disconnect when periods of inactivity; and call-back devices. Several of those controls don't well increase the protection of the system, however they are doing foster the notion that security is painful. As a result of users and managers don't see how round the inconveniences, security is usually utilized solely as a final resort, once a retardant has already occurred or a transparent threat exists.

False Solutions Impede Progress

The computer trade, like alternative industries, is subject to fads. Fads within the laptop security space will have a significant negative result on the general progress toward achieving sensible security, as a result of progress stops once folks suppose they need the solution. Since few folks have a decent understanding of security, security fixes are notably subject to snake-oil acquisition.

One thought (fortunately short-lived) concerned *data encryption*; that's, secret writing info employing a word or secret key in order that it cannot be deciphered by unauthorized people. Encoding is indispensable for communications and is beneficial for safeguarding the media accustomed store files, however it doesn't address the final laptop security downside. Few of the penetration techniques utilized by numerous "tiger teams" charged with finding security holes in systems would be unsuccessful by encoding. The first downside with file encoding is that it will nothing to extend the amount of trust within the software package; and if you are doing not trust your in operation system to safeguard your files, you cannot trust it to write your files in the least the correct times or to safeguard the encoding keys properly. Even so, oversimplified statements are still sometimes encountered that claim that securing associate software package makes no sense if all the files are encrypted.

A popular security device is that the *call-back modem*. The thought is that you simply telephone a computer from your home or workplace terminal and determine yourself (via a password) to the electronic equipment on the remote laptop through your terminal. The computer's electronic equipment verifies that the word is correct and tells you to hold up. The electronic equipment then appearance up your home signal in an exceedingly list, and calls you back. No one will dial into the system and masquerade as you, notwithstanding that person is aware of your word, unless that person additionally uses your phone. Call-back devices are enticing as a result of they are doing not need any modification to the system being protected a classic example of add-on security. The danger in these devices is that the risk of being lulled into satisfaction as a result of you is feeling that solely "good guys" will get to your system. You will decide that it's ne'er necessary to vary passwords or to enforce any management over the kinds of passwords folks use. You will become lax regarding access management among your system, permitting too several of your users access to an excessive amount of info. You will forget that half of your security downside may be a matter of keeping your users isolated from every other not keeping outsider out.

The worst downside with call-back modems, however, is that they will cause you to forget that there are alternative ways that folks will get into your system. Will your system have an association to a poster network from that users will log in? Are you able to trust all alternative systems with that your system communicates? If one among your users accesses your system via electronic equipment on a private laptop, however does one make sure that the non-public laptop has not been penetrated by associate outsider via that modem? Considering the issues that call-back modems cannot solve and consideration the price of those devices against easy measures like higher word management, it's laborious to envision their worth.

An example involving the employment of passwords shows however a security feature meant for one application will be applied unsuitably to a different. As a result of passwords are therefore sensible at dominant a user's access to the system, they're usually used for alternative varieties of access management access to certain applications in an exceedingly system, access to sure files, or freedom to hold out sure operations. Password schemes are enticing as a result of they're really easy to implement and to feature onto existing systems.

But passwords are inappropriate for several of those applications, particularly once one word is issued to many folks (for access to a typical file, as an example). Once one person within the cluster leaves the corporate, the word should be modified and also the new word manually distributed. If a by a business executive happens, it's not possible to inform United Nations agency is guilty. Another misuse of words involves the necessity on some systems that the user at a terminal reenter the password periodically supposedly to confirm that the meant user associated not a trespasser is at the terminal. This feature is dangerous for two reasons. First, recurrent entry of the word greatly will increase the danger that somebody is wanting over the user's shoulder once the word is entered. Second, the prompt for a word, showing at sudden times throughout a session, is extremely vulnerable to spoofing by a malicious program. In extra ways that within which passwords is also misused. The false sense of security created by inappropriate use of passwords weakens the impetus to hunt higher controls. The danger of exploitation such accidental solutions to deal with isolated issues is that one will lose sight of the basic issues.

The Problem is People, Not Computers

Many organizations believe that laptop security technology is digressive to real-world issues as a result of nearly all recorded cases of laptop abuse and frauds are non-technical. Computer crime typically involves exploitation of weaknesses in procedural or personnel controls, not weaknesses in internal controls. Hence, as long as comparatively simple, non-technical ways that exist to commit a criminal offense, technical controls are viewed as superfluous.

But these organizations usually fail to acknowledge that the computer will shield against blemished procedural controls. The technical controls will usually be accustomed ease the burden of procedural controls. it's distressing, as an example, to listen to claims that attacks by former staff represent personnel issues that the computer cannot solve, once the system will simply be instrumented to defend itself against this threat. Consider, too, what is going to happen once procedural controls are reinforced to the purpose that technical penetration becomes the trail of travail. Since a few years are required forming major security enhancements to existing systems, a abrupt explosion of technical crimes are terribly troublesome to counter.

Probably as a result of the computer trade remains in its infancy, enough data of computers to take advantage of technical flaws looks to be rare among the dishonest. However as data of computers becomes a lot of common, we tend to cannot assume that solely a couple of honest voters can possess the requisite skills to commit a significant crime. Given the low risk of obtaining caught and also the doubtless high payoff, refined laptop crime is probably going to become a lot of enticing within the future, particularly if the non-technical avenues to crime are sufficiently restricted.

One of the first arguments that laptops cannot forestall most cases of abuse relies on the observation that computer crimes committed by insiders typically don't involve a violation of internal security controls: the wrongdoer merely misuses info to that he or she ordinarily has access throughout, the course of traditional work responsibilities. One thing reminiscent of computing would be needed to find such abuse mechanically. however on nearer review, we frequently realize that individuals habitually gain access to a lot of info than they have, either as a result of the system's security controls don't give adequately fine-grained protection or as a result of implementing such protection among the bailiwick constraints of the system is simply too inconvenient or pricey. The matter seems to be only one among folks; however it's exacerbated by a technical deficiency of the system. The technical solutions aren't apparent as a result of associate organization's manner of doing business is usually influenced by the look (and limitations) of its computer system.

Technology is Oversold

There has long been the perception that true laptop security will ne'er be achieved in follow, therefore any effort is doomed to failure. This perception is due, in massive half; to the unhealthy press that variety of outstanding government funded secure laptop development programs have received. The explanations for the supposed failure of those developments are varied:

- Programs originally meant for analysis are wrong criticized for not fulfilling wants of production systems.
- Vying for scarce funding, researchers and developers usually promise quite they'll deliver.
- Funding for the programs has been unpredictable, and necessities could amendment because the programs are shuffled among agencies. Usually the necessities ultimately expressed are inconsistent with the initial goals of the program, resulting in unfortunate style compromises.
- Developments usually targeted to a selected model of laptop or software package, and inconsistent levels of funding have extended programs to the purpose wherever the initial target system is technologically obsolete by the time the program is prepared for implementation.
- The public doesn't understand that the primary version of associate software package invariably performs poorly, requiring important extra style and standardization before turning into acceptable. Vendors don't release such preliminary systems, suspending their "Version 1.0" announcement till the performance issues are self-addressed. Government programs are extremely visible, and any issues (even in early versions) tend to be viewed by critics as inherent characteristics. Worse, contracts are usually written in such some way that the primary version is that the final product and extra cash isn't on the market for performance standardization.
- Several massive government procurements have fixed the employment of security technology that was thought to be sensible at the time however really supported analysis still within the laboratory was. Once the analysis did not progress quick enough to satisfy the wants of the program, security necessities were waived and also the program lost its quality. Trade has understood for an extended time that developing a brand new software package involves way more than a one-time expense to make it; rather, a high level of continuous support is needed over the lifetime of the system. The central looks to own realized this, as well.

Not able to plan to open-ended support, the government has for the most part ceased direct funding for secure software package development, concentrating instead on specific applications and numerous seed efforts. A couple of business vendors are currently enterprise to fill the void.

Why Is Computer and Network Security Important?

It may appear absurd to raise the question. "Why is computer and network security important?" however it's crucial for organizations to outline why they need deliver computer security to see however they're going to achieve it. It's conjointly a useful to use once seeking senior management's authorization for security-related expenditures. Computer and network security is vital for the subsequent reasons.

- **To protect company assets:** One in all the first goals of laptop and network security is that the protection of company assets. By "assets," I don't mean the hardware and computer code that represent the company's computers and networks. The assets are comprised of the "information" that's housed on a company's computers and networks. Information could be an important structure quality. Network and laptop security is bothered, in particular else, with the protection, integrity, and accessibility of knowledge. Information is often outlined as information that's organized and accessible during a coherent and substantive manner.

- **To gain a competitive advantage:** Developing and maintaining effective security measures will offer a corporation with a competitive advantage over its competition. Network security is especially vital within the arena of web money services and e-commerce. It will mean the distinction between wide acceptance of a service and a mediocre client response.

- **To comply with regulatory requirements and fiduciary responsibilities:** Company officers of each company have a responsibility to make sure the protection and soundness of the organization. A part of that responsibility includes guaranteeing the continued operation of the organization. Consequently, organizations that have confidence computers for his or her continued operation should develop policies and procedures that address structure security needs. Such policies and procedures are necessary not solely to safeguard company assets however conjointly to safeguard the organization from liability. For-profit organizations should conjointly defend shareholders investments and maximize come back. In additionally, several organizations are subject to governmental regulation, which regularly stipulates needs for the protection and security of a corporation. For instance, most money establishments are subject to federal regulation. Failure to fits federal tips may end up within the seizure of an institution by federal regulators. In some cases, company officers United Nations agencies haven't properly performed their regulative and fiduciary responsibilities are in person responsible for any losses incurred by the institution that employs them.

- **To keep your job:** Finally, to secure one's position inside a corporation and to make sure future career prospects, it's vital to place into place measures that defend structure assets. Security ought to be a part of each network or systems administrator's job. Failure to perform adequately may end up in termination. Termination shouldn't be the automated results of a security failure, but if, once an intensive postmortem, it's determined that the failure was the results of inadequate policies and procedures or failure to fits existing procedures, then management must step in and build some changes.

One factor to stay in mind is that network security prices cash: It prices money to rent, train, associated retain personnel; to shop for hardware and computer code to secure an organization's networks; and to buy the multiplied overhead and degraded network and system performance that results from firewalls, filters, and intrusion detection systems (IDSs). As a result, network security isn't low cost. However, it's most likely cheaper than the prices related to having associate organization's network compromised.

Why Is Network Security Important?

- **Good Neighbor Policy:** Your mistakes are often somebody else's headaches. If your network is insecure and somebody takes management of one of your computers, they will use that machine to launch denial of service attacks on innocent third parties. They will conjointly flood the online with spam.

- **Patron Privacy:** Clearly, patron records are of preponderant importance. Trust between the library and its purchasers are often irreparably injured if these records are compromised.

- **Money and Time:** Chase down an epidemic or a worm and eliminating it from your network is frustrating and time consuming. You frequently ought to construct your machines from the bottom up, reinstalling the package and computer code and restoring information from backup tapes. Lax security will result in weeks of wasted time spent fix your network and fixing the portion.

NETWORK SECURITY POLICY

Security policy may be a definition of what it suggests that to be secure for a system, organization or different entity. For a company, it addresses the constraints on behavior of its members also as constraints obligatory on adversaries by mechanisms like doors, locks, keys and walls. For systems, the protection policy addresses constraints on functions and flow among them, constraints on access by external systems and adversaries together with programs and access to information by folks.

If it's vital to be secure, then it's vital to make sure all of the protection policy is implemented by mechanisms that are robust enough. There are several organized methodologies and risk assessment methods to assure completeness of security policies and assure that they're fully implemented. In complicated systems, like info systems, policies are often rotten into sub-policies to facilitate the allocation of security mechanisms to enforce sub-policies. However, this apply has pitfalls. It's too straightforward to easily go on to the sub-policies that are primarily the principles of operation and dispense with the highest level policy. That provides the false sense that the principles of operation address some overall definition of security after they don't. As a result of its therefore troublesome to assume clearly with completeness concerning security, rules of operation declared as "sub-policies" with no "super-policy" sometimes end up to be rambling rules that fail to enforce something with completeness. Consequently, a superior security policy is important to any serious security theme and sub-policies and rules of operation are unmeaning while not it.

A network security policy, or NSP, may be a generic document that outlines rules for electronic network access, determines however policies are implemented and lays out a number of the essential design of the corporate security/ network security atmosphere. The document itself is typically many pages long and written by a committee. A security policy goes way on the far side the straightforward plan of "keep the unhealthy guys out". It is a terribly complicated document, meant to manipulate information access, web-browsing habits, use of passwords and encoding, email attachments and a lot of. It specifies these rules for people or teams of people throughout the corporate.

Security policy ought to keep the malicious users out and additionally exert management over potential risky users at intervals your organization. The primary step in making a policy is to know what info and services are accessible (and to that users), what the potential is for harm and whether or not any protection is already in situ to forestall misuse. In addition, the protection policy ought to dictate a hierarchy of access permissions; that's, grant users access solely to what's necessary for the completion of their work. While writing the protection document are often a significant enterprise, a decent begin are often achieved by employing an example. National Institute for Standards and Technology provides a security-policy guideline. The policies might be expressed as a collection of directions that might be understood by special purpose network hardware dedicated for securing the network.

Good Security Thinking

Rather than dive straight into the strategies for implementing network security, let's take a high-level investigate six principles of security thinking. You will not notice these principles in an exceedingly book like a way to create Friends and Influence People; they're inevitably supported a philosophy of mistrust.

1. Do not talk over with anyone you do not understand.
2. Settle for nothing while not a guarantee.
3. Treat everybody as an enemy till established otherwise.
4. Do not trust your friends for long.
5. Use proven solutions.
6. Watch the bottom you're standing on for cracks.

The sixth principle could be a bit secret. The "ground" during this context refers to the pile of assumptions we tend to all stand on. As you'll see shortly, this sixth principle is that the real zone in security and one among the foremost fruitful for the enemy.

Do Not Talk Over With Anyone You Do Not Understand

In this state of affairs, you'll listen and you'll speak, however you've got no different means that to spot the individuals within the space. An easier (albeit a lot of boring) analogy could be a telephone call. In standard phone conversations, throughout that we will hear however not see the opposite person on the phone, we tend to perpetually convince ourselves that the opposite person is United Nations agency we expect he's. In most cases, we tend to do that subconsciously. at first we tend to assume the caller is United Nations agency he says he is; we tend to settle for his identity as expressed. However, before we tend to open our communications channels, we tend to take a look at that identity. If we all know the caller, we tend to acknowledge the voice and that we go straight to open mode. If we do not, we tend to cautiously open up as we tend to hear info that's in keeping with the person's expressed identity. Throughout the decision, we tend to still monitor and area unit tuned in to comments that sound strange or out of context.

Conference calls area unit tough as a result of a lot of individual's area unit concerned and you wish to perpetually establish United Nations agency is talking. Imagine that someone makes a comment that you simply do not quite hear and you say, "Could you repeat that?" The comment is continual, however are you able to make sure a similar person continual it, or that what was continual is that the same because the original comment?

The only reliable resolution to the present quandary is to need that the identities of all the decision participants be evidenced while not a doubt for each sentence they speak. For a Wi-Fi LAN, it's not enough to verify the identity of the opposite party. A Wi-Fi LAN should additionally verify that each message very came from that party. a straightforward methodology to attest somebody is to need that they understand a secret positive identification or key. This may be used at the beginning of communication to ascertain identity, and so a similar secret key will be incorporated into every message to make sure the message's credibleness. The concept is that, albeit enemies' area unit impersonating valid network addresses and different info, they cannot substitute rascal messages for authentic ones as a result of they do not understand the key that should be incorporated into each message. This approach was the premise of the first IEEE 802.11/Wi-Fi Security protocol known as WEP; however, as we are going to see later, it absolutely was too easy to be secure within the long-standing time.

Settle For Nothing While Not a Guarantee

Like "security," the word "guarantee" means that various things to completely different individuals. Within the context of network security, "guarantee" means that a guarantee of credibleness. In different words, it's proof that the message has not been modified. you recognize the sender should prove his identity before you settle for his message, however you furthermore may got to make sure that what you receive is that the message the sender supposed to send which the message has not been changed, delayed, or perhaps replaced with a brand new message. Consider the subsequent.

1.   A disciple sends a sound message to you.
2.   AN enemy intercepts the message before you receive it, modifies some bits, and so sends it on to you.
3.   You receive the message and check the sender's identity; however as a result of the enemy sent it last, you'll observe the interception, right?

As shown in Figure 2, the primary is that it assumes it's attainable to understand United Nations agency sent you the message. Bear in mind the concern is on the sender to supply proof for the receiver to envision. In an exceedingly wireless atmosphere, we tend to cannot expect the receiver to own a magic methodology of knowing United Nations agency sent the message aside from by reading its contents. Therefore, if AN enemy forwards a homogenous copy of a message sent by a disciple, however will the receiver probably understand that it's been handled in transit? Thus, you cannot observe that a message has been handled just by staring at it.

Figure 2. Modified message appears to destination from source

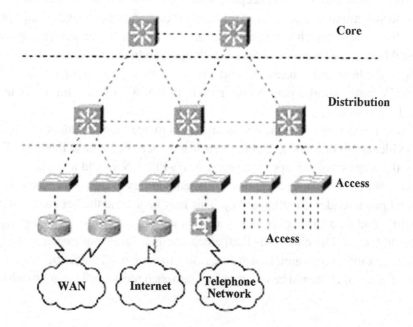

The second flaw is one among those hidden assumptions. We've assumed it's necessary for the enemy to receive and so resend the message. However, in an exceedingly wireless atmosphere, the enemy may discover how to change the message whereas the friend is sending it. Today, we do not understand any thanks to do this. However you may imagine that a rigorously regular burst of radio transmission from the enemy, colliding with the friendly transmission, may cause the receiver to interpret slightly to own a special worth, despite the fact that the remainder of the transmission came from the friend. During this case the enemy has tampered with a message while not retransmitting it in the slightest degree. In observe several security protocols use a way that has each identity proof and tamper-resistant packaging within the same algorithmic program. However, the rule still applies: settle for nothing while not a guarantee.

Treat Everybody As an Enemy Till Established Otherwise

A few years past a story circulated a couple of scam involving ATM machines (ATMs) (Neumann, 2001). We've since detected many versions of the story, therefore it would be urban story; however it's attention-grabbing all the same. Somebody obtained a previous ATM that had been taken out of service. The ATM was complete and still had its bank brand hooked up. This person put in the ATM in an exceedingly tiny trailer, ran it off a generator, and places it in an exceedingly busy downtown space. Shoppers assumed the bank was being proactive by introducing mobile ATMs and visited withdraw money. The machine displayed miscalculation message spoken language it absolutely was devoid of money; however it recorded the customers' ATM card info and private identification numbers (PINs). Each day, the criminal created copies of all the ATM cards used and withdrew the most allowed quantity from the important bank for each card, each day, till the scam was discovered and also the cards were disabled. This scam succeeded as a result of the purchasers assumed solely the important bank would originate AN ATM. The ATM cards didn't have the potential to envision the machine's credibleness either.

This example illustrates the importance of not giving info to anyone till that person has established identity. Arguably the purchasers during this example followed this rule; however their customary of proof was too low? They trustworthy the banks sign up the ATM!

This rule is vital in Wi-Fi wireless LAN applications. in an exceedingly wired LAN, for instance, you've got a fairly smart plan wherever you're connected as a result of you plug the cable into a hole within the wall, that either you or AN IT department maintains. Assumptive you retain your wiring closet fastened, you must be safe. However, by design, Wi-Fi LANs will search the airwaves probing for networks to affix. Access points advertise their handiness by sending beacon frames with their identity. It is, of course, trivial for AN enemy to start out up AN access purpose from a van and incorrectly advertise that he's a part of your network within the hope of casual a couple of wireless local area network cards into connecting. Later we are going to see however the new Wi-Fi security protocols work to make sure that you simply aren't caught during this lure.

Do not Trust Your Friends for Long

"Make new friends however keep the old…." What will it mean to "keep" a friend? The word "keep" implies a vigorous method, a method of affirmation. Suppose sooner or later you're walking down the road and you link up along with your supporter from high school. This is often a pleasant surprise as a result of you had lost contact and you hadn't seen this person for ten years. You grew up with this friend and shared all of your secrets. When reminiscing for a short time, you learn things aren't going well and you hear the frightening words, "Can you lend Maine some money? I fully promise I am going to pay you back." Why does one feel uncomfortable? 10 years past you may have forked over the money in complete confidence. Why not now? You've got not reaffirmed the friendship; you do not very understand United Nations agency this person is any longer. You'd have to be compelled to take time to alter trust before you were snug once more.

Applying this analogy to Wi-Fi security, friends area unit those devices you'll communicate with and enemies area unit everybody else. "Friends" in an exceedingly Wi-Fi LAN will be known as a result of they possess tokens like a secret key that may be verified. Such tokens, whether or not they area unit keys, certificates, or passwords, got to have a restricted life. You must keep reaffirming the connection by revitalizing the tokens. Failure to require this step may end up in unpleasant surprises.

There is a distinction between policy and protocol. In easy terms, the safety protocol is meant to implement the safety policy. Aiming to decide for your organization which individuals are "friends." you're additionally aiming to decide once those friends will access the network and, for multisite companies, wherever they're allowed access. It's then the work of the safety protocol, in conjunction with hardware and software package, to make sure that nobody will breach the policy. For instance, enemies ought to ne'er get access.

In the Wi-Fi LAN context, a disciple is sometimes someone or a laptop. If you're reproof some dedicated instrumentality, like a server or a network entryway, you wish to ascertain that the instrumentality is taken into account a disciple in your security policy. However, within the case of laptop computer or desktop computers, it would not be enough to spot the instrumentality. The laptop computer might need been taken or left unattended. In these cases, you wish to make sure the person victimization the computer is additionally legitimate. Memorizing a positive identification is that the commonest thanks to do that. Normally, well a minimum of in theory, those that work for your company area unit friends and it's acceptable to speak with them. In larger firms the notion of "friend" will be divided all the way down to departments or comes. Even after you area unit sure of the opposite party's identity, you may have to be compelled to check whether or not she has left the corporate or stirred off the project.

Corporations have security databases that area unit perpetually updated with the access rights or credentials of all prospective friends. Later we are going to investigate however Wi-Fi LAN security will be joined to those databases. However, accessing such information typically needs a big investment in time and resources, and in some cases, the info may be quickly inaccessible. To cut back overhead, it's common to verify another person's credentials and so assume these credentials area unit OK for a restricted amount of your time before checking once more. The particular quantity of your time will be set by the safety administrator and may vary from a couple of minutes to a couple of days.

Use Proven Solutions

A security guru can ne'er say that one thing is "totally secure." therefore what is the best you'll do? However are you able to ever develop trust in an exceedingly security protocol? A part of security science involves developing a high level of mistrust for the entire world new. To check however this affects people's attitudes, let's take encoding as AN example. The thing of encoding is to create the encrypted knowledge seem like utterly random noise. Suppose you're taking a discretionary message, pass it through the encoding algorithmic program, and send it over a communications link. Then repeat the method lots of times, causation a similar message over and over however encrypting it when before causation.

If the encoding algorithmic program is sweet, each transmission is going to be completely different and appearance completely random. If you may do that with no gaps within the transmission, no quantity of research on the output stream would reveal any pattern? Simply racket.

Now comes the onerous half. If you actually did convert the message to random racket, it might not be terribly helpful as a result of neither the friend nor the enemy would be ready to decrypt it. The trick is to create it seem like noise to the enemy whereas facultative the friend to extract the first knowledge. Several algorithms area unit on the market for achieving this goal, however are you able to tell which of them very work? If the message is to be decoded by the friend, it cannot be true noise? Somewhere there should be some info that enables the info to be extracted. Therefore however are you able to make sure an enemy cannot eventually understand that info and decrypt the message?

The answer to the present question has two elements. The primary involves mathematical analysis known as science. Science permits you to confirm however onerous it's to interrupt the encoding code by standard or well-known strategies. However, weaknesses may also return from unconventional strategies, like sudden relationships between computations within the algorithmic program or implicit hidden assumptions. Therefore, the second a part of developing confidence in an exceedingly new algorithmic program is that the smart previous "test of your time."

There is no shortage of encoding algorithms. Sometimes, terribly sometimes, algorithmic programs are going to be broken? That's, somebody figures out a way to decrypt a message while not victimization the computing power of all the computers within the universe. However, this is often not the first motivation for analysis into new strategies. It takes a particular quantity of computing power, energy, and memory to perform encoding and coding. Differing types of devices have completely different capabilities. For instance, the computing resources of a contemporary microcomputer area unit completely different from those of a transportable. Therefore, a lot of the analysis into new strategies is directed at craft strategies to the resources of real devices. There's no downside deploying an unbreakable encoding code if you've got limitless computing power and energy, however making a way that may be run on a powered PDA could be a challenge.

We tend to use "unbreakable" here within the globe sense. In theory all encoding algorithms area unit breakable with enough time and computing power accept the Vernam cipher, which uses pure random knowledge, completely different for each message.

The point here is that new strategies area unit still fabricated from time to time, and also the question then arises whether or not a brand new methodology is absolutely secure. Initially, security gurus area unit seemingly to be skeptical regarding the claims of any new algorithmic program. That's to not say that they lack interest or enthusiasm? It simply means that they will not provide it a seal of approval till the tactic contains a few miles on the milometer.

If you're introducing a brand new methodology, you rely heavily on the interest of the world's security specialists if you wish to induce the tactic accepted wide. Initial of all, the tactic should be in public on the market and sufficiently attention-grabbing to draw in experts' attention. If it's not novel, or if it includes mistakes, your methodology can get nothing quite a sniff. If you're a reputable guru and your methodology has some smart new tricks, the others may walk around and kick the tires. If you're very doing well, many of them can choose a take a look at drive. However before your methodology will become really accepted, it must be deployed within the globe for many years, hopefully in application that draws attacks. Once a way is deployed within the limelight, each hackers and bonafide security researchers can receive approval if they will break the system. For instance, once IEEE 802.11 WEP was broken, the story reached national newspapers, and also the researchers United Nations agency discovered the cracks attracted a lot of attention. But, if you survive a couple of years and nobody has broken your methodology, it is able to do the standing of trustworthy and mature. You most likely can, too.

You can see why it's therefore onerous to induce new strategies accepted and adopted. However you'll additionally see why it's necessary for this method to occur and why security gurus area unit correct to require a wait-and-see approach. Notice additionally that it's not enough to create an excellent methodology. Unless the tactic will attract the interest of the crypto logic analysis community and be deployed to draw in the interests of hackers, it will ne'er very be tested.

So what regarding the new Wi-Fi security strategies? However will we tend to make sure they're safe? It's true that the new security methods for Wi-Fi haven't had time within the field. However, the technology accustomed implement them relies where attainable on preceding and proven algorithms. It is often tempting for engineers to reinvent the wheel and is available up with some grand new theme of their own. Due to the expertise of the safety skilled concerned within the new Wi-Fi approach, this temptation has been resisted. Having aforesaid that, some new ideas are incorporated, and though they need been reviewed round the world, the "newness" risk will still apply.

Watch the Bottom You're Standing on for Cracks

Every day, we tend to create unnumberable assumptions. From our earliest days we've learned a way to investigate things and choose which of them area unit safe and which of them area unit dangerous. Over time we tend to perform several of those skills subconsciously; we tend to learn to trust, and for many folks, that trust is simply sometimes misplaced, generally painfully.

Humans mechanically transfer safe assumptions from acutely aware memory to subconscious behavior. The key word here is automatically; that's, individuals aren't aware this transfer happens. In fact, if it did not happen, we tend to couldn't operate, as our minds would be untidy with numerous checks and queries. However, this essential ability forever is that the open door that has been exploited by generations of con men, pickpockets, and tricksters in acting crimes. It's additionally the start line for hackers United Nations agency need to attack your network.

People style software package, hardware, and systems. Individuals write and assess international standards. Regardless of however subtle the planning tools, or what package software package is employed, the designers' assumptions still return shining through. Some area unit valid and a few false? And, a lot of hazardously, several area units applied subconsciously or implicitly.

Consider a medieval castle. The designers might specify thick walls, deep moats, and powerful gates. They might need that gallons of boiling oil be unbroken prepared in the slightest degree times. However would the castle folks fare against a contemporary heavier-than-air craft cruising overhead, dropping boiling oil on them? They'd have any defense as a result of the designers unconsciously assumed that attacks wouldn't return from the air. This assumption could be a hidden weakness of the castle style.

How is it attainable to safeguard against things that you simply cannot even imagine? However are you able to see the implicit assumptions and convey them forward for review and testing? There's no sure manner, however these challenges mildew the manner of thinking for security specialists. As a result, it will be tough to own standard conversations with security specialists. Here could be a easy take a look at to see whether or not you're reproof a security guru: raise him to call the safety system he considers to be the strongest within the world for causation secret knowledge by any methodology (wireless, wire, smoke signals, whatever). Then raise the subsequent question, "Would I be secure if I enforced this in my system?" If the solution is "yes," you're not reproof a true security guru. Security gurus ne'er say, "This is totally secure." they create statements like, "Based on the idea that attackers area unit restricted to process strategies and processor architectures like these days, it's computationally impossible to mount a [certain kind of attack] and no different varieties of attack area unit famous to be more practical at this point." generally they're ready to mention that one methodology is unquestionably as secure as another methodology, however the word "definite" does not get too several outings within the security expert's vocabulary.

Such hedging does not translate well to the shiny front of a product box, wherever customers merely rummage around for the words "this is secure." the most effective approach for a client is to know the strengths of the safety methodology used and, wherever attainable, the assumptions that were created within the style. If the assumptions area unit affordable, the tactic is simple, and lots of individuals area unit victimization it (to guarantee future support), the client will be snug.

The challenge for hackers, of course, is to appear for the limited cracks and crevices that result from hidden assumptions. Sadly for the remainder folks, this search is AN intriguing, fascinating, and motivating challenge for hackers. Some individuals wish to do problem puzzles, and a few individuals wish to play subtle problem-solving laptop games, typically wrapped in an exceedingly fantastical visual landscape. Hacking is another type of these mind games. Once inventing a brand new virus or a password-cracking program, the hacker is making an attempt to check into the mind of the designer and appearance for false assumptions that were created subconsciously. For instance, a recent virus known as "Code Red" (actually a worm) worked by exploiting the very fact that once internal memory buffers overflowed in an exceedingly laptop, info was accidentally left in memory in an exceedingly place that was accessible from outside. The system's designers created the false assumption that buffers don't overflow which, if they do, the surplus buffers area unit properly thrown away. Virtually actually this was a subconscious assumption; it absolutely was false and an offender found it.

HISTORY OF NETWORK SECURITY

The need for network security may be a comparatively new demand. Before the Nineteen Eighties most computers weren't networked. It had been undue to lack of need to network them; it had been additional a results of the shortage of technology. Most systems were mainframes or midrange systems that were centrally controlled and administered. Users interfaced with the mainframe through "dumb" terminals. The terminals had restricted capabilities. Terminals really needed a physical association on an avid port. The ports were typically serial connections that utilized the RS-232 protocol. It always needed one port for one terminal. IBM, Digital instrumentation, and different laptop makers developed variations on this design by utilizing terminal servers; however the essential thought was an equivalent. There was nothing comparable to what we have a tendency to expertise nowadays wherever tons of if not thousands of connections will reach a system on one network circuit.

In the Nineteen Eighties, the mixture of the event of the non-public laptop (computer), the event of network protocol standards, the decrease within the value of hardware, and therefore the development of latest applications created networking a way additional accepted follow. As a result, LANs, WANs, and distributed computing toughened tremendous growth throughout that amount.

When first deployed, LANs were comparatively secure-mainly as a result of they were physically isolated. They weren't typically connected to WANs, thus their standalone nature protected the network resources. WANs really preceded LANs and had been around for a few time, however they were typically centrally controlled and accessible by solely a couple of people in most organizations. WANs utilizing direct or dedicated in private owned or chartered circuits were comparatively secure as a result of access to circuits was restricted. To attach two locations (points A and B) typically needed a point-to-point (A-B) circuit. If you wished to attach a third location (point C) to each A and B, it needed two additional circuits (A-B, A-C, B-C).

Development of packet-switched protocols like X.25 and Transmission management Protocol/Internet Protocol (TCP/IP) reduced the price to deploy WANs, therefore creating them additional enticing to implement. These protocols allowed several systems to share circuits. Many folks or organizations may well be interconnected over the shared network. It had been now not necessary to attach systems in an exceedingly point-to-point configuration. Vulnerabilities were introduced with the preparation of this distributed setting utilizing shared, packet- switched networks using protocols like TCP/IP and therefore the thought of trustworthy systems. Systems on the network "trusted" one another. This case was oft created worse by connecting comparatively secure LANs to an unsecured WAN. Figure 3 illustrates the thought behind the packet-switched network. Basically, an organization's network connections enter into the cloud of the packet-switched network. Different organizations share the cloud, and on the packet-switched network one company's packets area unit intermixed with another organization's packets.

In this distributed setting the stress was on providing simple access and property. Security was an afterthought, if it had been thought of in the least. As a result, several systems were wide open and susceptible to threats that antecedently had not existed.

The Internet is that the largest and best better-known of this kind of network. The net utilizes TCP/IP and was primarily designed to attach computers in spite of their in operation systems in a straightforward and economical manner. Security wasn't a part of the first style of TCP/IP, and there are varieties of wide promulgated attacks that have exploited inherent weaknesses in its style. One well-known event was the network that brought the net to its knees back in 1986. Today, security should be additional necessary than simple access.

Figure 3. Packet switched WAN

Host A

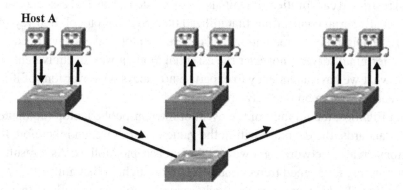

Brief History of Internet

The birth of the internet takes place in 1969 once *Advanced Research Projects Agency Network (ARPA-Net)* is commissioned by the *Department of Defense (DoD)* for analysis in networking. The ARPANET may be a success from the terribly starting. Though originally designed to permit scientists to share information and access remote computers, e-mail quickly becomes the foremost common application. The ARPANET becomes a high-speed digital post workplace as individuals use it to collaborate on analysis comes and discuss topics of assorted interests. The InterNetworking social unit becomes the primary of many standards-setting entities to control the growing network [10]. Vinton Cerf is electoral the primary chairman of the INWG, and later becomes called a "Father of the net."

In the 1980s, Bob designer and Vinton Cerf area unit key members of a team that make TCP/IP, the common language of all web computers. For the primary time the loose assortment of networks that created up the ARPANET is seen as Associate in Nursing "Internet", and therefore the web as we all know it nowadays is born. The mid-80s marks a boom within the computer and super-minicomputer industries. The mixture of cheap desktop machines and powerful, network-ready servers permits several firms to affix the net for the primary time. Companies begin to use the net to speak with one another and with their customers. In the 1990s, the net began to become out there to the general public. The globe Wide internet was born. Web browser and Microsoft were each competitive on developing a browser for the net. Web continues to grow and aquatics the net has become comparable to TV viewing for several users.

Security Timeline

Several key events contributed to the birth and evolution of laptop and network security. The timeline are often started as way back because the Nineteen Thirties. Polish cryptographers created an enigma machine in 1918 that regenerate plain messages to encrypted text. In 1930, mathematician, a superb scientist bust the code for the Enigma. Securing communications was essential in warfare II.

In the 1960s, the term "hacker" is coined by a few of Massachusetts Institute of Technology (MIT) students. The Department of Defense began the ARPANet, that gains quality as a passage for the electronic exchange of information and knowledge. This paves the means for the creation of the carrier network better-known nowadays because the web.

During the 1970s, the Telnet protocol was developed. This opened the door for public use of information networks that were originally restricted to government contractors and educational researchers.

During the 1980s, the hackers and crimes with reference to computers were starting to emerge. The 414 gang area unit raided by authorities when a nine-day cracking spree wherever they burgled top-secret systems. The computer Fraud and Abuse Act of 1986 were created owing to Ian Murphy's crime of stealing info from military computers. A collegian, financier, was guilty for unleashing the Morris Worm to over 6000 vulnerable computers connected to the internet. Supported issues that the Morris Worm ordeal may well be replicated, the *Computer Emergency Response Team (CERT)* was created to alert computer users of network security problems. Within the Nineties, web became public and therefore the security issues accumulated hugely. Roughly 950 million individuals use the net nowadays worldwide. On any day, there are unit roughly 225 major incidences of a security breach. These security breaches might additionally lead to financial losses of an outsized degree. Investment in correct security ought to be a priority for giant organizations yet as common users.

What is Network Security?

Network security consists of the provisions and policies adopted by a network administrator to forestall and monitor unauthorized access, misuse, modification, or denial of a electronic network and network-accessible resources. Network security involves the authorization of access to information during a network that is controlled by the network administrator. Users select or area unit appointed associate ID and watchword or different authenticating info that enables them access to info and programs among their authority. Network security covers a spread of laptop networks, each public and personal, that area unit utilized in chores conducting transactions and communications among businesses, government agencies and people. A network is non-public, like among an organization, et al. which could be hospitable public access. Network security is concerned in organizations, enterprises, and different styles of establishments. It will as its title explains: It secures the network, still as protective and overseeing operations being done. The foremost common and easy method of protective a network resource is by distribution it a novel name and a corresponding watchword.

Need for Network Security

The network wants security against attackers and hackers. Network Security includes two basic securities. The primary is that the security of information i.e. to shield the data from unauthorized access and loss. And also the second is computer security i.e. to shield knowledge and to thwart hackers. Here network security not solely suggests that security in an exceedingly single network rather in any network or network of networks.

Now our would like of network security has broken into two wants. One is that they would like of data security and different is that they would like of computer security. On internet or any network of a company, thousands of vital info is changed daily. This information is often victimized by attackers. The data security is required for the subsequent given reasons.

1. To shield the key info users on world wide web solely. No different person ought to see or access it.
2. To shield the data from unwanted written material, accidently or by choice by unauthorized users.
3. To shield the data from loss and build it to be delivered to its destination properly.
4. To manage for acknowledgement of message received by any node so as to shield from denial by sender in specific things. As an example let a client orders to buy a couple of shares xyz to the broader and denies for the order when 2 days because the rates go down.
5. To limit a user to send some message to a different user with name of a 3rd one. As an example a user x for his own interest makes a message containing some favorable directions and sends it to user y in such a way that y accepts the message as coming back from z, the manager of the organization.
6. To shield the message from unwanted delay within the transmission lines/route so as to deliver it to needed destination in time, just in case of urgency.
7. To shield the data from wandering the info packets or information packets within the network for infinitely durable and so increasing congestion within the line just in case destination machine fails to capture it as a result of some internal faults.

Another part of network security includes the pc security. Computer security suggests that to shield your automatic data processing system from unwanted damages caused owing to network. One in every of the most important reason for such damages are the viruses and spywares which will wipe off all the data from your hard disc or generally they will be enough harmful and will cause hardware issues too. Definitely the network should be protected against such kind of damaging computer code. The network computers are a part of it; therefore the laptop security from Hackers is additionally a region of network security. The requirements of laptop security from Hackers are as follows:-

- It ought to be protected against replicating and capturing viruses from infected files.
- It wants a correct protection from worms and bombs.
- There could be a would like of protection from Trojan Horses as they\'re enough dangerous for your laptop.

Security has one purpose: to shield assets. For many of history, this meant building robust walls to prevent the enemy and establishing tiny, well-guarded doors to supply secure access for friends. This strategy worked well for the centralized, fortress-like world of mainframe computers and closed networks, as seen in Figure 4.

The closed network generally consists of a network designed and enforced in an exceedingly company surroundings and provides property solely to identified parties and sites while not connecting to public networks. Networks were designed this manner within the past and thought to be fairly secure as a result of no outside property. With the appearance of private computers, LANs, and also the wide-open world of the net, the networks of nowadays are a lot of open, as shown in Figure 5.

As e-business and net applications still grow, the key to network security lies in shaping the balance between a closed and open network and differentiating the great guys from the unhealthy guys. With the increased variety of LANs and private computers, the net began to form much numbers of security risks.

Figure 4. Closed network

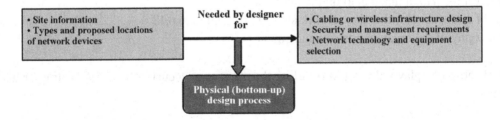

Figure 5. Open network

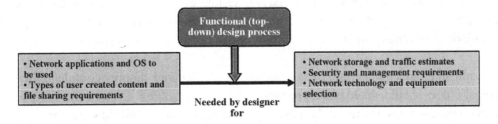

Firewall devices, that are computer code or hardware that enforce AN access management policy between two or a lot of networks, were introduced. This technology gave businesses a balance between security and straightforward outward access to the internet that was principally used for e-mail and net surfing.

This balance was temporary because the use of extranets began to grow, that connected internal and external business processes. Businesses were presently realizing tremendous price savings by connecting supply-chain management and enterprise resource designing systems to their business partners, and by connecting sales-force automation systems to mobile workers, and by providing electronic commerce connections to business customers and customers. The firewall began to incorporate intrusion detection, authentication, authorization, and vulnerability-assessment systems. Today, triple-crown firms have once more smitten a balance by keeping the enemies out with progressively advanced ways that of belongings friends in.

Most people expect security measures to make sure the following:

- Users will perform solely approved tasks.
- Users will acquire solely approved info.
- Users cannot cause harm to the info, applications, or in operation surroundings of a system.

The word security suggests that protection against malicious attack by outsiders (and by insiders). Statistically, there are a lot of attacks from within sources. Security additionally involves dominant the consequences of errors and instrumentality failures. Something that may defend against AN attack will in all probability stop random misfortunes, too.

Evaluating Security Needs

Before you'll develop a security arranges and policies for your organization, you want to assess the safety desires, which is able to typically be supported the subsequent broad considerations:

- Sort of business within which the organization engages
- Sort of information that's hold on the network
- Sort of connection(s) that the network should different networks
- Philosophy of the organization's management

Each of those can play a district in deciding the amount of security that's fascinating or necessary for your network.

Assessing the Sort of Business

Certain fields have inherent high-security needs. A visible example is that the military, or different government agencies that upset defense or national security problems. Personal firms with government defense contracts additionally are this class. Others could also be less obvious:

- Law companies area unit certain by law and ethics to safeguard shopper confidentiality.
- Medical offices should shield patient records.
- Enforcement agencies, courts, and different governmental bodies should secure info.

- Instructional establishments store student records.
- Firms that gather info from people or organizations guarantee that the information are unbroken confidential.

The competitive nature of the business is additionally a thought. In an exceedingly field like propagation analysis, that may be a "hot" market wherever new developments area unit being created on a day to day, any of that might involve vast profits for the corporate that patents the thought, protective trade secrets becomes vitally necessary. Most businesses can have some information of a confidential nature on the network's laptop systems, however the safety needs in some fields area unit abundant on top of others. This could be thought of as you start to develop your security arrange.

Assessing the Sort of Information

The second question to think about is what sort of information is hold on your network, and where. You will notice that a better level of security is required in one department or division than another. You may, in fact, need to divide the network physically, into separate subnets, to permit you to higher management access to totally different components of the corporate network severally.

Generally, payroll and human resource records (such as personnel files and claim documents), company money records (accounting documents, money statements, tax documents), and a spread of different common business records can have to be compelled to be protected. Even in cases wherever these documents area unit needed to be created public, you'll need to require steps to confirm that they can't be changed or destroyed. Bear in mind that information integrity, yet as information confidentiality and convenience, is protected by a decent security arrange.

Assessing the Network Connections

Your exposure to outside intruders is another thought in coming up with a way to implement security on your network. A computer network that's self-contained and has no neither web property, nor any modems or different outside connections won't need the degree of protection (other than physical security) that's necessary once there are a unit several avenues "in" that an trespasser will take.

Dialup electronic equipment connections benefit special thought. Whereas a dialup association is a smaller amount receptive intrusion than a fulltime dedicated association – each as a result of its connected to the surface for a shorter period of time, reducing the window of chance for intrusion, and since it'll typically have a dynamic IP address, creating it tougher for Associate in Nursing trespasser to find it on multiple occasions – permitting workstations on your network to own modems and phone lines will produce a large security risk.

If improperly designed, a laptop with a dialup association to the net that's additionally cabled to the interior network will act as a router, permitting outside intruders to access not simply the digital computer connected to the electronic equipment, however different computers on the computer network.

One reason for permitting modems at individual workstations is to permit users to dialup connections to different personal networks. A safer thanks to do that is to get rid of the modems and have the users established a virtual personal networking (VPN) reference to the opposite personal network through the LAN's web association. The best security policy is to own as few connections from the interior network to the surface as doable, and management access at those entry points (called the network perimeter).

Assessing Management Philosophy

This last criterion is that the most subjective, however will have an incredible influence on the safety level that's applicable for your organization. Most firms area unit supported one (or a mix of over one) management model.

Understanding Management Models

Some firms institute a extremely structured, formal management vogue. Workers area unit expected to respect a strict chain of command, and knowledge is usually disseminated on a "need to know" basis. Governmental agencies, particularly people who area unit law-enforcement connected, like police departments and investigatory agencies typically follow this philosophy. This can be typically cited because the paramilitary model.

Other firms, notably those within the IT trade and different fields that area unit subject to very little state regulation, area unit designed on the alternative premise: that each one workers ought to have the maximum amount info and input as doable, that managers ought to perform as "team leaders" instead of authoritarian supervisors, which restrictions on worker actions ought to be obligatory only necessary for the potency and productivity of the organization. This can be typically referred to as the "one huge happy family" model. Creativeness is valued over "going by the book," and job satisfaction is taken into account a crucial facet of enhancing worker performance and productivity.

In business management circles, these 2 diametrically-opposed models area unit referred to as Theory X (traditional paramilitary style) and Theory Y (modern, team-oriented approach). Though there are a unit varied different management models that are popularized in recent years, like Management by Objective (MBO) and Total Quality Management (TQM), every company's management vogue can fall somewhere on the time between Theory X and Theory Y. The management model is predicated on the non-public philosophies of the company's high decision-makers concerning the connection between management and workers.

The management model will have a profound influence on what's or isn't acceptable in coming up with security for the network. A "deny all access" security policy that's viewed as applicable in an exceedingly Theory X organization could meet with most ill will and worker discontentment in an exceedingly Theory Y company that it disrupts business operations. Forever contemplate the corporate "atmosphere" as a part of your security coming up with. If you've got smart reasons to implement strict security in an exceedingly Theory Y atmosphere, understand that you just can most likely need to justify the restrictions to management and "sell" them to workers, whereas those self same restrictions can be accepted while not question in an exceedingly additional ancient organization.

Designating Responsibility for Network Security

In any enterprise as complicated because the development and implementation of a comprehensive company security arrange and concomitant policies, it's important that areas of responsibility be clearly selected. Best practices dictate that nobody person ought to have complete authority or management, and in an enterprise-level network, it'd be troublesome for any single person to handle all aspects of developing and implementing the safety arrange anyway.

Responsibility for Developing the Safety Arrange and Policies

The initial creation of a decent security arranges would require an excellent deal of thought and energy. The policy can impact those in the least levels of the organization, and soliciting input from as several representatives of various departments and job descriptions as is sensible is fascinating. An efficient approach is to make a committee consisting of persons from many areas of the organization to be concerned in making and reviewing the safety arrange and policies.

The Security coming up with Committee would possibly embrace some or all of the following:

1. The network administrator and one or additional assistant directors
2. The site's security administrator
3. Department heads of assorted company departments or their representatives
4. Representatives of user teams which will be compact by the safety policies (for example, the assistant workers or the information process center)
5. A member of the legal department World Health Organization makes a specialty of laptop and technology law
6. A member of the finance or budget department

Responsibility for Implementing and Imposing the Safety Arrange and Policies

Security policies can typically be enforced and implemented by network directors and members of the IT workers. Job descriptions and policies ought to designate specifically World Health Organization is chargeable for the implementation of that components of the arrange. There ought to be a clear-cut chain of command that specifies whose call prevails just in case of conflict.

In some cases – like physical penetration of the network – the corporate staff can get involved. There ought to be written, clearly developed policies that stipulate that department has responsibility that task in such things. The safety arrange ought to additionally address the procedures for coverage security breaches, each internally, and if the police or different outside agencies area unit to be brought in (as well as World Health Organization is chargeable for or has the authority to decision in outside agents).

One of the foremost necessary factors in an exceedingly smart security policy is that it should be enforceable, and going a step any, it should be implemented. This can be necessary for legal yet as sensible reasons. If your company has policies in situ that they habitually fail to enforce, this could be seen as an off-the-cuff elimination of the policy, exploit the corporate lawfully to blame for the actions of workers World Health Organization violate the policy. If the policy are often implemented through technological suggests that, this can be most well-liked. If the policies should be implemented through reprimand or different actions against workers World Health Organization violate them, there ought to be clearly worded, universally distributed written documentation of what constitutes a violation and what sanctions can result, yet as World Health Organization is chargeable for imposing such sanctions.

The Goals of Network Security

Regardless of the access medium and therefore the coverage of a network, network security is often thought of through the accomplishment of two security goals: system security and communication security.

The computer system security is to safeguard info assets against unauthorized or malicious uses, yet on shield the knowledge hold on in laptop systems from unauthorized revealing, modification or destruction. The communication security is to safeguard info throughout its transmission through a communication medium, from unauthorized revealing, modification or destruction.

In order to realize the goals of network security in any network, the subsequent steps should be followed:

- *Define the assets to be protected and therefore the perimeter of the network.* Before implementing any security measures, the assets of the network should be known and assessed. Moreover, the perimeter of the network to be protected should be outlined, so as to differentiate the interior or personal network from the external or unreliable network.

- *Define the doable security threats and attacks.* When the network assets and therefore the network perimeter are outlined, the doable security attacks that threat the network should be outlined and evaluated. This can facilitate in that specialize in the protection from the foremost doable threats. During this method vital to consult specialized websites that specialize in the network security and security threats, either of proprietary product or from security threats and vulnerabilities databases.

- *Evaluate the safety risks and outline the required security level.* The subsequent steps to be appraise the examined threats in conjunction with existing vulnerabilities and assets. This could be performed by mistreatment the safety risk analysis methodology. Then, when the risks against network security are known, the required security level should be outlined, so as to line up the appropriate security measures.

- *Define the safety policies that formally came upon desired security level.* The required security level should then be formalized through network security policies. These policies area unit a proper thanks to outline what security services should be provided, so as to succeed in the network security goals and scale back the risks to desired and acceptable level?

- *Define the safety services and implement the correct security mechanism.* The safety services outline what security services should be maintained in every part of the network, like authentication and access management. The safety mechanism defines the means which will implement the practicality of the outlined security services. Additional detail concerning network security services and mechanisms area unit provided within the following sections. Note but that aside from the technical security mechanisms, different non technical security measures are outline so as to realize the required security level that's formally represented within the security policies. These non-technical measures area unit largely security procedures.

- *Periodically assure that the correct security policies, services and mechanisms area unit in situ.* Though the safety threats could are properly recognized and security policies could enforces the required security level with security mechanisms and controls, it's necessary to sporadically assure that everything is about up properly. Issues could arise attributable to new security threats and vulnerabilities, new security desires or attention of the prevailing security mechanisms. The amount that every of the higher than should be examine differs, since attributable to technology changes it's typically needed to look at the safety mechanisms additional oft than the safety policies or services, or the required security level.

Security Terms

Every trade has its own "language," the jargon that describes ideas and procedures peculiar to the sphere. Laptop networking is notorious for the "technotalk" and therefore the proliferation of acronyms that always mystify outsiders. Specialty areas inside and trade typically have their own brands of jargon, as well, and therefore the laptop security sub-field is not any exception.

It is out of the question to supply an entire gloss of security-related terms inside the scope of this chapter, however during this section, we'll outline a number of the additional common words and phrases that you just could encounter as you start to explore the fascinating world of laptop security:

- **Attack:** Within the context of computer/network security, and attack is an endeavor to access resources on a laptop or a network while not authorization, or to bypass security measures that area unit in situ.
- **Audit:** To trace security-related events, like work onto the system or network, accessing objects, or workout user/group rights or privileges.
- *Availability* of data, reliable and timely access to data.
- **Breach:** With success defeating security measures to realize access to information or resources while not authorization, or to create information or resources out there to unauthorized persons, or to delete or alter laptop files.
- **Brute Force Attack:** Commit to "crack" passwords by consecutive attempting all doable mixtures of characters till the proper combination works to permit access.
- **Buffer:** A holding space for information.
- **Buffer Overflow:** How to crash a system by golf shot additional information into a buffer than the buffer is in a position to carry.
- **CIA Triad:** Confidentiality, Integrity, and convenience of information. Guaranteeing the confidentiality, integrity, and convenience of information and services area unit primary security objectives that area unit typically associated with one another. See also convenience of information, confidentiality of information, and integrity of information.
- **Confidentiality of Data:** Guaranteeing that the contents of messages are unbroken secret. See also integrity of information.
- **Countermeasures:** Steps taken to forestall or reply to an attack or malicious code.
- **Cracker:** A hacker who makes a speciality of "cracking" or discovering system passwords to realize access to laptop systems while not authorization. See also hacker.
- **Crash:** Explosive failure of a system, rendering it unusable.
- **Defense-in-Depth:** The follow of implementing multiple layers of security. Effective defense-in-depth ways don't limit themselves to that specialize in technology, however additionally specialize in operations and other people. For instance, a firewall will shield against unauthorized intrusion, however coaching and therefore the implementation of well-considered security policies facilitate to confirm that the firewall is correctly designed.
- **Denial of Service Attack:** A deliberate action that keeps a laptop or network from functioning as meant (for example, preventing users from having the ability to log onto the network).

- **Exposure:** A live of the extent to that a network or individual laptop is receptive attack, supported its specific vulnerabilities, however acknowledge it's to hackers, and therefore the time length throughout that intruders have the chance to attack. For instance, a laptop employing a dialup analog association has less exposure to attack coming back over the net, as a result of its connected for a shorter amount of your time than those mistreatment "always-on" connections like cable, telephone circuit or T-carrier.

- **Hacker:** Someone World Health Organization spends time learning the small print of computer programming and in operation systems, a way to take a look at the bounds of their capabilities, and wherever their vulnerabilities lie. See also cracker.

- **Integrity of Information:** Guaranteeing that data has not been changed or altered, that the information received is similar to the information that was sent.

- **Least Privilege:** The principle of least privilege needs that users and directors have solely the minimum level of access to perform their job-related duties. In military formulation, the principle of least privilege is cited as have to be compelled to apprehend.

- **Malicious Code:** A malicious program or script that performs and action that designedly damages a system or information that performs another unauthorized purpose, or that gives unauthorized access to the system.

- **Penetration Testing:** Evaluating a system by making an attempt to avoid the computers or network's security measures.

- **Reliability:** The likelihood of a system or network continued to perform in an exceedingly satisfactory manner for a particular period of time underneath traditional in operation conditions.

- **Risk:** The likelihood that particular security threats are able to exploit system vulnerability, leading to injury, loss of information, or different unsought results. That is, a risk is that the total of the threat and the vulnerability.

- **Risk Management:** The method of characteristic, dominant and either minimizing or fully eliminating events that create a threat to system reliability, information integrity, and information confidentiality.

- **Sniffer:** A program that captures information because it travels across a network. Additionally referred to as a packet someone.

- **Social Engineering:** Gaining unauthorized access to a system or network by subverting personnel (for example, motility as a member of the IT department to convert users to reveal their passwords).

- **TCSEC:** Trusted Computer System Evaluation Criteria. A method of evaluating the amount of security of a system.

- **Technical Vulnerability:** A flaw or bug within the hardware or package elements of a system that leaves it susceptible to security breach.

- **Threat:** A possible danger to information or systems. A threat agent is often a virus; a hacker; a phenomenon, like a tornado; a discontented employee; a rival, and different menaces.

- **Trojan Horse:** A malicious program that seems to perform a fascinating performs however contains hidden code that's meant to permit unauthorized assortment, modification or destruction of information.

- **Virus:** A program that's introduced onto a system or network for the aim of performing an unauthorized action (which will vary from doping up a harmless message to destroying all information on the laborious disk).

- **Vulnerability:** A weakness within the hardware or package or security arranges that leaves a system or network receptive threat of unauthorized access or injury or destruction of information.
- **Worm:** A program that replicates itself, spreading from one machine to a different across a network.

Once you're snug with the language, you'll begin to deal with the individual objectives which will assist you in realizing your goal to make a secure network setting.

Principles of Network Security

Following area unit a number of the rules issued by Economic Cooperation and Development meant for development of laws and policies:

- **Accountability:** Everyone committed the safety of data should have specified responsibility towards actions.
- **Awareness:** Everybody from the organization should be able to access the data referring to security measures, practices and procedures and every one effort shall be created in building confidence in info systems.
- **Ethics:** The strategy within which info systems and their associated security mechanisms area unit operated should be able to respect the privacy, rights and legit interests of users.
- **Multidisciplinary Principle:** All the aspects and opinion should be thought of within the development of policies, procedures and techniques. These should embrace legal, technical, body, structure, operational, business and academic aspects.
- **Proportionality:** Security measures should be supported the worth of data and therefore the level of risk concerned.
- **Integration:** Security measures should be integrated to figure along and establish defensive depth within the security system.
- **Timeliness:** everybody ought to act along in coordinated and timely fashion once a security breach happens.
- **Reassessment:** Security mechanisms and desires should be reassessed sporadically to confirm that organizations needs area unit being met.
- **Democracy:** The safety of the data and therefore the systems wherever its hold on should be in line with the legitimate use and knowledge transfer of that information.

In addition to those security principles, some extra principles area unit necessary once is shaping policies. These include:

- **Individual Accountability:** People area unit unambiguously known to the safety systems and user's area unit command in charge of their actions.
- **Authorization:** The safety mechanisms should be able to grant authorization for access to specific info or systems supported the identification and authorization of the user.
- **Least Privilege:** People should be able to access the knowledge that they have for the completion of their connected task or job responsibilities, and just for as long as they are doing that job or complete various task.

- **Separation of Duty:** Functions should be divided between individuals to confirm that no single person will commit a fraud, which may go undiscovered.
- **Auditing:** The work being done, the associated results should be monitored to confirm compliance with established procedures and therefore the correctness of the work being performed.

Identifying Potential Risks to Network Security

A risk analysis ought to determine the risks to the network, network resources, and data. The intent of a risk analysis is to spot the parts of the network, judge the importance of every element, and so apply associate degree acceptable level of security. This analysis helps to keep up an executable balance between security and needed network access. The secret is to spot what has to be secured and at what value. Extra money associate degreed assets would be allotted making certain the safety of a pricy automobile versus a recent Prussian, for instance.

Asset Identification

Before the network is often secured, you want to determine the individual parts that compose the network. You would like to form associate degree plus inventory that has all the network devices and endpoints, like hosts and servers.

Vulnerability Assessment

After you've got known the network parts, you'll assess their vulnerabilities. These vulnerabilities may well be weaknesses within the technology, configuration, or security policy. Any vulnerability you discover should be addressed to mitigate any threat that would cash in of the vulnerability. Vulnerabilities are often fastened by varied ways, as well as applying software package patches, reconfiguring devices, or deploying countermeasures, like firewalls and antivirus software package. Several websites list the vulnerabilities of network parts, and also the makers of operative systems and parts that list vulnerabilities of their product sponsor several websites.

Threat Identification

A threat is an incident that may cash in of vulnerability and cause a negative impact on the network. Potential threats to the network have to be compelled to be known, and also the connected vulnerabilities have to be compelled to be addressed to attenuate the danger of the threat.

Network Design Overview

Computers and knowledge networks are important to the success of companies, each massive and tiny. They connect folks, support applications and services, and supply access to the resources that keep the companies running. To satisfy the daily needs of companies, networks themselves have become quite advanced.

Network Design Process

A structure network needs many sorts of style, every specializing in a particular characteristic of the network. For instance, one style will detail network traffic flows, whereas another illustrates the physical location of every network device.

Functional Design Process

Functional style is additionally observed as top-down style. During this method, the network designer begins with associate degree assessment of the categories of users and applications probably to be supported by the projected network. Other factors, as well as the projected network package (NOS) and also the expected volume of information to be generated by users, also are evaluated. Upon analysis of the knowledge gathered, the designer will generate preliminary needs for network process and storage, expected traffic patterns and levels, and also the body infrastructure, as shown in Figure 6. This info is then wont to choose the acceptable network technologies and product.

Physical Design Process

Physical style is additionally observed as bottom-up style. During this method, the network designer begins with associate degree assessment of the site(s) wherever the projected network is to be deployed. Details like the physical characteristics of the premises, security needs, and expected distances between network devices are assessed, as shown in Figure 7.

Figure 6. Functional (top-down) design

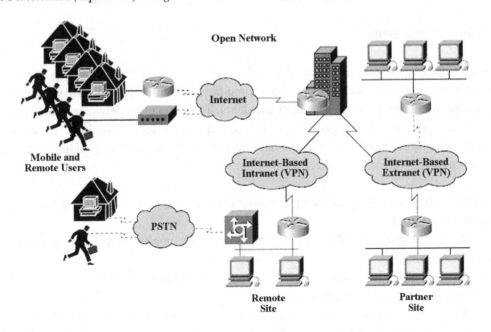

Figure 7. Physical (bottom – up) design

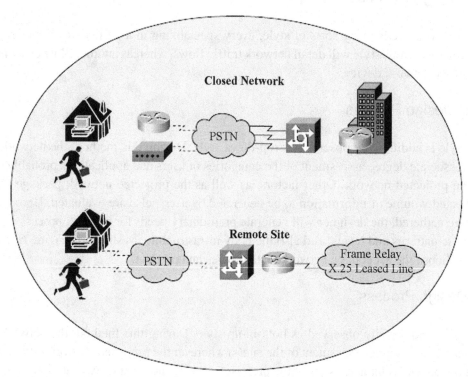

Upon analysis of the knowledge gathered, acceptable picks are often created for the categories of network property and product needed at the site(s). Note: The physical style method is employed in cases wherever careful network characteristics aren't accessible (e.g., new multi-tenant business buildings).

Network Requirements

Today, the Internet-based economy usually demands nonstop client service. This suggests that business networks should be accessible nearly one hundred computer of the time. They have to be sensible enough to mechanically shield against sudden security incidents. These business networks should even be able to fits ever-changing traffic masses to keep up consistent application response times. It's not sensible to construct networks by connecting several standalone parts while not careful designing and style. Most businesses even have solely many needs for his or her network:

- The network ought to sit up all the time, even within the event of unsuccessful links, failure, and overloaded conditions.
- The network ought to faithfully deliver applications and supply affordable response times from any host to any host.
- The network ought to be secure. It ought to shield information that's transmitted over it and data hold on the devices that hook up with it.
- The network ought to be simple to switch to adapt to network growth and general business changes.
- Because failures often occur, troubleshooting ought to be simple. Finding and fixing a drag shouldn't be too long.

Building a Good Network

Good networks don't happen out of the blue. They're the results of exertions by network designers and technicians, United Nations agency determine network needs and choose the simplest solutions to satisfy the requirements of a business.

The steps needed to style a decent network are as follows:

1. Verify the business goals and technical needs.
2. Verify the options and functions needed to satisfy the requirements known in Step one.
3. Perform a network-readiness assessment.
4. Produce an answer and web site acceptance check set up.
5. Produce a project set up.

After the network needs are known, the steps to coming up with a decent network are followed because the project implementation moves forward. Network users usually don't suppose in terms of the quality of the underlying network. They consider the network as the way to access the applications they have, after they would like them.

Fundamental Design Goals

When examined rigorously, these needs translate into four elementary network style goals:

- **Scalability:** ascendable network styles will grow to incorporate new user teams and remote sites and might support new applications while not impacting the extent of service delivered to existing users.
- **Availability:** A network designed for accessibility is one that delivers consistent, reliable performance, twenty four hours every day, seven days every week. Additionally, the failure of one link or piece of kit shouldn't considerably impact network performance.
- **Security:** Security may be a feature that has got to be designed into the network, not value-added on once the network is complete. Designing the placement of security devices, filters, and firewall options is important to safeguarding network resources.
- **Manageability:** Despite however sensible the initial network style is, the accessible network workers should be able to manage and support the network. A network that's too advanced or troublesome to keep up cannot operate effectively and expeditiously.

Hierarchical Network Design

In networking, a graded style is employed to cluster devices into multiple networks. The networks are organized in an exceedingly superimposed approach. The graded style model has three basic layers:

- **Core Layer:** Connects distribution layer devices
- **Distribution Layer:** Interconnects the smaller native networks
- **Access Layer:** Provides property for network hosts and finish devices

Hierarchical networks have benefits over flat network styles. The good thing about dividing a flat network into smaller, additional manageable graded blocks is that native traffic remains native. Solely traffic destined for different networks is rapt to a better layer. Layer two devices in an exceedingly flat network offer very little chance to manage broadcasts or to filter undesirable traffic. As additional devices and applications are value-added to a flat network, response times degrade till the network becomes unusable. Figures 8 and 9 show the benefits of a graded network style versus a flat network style.

Figure 8. Flat networks

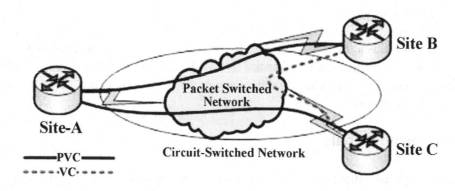

Figure 9. Hierarchical networks

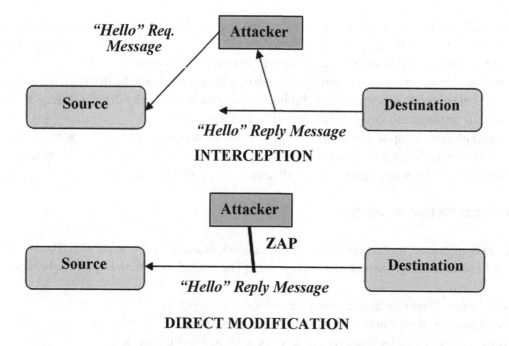

The Benefits of a Hierarchical Network Design

To meet the several elementary style goals, a network should be engineered on associate degree design that permits for each flexibility and growth.

- **Scalability:** Hierarchical networks scale very glowing. The modularity of the design permits you to duplicate design parts because the network grows. As a result of every instance of the module is consistent, growth is simple to set up and implement. for instance, if your style model consists of two distribution layer switches for each ten access layer switches, you'll be able to still add access layer switches till you've gotten access layer switches cross-connected to the two distribution layer switches before you wish to feature further distribution layer switches to the constellation. Also, as you add additional distribution layer switches to accommodate the load from the access layer switches, you'll be able to add further core layer switches to handle the extra load on the core.

- **Redundancy:** As a network grows, availableness becomes additional necessary. You'll be able to dramatically increase availableness through straightforward redundant implementations with stratified networks. Access layer switches area unit connected to two completely different distribution layer switches to confirm path redundancy. If one amongst the distribution layer switches fails, the access layer switch will switch to the opposite distribution layer switch. In addition, distribution layer switches area unit connected to two or additional core layer switches to confirm path availableness if a core switch fails. The sole layer wherever redundancy is proscribed is at the access layer. Typically, finish node devices, like computers, printers, and information science phones, don't have the power to attach to multiple access layer switches for redundancy. If associate degree access layer switch fails, simply the devices connected to it one switch would be littered with the outage. The remainder of the network would still operate unaffected.

- **Performance:** Communication performance is increased by avoiding the transmission of information through low-performing, intercessor switches. Information is distributed through collective switch port links from the access layer to the distribution layer at close to wire speed in most cases. The distribution layer then uses its high performance change capabilities to forward the traffic up to the core, wherever it's routed to its final destination. As a result of the core and distribution layers perform their operations at terribly high speeds, there's less competition for network information measure. As a result, properly designed stratified networks are able to do close to wire speed between all devices.

- **Security:** Security is improved and easier to manage. Access layer switches are often designed with varied port security choices that give management over that devices area unit allowed to attach to the network. You furthermore may have the flexibleness to use additional advanced security policies at the distribution layer. You will apply access management policies that outline that communication protocols area unit deployed on your network and wherever they're permissible to travel. For instance, if you would like to limit the utilization of HTTP to a selected user community connected at the access layer, you may apply a policy that blocks HTTP traffic at the distribution layer. Limiting traffic supported higher layer protocols, like information science and HTTP, needs that your switches area unit able to method policies at that layer. Some access layer switches support Layer three practicality, however it's sometimes the duty of the distribution layer switches to method Layer three information, as a result of they will method it way more with efficiency.

- **Manageability:** Manageability is comparatively straightforward on a stratified network. Every layer of the stratified style performs specific functions that area unit consistent throughout that layer. Therefore, if you wish to vary the practicality of associate degree access layer switch, you may repeat that amendment across all access layers switches within the network as a result of the presumptively perform a similar functions at their layer. Readying of latest switches is additionally simplified as a result of switch configurations are often traced between devices with only a few modifications. Consistency between the switches at every layer permits for fast recovery and simplified troubleshooting. In some special things, there can be configuration inconsistencies between devices, thus you must make sure that configurations area unit well documented in order that you'll be able to compare them before readying.

- **Maintainability:** Because stratified networks area unit standard in nature and scale terribly simply, they're straightforward to take care of. With different constellation styles, flexibility becomes progressively sophisticated because the network grows. Also, in some network style models, there's a finite limit to however massive the network will grow before it becomes too sophisticated and dearly-won to take care of. Within the stratified style model, switch functions area unit outlined at every layer, creating the choice of the proper switch easier. Adding switches to one layer doesn't essentially mean there'll not be a bottleneck or different limitation at another layer. For a full mesh constellation to attain most performance, all switches got to be superior switches, as a result of every switch has to be capable of acting all the functions on the network. Within the stratified model, switch functions area unit completely different at every layer. you'll be able to economize by mistreatment less costly access layer switches at very cheap layer, and pay additional on the distribution and core layer switches to attain high performance on the network.

Network Design Methodology

Large network style comes are commonly divided into three distinct steps:

1. Determine the network needs.
2. Characterize the prevailing network.
3. Style the configuration and solutions.

Step 1: Determine the Network Needs

The network designer works closely with the client to document the goals of the project. Figure 10 depicts a gathering between the designer and also the business owner. Goals are sometimes separated into two categories:

- **Business Goals:** Target however the network will create the business additional prosperous
- **Technical Requirements:** Target however the technology is enforced inside the network

Figure 10. Client interaction

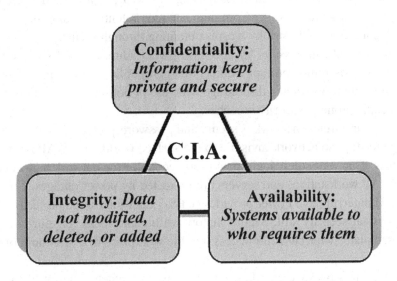

Step 2: Characterizing the Prevailing Network

Information regarding the present network and services is gathered and analyzed. It's necessary to check the practicality of the prevailing network with the outlined goals of the new project. The designer determines whether or not any existing instrumentality, infrastructure, and protocols are often reused, and what new instrumentality and protocols are required to complete the planning.

Step 3: Style the Configuration and Solutions

A common strategy for network style is to require a top-down approach. During this approach, the network applications and repair needs are known, and so the network is meant to support them. When the planning is complete, a paradigm or proof-of-concept check is performed. This approach ensures that the new style function needless to say before it's enforced.

Network Security Measures, Mechanisms

Network Security Measures

IT professionals are charged with making certain that company knowledge are unbroken secure which workers follow security protocols. The latter are often notably difficult however there are software package and best practices that may improve compliance with security measures.

Here may be a list of measures that may be simply adopted throughout a company:

- Activate firewalls and modify administrator settings on every terminal to stop workers from disabling them.
- Go into management panels and guarantee settings important for security will solely be modified by directors.

- Install port block and IP block software package to stop phishing and adware from slippery through antivirus software package. Communicate any potential weaknesses with workers, like email alerts regarding notably sneaky worms obtaining through security.
- Email is often created super-secure by specifying what addresses it'll settle for. If this is often not an appropriate possibility, prompt workers that non-public emails sent through the system are technically company property and discourage wide use of non-public emailing. Prompt them that email is especially prone to security breaches.
- Make positive your wireless network is secure and password-protected. You'll conjointly set software package to stay the network invisible to the surface world. Use WAP or WPA or WPA2 for secure wireless. This way, solely legitimate users recognize the network name and watchword.
- Make positive all workstations and servers are protected by power outages. Computer Magazine recommends Uninterruptable Power provides (UPS) rather than surge protectors.
- Look into physical security still. Secure laptops with cable locks. If your company is massive enough, contemplate swipe cards for access into the workplace or a minimum of the server area.

Finally, install antivirus packages. Packages like Norton are much better at block malware than at cleansing them out. (Ulanoff, 2010) They conjointly offer regular updates that may be simply shared throughout a network.

Security Mechanisms

A security policy describes precisely which actions the entities in a system are allowed to take and which ones are prohibited. Entities include users, services, data, machines, and so on. Once a security policy has been laid down, it becomes possible to concentrate on the security mechanisms by which a policy can be enforced. Important security mechanisms are:

1. Encryption
2. Authentication
3. Authorization
4. Auditing

Encryption is fundamental to computer security. Encryption transforms data into something an attacker cannot understand. In other words, encryption provides a means to implement confidentiality. In addition, encryption allows us to check whether data have been modified. It thus also provides support for integrity checks.

Authentication is used to verify the claimed identity of a user, client, server, and so on. In the case of clients, the basic premise is that before a service will do work for a client, the service must learn the client's identity. Typically, users are authenticated by means of passwords, but there are many other ways to authenticate clients.

After a client has been authenticated, it is necessary to check whether that client is authorized to perform the action requested. Access to records in a medical database is a typical example. Depending on who accesses the database, permission may be granted to read records, to modify certain fields in a record, or to add or remove a record.

Auditing tools are used to trace which clients accessed what, and which way. Although auditing does not really provide any protection against security threats, audit logs can be extremely useful for the analysis of a security breach, and subsequently taking measures against intruders. For this reason, attackers are generally keen not to leave any traces that could eventually lead to exposing their identity. In this sense, logging accesses makes attacking sometimes a riskier business.

CASE STUDY: MOBILE DEVICE SECURITY – UNDERSTANDING VULNERABILITIES AND MANAGING RISKS

Introduction

Over the past two decades, we have witnessed significant technology advances in mobile devices, from the personal data assistants (PDAs) of the late 1990s and early 2000s to the ubiquitous and multifunctional smartphones of today. These advances have extended the virtual boundaries of the enterprise, blurring the lines between home and office and coworker and competitor by providing constant access to email, enabling new mobile business applications and allowing the access to, and storing of, sensitive company data.

History

When the first BlackBerry smartphone was released in the early 2000s, corporations recognized the benefits of remote email and calendar access and began providing smartphones with network access to a large percentage of their workforce, effectively establishing the idea of 24-hour connectivity.

The popularity of smartphones extended beyond business users with the release of Apple's iPhone and later devices running Android, BlackBerry, Windows Mobile and Windows Phone 7 operating systems. Features expanded beyond just email and web browsing; mobile devices now have the ability to take photos, run custom applications, view rich content websites with Flash and JavaScript, connect to other devices and networks wirelessly, establish virtual private network (VPN) connections, and act as data traffic conduits for other devices (known as tethering).

Vulnerabilities and Security Challenges

With the increase in mobile device capabilities and subsequent consumer adoption, these devices have become an integral part of how people accomplish tasks, both at work and in their personal lives. Although improvements in hardware and software have enabled more complex tasks to be performed on mobile devices, this functionality has also increased the attractiveness of the platform as a target for attackers. Android's "open application" model has led to multiple instances of malicious applications with hidden functionality that surreptitiously harvest user data. Similarly, third-party Android application markets in China have been identified as hosting applications with administrative remote command execution capability.

Many organizations are concerned about data integrity, and increased regulation and data protection requirements have placed further obligations on organizations to properly secure data that interacts with mobile devices. As a result, higher levels of security and data protection assurance are required — potentially more than vendors or the platforms themselves are currently able to provide.

Mobile Device Risks

The ubiquity of mobile devices in the corporate environment has allowed the further expansion of the corporate office. From a security perspective, the risks and potential effects of deploying and supporting mobile devices as a corporate tool must be understood.

Trusted Clients

Mobile devices often have elevated levels of trust due to inherently strong client identification mechanisms. In the BlackBerry Enterprise Server architecture, a BlackBerry device is authenticated through a triple-DES shared-key infrastructure. This ensures that the BlackBerry unit accessing the server is a valid device (as long as the key remains uncompromised), but it does not speak to the intentions of the user. This trust also applies to other devices connected via secure channels to the environment. Due to this inherent trust of the connection, safeguards normally in place for external connections are disabled or infrequently implemented.

The iPhone application model also relies to a degree on users downloading applications from a trusted source. However, owners may bypass device restrictions through a method known as "jail breaking". Once users jailbreak their iPhones, they can remove any policy requirements on the phone, install unapproved applications and potentially be exposed to additional security threats.

Network Architecture

In a mobile device implementation, the infrastructure to control and manage mobile device connections often exists within the corporate intranet instead of a demilitarized zone (DMZ). This flat network strategy to provide mobile device data access presents the same security risks as a single-tiered wired intranet. In addition, weaknesses in vendor-advertised controls can create unexpected vulnerabilities in the security of the implementation.

Policy Implementation

Compared to laptops, mobile devices often contain stronger client-side controls that can shift the security concern away from infrastructure lockdown to device lockdown. The inherent trust partly established from the tendency to trust the owners of mobile devices is fully realized when client-side controls are in place. However, an attacker can easily bypass incorrect, insufficient or weakly implemented controls, thereby leveraging the internal network's trust in the device. For example, BlackBerry devices supported by the appropriate version of BlackBerry Enterprise Server can act as modems for a laptop to access the intranet. This would bypass some device restrictions and allow a malicious user to attack the internal network from the much more functional platform of a PC.

Stolen or Lost Devices

A fundamental problem of mobile devices is physical access control. By their design, mobile devices are most useful outside of the office and on the move with the owner. This presents several concerns for a security administrator, as the device on the move is more likely to be lost or stolen — and subsequently used by a malicious attacker. Considering these risks, Ernst & Young recommends assessing devices using a testing methodology specific to the risks inherent in these types of devices.

Vulnerability Identification

We recommend a structured approach, consisting of both manual testing and automated reviews aimed at identifying and exploiting vulnerabilities. Specifically, we recommend assessing mobile device configurations using the following approaches:

- Network accessibility
- Policy configuration

Mobile Device Application Gray Box Assessment

Mobile device application gray box assessments combine traditional source code reviews (white box testing) with front-end (black box) testing techniques. The application's codebase should be examined for critical areas of functionality and for symptoms of common poor coding practices. Each of these "hot spots" in the code should be linked to the live instance of the application where manual exploit techniques can verify the existence of security vulnerability. The recommended approach also follows this process in reverse order by reviewing the application according to our black box methodology and linking identified vulnerabilities to their cause in the codebase. Mobile code gray box assessments are designed to:

- Prioritize high-risk areas of code
- Maximize code coverage
- Identify root causes of identified vulnerabilities

The assessment approach follows the steps outlined below.

Threat Modeling

Threat modeling allows the testing team to identify first those threats that have the greatest potential impact to the application. This phase should be used to prioritize specific application components or areas of code during later phases. Using the application architecture documents provided with the application, the testing team should familiarize themselves with the general architecture and usage scenarios for the application.

Gather Information

Through collaboration with the mobile application development team, documents required to assist in understanding the design and functionality of the application should be obtained. Details described in these documents will provide the foundation for all of the steps in the threat modeling process.

Undertake Reconnaissance and Application Mapping

Understanding how the mobile application is intended to function is vital to creating a model of the application to which threats can be applied. During this step, the testing team should manually crawl and explore the live instance of the application. The team should then explore both the anonymous and authenticated portions of the application while focusing on areas of the application that handle sensitive data and functionality. The architecture, configuration, processes, users and technologies are all documented in this step and leveraged in later steps. The areas that will be flagged for targeted testing during the next phase include:

- Administrative interfaces
- Multipart forms
- Transmission of sensitive information
- Interfaces to external or third-party applications
- Use of mobile protocols, such as SMS, MMS and WAP

Every request and response during this stage should be logged for later analysis using a combination of local proxy tools and network sniffers.

SUMMARY

This chapter covers an awfully massive and necessary space of network security. Because the world becomes a lot of connected by networks, the importance of network security will definitely still grow. Security problems for networks are visible and necessary, however their analysis is comparable to the analysis in hot water different aspects of security. Security in networks is that the combination and fruits of everything we all know concerning security, and positively everything we've got mentioned during this chapter.

Network security is an important field that is increasingly gaining attention as the internet expands. Secure network environments are an ever-growing need. Weaknesses within the network have lead to the rapid growth of identity theft and daily computer virus outbreaks. Software developers and network administrators are being held accountable for compromises within their systems, while attackers remain anonymous. Network security is the process by which digital information assets are protected. The goals of network security square measure as follows:

- Protect confidentiality
- Maintain integrity
- Ensure availability

Understand the fundamentals needs of network security. These include the definition of security, computer security, security and privacy, network security important. The critical characteristics of information, among them confidentiality, integrity, and availability (the C.I.A. triangle), must be protected at all times; this protection is implemented by multiple measures (policies, education training and knowledge, and tools).

Reviews the importance of network security and presents some relevant background and history. It also introduces some basic terminology that is used throughout the chapter to define network, information, and computer security, security timeline, goals and fundamentals framework for Network Security.

A structure network needs many sorts of style, every specializing in a particular characteristic of the network. For instance, one style will detail network traffic flows, whereas another illustrates the physical location of every network device. The process of designing a good network requires concerted efforts by network designers and technicians, who identify network requirements and select the best solutions to meet the needs of a business. The four fundamental technical requirements of network design are scalability, availability, security, and manageability. In the hierarchical design model, it is easiest and usually least expensive to control the size of a failure domain in the distribution layer. Redundancy at the distribution layer ensures that failure domains remain small. As a network designer, it is extremely important that these goals and considerations be used from the very beginning of the network design methodology. From the topology used to the level of physical access given to personnel can mean the difference between a successful network implementation and a dismal failure.

The final section, we will outline means by which many of these risks may be mitigated through technical device controls, third-party software, and organizational policy. These components all contribute to an enterprise-grade mobility management program that will ultimately serve as a guide in the rapidly evolving mobile environment.

REFERENCES

Ashland, R. E. (1985). B1 Security for Sperry 1100 Operating System. In *Proceedings of the 8th National Computer Security Conference* (pp. 105–7). Gaithersburg, MD: National Bureau of Standards.

Best Practices for Network Security in Emerging Businesses. (n.d.). Productive Corporation.

Blotcky, S., Lynch, K., & Lipner, S. (1986). SE/VMS: Implementing Mandatory Security in VAX/VMS. In *Proceedings of the 9th National Computer Security Conference* (pp. 47–54). Gaithersburg, MD: National Bureau of Standards.

Department of Defense. (1985). DoD Trusted Computer System Evaluation Criteria. DOD 5200.28-STD. Washington, DC: Department of Defense. (U.S. Government Printing Office number 008-000-00461-7)

Douligeris, & Kotzanikolaou. (n.d.). Network Security. *Telecommunication Systems and Technologies, 2*.

Douligeris, C., & Serpanos, D. (Eds.). (2006). Network Security: Current Status and Future Directions. Wiley–IEEE.

Fraim, L. J. (1983). SCOMP: A Solution to the Multilevel Security Problem. Computer, 16(7), 26–34.

Glossary of Terms Used in Security and Intrusion Detection by SANS Institute. (n.d.). Accessed online at www.sans.org/resources/glossary.php

Internet History Timeline. (n.d.). Retrieved from www3.baylor.edu/~Sharon_P_Johnson/etg/inthistory.htm

National Computer Security Center. (1987). *Trusted Network Interpretation. NCSC-TG-005*. National Computer Security Center.

National Security Telecommunications and Information Systems Security. (1994). *National Training Standard for Information Systems Security (Infosec) Professionals*. Accessed 8 Feb 2007 from www.cnss.gov/Assets/pdf/nstissi_4011.pdf

Organick, E. I. (1972). *The Multics System: An Examination of Its Structure*. Cambridge, MA: MIT Press.

Peltier, T. R. (2001). *Information security risk analysis*. Auerbach Publications.

RFC 2828–Internet Security Glossary from the Internet RFC/STD/FYI/BCP Archives. (n.d.). Accessed online at www.faqs.org/rfcs/rfc2828.html

Schell, R. R., Tao, T. F., & Heckman, M. (1985). Designing the GEMSOS Security Kernel for Security and Performance. In *Proceedings of the 8th National Computer Security Conference* (pp. 108–19). Gaithersburg, MD: National Bureau of Standards.

Security. (n.d.). In *Merriam-Webster Online*. Accessed 8 February 2007 from www.m-w.com/dictionary/security

Security Overview. (n.d.). Retrieved from www.redhat.com/docs/manuals/enterprise/RHEL-4-Manual/security-guide /ch-sgs-ov.html

Simmonds, A., Sandilands, P., & van Ekert, L. (2004). An Ontology for Network Security Attacks. Lecture Notes in Computer Science, 3285, 317–323. Doi: doi:10.1007/978-3-540-30176-9_41

Ulanoff, L. (2010, November). Computer Trouble Isn`t Always What You Think It Is. *PC Magazine*.

Whitmore, J., Bensoussan, A., Green, P., Hunt, D., Kobziar, A., & Stern, J. (1973). Design for Multics Security Enhancements. ESD-TR-74-176. Hanscom AFB, MA: Air Force Electronic Systems Division.

Chapter 2
Security Issues in Mobile Wireless Networks

Arif Sari
Girne American University, Cyprus

ABSTRACT

The varieties of studies in literature have been addressed by the researchers to solve security problems of Mobile Wireless Ad Hoc Networks (MANET) against denial of service (DoS) and distributed denial of service (DDoS) attacks. Attackers have proposed variety of methods and techniques by considering weaknesses of the wireless nature of the channels and specific characteristics of mobile wireless networks. This chapter evaluates variety of attacks proposed in the literature against MANET by classifying variety of security strategies and mechanisms proposed by the researchers. The algorithms are discussed and explained separately. All these attacks are classified in different categories and security strategies proposed by the researchers have been explained.

INTRODUCTION

Security is one of the major problems of network systems. Secure communication becomes significant challenge for Mobile Wireless Ad Hoc Networks (MANET) due to their dynamic network topology and lack of centralized infrastructure. The varieties of attacks cause potential threats from different aspects, however, Denial of Service attacks (DoS) or Distributed Denial of Service attacks (DDoS) are two of the most harmful attacks against functionality and stability of network systems and MANETs are more vulnerable to these attacks due to limited resources that forces them to be greedy in resource utilization. These attacks aims to paralyze the member of the network (a node) or the entire network, by flooding excessive volume of traffic to consume the key resources of the member of the network or the entire network.

Solving security issues in these networks become more critical since financial aspects of the DoS and DDoS attacks becomes noticeable and since the application areas covers military, disaster relief operations, mine site operations and robot data acquisitions. Such networks can be used to enable next generation of battlefield applications envisioned by the military including situation awareness systems

DOI: 10.4018/978-1-4666-8761-5.ch002

for maneuvering war fighters, and remotely deployed unmanned micro-sensor networks. MANETs can provide communication for civilian applications, such as disaster recovery and message exchanges among medical and security personnel involved in rescue missions.

Majority of the research efforts in the literature have been taken to solve an effective and applicable security mechanism problems of MANETs, which would detect the flooding attack, mitigate the effects and provide traceback mechanism. Research efforts on MANETs provided security through different mechanisms.

Based on the wide range of survey and analysis of current MANETs DDoS attacks and security system strategies, the major purposed solutions composed of two-tier architecture which has a little complexity that obeys the nature of MANETs. On many surveys, the proposed solutions require some modifications on routing protocols (such as AODV, DSR, DSDV), or require some cooperation or support from non-system node(s), or in some studies controlling the access and authorization through assigning through certification authorities (CA). These proposed solutions and strategies against DoS attacks can be classified under different categories and especially Jamming attacks are investigated by the researchers in the literature since these attacks consume the nodes power and processing abilities to keeping them busy by injecting huge amount of traffic on the network (Nguyan, et.al, 2000).

DoS defence methods have been proposed since long time, but most of them remain theoretical with no actual implementation or could not produce satisfied results and performance when applied on MANETs. Many of these methods need to be implemented simultaneously and collaboratively on several nodes, making them difficult to implement especially on nodes which are distributed and need to maintain round-the-clock Internet connectivity. In addition to this, this implementation becomes more difficult once we consider distributed framework and the stability of Internet connection problems arises on MANETs. Moreover, adopted solutions introduce relative complexity, overhead and delay to the network, by adding features such as digital signatures and encryption. The security methods rely on random or probabilistic means to detect legitimate traffic and discard it, which necessities that a certain percentage of legitimate packets would be dropped in the process. While this might not be a serious downside, it reduces the overall Quality of service on providing security.

Recent wireless research indicates that the wireless MANET presents a larger security problem than conventional wired and wireless networks. A Jamming attacks exhausts the victim's network resources such as bandwidth, computing power, battery etc. The victim is unable to provide services to its legitimate clients and network performance is greatly deteriorated. This chapter provides a wide range of literature survey of existing methods and approaches to providing security in MANETs.

Security Threat Aspects and Design Challenges of Mobile Ad Hoc Networks

In recent years, home or small office networking and collaborative computing with laptop computers in a small area have also emerged as other major potential areas of where the use of MANET could be useful. In this introductory chapter on ad-hoc networks we discuss some of the issues related with security aspects and along with some general and foundation topics that provide context for the rest of the chapters that follow in this thesis. This chapter begins by first looking into the security aspects and design challenges of MANETs. The continuation of this section covers discussion of different types of vulnerabilities in MANET environment. Section 2.2 provides a detailed comparative survey of existing methods and techniques of implementing security on MANETs. In section 2.3, previous studies on securing MANETs and examples of specific security strategies against DDoS and DoS attacks are highlighted and classified.

There is variety of research conducted on securing mobile ad hoc networks in the literature. The Mobile ad hoc network is an active mobile device is called node which is free to move independently in any location the users wants to take it, and will of course repeatedly change its links to the other devices (Katz, 2002). Because of several characteristics which makes MANETs vulnerable against attacks from variety of perspectives, researchers face difficulties of implementing proper security scheme on MANETs.

The security threats that prevail in a traditional wired and wireless network environment also hold true for wireless ad-hoc networks but are further aggravated due to unpredictable and dynamic nature of such networks. There are also some security issues that are peculiar only to MANET such as a nasty neighbour relaying packets or a malicious node disrupting the routing infrastructure. Further, wireless link characteristics also introduce reliability problems due to limited wireless transmission range, the broadcast nature of the wireless medium, mobility induced packet losses, and data transmission errors (Zhou & Haas, 1999).

MANETs require the four standard attributes in order to provide wide range of security on the network (Gasser et al., 1989). These are the; Availability; which requires that the system stays up and in a working state, and provides the right access and functionality to each user. This security aspect is the target of DoS or DDoS attacks. Confidentiality; which requires that the information will not be read or copied by unauthorized parties. Authentication and other access control techniques are also used to achieve this goal. Authenticity, which requires that the communication peer is really the legitimate node and is exactly whom we expect to talk to (not an unauthorized node), and that the content of a message is valid. Integrity, which requires that communication data between nodes must not be modified by any unauthorized, unanticipated or unintentional parties.

There are varieties of threats available on the field of Mobile ad-hoc Networks. In this section, several security threats will be discussed that are prevalent in an ad-hoc network environment (Rafique, 2002).

Denial of Service is the first and the most famous threat for MANETs. This threat prevents the normal use of management or communication facilities of the network. This is a threat against the availability of the system. Availability means that all necessary components are operable and all the necessary services are available when a user requires them. In ad-hoc environment, Availability concept has 2 different aspects, i.e., is the medium available when it is needed and is the services offered by a node available to its users when expected, in spite of attacks (Kong et al., 2001). In the DoS attack, the attacker can deny service to the nodes in a given area by jamming the radio frequencies they use. On the other hand, the attack can be internal or external from the node's perspective. In an internal attack a legitimate node behaves maliciously to subvert the communication between two or more nodes. In an external attack, an unauthorised node attempts to break or prevent the message flow between two nodes. Such nodes may generate incorrect routing information, replay old routing information or even deform old routing information (Luo et al., 2000). In the former case, appropriate mechanisms and services must exist to detect and eliminate the compromised malicious node. In the latter case, appropriate authentication and authorisation services must exist to prevent an unauthorised node from participating in the network.

In Unauthorised Disclosure of Information attacks, an attacker tries to learn the contents of the transmitted message. A confidentiality service is necessary to protect the transmitted data from such attacks and protect the contents of the data. Several levels of protection can be identified. The broadest service protects all the data transmitted in the network for a period of time. However complexity and applicability must be taken into consideration in such cases. Narrower forms of this service can also be defined, including protection of a single message or even specific fields within a message. This type of solution will protect only the transmitted message and not the entire communication line. In an ad-hoc network, the links are wireless and are error prone. Use of such wireless links renders an ad-hoc network susceptible to link attacks ranging from passive eavesdropping to active impersonation. The other aspect of confidentiality is the protection of traffic flow from analysis. The protection mechanisms that maintain confidentiality requires attacker not be able to observe the characteristics of the network traffic such as transmission of source and destination address, frequency, length or other characteristics. The leakage of such information could have fatal consequences. For instance, in battlefield ad-hoc networks, traffic analysis can have devastating effects. In such situations, the routing information must also remain confidential because this information might be valuable to enemies to identify and locate their targets in a battlefield (Luo et al., 2000).

As mentioned before, the security of transmitted message is one of the important aspects of confidentiality. Appropriate encryption (symmetric or public key) must be in place to protect the secrecy of transmitted information. Through the help of efficient key management infrastructure, these encryption mechanisms provide secrecy of the message. There are several issues in providing such an infrastructure for ad-hoc networks. We discuss these issues later sections of this study.

The Unauthorised Modification of Information means that some portion of the legitimate message is altered somehow, or that message are delayed or reordered, to produce an unauthorised effect. An integrity service is necessary to ensure that a message being transferred (with or without encryption) is never corrupted. In an ad-hoc network environment, a message could be corrupted because of benign failures, such as radio propagation impairment, or because of malicious attacks on the network (Luo et al., 2000). The applicability of Integrity can be possible for a single message, selected fields within a message or to a stream of messages. When integrity is applied to a stream of messages then this process is called connection-oriented integrity (Luo et al., 2000). This approach ensures that messages are received as sent, with no duplication, insertion, modification, reordering, or replays. The links in ad-hoc networks are vulnerable to errors and prone to active attacks, and hence the use of connection-oriented integrity can be justified. An integrity service is often implemented using so called Checksums and hashing functions. Checksum or hashing-hash sum is a count of number of bits in a transmission unit that is included with the unit so the receiver can check to see whether the same number of bits was received. TCP and UDP layers provide checksum and hash-sum functions to ensure integrity.

Unauthorised Access to Information includes unauthorised access to resources on the network as well as within a system. This may occur in conjunction with a masquerading attack. The attacker has successfully masqueraded himself with another entity, and gain access to resources of the network which are otherwise denied to it. An access control service provides the ability to limit and control access to host systems applications, resources and networks, and to limit what entity might do with the information contained. In ad-hoc networks access control can involve mechanisms with which the formation of groups is controlled (Zhang & Lee, 2000). For example, in cluster driven ad-hoc networks, an access control service must exist that determines when nodes may form, destroy, join, or leave clusters. This makes a strict control for joining into network or make modification on the network resources.

Access Control Service is represented by an access control policy that is essentially a set of rules that define the conditions under which initiators may access targets (Zhang & Lee, 2000). The access control rules are used to determine the requests decisions whether to accept or deny. The variety of access control approaches mentioned in the literature by the researchers. For example Discretionary access control (DAC) allows the restriction of access to objects based on the identity of subjects or groups of subjects. The Mandatory access control (MAC) contains formal authorisation policy that controls the access to the objects. While MAC is more general than DAC and controls the operations of DAC, and DAC used by the user to control access to other subjects, both DAC and MAC are often applied together for efficient and effective security. In addition to that Role Based Access Control (RBAC) applies the concept of roles within subjects (Zhang & Lee, 2000).

A masquerading attack takes place when one entity pretends to be another entity. An authentication scheme must be in place to the recipient that a message is from the source that it claims to be. In an ad-hoc network a node performs routing functions apart from being an end recipient for a transmission flow. The malicious node that attacks to network can misdirect or modify the routing information thus causes interruption on the communication among nodes in the network. For better security inter node authentication is required which means, each node must authenticate each other prior to exchange routing information and after this step, end to end authentication step should be followed. It must also be ensured that the communication between these two nodes is not interfered with in such a way that a third node can masquerade as one of the two legitimate parties for the purpose of unauthorized transmission and reception.

Repudiation of Actions is a kind of a threat against accountability and occurs when the sender (or the receiver) denies having sent (or received) the information. A no repudiation service must be in place that prevents either the sender or receiver from denying a transmitted message. For that reason, when a message is sent, the receiver can prove that the message was in fact sent by the alleged sender. Similarly, when a message is received, the sender can prove that the alleged or presumed receiver in fact received the message. When one node receives a false message from another node, this service allows it to blame the other node of sending the false message and enables all the other nodes to know that the offending node is compromised (Kong et al., 2001).

A key management is another issue once the above mentioned problems are highlighted. A problem in providing the above mentioned security services are to facilitate the provision of a key management infrastructure. Key management addresses the problem of creation, generation and distribution of keys that are necessary for the implementation of a security service. Wired and traditional wireless networks assign the responsibility of key management to a static and trusted authority, which normally is a part of fixed infrastructure. Such an entity does not exist in an ad-hoc environment where the nodes dynamically form a network without the support and power of any fixed authority or infrastructure. The dynamic nature of ad-hoc networks insinuate that nodes move in an out of the networks frequently making it necessary to change the keys in securing communications more often than in other networks. This also indicates that the regular key management framework used in traditional networks will not be applicable to this situation. There are several approaches to providing a key management service mentioned in the literature by the researchers. Often a public key infrastructure is deployed because of its superiority in distributing keys and in achieving integrity and non-repudiation (Luo et al., 2000). However, a public key infrastructure based scheme requires the presence of a certification authority (CA) for key management (Schwingenschlögl & Horn, 2002). The CA has a public/private key pair, with its public key known to every node in the network, and signs certificates binding public keys to nodes. The public key system requires that the Certification Authority (CA) be available on line, to confirm and revoke public key certificates. The presence of a single CA leads to bottleneck problems leading to a single point of failure in the network. It also becomes the most obvious point of attack since a compromise of the CA compromises the entire network. Finally, such an infrastructure requires that a single reliable, trusted entity is available on-line, an assumption that appears unrealistic in an ad-hoc environment. The problem of key management is further provoked in multicast based communications i.e., situations involving multi-party communications. Any key management scheme deployed for such networks must have the following properties:

- **Scalability:** To accommodate dynamic groups of arbitrary size.
- **Low Computational Complexity:** To accommodate nodes having limited resources.
- **Not Relying on Dedicated Trusted Nodes:** To accommodate rapidly changing topological conditions.

In the above section, we have identified the types of threats that can rise in a mobile ad-hoc environment. For a particular environment, one needs to determine which threats are more applicable. For instance, in group-based communication, uttermost care must be taken to prevent the key management infrastructure from being compromised by attackers. In military based communication, care should be taken to protect the information flow from traffic analysis. For commercial scenarios like a wireless payment system over mobile ad-hoc, strong authentication and authorization schemes must coexist with the confidentiality service. In most of the cases, physical attacks against the nodes must also be considered. This can be a very serious security fact that as the attacker can get access to hardware and software known to the network and can possibly perform successful authentication, eavesdrop messages or inject arbitrary or malicious data into the network which may lead to collapse in entire network (Rabin, 1998). It may be necessary for such networks to deploy Intrusion Detection Systems (IDS) to detect and respond to computer misuse and attacks conducted by the adversary.

Counteracting the relevant security threats involves provision and enforcement of appropriate security services and mechanisms as discussed above. The overall set of security measures required to neutralize the identified threats forms the security policy. The security architecture supported by this policy must be able to support a wide range of systems and applications, and therefore it is intended that it should support a wide range of security services that can be used and combined in different ways to meet different security policies in the entire network.

In conclusion of this section, design and deployment of the effective security framework for wireless ad-hoc networks requires investigation of various criteria. For that reason, this thesis contains the investigation of different attacks and security mechanisms in MANETs, proposed security architectures by researchers in the literature, e.g., network architectures and routing protocols that are specifically targeted to assist in security, determination and classification of compromised nodes and establishing the trusted node

Detailed Comparative Analysis of Existing Methods and Techniques of Implementing Security in MANETs

In this section, an overview of the existing methods and techniques are criticized and compared in the field of MANET security issues.

The paper by the researcher presented a short literature study over papers on ad-hoc networking to show that many of the new generation ad-hoc networking proposals are not yet able to address the actual security problems they face (Shoup, 2000). The author indicates that ad hoc networking proposals of modern era up till now are not able to completely describe the security problems of ad hoc networks.

According to the author, environment-specific implementations of the required approaches in implementing security have not yet been fully realised.

Researchers have examined the major security issues related to the wireless ad-hoc networks (Desmedt & Frankel, 1990). According to them that from the time ad-hoc environment of network are controlled by tight bounds on power budget and the CPU cycles, and by the communication of intermittent nature, this combination builds an authentication, naming and denial of service irrelevant. The combination identifies some of the recently originated attacks i.e. sleep deprivation torture, & shortfalls of the acceptable primitives for the cryptographic protocols. According to the researchers, providing confidentiality is not a more difficult task compared to providing authentication. They mentioned that if the problems regarding to authentication are solved, protecting confidentiality becomes very simply by just encrypting the session, no matter what material related to keying is available. They present the secure transient association approach which indicates the association between the controller and the peripheral device. This relationship indicates the capacity of a controller to control a peripheral device during its ownership duration of the peripheral device. When device controlled by the new controller, it does as new master orders to act and stop obeying the previous one consequently makes this relationship transient.

As it is mentioned above, researcher claims that one way of securing the ad hoc network is a "duckling model" (Stajano & Anderson, 1999). In this model, duckling is the slave device and duck is the mother which is the master controller. Firstly, duckling recognizes it's as first entity which sends it a secret key on a secure channel fro example by physical contact. This entire process is called imprinting. The duckling slave device always obeys its mother, which tells it whom to talk to by reference to an access control list. The bond between mother and duckling is broken by death after which the duckling accepts another imprinting. Death may be caused by the mother itself, a timeout or any specific event. The whole security chain corresponds to a tree topology formed of hierarchical master-slave relationships. The root of the tree is a human being controlling all devices in its subtree. As it is well known that, in hierarchical networks there are nodes that have different roles than others (Desmedt & Frankel 1990).

However this specific approach proposed by researchers for providing security has some issues. For example if there is a breakage in one relationship then the relationship of the whole subtree is broken. So, it requires the constant involvement of a human for the maintenance of security, which is not be feasible in a lot of cases. So network maintenance should be considered while designing a proposed solution for mobile ad hoc network environments.

According to research by authors has proposed a scalable intrusion tolerant security solution for infrastructureless wireless mobile ad hoc networks (Venkatraman & Agrawal 2001). The proposed system has designed to be fully decentralized in order to operate in a large-scale network. The main idea behind this scheme is to maximise the service availability in each network locality which is crucial for supporting ubiquitous services for mobile users. If this proposed method investigated from the cryptographic perspective, the design is based on the concepts of threshold secret sharing and secret share updates. From the system aspect, the architecture is fully distributed and localised.

However, there are several drawbacks associated with this scheme. In this scheme researchers used k-bounded coalition offsetting technique to enable scalable distributed certificate generation. But when a node V_j receives a certificate request from V_i, its records may not provide enough information on V_i. This may be because the interaction between V_i and V_j does not last long enough. Moreover, V_i may not exist in V_j records at all if they just met. At this point, there are 2 possibilities. First, V_j may serve to the V_i's request since it has not bad records about V_i. Other option is to drop the request since there is no reliable information available about the request owner. In addition to that, the simulation experiment conducted by the researchers shows that for both centralised and hierarchical solutions incur in high delay which entails difficulties in predicting future expiration time in certificate renewal.

Researchers have followed the design guidelines provided in other researchers (Venkatraman & Agrawal 2001), and proposed a new scheme with a number of new contributions (Binkley & Trost, 2001). The proposed scheme makes a local trust model by expanding the adversary model which a system can handle. In his trust model, an entity (for example entity K) is trusted in the condition that trusted entities claim within a specified duration "Tcert". These K entities are in general are among the entity's one-hop neighbours. The authors claim that the proposed scheme is self-securing design approach in which multiple nodes collaboratively provide authentication services for any node in the network. The proposed scheme is designed to handle DoS attacks and node break-ins (Binkley & Trost, 2001).

There are quite a few deficiencies in this approach. The model assumes that each node has minimum K number of legitimate neighbours. The theory is critical for certification services to be strong against the adversaries. Availability of the services is also determined by the parameter K. The three mentioned factors of the model are joined and characterized by a single parameter K. This sort of coupling effect to reduces the flexibility of the model's scheme. In a specific scenario, these factors aspects may have contradictory goals. For example, security may require K to be minimum 10, but the service availability may require the K to be maximum 7, where as network can only certify 5 legitimate neighbours. This situation creates new challenges that need to be addressed. The model also makes an unrealistic assumption that each node is equipped with a few local detection mechanisms to recognize the misbehaving nodes among its one hop neighbourhood (Binkley & Trost, 2001).

The research shows a survey for intrusion detection and trace back response techniques against attacks (Marti et al., 2000). This research inspected the weaknesses of ad-hoc networks and gives a conclusion that an ad-hoc network is mainly exposed to DoS attack, because of its features including open medium, cooperative algorithms, dynamic changing topology, lacking the centralised monitoring and management point, and lacking a clear line of defence. According to researchers, building a highly secure wireless ad hoc network, a suitable intrusion detection and response technique must be applied. They claim that there is need of further research to adapt the intrusion detection and response technique to any ad-hoc network environment. The recent intrusion detection techniques discussed which is distributed and co-operative and also uses an approach of statistical anomaly detection. According to them the processes of trace analysis & anomaly detection must be done locally of each node and by the cooperation with each node in the network if possible. Further, the process of intrusion detection must take place in all the networking layers in the integrated cross layer manner. This technique is specified to intrusion detection and cannot be used as a generic security model (Marti et al., 2000).

The paper by researchers suggests some algorithms to use as build blocks against the DoS attacks on ad-hoc networks (Johnson & Maltz, 1996). Given the self-controls faced by such networks, the paper also inspects the feasibility of such algorithms on the environments of mobile ad-hoc network. It mentions that different algorithms can be used which can deal with the secret and function sharing and RSA threshold schemes like Capkun et al. (2003) and Hubaux et al. (2001). The paper also describes that how these algorithms can meet the given demands of ad-hoc networks.

Researchers proposed a new security mechanism by identifying the new challenges and opportunities faced by the ad-hoc networking environment and proposed so called threshold cryptography scheme to provide secure communication within network (Luo et al., 2000). The proposed secure communication method is inspired from the study of another proposed security method (Asokan & Ginzboorg, 2000). The paper mainly discusses on secure routing and secure key management establishment concepts.

In particular techniques to prevent denial of service attacks from occurring in the routing process are discussed. These techniques take advantage of the redundancies in ad-hoc network topology and use diversity coding on multiple routes to tolerate both benign and Byzantine failures.

According to the researchers, this work represents the first step of their research to analyse the security threats, to understand the security mechanisms for ad-hoc networks, and to identify existing techniques, as well as to propose new mechanisms to secure ad-hoc networks (Luo et al., 2000). The idea suggested by this approach is to distribute trust to a set of nodes by letting them share the key management service, in particular the ability to sign certificates. This is done using threshold cryptography which proposed by the researchers in the literature (Asokan & Ginzboorg, 2000). An (n, t+1) threshold cryptography scheme allows parties to share the ability to perform a cryptographic operation so that any t+1 parties can perform this operation jointly whereas it is infeasible for at most t parties to do so. Using this scheme, the private key k of the CA (certification authority) is divided into n shares (s1, s2, …,sn), each share being assigned to a special node. Using this share, a set of t+1 special node is able to generate a valid certificate. As long as t or less special nodes are compromised and do not participate in generating certificates the service can operate. Even if the compromised nodes deliver incorrect data the service is able to sign certificates (Luo et al., 2000).

In the proposed method (Luo et al., 2000) the user identity is authenticated by CA. In a case of single centralised CA, this scheme works well. But this proposed scheme may face problems in a distributed CA environment. This scheme shows a scenario in which, collaborative CAs are arranged and deployed as access point for the security services. So, the users have to prove their identity to all the special nodes to prevent compromised node passing on the faulty information but if it signs that the certificates without proving the identity the model cannot be used for highly-value transactions. There are a number of characteristics of this model which make it ineffective. High mobility makes frequent route changes thus in this way contacting the local CA in a timely manner is insignificant. Moreover, in an ad-hoc network, a local CA can be multihops away and also can move. This situation not only complicates the dynamic repartitioning of a network, but also complicates the problem of tracing and tracking the local CA server. Multihop communication over an error-prone wireless channel depicts the data transmission to a high loss rate. The whole act reduces the success ratio sand which increases the average service latency.

According to the work mentioned by Bellovin and Merrit (1992), an effective operation of the ad-hoc networks is mainly dependant on maintaining the appropriate routing information in a distributed way to avoid a malicious node from becoming misrepresented, suppressing or misrouting the data packets. To work against this attack, researcher has introduced a technique for inter-router authentication and meanwhile problems like handle replay that can prevail using existing the schemes. This technique has been integrated into a routing protocol to minimize the security threats to routing protocols. According to author the technique uses Ad Hoc On-Demand Distance Vector Routing (AODV) routing protocol and is evenly applicable to other demand driven routing protocols.

The scheme in Bellovin and Merrit (1992) works whenever the route from a source A to a destination B needs to be found, the route discovery process is initiated. The process has several steps that contain route discovery messaging between the source and destination or intermediate nodes. The scheme provides a means for authenticating route discovery messages to ensure that route table does not contain any false routing information. Researchers have simulated this scheme and shown the results. This technique has a drawback that it does not perform a good authentication during the time propagation of route requests but optionally it provides reliability by using message authentication codes. Unfortunately, a message authentication code can only approves for the integrity but cannot stop the replay attack.

Researchers has acknowledged some security goals of modern ad-hoc routing protocols, and anticipated some causes of threats to the mentioned routing protocols (Kong et al., 2001). For that reason, it has suggested some possible approaches to prevent the routing attacks in mobile ad-hoc networks with a key management framework. Specifically, researcher suggested some solutions for protecting the internal and external attacks to these ad-hoc networks. He suggests "that encrypting routing messages with a private key algorithm and authenticate them by using the digitally signed message digests with windowed sequence numbers can prevent the external attack. For internal attacks he suggests that redundant paths, "aging out of false routing information, and dismiss the routing information at each node are all employed to combat against internal attacks.

For the ad-hoc networks (Diffie & Hellman 1976), has designed an authenticated routing protocol at the link layer which specifically addresses the link security issues. He presents two key ideas in his research report. First of all, he suggests providing a fix to decrease the spoofing problems linked with the Address Resolution Protocol. Providing a fix and exchanging the Address Resolution Protocol with a protocol where beacons are used to verify approach. This type of protocol is always naturally integrated with the Mobile IP as the agent already uses a beacon system for communicating. In the second solution he provides, "the beacons binding IP and MAC addresses are authenticated". This stops the unauthorised entities to access the network resources and also reduce the danger of attacks like link-layer spoofing. These authentication beacons improve the Mobile IP security. These approaches by researcher also do not deal with the threats of replay attacks. The attackers can record a link layer authenticated beacon at one foreign agent and later he can retransmit it. In the result, the victim may not be presented and remains unaware of the attack. The protocol described in this approach just protects the routing connectivity but unable to protect the user data. An attacking host may just simply listen to the passing traffic. This work is very easy to do and extremely difficult to detect, and it works despite the consequences that how a hosts learn will each other's MAC addresses (Diffie & Hellman 1976).

The paper has suggested the Pathrater technique for the prevention of DoS attacks on ad hoc networks (Weimerskirch & Thonet, 2001). This study has inspired from the paper presented by Torgerson and Leeuwen (2001), which related with Dynamic Source Routing in Ad-hoc networks. In this technique run by each node on an ad hoc network combines the knowledge of misbehaving nodes with the link of reliability of data to pick the most reliable route expectedly. The author suggests a method to prevent misbehaving or malicious nodes to participate in the network. Through categorising nodes based on their dynamically measured behaviour. The watchdog method is proposed by the researchers to detect misbehaving nodes and a Pathrater that helps routing protocols to avoid these nodes. As mentioned before, these two features are added as extensions to Dynamic Routing Algorithm (DSR) by Torgerson and Leeuwen (2001). A drawback with this technique is that as the Pathrater cannot detect a misbehaving node in the existence of different types of collisions such as ambiguous collisions, receiver collisions, limited transmission power, false misbehaviour and partial dropping. The limitation with this method is since it depends on knowing the exact path a data packet has passed through, so implementation of this is only possible on top of a source routing protocol.

To prevent Mobile Ad Hoc Networks from the DoS attacks researchers has proposed several repository construction algorithms (Papadimitratos & Haas, 2002). These algorithms take into consideration the features of certificate graphs in the sense that the choices of certificates which are stored by each service user depends on the connectivity of that user and also depends on his certificate graph neighbours. The success or failure of this technique extremely dependent on construction of some local certificate repositories and depends on the features of certificate graphs. A certificate graph is a type of graph whose vertices are represented by the public keys of the users and the edges are represented by the public key certificates issues by the service users. Like in the any of the approach which uses certificate chains, this approach also assumes that trust is transitive that is not practiced quite regularly in the real life situation. The author suggests fixing to this problem by assuming the paths of multiple certificates and by using the authentication metrics.

The study by Levijoki (2000), describes some problems related to the securing ad hoc networks form DoS attack. The work presented here is similar to the presented in Papadimitratos and Haas (2002) with more detailed description of algorithms. The proposed method suggest to develop the idea of a self-organized public key infrastructure and certificates are stored and distributed by the users instead of using certificate directory.

This proposed system offered by researchers has several drawbacks. First of all, to ensure the safety of system, each entity's identity should be checked in real times before the certificates are issued to users. Additionally the approach assumes that each node in the recommendation chain is completely checked by the certificate requester trusts. In the end a considerable amount of computing power and considerable time is consumed to get a certificate which is passing through the chain of certificates. In the process of checking the received certificate for authentication and signing it before forwarding it each node in the chain must perform the operations of public key. This process cannot be prepared parallel but can only be done one after the other (Levijoki, 2000).

In a paper by Patrikakis, Masikos and Zouraraki (2004), a new key agreement scenario is described and various solutions to the key agreement problem in this scenario are examined. The encrypted key exchange method presented in a research paper is extends to multi-party case (Royer & Toh, 1999). This method is based on the assumption that the composition of the group does not change during the session. On the other hand, this work has similarity which has presented a fault-tolerant version of multiparty Diffie-Hellman Key agreement protocol (Wood & Stankovic, 2002). The particular scheme addressed the scenario of group of people who want to set up a secure session in a meeting room without any support infrastructure.

The major disadvantage of this proposed scheme, authentication is done outside the IT system e.g., the group members authenticate themselves by showing their passports or through common knowledge like friendship or knowing each other. So this method may not be applicable for those situations when there are more than one group exist or the group of people don't know each other.

The work proposed by researchers provided an authentication service in an ad-hoc network environment and claims that authentication is a core element for secure communication (Nichols & Lekkas, 2002). This scheme is proposed for low value transactions and cooperation and feedback system introduces quality and responsibility while hardware requirements for the devices are quite low. However, there are some problems with this approach. In this approach, for preventing channel establishment, a path in the network of trusted entities is replaced by the shared knowledge or is trusted with third party. There is as high probability of any malicious entity in the network of trusted entities as much as longer the particular path stays. Thus there is a lot of effort required to find out the efficient algorithms and making a well-sized repository lists. Another challenge in this approach is the essential feedback system. The proposed feedback system has to work to detect fraud quickly and take appropriate action to prevent repeated attacks.

The report prepared by Sandia laboratories, is focused on security issues arise from wrapping authentication mechanisms around ad hoc routing data (Schuller, 2003). The researchers indicate that, appending signatures to the routing messages of currently existing protocols is not sufficient to prevent adversaries to insert false routing information into network. In this report, the authors have illustrated a repeater attack and prove that even if the network has sophisticated authentication mechanisms placed on the routing messages, the adversary can bring down the entire multi-hop network. This happens through the distributed repeaters that placed by the adversary throughout the network and hears the network traffic and transmits the traffic to all other repeaters that in the network. The routing protocol may behave as though nothing had happened since the adversary's repeaters have only increased the broadcast range and not violated any security features. These adversary's repeaters broadcast the messages to all other repeaters and this action gives the nodes the false belief that the diameter of the network is much smaller than that it actually is.

The authors argue that the provision of comprehensive secure communication requires that both discovery and data forwarding be safeguarded (Wenyuan et al, 2005). The scheme proposes a secure routing protocol (SRP) that counters malicious behaviour that targets the discovery of topological information. The authors proposed a protocol called Secure Message Transmission protocol (SMT) to provide flexible, end to end secure data forwarding scheme that naturally compliments SRP. In essence, this work is proposed to secure against non-colluding adversaries and does not aim to authenticate intermediate nodes that forward "Route requests" and thus do not handle authorization.

In a research proposed by Blum and Eskandarian (2004), is identified some of the challenges in providing authentication, authorisation and accounting in wireless ad hoc networks through classifying them. This is a review paper that cites the work of another research paper, to propose some remedial solutions (Luo et al., 2000).

Previous Studies on Securing MANETs against DoS and DDoS Attacks

A DoS attacker can cause the congestion in a network by either producing an unnecessary amount of traffic by itself, or generating the excessive amount of traffic by the other nodes. In the wireless networks, DoS attacks are very difficult to prevent or protect. These attacks can cause a harsh degradation on performance of network. In this section, the types of DoS and DDoS attacks and the possible preventions against these attacks are discussed.

According to the research study, master minds of DoS attacks usually target the sites or services hosted on the high-profile web servers like banks, gateways of credit card payment, and also the root name servers (Stubblefield, Ioannidis & Rubin, 2002). A common way of attack is saturating the target machine with external communications requests, like it can't respond to the legitimate traffic, or it may respond so slowly as to be made effectively unavailable. According to these authors attacks like these generally lead to an overload of server. According to these authors generally, DoS and DDoS attacks are implemented either by forcing the targeted network to reset, or consuming that particular network's resources with the intention that it no longer is able to provide its intended service or block the communication media between its intended users or the victim to obstruct adequate communicate (Stubblefield, Ioannidis & Rubin, 2002).

As variety of prevention and detection methods discussed and analysed in the section 2.2, the variety of attacks can be clearly understood in the light of comparative critical analysis. Because of the variety of attacks in MANETs, the attacks are classified based on different aspects. This section mainly covers DoS and DDoS attacks in order to provide an insight about the importance of problem in this field of science and importance of proposed solution. The attacks are classified and categorized in this section as well. On the other hand, the security strategies against these attacks proposed by researchers are also categorised according to their characteristics.

The attack types are classified and categorised as follows; Legitimate Based Classification, Interaction Based Classification, Network Protocol Stack Based Attack Classification, Cryptography Attacks, and AODV protocol Attacks. Each and every attack category will be discussed in the further subsections. As it is mentioned in the section 2.1, MANETs required four standard security attributes and these attributes were availability, confidentiality, authenticity and integrity. In order to provide a secure MANET environment, the existence of such attributes is compulsory. Each of these concepts has explained in the section 2.1. In addition to this, likewise the attack classification, the security strategies against DDoS and DoS attacks proposed by researchers are also classified.

These strategies are classified as attacker side strategies, victim side strategies, and intermediate strategies.

In legitimate based classification, according to the legitimate status of a node, an attack could be external or internal. The external attacks are committed by nodes that are not legal members of the network or group, while the internal attacks are from a compromised member inside the network called as "selfish node". These attackers are aware of the security strategies and are even protected by them. The internal attacks pose a higher threat to the network.

Interaction based classification is another category. In terms of interaction, an attack could be passive or active. The Figure 1 illustrates the categorisation of active and passive attacks. Passive attacks do not disrupt the communication. Instead, they intercept and capture the packets to read the information where this information might be personal or related with security issues. On the other hand, active attackers inject packets into the network to interfere or interrupt the network communication among nodes, overload the network traffic; fake the legitimate node or package, consume the participating nodes processing power and battery, obstruct the operation or cut off certain nodes from their neighbours so they cannot use the network services effectively anymore. Denial of Service or Distributed Denial of Service attacks are active attacks as shown in the Figure 1.

The attacks could also be classified according to the target layer in the protocol stack. The Table 1 illustrates the protocol based attack classification. As it is shown on the Table 1, the protocol stack layer is separated according to attack types. Each and every attack belongs to one of the layer in the stack layer.

Figure 1. Taxonomy of MANET attacks

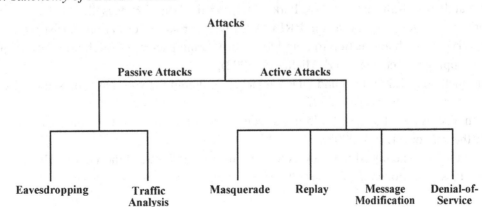

Table 1. MANET protocols and attacks classification

Application Layer Attacks	⇒	Repudiation, Backdoor, Virus, Data corruption or deletion
Transport Layer Attacks	⇒	Session hijacking, SYN flooding, Desynchronization
Network Layer Attacks	⇒	Black hole, Byzantine, Misdirection, Resource consumption, Flooding, Location disclosure, packet dropping, Rushing, Spoofing, Wormhole, Selfish
Link Layer Attacks	⇒	Collision, Disruption MAC(802.11), Unfairness, Exhausting, Monitoring
Physical Layer Attacks	⇒	Eavesdropping, Interceptions, Jamming, Tampering
Multi-Layer Attacks	⇒	DoS, impersonation, replay, man-in-the-middle

The stack layer contains layers which are Application Layer Attacks, Transport Layer Attacks, Network Layer Attacks, Link Layer Attacks, Physical Layer Attacks and Multi-Layer Attacks (Katz, 2002).

The physical layer attacks are targeting the physical layer of a wireless node, an attacker can easily intercept and read the message contents from open radio signals (Ramaswamy et al., 2003; Barbir, Murphy & Yang, 2004). An attacker can interfere the communication by generating powerful transmission to overwhelm the target signals. The jamming signals do not follow the protocol definition, and they can be meaningless random noise and pulse (Yi et al., 2005).

The network layer is responsible of taking traffic from the transport layer and prepare it for the data link layer which leads to realization of end-to-end delivery of packets between nodes. The attackers are targeting the link layer and generate meaningless random packets to grab the channel and cause collisions (Vigna, 2004). In such situation, if the impacted node keeps trying to resend the packet, it will exhaust its power supply; The attacker can passively eavesdrop on the link layer packets; The link security protocol Wireless Encryption Protocol (WEP) is vulnerable too, the initialization vector (IV) flaw in the WEP protocol makes it easier for an attacker to launch a cryptanalytic type attack (CERT, 1998).

Variety of new protocols introduced in MANETs, different types of attacks are targeted these vulnerabilities of these protocols. "Black hole" attacks targeted Distance Vector type routing protocols (Ramaswamy, et al., 2003; Just, Kranakis & Wan 2003). The black hole attacker responds to all Route Requests (RREQ) with a shortest Route Reply (RREP). Once the black hole attacker grabs the route, it may drop all the packets, or selectively forward some of the packets to hide the malicious nature. It is also the first step in the man-in-the-middle attacks which is illustrated in the Figure 2 (Hu, Perrig, & Johnson, 2003).

In Figure 2 Black hole attack, Attacker A claims to have shortest route to N1, N2, and N3

Cooperative black hole attacks over AODV and defence system is investigated and discussed in the study by researchers (Al-Shurman, Yoo & Park, 2004; Conti, Gregori & Maselli, 2003).

"Byzantine" attackers respond to the RREQ with wrong route information to disrupt or degrade the routing services, such as creating routing loops, forwarding packets through non-optimal paths, or selectively dropping packets (Molva & Michiardi, 2002).

Flooding methods used by DoS and DDoS attackers in wired network have the same effect on the MANET environment (Stoica et al., 2002).

"Location disclosure" attackers disclose the security-sensitive location information of nodes or the topology of the network (Lazos, 2005).

"Misdirection" attackers lead the packets to a wrong way and toward the victim. This is similar to the "Smurf attack" mentioned in (Charles, 2005).

Figure 2. Man-in-the-middle attack: - Black hole attack

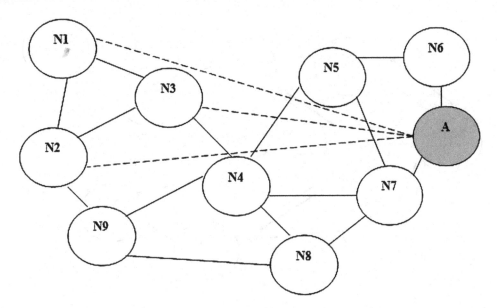

"Packet dropping" attackers disrupt the network communication, and they are very difficult to detect. This attack is often working alone with other attack methods to amplify and increase the damage (Lawson, 2005).

"Resource consumption" or so-called "Sleep deprivation" attackers try to waste the power of the legitimate nodes by requesting excessive route discovery, forwarding useless packets to the victim node, or endlessly "dangling" useless packets between two distant attackers.

"Rushing" attackers have more power and quicker links than legitimate nodes in the network. They may forward RREQ and RREP faster and this allows them to be involved in the routes always as attacker A follows this method which is faster and more powerful than other nodes. The Figure 3 illustrates the Rushing Attack (Hu, Perrig, & Johnson, 2003; Graf, 2005).

The "Selfish" nodes, as mentioned before, join into network but do not cooperate. These nodes save the battery life, CPU cycles and other resources for their own packets and processes. This behaviour cause inefficient networking while not damaging other participating nodes of the network. There are varieties of researches conducted to differentiate selfish or misbehaving nodes in the network (Black Box Corp, 2003).

The "Spoofing" attackers impersonate a legitimate node to misrepresent the network topology to cause network loops or partitions (Ferguson & Senie, 2000 ; Humphries & Carlisle, 2002). As it is shown in the Figure 4, the "Wormhole" attackers forward packets between each other by a tunnel instead of hop based routing method defined by the protocol in the research paper (Lazos et al., 2005; Min, 2004). This tunnel control messages may cause interruption on routing. The Wormhole attacks are harsh threats for MANETs on- demand routing protocols. This attack may cause prevention of discovery actual routes other than through the wormhole. The Figure 4 illustrates the Wormhole attack. In the literature, research papers mention about defence strategies against Wormhole attack. However these strategies are often based on space or time relativity, such as geographical leashes, temporal leashes or a graph theoretic approach (Min, 2004; Wang, 2004).

Figure 3. Rushing attack

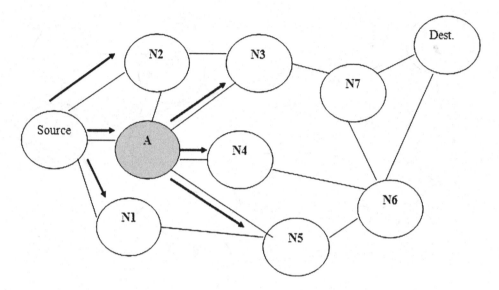

All these attacks that are mentioned above related with Physical layer attacks. The second layer is Transport Layer. The "desynchronization" attackers sends fabricated packets exceeding the sequence number to either node of the connection and break an existing connection between two nodes. This may lead one of the nodes to send retransmission request for the missed frames which may cause an unnecessary traffic (Kaufman, Perlman & Speciner, 2002).

Another transport layer attack is a "Session Hijacking" attack. The attacker impersonates the victim node and takes over the TCP session between the victim and the server (Chen, Deng & Varshney, 2003; Lawson, 2005).

The application layer attackers execute a "Repudiation" attack that treats companies that relies on electronic traffic. Some of the cases described in a research paper in literature (Xu et al., 2005). Other

Figure 4. The Wormhole attack

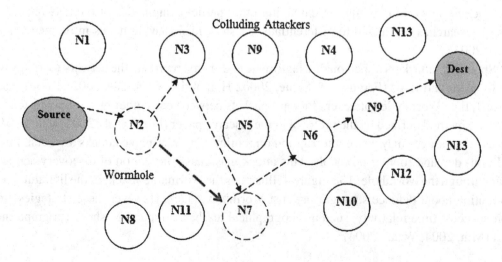

application layer attacks such as worms, Trojans, spywares, backdoor, viruses, and data corruption and deletion, target either application layer protocols, such as File Transfer Protocol (FTP), Hyper Text Transfer Protocol (HTTP) and Simple Mail Transfer Protocol (SMTP) or applications and data files on the victims (Katz, 2002; Xu et al., 2005).

The Cryptography Attacks targeted vulnerabilities of encryption algorithms on the related protocols. The Digital Signature attacks target RSA public-key encryption algorithms (Min, 2004; Convery, Miller & Sundaralingam, 2003). Attacker constructs a message based on the signature of a legitimate message. There are 3 types of Digital Signature Attacks exist in literature which are known-message, chosen-message and key-only attacks. The "Known-message" attacker knows a list of messages previously signed by the victim. The "Chosen-message" attacker can choose a specific message that it wants the victim to sign. The "Key-only" attacker knows the public verification algorithm only (Min, 2004).

The "Hash collision" attacks target hash algorithms, such as SHA-1, MD4, MD5, HAVAL-128, and RIPEMD, to construct a valid certificate corresponding to the hash collision (Wang, et al., 2003).

Pseudorandom number attacks reverse engineer the pseudorandom number generator used by the public key mechanisms in order to break the cryptography (Humphries, Jeffrey and Carlisle, 2002).

The AODV protocol is specifically designed as a routing protocol for MANETs and other ad-hoc networks. This protocol has many advantages while it is intrinsically vulnerable to many attacks. The classification is illustrated in the Figure 5 (Lazos et al., 2005).

The vulnerability on DoS attacks in link layer IEEE 802.11 has been investigated widely by the researchers in the literature (Karygiannis & Owens, 2002). The malicious or misbehaving node keeps the most of binary exponential back off scheme. In order to happen as expected malicious node damage frame easily by putting few extra bits on the frame and transmits the package to the network through other participating nodes. Malicious node keep the wireless medium busy and start loaded frames transmitting which tend to capture the wireless channel by sending data non-stop as result neighbours nodes back-off endlessly. Therefore other nodes find the wireless medium busy and keep back-off so the performance of the network degrades this way.

The most popular attack model of IEEE 802.11 is Jamming Attacks. Jamming is defined as a DoS attack that interferes with the communication between nodes. The objective of the adversary causing a jamming attack is to prevent a legitimate sender or receiver from transmitting or receiving packets on the network. Adversaries or malicious nodes can launch jamming attacks at multiple layers of the protocol suite. In the later section of this thesis, the Jamming attacks are simulated on MANETs that results in collisions in the mobile wireless network. The jamming is divided into two categories as Physical and Virtual Jamming attacks. The physical jamming is launched by continuous transmissions and/or by causing packet collisions at the receiver. Virtual jamming occurs at the MAC layer by attacks on control frames or data frames in IEEE 802.11 protocol (Chen, Deng, & Varshney, 2003).

Physical or Radio jamming in a wireless medium is a simple but disruptive form of DoS attack. These attacks are launched by either continuous emission of radio signals or by sending random bits onto the channel (Xu et al., 2005). The jammers causing these attacks can deny complete access to the channel by monopolizing the wireless medium. The nodes trying to communicate have an unusually large carrier sensing time waiting for the channel to become idle. This has an adverse propagating effect as the nodes enter into large exponential back-off periods.

Virtual Jamming Attacks can be launched at the MAC layer through attacks on the RTS/CTS (Request to Send/Clear to Send) frames or DATA frames (Chen, Deng & Varshney, 2003; Thuente & Acharya, 2006). A significant advantage of MAC layer jamming is that the attacker node consumes less power

Figure 5. Attacks on AODV Protocol in MANETs

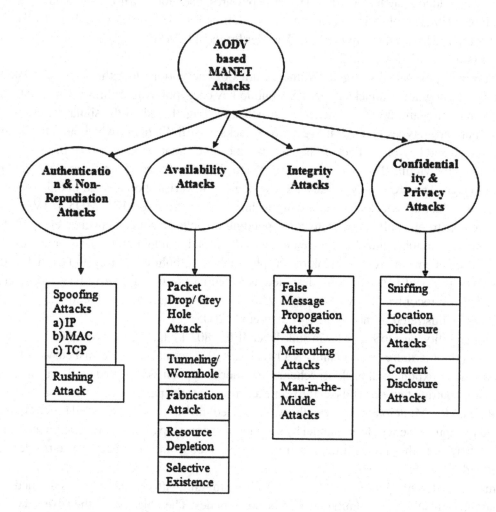

in targeting these attacks as compared to the physical radio jamming. Here, we focus on DoS attacks at the MAC layer resulting in collision of RTS/CTS control frames or the DATA frames. In virtual jamming attack malicious node sent RTS packets continuously on the transmission with unlimited period of time. During this entire process malicious node effectively jam the transmission with a large segment of transmission on the wireless channel with small expenditure of power. This attack is much effective than physical layer jamming as this attack consume less battery power compare to the other physical layer jamming attack. For example node M is a malicious node and it starting sending a false RTS packet to node R with a large frame. When nodes G and H receive packet on wireless channel they both become blocked for a certain amount of time as apply for node M as shown in the Figure 6 (Rahman & Gburzynski, 2006).

The jammers used in jamming attacks are also categorized into 4 categories. These are constant jammers, deceptive jammers, random jammers and reactive jammers. The constant jammer continuously emits radio frequency signals in form of random generated packets devoid of any MAC-layer protocol or rules. A high RF signal emitted into the wireless channel creates a busy channel such that the sender

Figure 6. Virtual Jamming attack

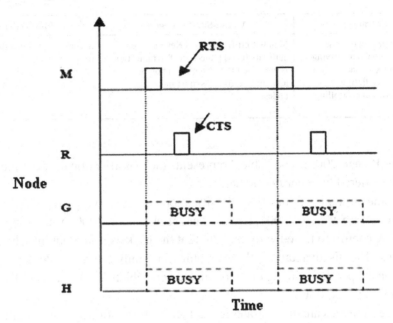

senses the medium as busy. The constant jammer specifically does not imply the carrier sense scheme; this means that it does not wait for the channel to be idle before transmitting. The deceptive jammers perform its activities by deception as it constantly injects regular packets to the channel between sequential transmissions without any interval of time instead of sending out random bit. It transmits semi-valid packets that contains valid message header but useless pay load. This behaviour leads to a deceptive environment that all other participating nodes notice that the channel contains a valid traffic. Random jammers send radio signals within specific periods. These periods are specified as "awake" and "sleep". Once the jammer is awake, it transmits the signals and once it's in "sleep" condition, it does not transmit any signals. The major aim of such mechanism is to create an energy efficient attack while saving its energy during sleeping mode by turning its radio off. Reactive Jammers targeting receiver channel by sending radio signal when it detects that the channel is busy which means that the reactive jammers do not conserve energy unless they detect the channel.

Security Strategies against DoS and DDoS Attacks on Mobile Ad Hoc Networks

As mentioned in the section 2.1, the provision of effective and efficient security can be provided through considering availability, confidentiality, authenticity and integrity concepts. A practically operating MANET must consider the trade-off between the deployment feasibility of a security patch and the system efficiency. And often, the feasibility is considered over the efficiency (Ferguson & Senie, 2000; Sans, 2000). The feasibility of a deployment (accessibility and cost) mostly depends on the deployment location. Based on this concept, the security strategies are classified as attacker-side strategies, victim-side strategies, and intermediate strategies (Lakshminarayanan, 2003). This taxonomy makes more practical sense to evaluate a security strategy than other taxonomies, e.g. activity level or cooperation degree

Table 2. Classification of Strategies against DoS attacks

Attacker-Side Strategies	Victim-Side Strategies	Intermediate Strategies
Mostly Protocol based protection. The protection is provided through modifying the communication protocols and analyze/differentiate the authorized traffic transmitted over network and controlling e.g. AODV, DSR.	Mainly Certification and Key management authority based protection. The protection is provided through authorization by assigning certificates to participating nodes.	Security is provided through participated nodes in the network. These nodes called intermediate nodes.

(Mirkovic, Prier & Reiher, 2002). The Table 2 represents the classification of the strategies with sample proposed examples offered by other researchers.

The Attacker-side strategies is the first classification for classifying attacks (Zhou, Schneider & Renesse, 2002; Benccsath & Vajda 2004; Leiwo, Aura & Nikander, 2000; Yau, Wang & Karim, 2002). It puts the incoming control to the edge routers. So that the packets going out into the network are only the legitimate ones. The disadvantage is that it requires not only a large-scale deployment of ingress control, but also the cooperation among the network clusters which requires a complex architecture that is against the nature for MANETs.

The Victim-side strategies are those strategies that an authentication system is built up by the victim, then it may let only the legitimate traffic have the access, or allocate resources to the requests only after they are authenticated (Li et al., 2004; Ioannidis & Bellovin, 2002; Savage et al. 2000). The disadvantages are that it requires the client to take extra legitimate application for the access, and DoS congestion may occur before the traffic reaches the victim so the strategy fails. The implementation of such strategy must be taken into consideration carefully against DDoS attacks.

Intermediate strategies require multiple intermediate nodes to support the secure system for the target. These intermediate nodes can work as a proxy to forward and filter the packets, or as the traffic monitors to detect the attack patterns. Another usage of the intermediate nodes is to form a multi-tier architecture, which can provide a unified security service (or other MANET services) interface towards client nodes (Schnackenberg, Djahandari, & Sterne, 2000). In our architecture, we will be also using participating nodes in the network in order to provide security against DoS attacks.

The effective strategy can be a combination of the characteristics of the above mentioned strategies which requires large amount of testing and verifying to solve the dilemma of performance and complexity.

The strategies and methods proposed by researchers to provide security, detection and backtracing against DoS and DDoS attacks are classified in this study. The DoS and DDoS strategy examples are given in the light of the strategy classification shown in the Table 2.

In addition to this Figure 7 illustrates the classification of known detection methods and each of the method that researchers have proposed in the literature.

Researchers have proposed variety of methods to provide security in MANETs against DoS and DDoS attacks. In addition to security, the methods proposed by researchers focus on providing backtracing facilities in order to detect the source of the attack and block the incoming attack from the point of inception. Statistical-based Detection and Backtracing methods are proposed by Yaar,, Perrig,, and Song, (2004) and used packet header marking in order to reduce overhead problem in the network for detection and backtracing facilities. This strategy works through packet sampling and picks particular percentage of the packets on the network in order to analyze and provide security. When DoS attack happens, the flood of attack packets can rapidly provide sufficient information about incoming packages through packet

Figure 7. Classification of detection mechanisms

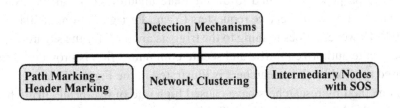

header marking and it gives sufficient information for backtracing purposes. In addition to this, other researchers also proposed similar security strategies through header marking or path marking methods mentioned in the literature (Anderson, Roscoe & Wetherall, 2004; Keromytis & Rubenstein, 2002).

The Network Clustering is another proposed method by the researchers in the literature which works through clustering the nodes into small groups called community and puts the boundary controllers at the edge of each community. This controllers help nodes to communicate with each other among different clusters and provide information to trace back the DoS attacks. In order to provide such mechanism, researchers have proposed Intruder Detection and Isolation Protocol (IDIP) (Schnackenberg, Djahandari, & Sterne, 2000). The Figure 8 represents the groups-communities and Intruder detection system and Isolation Protocol working mechanism.

On the other hand, researchers have proposed another strategy method so called "mobile-agent-based architecture" which is fully distributed and randomly selecting the migration path (Stoica et al. 2002; Bencsáth, & Vajda, 2004; Leiwo, Aura & Nikander, 2000). As it is represented on Table 2 security in

Figure 8. IDIP intrusion detection system

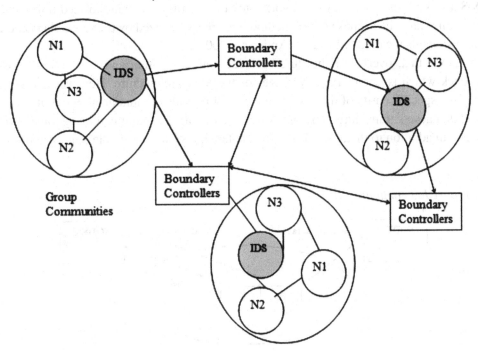

MANETs can be provided through managing authorization and differentiation of authorized traffic. The researchers have proposed a method to differentiate unauthorized traffic through specifying an authorization key to the important service requesters (Yaar,, Perrig,, & Song, 2004; Anderson, Roscoe & Wetherall, 2004). However it does nothing to the triggers are used for the secure and efficient routing (Min, 2004). The secure authorized traffic and secure communication is provided through this mechanism. The proposed method by the researchers is illustrated in the Figure 9.

This proposed method by researchers have caused high rate of overhead during handshake process of specification of authorization key problem. On the other hand, the public triggers must be known by the clients or the specified servers have to announce them which lead to the DoS attacks. On the other hand, this method has not implemented in the Application Layer, which requires modification on the Network Layer for all other actors of the network such as client nodes and server nodes. It is compulsory to consider the Wormhole attacks which belongs to Network Layer and as it has mentioned that strategy is not modified for the Application layer which contains Backdoors and Trojans and Viruses, the all other actors will be vulnerable to these attacks.

The traceback mechanism is provided through edge routers and tracking routers. The suspicious traffic is rerouted by the edge routers and tracking routers distinguish between the malicious packets and authorized packets. However, this process requires high rate of bandwidth and in the case of DoS attack, the networking overhead would increase the effects of a DoS attack.

Researchers have proposed Secure Overlay Services (SOS) that hides the overlay nodes and opens a couple of access points for communication (Keromytis & Rubenstein, 2002). The architecture is shown in the Figure 10. In this architecture, the system assumed that the requests arrive from the nodes that know the architecture and the access point. So no unauthorized access is possible. On the other hand, the architecture contains an access point called Secure Overlay access point (SOAP) for the outside requests. These outside requests are forwarded by the access point to the forwarding proxy nodes called "Secret Servlets" in the architecture. These secret servlets nodes deliver the requests to the service provider. When a DoS attack is generated on the network, only the legitimate and authorized traffic can get into the system by this way. The proposed SOS method is more generalized by the researchers and proposed as a security mechanism called "Mayday" (Andersen, 2003).

As it is known that, overlay architectures provide communication and connectivity even though under the attack which is one of the advantages of the SOS architecture. However the SOS strategy protects only the specific entity of the system and cannot provide communication out of the overlay. In addition to this, packets transmitted through secure overlay access point can be spoofed and attack to secret servlets. In addition to that, there is not load balancing system available among nodes to provide

Figure 9. Proposed i3 communication

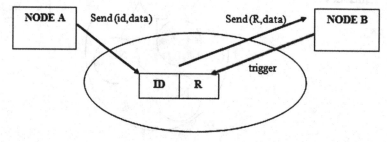

Figure 10. SOS architecture

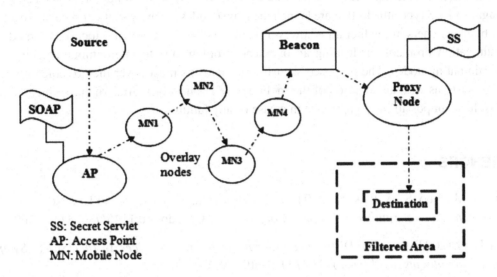

SS: Secret Servlet
AP: Access Point
MN: Mobile Node

equal workload share. So system may even crash with more complex flow of traffic. The SOS method is also proposed for the Internet and it will have performance, mobility and deployment problems for implementing in Mobile Ad Hoc Networks. The proposed SOS method is useful and effective in wired networks but faces mobility and adaptability problems in MANET environment.

Therefore, this thesis attempts to provide and original solution which ensures a minimum impact on the network infrastructure and topology which makes the implementation phase inexpensive with reasonable overhead, security and network performance.

FUTURE RECOMMENDATION

The most of the proposed methods by researchers discussed in this chapter required modification on communication protocols or architecture or even both. The modification and upgrade of the communication protocols seems like an absolute solution for prevention against DoS and DDoS attacks. However, the process of implementing such project may fail because of non-participating nodes refuse the upgrade or modification. On the other hand, network protocol modifications may fail the applications running on the network. For instance, modification on network layer affects the link layer and layers above it and interfaces between them. Controlling the attack traffic through edge routers and using tunnels to forward this traffic is useful. However it requires protocol modification and it may require high rate of bandwidth which may lead an amplification effect of DoS attack on the network. It is compulsory to take all these into account for designing and novel security algorithm to for mobile wireless networks.

CONCLUSION

Significant research on MANET has done so far and are most likely to grow more and get bigger presence in future communication infrastructure. As the use of MANET technology is increase, there's become a security concern as a large number of research showed that MANET are vulnerable when it concerns the security against DoS type attacks that are launched against nodes easily. Variety of security mechanisms proposed by researchers in the literature however majority of these researches focused on modification of communication protocols or leading an overhead problem due to intercommunication processes among participating nodes. The proposed security mechanisms must cover the possible drawbacks of the existing systems with an adoption of the mobile wireless network infrastructure which is dynamic and it must have an possibility to optimize in a case of any failure.

REFERENCES

Al-Shurman, M., Yoo, S., & Park, S. (2004). Black Hole Attack in Mobile Ad Hoc Networks. In *Proceedings of 42nd Annual Southeast Regional Conference*. ACM. doi:10.1145/986537.986560

Andersen, D. G. (2003). *Mayday: Distributed Filtering for Internet Services*. In *4th USENIX Symposium on Internet Technologies and Systems (USITS)*, Seattle, WA.

Anderson, T., Roscoe, T., & Wetherall, D. (2004). Preventing Internet Denial-of-Service with Capabilities. *Computer Communication Review*, *34*(1), 39–44. doi:10.1145/972374.972382

Asokan, N., & Ginzboorg, P. (2000). Key Agreement in Ad-hoc networks. *Computer Communications*, *23*(17), 1627–1637. doi:10.1016/S0140-3664(00)00249-8

Barbir, A., Murphy, S., & Yang, Y. (2004). *Generic Threats to Routing Protocols 2004, IETF Internet draft*. Available at: http://www.ietf.org/internet-drafts/draft-ietfrpsec-routing-threats-07.txt

Bellovin, S. M., & Merrit, M. (1992). Encrypted Key Exchange*: Password-Based Protocols Secure Against Dictionary Attacks. IEEE Symposium on Research in Security and Privacy*.

Bencsáth, B., & Vajda, I. (2004). *Protection Against DDoS Attacks Based On Traffic Level Measurements*. In *International Symposium on Collaborative Technologies and Systems,* San Diego, CA.

Binkley, J., & Trost, W. (2001). Authenticated Ad-hoc Routing at the Link Layer for Mobile Systems. *Wireless Networks*, *7*(2), 139–145. doi:10.1023/A:1016633521987

Black Box Corp. (2003). *Network Security, A White Paper*. Available at: http://www.blackbox.com/Tech_Support/White-Papers/Network-Security2.pdf

Blum, J., & Eskandarian, A. (2004). The Threat of Intelligent Collisions. *IT Professional*, *6*(1), 24–29. doi:10.1109/MITP.2004.1265539

20. Capkun, S., Buttyan, L., & Hubaux, J. P. (2003). Self Organized Public-Key Management for Mobile Ad Hoc Networks. *IEEE Transactions on Mobile Computing*, *2*(1), 52–64. doi:10.1109/TMC.2003.1195151

CERT. (1998). *Smurf Attack CERT Annual Report*. Available at CERT: http://www.cert.org/advisories/CA-1998-01.html

Charles, C. T. (2005). *Security Review of the Light-Weight Access Point Protocol. 2005*. IETF CAPWAP Working Group.

Chen, D., Deng, J., & Varshney, P. K. (2003). Protecting wireless networks against a denial of service attack based on virtual jamming. In *MOBICOM -Proceedings of the Ninth Annual International Conference on Mobile Computing and Networking*. ACM.

Conti, M., Gregori, E., & Maselli, G. (2003). Towards Reliable Forwarding for Ad Hoc Networks. In *Personal Wireless Communications, IFIP-TC6 8th International Conference, PWC 2003*. Venice, Italy: Springer. doi:10.1007/978-3-540-39867-7_71

Convery, S., Miller, D., & Sundaralingam, S. (2003). *Cisco SAFE: Wireless LAN Security in Depth 2003*. CISCO Whitepaper.

Desmedt, Y., & Frankel, Y. (1990). Threshold Cryptosystem. Springer Verlag. doi:10.1007/0-387-34805-0_28

Diffie, W., & Hellman, M. (1976). New Directions in Cryptography. *IEEE Transactions on Information Theory, IT, 22*(6), 644–654. doi:10.1109/TIT.1976.1055638

Ferguson, P., & Senie, D. (2000). *Network Ingress Filtering: Defeating Denial of Service Attacks Which Employ IP Source Address Spoofing*. Available on http://www.rfc-archive.org/getrfc.php?rfc=2827

Fletcher, T., Richardson, H. W. K., Carlisle, M. C., & Hamilton, J. A. (2005). Simulation Experimentation with Secure Overlay Services. In *Summer Computer Simulation Conference*, Philadelphia, PA.

Gasser, M., Goldstein, A., Kaufman, C., & Lampson, B. (1989). The Digital distributed system security architecture. In *Proceedings of the National Computer Security Conference*.

Graf, K. (2005). *Addressing Challenges in Application Security*. Watchfire White Paper. Retrieved from http://www.watchfire.com

Hu, Y-C., Perrig, A., & Johnson, D. B. (2003). Rushing Attacks and Defense in Wireless Ad Hoc Network Routing Protocols. In *2nd ACM Wireless Security* (WiSe'03).

Hubaux, J. P., Gross, T., Boudec, J. Y., & Vetterli, M. (2001, January). Toward self-organized mobile ad hoc networks: The terminodes project. *IEEE Communications Magazine, 39*(1), 118–124. doi:10.1109/35.894385

Humphries, J. W., & Carlisle, M. C. (2002). Introduction to Cryptography. *ACM Journal of Educational Resources in Computing, 2*(3), 2.

Ioannidis, J., & Bellovin, S. M. (2002). *Implementing Pushback: Router-Based Defense Against DDoS Attacks*. In *Network and Distributed System Security Symposium*, San Diego, CA.

Johnson, D. B., & Maltz, D. A. (1996). Article. In T. Imielinski & H. Korth (Eds.), Dynamic source routing in ad hoc wireless networks, in mobile Computing (pp. 153–181). Kluwer Academic Publishers.

Just, M., Kranakis, E., & Wan, T. (2003). Resisting Malicious Packet Dropping in Wireless Ad Hoc Networks. In ADHOCNOW'03, Montreal, Canada. doi:10.1007/978-3-540-39611-6_14

Karygiannis, T., & Owens, L. (2002). *Wireless Network Security 802.11 Bluetooth and Handheld Devices*. National Institute of Standards and Technology Special Publication, 800-48. Available at: http://csrc.nist.gov/publications/nistpubs/800-48/NIST_SP_800-48.pdf

Katz, J. (2002). *Efficient Cryptographic Protocols Preventing "Man-in-the-Middle" Attacks*. (PhD Dissertation). Columbia University.

Kaufman, C., Perlman, R., & Speciner, M. (2002). *Network Security Private Communication in a Public World*. Prentice Hall PTR.

Keromytis, A. D., & Rubenstein, D. (2002). SOS: Secure Overlay Services. In ACM SIGCOMM'02, Pittsburgh, PA.

Kong, J., Zerfos, P., Luo, H., Lu, S., & Zhang, L. (2001). Providing Robust and Ubiquitous Security Support for Mobile Adhoc Networks. In *Ninth International Conference on Network Protocols* (ICNP). Available at http://citeseer.nj.nec.com/kong01providing.html

Lakshminarayanan, K., Adkins, D., Perrig, A., & Stoica, I. (2003). Taming IP Packet Flooding Attacks. In *2nd ACM Workshop on Hot Topics in Networks*. Cambridge, MA: ACM Press. doi:10.1145/972374.972383

Lawson, L. (2005). *Session Hijacking Packet Analysis*. SecurityDocs.com Report.

Lazos, L., Poovendran, R., Meadows, C., Syverson, P., & Chang, L. W. (2005) Preventing Wormhole Attacks on Wireless Ad Hoc Networks: A Graph Theoretic Approach. In *IEEE Wireless Communications and Networking Conference*. doi:10.1109/WCNC.2005.1424678

Leiwo, J., Aura, T., & Nikander, P. (2000). *Towards Network Denial Of Service Resistant Protocols*. In 15th International Information Security Conference, Beijing, China. doi:10.1007/978-0-387-35515-3_31

Levijoki, S. (2000). *Authentication, Authorization and Accounting in Ad-hoc networks*. Department of Computer Science Helsinki University of Technology. Retrieved from http://www.hut.fi/~slevijok/aaa.htm

Li, J., Sung, M., Xu, J., & Li, L. E. (2004). *Large-Scale IP Traceback in High-Speed Internet: Practical Techniques and Theoretical Foundation*. In IEEE Symposium on Security and Privacy, Oakland, CA.

Luo, H., Kong, J., Zerfos, P., Lu, S., & Zhang, L. (2000). *Self Securing Ad-hoc Wireless Networks. IEEE Symposium on Computers and Communications (ISCC'02)*.

Marti, S., Giuli, T., Lai, K., & Baker, M. (2000). Mitigating Routing Misbehaviour in Mobile Ad-hoc Networks. In *Proceedings of the ACM International Conference on Mobile Computing and Networking MobiCom*.

Min, S. (2004). *A Study on the Security of NTRUSign Digital Signature Scheme*. (Master Thesis). Information and Communications University, Korea.

Mirkovic, J., Prier, G., & Reiher, P. (2002). Attacking DDoS at the Source. In *Proceedings of 10th IEEE International Conference on Network Protocols*. IEEE Computer Society.

Molva, R., & Michiardi, P. (2002). Security in Ad Hoc Networks. In *Personal Wireless Communications, IFIP-TC6 8th International Conference*. Venice, Italy: Springer. doi:10.1007/978-3-540-39867-7_69

Nguyan, D., Zhao, L., Uisawang, P., & Platt, J. (2000). Security Routing Analysis For Mobile Ad-hoc Networks. Interdisciplinary Telecommunications Program of Colorado University.

Nichols, R. K., & Lekkas, P. C. (2002). Wireless Security: Models, Threats, and Solutions. McGraw-Hill Professional.

Papadimitratos, P., & Haas, Z. J. (2002). Secure Routing for Mobile Ad-hoc Networks. In *Proceedings of the SCS Communication Networks and Distributed Systems Modelling and Simulations Conference (CNDS 2002)*.

Patrikakis, C., Masikos, M., & Zouraraki, O. (2004). Distributed Denial of Service Attacks. *The Internet Protocol J.*, *7*(4), 13–35.

Rabin, T. (1998). A Simplified Approach to Threshold and Proactive RSA. In *Advances in Cryptology – Crypto 98 Proceedings* (LNCS), (Vol. 1462, pp. 89–104). Springer-Verlag. doi:10.1007/BFb0055722

Rafique, K. (2002). *A Survey of Mobile Ad Hoc Networks*. Available at: http://www.columbia.edu/itc/ee/e6951/2002spring/Projects/CVN/report13.pdf

Rahman, A., & Gburzynski, P. (2006). *Hidden Problems with the Hidden Node Problem*. Available at: http://citeseerx.ist.psu.edu/viewdoc/download?doi=10.1.1.61.365&rep=rep1&type=pdf

Ramaswamy, S., Fu, H., Sreekantaradhya, M., Dixon, J., & Nygard, K. (2003). Prevention of Cooperative Black Hole Attack in Wireless Ad Hoc Networks. In *Proceedings of International Conference on Wireless Networks*.

Royer, E., & Toh, C. (1999). A Review of Current Routing Protocols for Ad Hoc Mobile Wireless Networks. *IEEE Personal Communications*, *6*(2), 46–55. doi:10.1109/98.760423

Sans. (2000). *Egress Filtering v 0.2*. Available at: http://www.sans.org/y2k/egress.htm

Savage, S., Wetherall, D., Karlin, A., & Anderson, T. (2000). *Practical Network Support for IP Traceback*. In the 2000 ACM SIGCOMM Conference, Stockholm, Sweden.

Schnackenberg, D., Djahandari, K., & Sterne, D. (2000). Infrastructure for Intrusion Detection and Response. In DARPA Information Survivability Conference and Exposition.

Schuller, J. (2003). *Understanding Wireless LAN Technology and Its Security Risks*. Available at GIAC: http://www.giac.org/practical/GSEC/Julie_Schuller_GSEC.pdf

Schwingenschlögl, C., & Horn, M.-P. (2002). Building Blocks for Secure Communication in Ad-hoc Networks. In *Proceedings of the 4th European Wireless (EW'02)*.

Shoup, V. (2000). Practical Threshold Signatures. In *Advances in Cryptology-Eurocrypt 2000 proceedings (LNCS)*, (Vol. 1807, pp. 207–221). Springer Verlag. doi:10.1007/3-540-45539-6_15

Stajano, F., & Anderson, R. (1999). The Resurrecting Duckling: Security Issues for Ad-Hoc Wireless networks. In *Proceedings of the 7th International Workshop on Security Protocols*.

Stoica, I., Adkins, D., Zhuang, S., Shenker, S., & Surana, S. (2002). *Internet Indirection Infrastructure*. In ACM SIGCOMM Conference, Pittsburgh, PA.

Stubblefield, A., Ioannidis, J., & Rubin, A. D. (2002). *Using the Fluhrer, Mantin, and Shamir attack to break WEP*. In Symposium on Network and Distributed System Security. Available at http://www.isoc. org/isoc/conferences/ndss/02/proceedings/papers/stubbl.pdf

Thuente, D., & Acharya, M. (2006). Intelligent jamming in wireless networks with applications to 802.11b and other networks. In *Proceedings of the 25th IEEE Communications Society Military Communications Conference (MILCOM)*.

Torgerson, M. & Leeuwen, B.V. (2001). *Routing Data in Wireless Ad-hoc Networks*. Sandia laboratories report SAND2001-3119 October 2001.

Venkatraman, L., & Agrawal, D. P. (2001). An Optimized Inter-Router Authentication Scheme for Ad-hoc networks. In *Proceedings of the 13th International Conference on Wireless Communications*.

Vigna, G., Gwalani, S., Srinivasan, K., Elizabeth, M., Royer, B., & Kemmerer, R. (2004). An Intrusion Detection Tool for AODV-based Ad hoc Wireless Networks. In *Proceedings of 20th Annual Computer Security Applications Conference* (ACSAC'04). IEEE Computer Society.

Wang, X., Feng, D., Lai, X. & H. Yu (2004). *Collisions for Hash Functions MD4, MD5, HAVAL-128 and RIPEMD*. Cryptology ePrint Archive.

Weimerskirch, A., & Thonet, G. (2001). A Distributed Lightweight Authentication Model for Ad-hoc Networks. In *Proceedings of the 4th International Conference on Information Security and Cryptology* (ICICS 2001).

Wood, A. D., & Stankovic, J. A. (2002). Denial of Service in Sensor Networks. *Computer, 35*(10), 54–62. doi:10.1109/MC.2002.1039518

Xu, W., Wade, T., Yanyong, Z., & Timothy, W. (2005). The Feasibility of Launching and Detecting Jamming Attacks in Wireless Networks. In *Proceedings of 6th ACM International Symposium on Mobile Ad Hoc Networking and Computing 2005*. Urbana-Champaign, IL: ACM Press.

Xu, W., Trappe, W., Zhang, Y., & Wood, T. (2005). The feasibility of launching and detecting jamming attacks in wireless networks. In *Proceedings of the 6th ACM international symposium on Mobile ad hoc networking and computing*.

Yaar, A., Perrig, A., & Song, D. (2004). SIFF: A Stateless Internet Flow Filter to Mitigate DDoS Flooding Attacks. In *Proceedings of the IEEE Security and Privacy Symposium*. Philadelphia, PA: ACM Press. doi:10.1109/SECPRI.2004.1301320

Yau, S. S., Wang, Y., & Karim, F. (2002). Development of Situation-Aware Application Software for Ubiquitous Computing Environment. In *Proceedings of 26th International Computer Software and Applications Conference on Prolonging Software Life: Development and Redevelopment*. IEEE Computer Society. doi:10.1109/CMPSAC.2002.1044557

Yi, P., Dai, Z., Zhong, Y., & Zhang, S. (2005). Resisting Flooding Attacks in Ad Hoc Networks. In *Proceedings of the International Conference on Information Technology: Coding and Computing* (ITCC'05).

Zhang, Y., & Lee, W. (2000). Intrusion detection in wireless ad-hoc networks. In *Proceedings of the 6th Annual International Conference on Mobile Computing and Networking*.

Zhou, L., & Haas, Z. J. (1999, November/December). *Securing Ad-hoc Networks. IEEE Networks*, 24–30.

Zhou, L., Schneider, F. B., & Renesse, R. V. (2002). COCA: A Secure Distributed On-line Certification Authority. *ACM Transactions on Computer Systems, 20*(4), 329–368. doi:10.1145/571637.571638

Chapter 3
Virtual Private Networks

Alok Vishwakarma
Sysbiz Technologies Pvt. Ltd., India

ABSTRACT

Virtual Private Network, Its 'Virtual', Its 'Private' and it's a 'Network'. A virtual private network (VPN) provides a secure connection between a sender and a receiver over a public non-secure network such as the Internet. A secure connection is generally associated with private networks. (A private network is a network that is owned, or at least controlled via leased lines, by an organization.). We can define a VPN by the following relationship: VPN = Tunneling + Security + QoS Parameters. This Chapter deals with Advantages of VPNs, Types of VPNs, VPN Architectures, VPN Models, VPN Devices, Technologies and Protocols Used to Enable Remote Access VPNs.

INTRODUCTION

What Makes a VPN?

A well-designed VPN can greatly benefit a company (see Figure 1). For example, it can:

- Extend geographic connectivity • Improve security • Reduce operational costs versus traditional WAN
- Reduce transit time and transportation costs for remote users
- Improve Productivity
- Simplify Network Topology
- Provide global networking opportunities
- Provide telecommuter support
- Provide broadband networking compatibility
- Provide faster ROI (return on investment) than traditional WAN

DOI: 10.4018/978-1-4666-8761-5.ch003

Figure 1. VPN architecture diagram

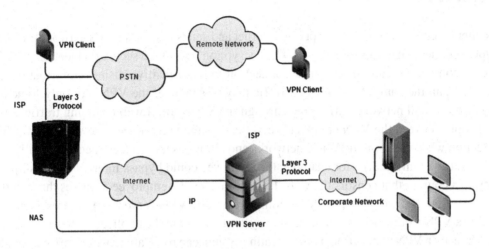

VPN Architecture

Background

A VPN can transform the characteristics of a public non-secure network into those of a private secure network. VPNs reduce remote access costs by using public network resources. Compared to other solutions, including private networks, a VPN is inexpensive. VPNs are not new. In fact, they have been used in telephone networks for years and have become more prevalent since the development of the intelligent network (Web ProForum Tutorials, n.d.). Frame relay networks, which have been around for some time, are VPNs. Virtual private networks are only new to IP networks such as the Internet. Therefore, some authors use the terms Internet VPN and virtual private data network to distinguish the VPN described in this chapter from other VPNs. In this book, the term VPN refers to Internet VPN. The goal of a VPN is to provide a secure passage for users' data over the non-secure Internet. It enables companies to use the Internet as the virtual backbone for their corporate networks by allowing them to create secure virtual links between their corporate office and branch or remote offices via the Internet. The cost benefits of VPN service have prompted corporations to move more of their data from private WANs to Internet- based VPNs.

Technologies and Protocols Used to Enable Remote Access VPNs

- The Layer Two Forwarding (L2F) Protocol—L2F
- The Point-to-Point Tunneling Protocol (PPTP)
- The Layer 2 Tunneling Protocol versions 2 and 3 (L2TPv2/L2TPv3
- IPsec
- The Secure Sockets Layer (SSL)

How a VPN Works?

The VPN client communicates over the public Internet and sends the computer's network traffic through the encrypted connection to the VPN server. The encryption provides a secure connection, which means the business's competitors can't snoop on the connection and see sensitive business information. Depending on the VPN, all the computer's network traffic may be sent over the VPN – or only some of it may (generally, however, all network traffic goes through the VPN). If all web browsing traffic is sent over the VPN, people between the VPN client and server can't snoop on the web browsing traffic. This provides protection when using public Wi-Fi networks and allows users to access geographically-restricted services (Seada & Helmy, n.d.) – for example, the employee could bypass Internet censorship if they're working from a country that censors the web. To the websites the employee accesses through the VPN, the web browsing traffic would appear to be coming from the VPN server (see Figures 2 and 3).

Crucially, a VPN works more at the operating system level than the application level. In other words, when you've set up a VPN connection, your operating system can route all network traffic through it from all applications (although this can vary from VPN to VPN, depending on how the VPN is configured). You don't have to configure each individual application.

Figure 2. Connecting a VPN at workplace

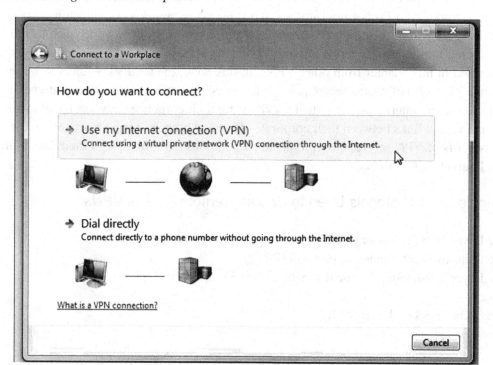

Figure 3. Connecting a VPN at workplace

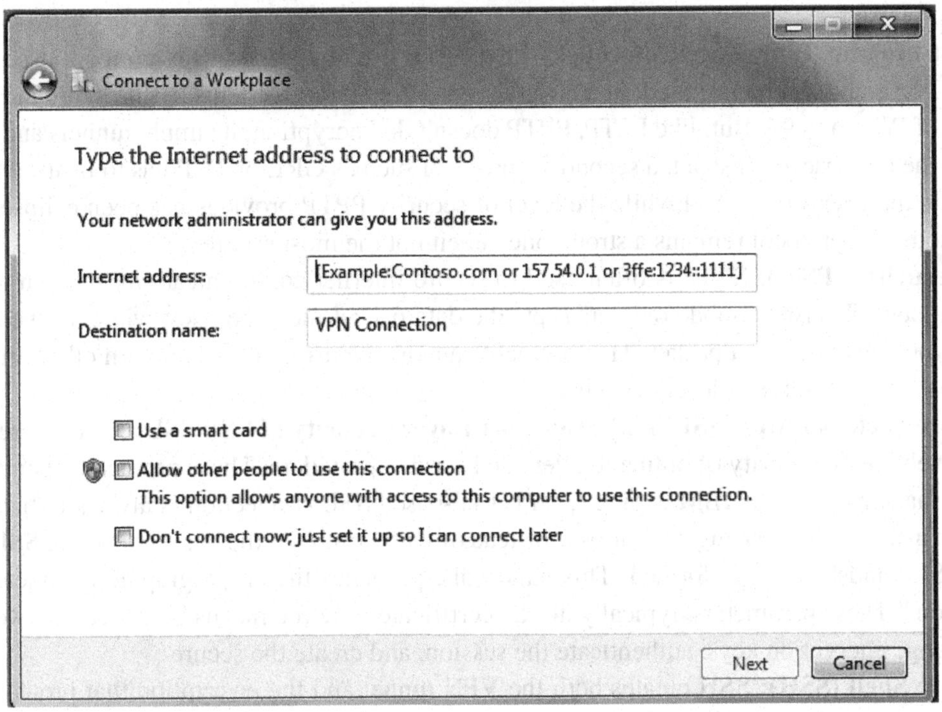

MAIN FOCUS OF THE CHAPTER

Issues, Controversies, Problems

There are several Issues, Controversies and Problems while setting up a VPN. Some of them will be addressed in this chapter. They are as follows:

- Security
- Reliability
- Scalability
- Network management
- Policy management

Security

Many security protocols (Miltchev, Ioannidis, & Keromytis, n.d.) have been developed as VPNs, each offering differing levels of security and features. Among the more common are:

1. **Layer 2 Tunneling Protocol (L2TP)/IPsec:** The L2TP and IPsec protocols combine their best individual features to create a highly secure VPN client. Since L2TP isn't capable of encryption, it instead generates the tunnel while the IPSec protocol handles encryption, channel security, and

data integrity checks to ensure all of the packets have arrived and that the channel has not been compromised.

2. **Point-to-Point Tunneling Protocol (PPTP):** PPTP is a ubiquitous VPN protocol used since the mid-1990s and can be installed on a huge variety of operating systems has been around since the days of Windows 95. But, like L2TP, PPTP doesn't do encryption, it simply tunnels and encapsulates the data packet. Instead, a secondary protocol such as GRE or TCP has to be used as well to handle the encryption. And while the level of security PPTP provides has been eclipsed by new methods, the protocol remains a strong one, albeit not the most secure.

3. **IP security (IPSec):** IPSec is often used to secure Internet communications and can operate in two modes. Transport mode only encrypts the data packet message itself while Tunneling mode encrypts the entire data packet. This protocol can also be used in tandem with other protocols to increase their combined level of security.

4. **Secure Sockets Layer (SSL) and Transport Layer Security (TLS):** SSL and TLS are used extensively in the security of online retailers and service providers. These protocols operate using a handshake method. As IBM explains, "A HTTP-based SSL connection is always initiated by the client using a URL starting with https:// instead of with http://. At the beginning of an SSL session, an SSL handshake is performed. This handshake produces the cryptographic parameters of the session." These parameters, typically digital certificates, are the means by which the two systems exchange encryption keys, authenticate the session, and create the secure

5. **Secure Shell (SSH):** SSH creates both the VPN tunnel and the encryption that protects it. This allows users to transfer information unsecured data by routing the traffic from remote fileservers through an encrypted channel. The data itself isn't encrypted but the channel it's moving through is. SSH connections are created by the SSH client, which forwards traffic from a local port one on the remote server. All data between the two ends of the tunnel flow through these specified ports.

Solutions and Recommendations

We have certain solutions and recommendations in dealing with the issues, controversies and Problems.

- VPN Security: Firewalls
- VPN Security: Encryption
- VPN Security: AAA Servers

Now we will see the detailed description of these security protocols which offers security to Virtual Private Network

1. THE LAYER TWO FORWARDING (L2F) PROTOCOL—L2F

Layer Two Forwarding (L2F) is a Cisco tunneling protocol that uses virtual dial-up networks for secure data packet transport. L2F functionality is similar to the Point-to-Point Tunneling Protocol (PPTP), which was developed by the Microsoft-led PPTP Forum. L2F is part of the Layer 2 Tunneling Protocol (L2TP) standard (RFC 2661).

L2F creates point-to-point (PPP) network and user connections and allows high-level protocols to create tunnels via the link layer, including High-Level Data Link Control (HDLC) or SLIP frames (Vanguard Managed Solutions, n.d.). These tunnels separate server and termination points to facilitate network access.

1.1. How it Works?

When using PPP with L2F, for example, PPP provides the connection between a dial-up client and the network access server (NAS) that receives the call. A PPP connection initiated by a client terminates at a NAS (IMEX, n.d.) located at a PPP service provider, usually an Internet service provider (ISP). L2F allows the termination point of the connection to be extended beyond the NAS to a remote destination node, so the client's connection appears to be directly to the remote node instead of to the NAS. The function of the NAS in L2F is simply to project or forward PPP frames from the client to the remote node. This remote node is called a home gateway in Cisco networking terminology.

1.2. Troubleshooting Layer Two Forwarding Protocol VPNs

The Layer Two Forwarding (L2F) Protocol is a Cisco proprietary protocol that facilitates the transparent forwarding of Point-to-Point Protocol (PPP) and Serial Line Internet Protocol (SLIP) across an IP backbone.

L2F, which is defined in RFC 2341 (Valencia, Littlewood, & Kolar, 1998), allows the separation of the functionality of the traditional Network Access Server (NAS), with call reception on a NAS, but termination of the PPP or SLIP connection on a device called a Home Gateway. The Home Gateway is geographically separated from the NAS. This means that an enterprise can outsource call reception to an Internet service provider (ISP) but still terminate PPP/SLIP connections within the corporate network. This allows the enterprise to save or minimize on call charges because remote access clients are no longer required to dial directly to the enterprise. They are instead able to dial in to the ISP's nearest Point-of-Presence (POP). Figure 4 illustrates this concept.·

1.3. Technical Overview of L2F

As previously described, L2F (Government of the Hong Kong Special Administrative Region, 2008) is a protocol that allows the tunneling of PPP and SLIP frames across a IP backbone between a NAS and

Figure 4. L2F topology

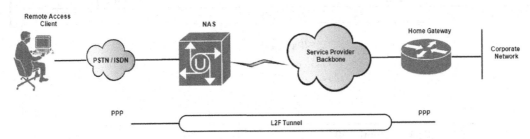

Table 1. Relationship between IP, UDP, and L2F

IP Header
UDP Header
L2F Header
L2f Payload
L2F CRC (Optional)

a Home Gateway. This chapter focuses on the tunneling of PPP frames because, to a great extent, PPP has superseded SLIP as the remote access protocol of choice.

The protocol itself uses the User Datagram Protocol (UDP), on top of which sits the L2F packet (header, payload, and optional CRC) itself. Table 1 illustrates the relationship between IP, UDP, and L2F.

Note that L2F packets utilize UDP port 1701. This will be relevant when troubleshooting L2F.

Now take a closer look at the L2F Protocol packet header itself in Figure 5.

The following list provides an analysis of the L2F header, starting with the header flags.

The F, K, S, and C bits, if set to 1, indicate that the optional fields (shown as opt in Figure 2-3) should be present:

- F, if set, indicates that the Offset field should be present.
- K, if set, indicates that the Key field should be present.
- S, if set, indicates that the Sequence number should be set.
- Finally, C, if set, indicates that the Checksum should be present.

The P bit, if set, indicates that this L2F packet is a priority packet. RFC 2341 does not specifically define what type of packet should constitute a priority packet but instead leaves this up to the implementer.

The Version (Ver) field is a 3-bit field and should be set to 001 binary = 1 decimal. No other value is valid, at least as far as L2F is concerned.

Figure 5. Overall L2F packet format

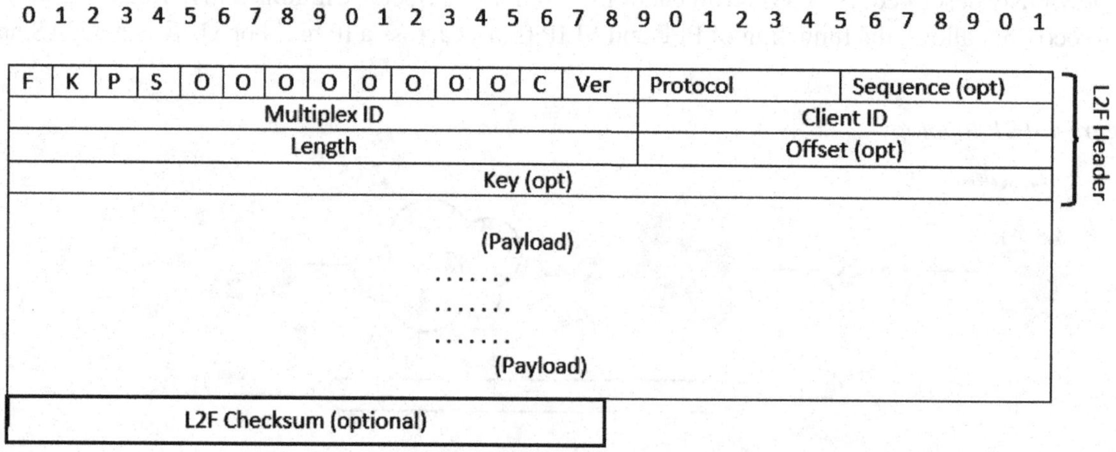

Table 2. Summarizes protocol field values

Value	Type	Description
0x00	L2F_ILLEGAL	Illegal protocol type
0x01	L2F_PROTO	Management packets
0x02	L2F_PPP	Payload carries tunneled PPP
0x03	L2F_SLIP	Payload carries tunneled SLIP

The 8-bit Protocol field has only three legal values, 0x01, 0x02, and 0x03 (see Table 2). The value 0x1 indicates that this is an L2F management packet (type L2F_PROTO), the value 0x2 indicates that this packet contains PPP tunneled within L2F (type L2F_PPP), and the value 0x3 indicates that the packet contains SLIP tunneled within L2F (type L2F_SLIP).

If the value in the Protocol field specifies a management packet, then various options and sub options are carried within the L2F payload. Options specify an overall message type, with sub options carrying data associated with the message type.

Options and sub options are discussed in the section "L2F Management Messages."

The 8-bit Sequence field is present only if the S-bit is set. The S-bit must be set, and therefore, sequence numbering must be used, for L2F management packets.

RFC 2341 allows a degree of flexibility with regard to the Sequence number field. Packets other than management packets can use sequence numbers, but it is not mandatory. Some protocols might be sensitive to packets arriving out of sequence, and sequence numbering can be useful in this case. If sequence numbering is used, it must be present in every packet for a particular session (for every packet with the same multiplex ID [MID]).

The MID is a 16-bit field, and it is used to distinguish between different sessions (connections) within the overall L2F tunnel from a NAS to a Home Gateway (Hätönen, Nyrhine, et al., n.d.).

Figure 6 illustrates an L2F tunnel between a NAS and Home Gateway with multiple sessions within it, each from a different remote access client.

Figure 6. Multiple session within the L2F tunnel

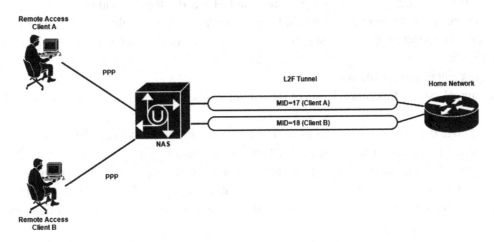

In Figure 6, two remote access users are connected to the NAS. Their PPP connections are tunneled via L2F from the NAS to the Home Gateway.

The Home Gateway has to be able to distinguish between the two sessions, and this is done using unique MIDs. Remote access user A's PPP connection uses MID 17, and user B's PPP connection uses MID 18. Note that MID 17 and 18 have no special significance and are used purely for illustrative purposes.

The MID 0 is reserved for L2F management (L2F_PROTO) packets, leaving a theoretical $2^{16}-1$ (65535) MIDs for client sessions.

The Client ID (CLID) is a 16-bit field, and it is used to uniquely identify a particular tunnel from a NAS to a Home Gateway and vice-versa. At any one time, a Home Gateway might be terminating L2F tunnels from a number of NASs. Similarly at any one time, a NAS might have tunnels to several Home Gateways. To allow the Home Gateway (or NAS) to distinguish between the packets coming through tunnels from different NASs (or Home Gateways), a CLID is used.

The CLID assigned to a particular tunnel is communicated during the tunnel setup. It is communicated via the Assigned CLID field in a L2F_CONF packet (see the section "L2F Tunnel Establishment"). The receiving device then uses the CLID to distinguish inbound packets belonging to different tunnels.

For example, a NAS with hostname NAS1 receives a call from an employee of the Perris Corporation. Having no existing L2F tunnel to the Home Gateway for the Perris Corporation (PERRIS_HGW1), NAS1 needs to set one up. Tunnel setup begins from NAS1 to PERRIS_HGW1. PERRIS_HGW1 is already terminating an L2F tunnel from NAS2, and this tunnel is identified by the CLID 1. PERRIS_HGW1 needs to distinguish inbound packets on the tunnel from NAS1 from those inbound from NAS2. During tunnel setup to NAS1, therefore, PERRIS_HGW1 assigns the unique CLID 2 and communicates this to NAS1 via the Assigned CLID field in a L2F_CONF message. Thereafter, whenever NAS1 needs to send L2F tunnel packets to PERRIS_HGW1, it puts the number 2 in the Client ID field.

In simple terms, during tunnel setup, PERRIS_HGW1 says to NAS1, "Whenever you want to send tunnel packets to me, please uniquely identify them with the CLID 2 so that I will know that they are packets from you." Remember that this process is bidirectional, so NAS1 also communicates a locally unique CLID to PERRIS_HGW1.

In Figure 7, PERRIS_HGW1 is receiving L2F tunnel packets from both NAS1 and NAS2. It is able to distinguish these packets by examining the CLID field.

The next field in the packet header is Length. The Length field is 16 bits long, and it reflects the length of the header and payload but does not include the checksum if one is present. The Offset field, if present, is used to specify how many bytes after the L2F header the payload starts.

For some transport architectures, it might be more efficient if the payload is aligned with a 32-bit boundary, and the Offset field can be used to ensure this (with an offset of 0). The Offset is present only if the F bit is set.

The Key is calculated as follows:

During tunnel establishment, each end of the tunnel sends a challenge to its peer in an L2F_CONF message.

This challenge contains a random number. The recipient of this challenge calculates a 128-bit hash value based on the random number and a shared password (tunnel secret).

The recipient then breaks the 128-bit hash into four parts, exclusive-ORs (XORs) them together, and sends the resultant hash value in the Key field back to its tunnel peer (NAS or Home Gateway). Note that the original 128-bit hash value is also sent to the tunnel peer during tunnel authentication.

Figure 7.

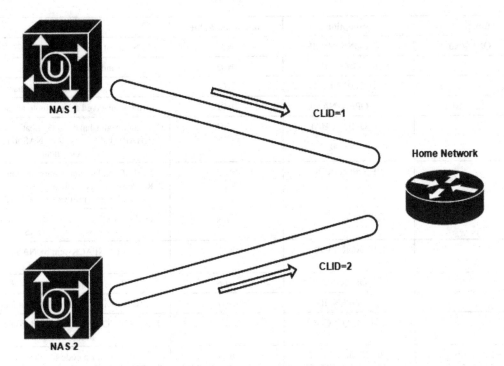

The originator of the challenge calculates its own hash value based on the same random number and the shared password and compares it to the hash value received. If the two hash values match, authentication is successful.

The 32-bit Key, once calculated, is carried in all tunnel packets for the duration of its lifetime.

Next in the packet comes the L2F payload. This is used to carry either L2F management messages or PPP frames depending on the packet type. Finally, if the C bit is set, a 16-bit checksum is appended to the packet. The checksum is calculated over the entire L2F packet, starting with the header and including the payload.

1.4. L2F Management Messages

As previously mentioned, if the L2F header has a value of 0x01 (L2F_PROTO) in the Protocol field, the packet is a tunnel management packet. Within the payload of a tunnel management packet, various options and sub options can be carried. The option specified dictates what kind of management message the packet is, whereas the sub options carry any data associated with that particular message type (see Table 3).

As you can see, if a L2F_CONF message is sent, three suboptions can be carried along with it: L2F_CONF_NAME, L2F_CONF_CHAL, and L2F_CLID. Similarly, if the message is an L2F_OPEN, the suboptions that can be carried range from L2F_OPEN_NAME to L2F_REQ_LCP0. When an L2F_CLOSE message is sent, the two suboptions can be carried are L2F_CLOSE_WHY and L2F_CLOSE_STR. Finally, if the message is either an L2F_ECHO or an L2F_ECHO_RESP, no suboptions can be carried.

The sections that follow describe the function of the options and suboptions in greater detail.

Table 3. Summarizes the available options and their corresponding sub options

Option	Suboption	Suboption Value	Description
L2F_CONF (0x01)	L2F_CONF_NAME	0x02	Name of peer sending L2F_CONF
	L2F_CONF_CHAL	0x03	Random number challenge
	L2F_CONF_CLID	0x04	Assigned CLID for peer use
L2F_OPEN (0x02)	L2F_OPEN_NAME	0x01	Username received from remote access client
	L2F_OPEN_CHAL	0x02	Challenge Handshake Authentication Protocol (CHAP) challenge sent by NAS to remote access client
	L2F_OPEN_RESP	0x03	1. Tunnel authentication response 2. Response from remote access client to NAS challenge (hash value, if CHAP)
	L2F_ACK_LCP1	0x04	Last LCP CONFACK received from remote access client by NAS
	L2F_ACK_LCP2	0x05	Last LCP CONFACK sent by NAS to remote access client
	L2F_OPEN_TYPE	0x06	Type of authentication used
	L2F_OPEN_ID	0x07	ID associated with CHAP challenge
	L2F_REQ_LCP0	0x08	First LCP CONFREQ received from remote access client
L2F_CLOSE (0x03)	L2F_CLOSE_WHY	0x01	Reason code for close
	L2F_CLOSE_STR	0x02	ASCII string description of close reason
L2F_ECHO (0x04)	(no suboptions)		Keep alive
L2F_ECHO_RESP (0x05)	(no suboptions)		Response to L2F_ECHO

1.5. L2F Tunnel Establishment

Tunnel establishment begins with the reception of a PPP connection by the NAS. At this stage, the NAS goes through the Link Control Protocol (LCP) negotiation phase with the remote client, with options such as compression, callback, and authentication protocol being negotiated. As soon as the LCP negotiation phase has been completed, the NAS and the remote client move onto authentication. A Challenge Handshake Authentication Protocol (CHAP) (Leduc, n.d.) challenge is now sent by the NAS to the client. Note that although either CHAP or Password Authentication Protocol (PAP) could be used for authentication, this chapter assumes that CHAP is used. Upon receipt of the CHAP challenge, the remote client takes the random number in the challenge (call it Random3), the Challenge ID, and the CHAP password and calculates a Message Digest 5 (MD5) (Hossain, Islam, Das, & Nashiry, n.d.) hash value (call it Hash3). This hash value is transmitted back to the NAS via a CHAP response message.

At this point, the NAS performs a partial authentication on the CHAP response. The NAS does not examine the hash value contained within the CHAP response packet as it normally would but looks at the sender's name (which is also contained within the response). If this PPP connection is one that should be tunneled to a Home Gateway, the sender's name should be in the format username@domain_name. The domain name indicates to the NAS to which Home Gateway this PPP connection should be tunneled.

It is worth noting that this delimiter character (@) can be modified on the NAS using the command vpdn domain-delimiter.

This association of user to tunnel can also be based on the Dialed Number Information Service (DNIS) string. The DNIS (Dialed Number Identification Service, n.d.) is the dialed number, and it is present in ISDN Q.931 messages passed from the ISDN switch to the NAS during call setup. This means that, for example, if a remote access client dials the number 555-1234 to access the NAS, the NAS will use this number to associate the user to a L2F tunnel.

1.6. The Layer 2 Tunneling Protocol Version 2

Short for Layer 2 Tunneling Protocol, L2TP is a tunneling, Session Layer protocol, using the UDP port 1701 on a Virtual Private Network (VPN) (Berger, 2006). It does not include any encryption and relies on other methods to provide data security and privacy, such as IPsec.

L2TP can be used as a tunneling mechanism to resell ADSL connectivity, by cable providers to resell connectivity, and by companies providing a connection for their employees to their private network from outside the office.

Layer Two Tunneling Protocol (L2TP) version 2 is defined in RFC 2661 and combines the best features of Layer Two Forwarding (L2F) and Point-to-Point Tunneling Protocol (PPTP). L2TP, like L2F and PPTP, is designed to separate the functionality of the traditional Network Access Server (NAS). Calls from remote access clients are terminated at a local access concentrator known as the L2TP Access Concentrator (LAC), but PPP connections are terminated on a separate device called an L2TP Network Server (LNS). PPP connections are tunneled from the LAC to the LNS over an intervening network. This separation of traditional NAS functionality can potentially lead to cost savings because calls no longer need to be made directly to a distant NAS but, instead, can be made to a LAC at the local service provider Point-of-Presence (POP) (Doverspike, Ramakrishnan, & Chase, n.d.). It is worth noting that the LAC could, for example, be a traditional dial-in access server or could be a digital subscriber line access multiplexer (DSLAM). The functionality of L2TP can extended to allow separate links in a Multilink PPP group to be terminated on different NASs and then bundled together by tunneling them to one device using L2TP. On Cisco routers, Multichassis Multilink PPP (MMP) provides this functionality.

L2TP operates in two different modes, compulsory tunnel mode and voluntary tunnel mode. In compulsory tunnel mode, the LAC terminates calls from remote access clients locally and tunnels their PPP sessions across the intervening network to an LNS. This mode does not require the remote access clients to have any knowledge of L2TP. Remote access clients simply need to dial into the LAC using PPP (see Figure 8 and Figure 9).

Figure 8. L2TP compulsory tunnel mode

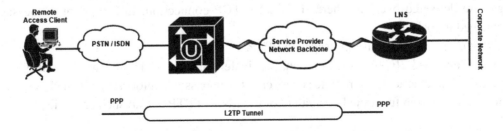

Figure 9. L2TP voluntary tunnel mode

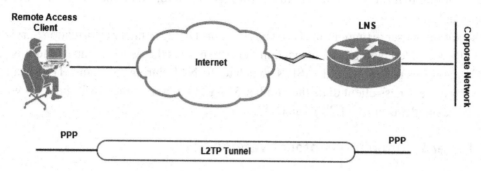

As previously mentioned, L2TPv2 is derived from L2F and PPTP. Some of the main similarities and differences between L2TPv2 and L2F/PPTP are as follows:

- L2F was developed by Cisco Systems, and PPTP (Microsoft Corporation, 2014) was developed by a consortium of vendors. L2TPv2 is an industry standard and was developed within the Internet Engineering Task Force (IETF).
- L2TP is more easily extensible than L2F and PPTP because L2TP control messages are made up of attribute-value-pairs (AVPs).
- L2TPv2 and PPTP are designed to tunnel PPP. L2F, on the other hand, can tunnel both PPP and SLIP. Note that L2TPv3 is designed to tunnel a wide variety of Layer 2 protocols.
- L2TPv2 is similar to L2F with regard to its control connection. In both L2TP and L2F, control messages are transmitted in-band (using the same transport mechanism as data messages, UDP in an IP network), whereas in PPTP, control messages are transmitted out-of-band over a separate TCP connection
- Both L2TPv2 and PPTP include the capability to make outgoing calls, whereas L2F does not.
- L2TPv2 and PPTP can operate in both compulsory and voluntary tunnel modes. L2F, on the other hand, can operate only in compulsory tunnel mode.
- Both L2TPv2 and L2F support authentication of tunnel endpoints (LAC/LNS and L2F NAS/ Home Gateway in L2TPv2 and L2F, respectively) during tunnel setup, whereas PPTP does not (it relies on authentication of PPP peers instead).
- L2TPv2 and L2F both transport data and control messages over UDP in an IP network (using UDP port 1701). The L2TPv2 and L2F headers are both derived from Generic Routing Encapsulation (GRE). PPTP data messages are transported over Enhanced GRE (SANS Institute, n.d.) (IP protocol 47), and PPTP control messages are transported over TCP (using port 1723).
- Reliable delivery of control messages is included in L2TPv2, PPTP, and L2F, but is implemented in different ways. L2TP uses both implicit or explicit acknowledgment, and PPTP control messages are delivered over an inherently reliable TCP connection. In L2F, control messages are exchanged in lock-step.
- L2TPv2 uses similar control messages to PPTP.
- The LAC and the L2F NAS (the functional equivalent of the LAC) both have the ability to negotiate LCP and authenticate the remote access client then pass this information to the LNS or the L2F Home Gateway (the functional equivalent of the LNS). PPTP has no such capability.

- L2TPv2 has the built-in capability to hide the content of control messages (AVP hiding), whereas L2F and PPTP do not.

1.7. Layer 2 Tunneling Protocol Version 3

It is an IETF standard related to L2TP that can be used as an alternative protocol to Multiprotocol Label Switching (MPLS) for encapsulation of multiprotocol Layer 2 communications traffic over IP networks. Like L2TP, L2TPv3 provides a 'pseudo-wire' service (Cisco, n.d.), but scaled to fit carrier requirements.

The Layer 2 Tunnel Protocol Version 3 feature expands on Cisco support of the Layer 2 Tunnel Protocol Version 3 (L2TPv3). L2TPv3 is an Internet Engineering Task Force (IETF) l2tpext working group draft that provides several enhancements to L2TP for the capability to tunnel any Layer 2 payload over L2TP. Specifically, L2TPv3 defines the L2TP protocol for tunneling Layer 2 payloads over an IP core network using Layer 2 virtual private networks (VPNs). Benefits of this feature include the following:

- L2TPv3 simplifies deployment of VPNs
- L2TPv3 does not require Multiprotocol Label Switching (MPLS)
- L2TPv3 supports Layer 2 tunneling over IP for any payload

How to Configure Layer 2 Tunnel Protocol Version 3

This section contains the required procedures:

- Configuring the L2TPv3 Pseudowire (required)
- Configuring the Xconnect Attachment Circuit (required)
- Manually Configuring L2TPv3 Session Parameters (required)

Configuring the L2TPv3 Pseudowire

The pseudowire class configuration procedure creates a configuration template for the pseudowire. You use this template, or class, to configure session-level parameters for L2TPv3 sessions that will be used to transport attachment circuit traffic over the pseudowire.

The pseudowire configuration specifies the characteristics of the L2TPv3 signaling mechanism, including the data encapsulation type, the control protocol, sequencing, fragmentation, payload-specific options, and IP properties. The setting that determines if signaling is used to set up the pseudowire is also included.

Summary Steps

1. enable
2. configure terminal
3. pseudowire-class [pw-class-name]
4. encapsulation l2tpv3

5.   protocol {l2tpv3 I none} [l2tp-class-name]
6.   ip local interface interface-name
7.   ip pmtu
8.   ip tos {value value I reflect}
9.   ip dfbit set
10.   ip ttl value
11.   ip protocol {l2tp I uti I protocol-number}
12.   sequencing {transmit I receive I both}

Configuring the Xconnect Attachment Circuit

This configuration procedure binds an Ethernet, 802.1q VLAN, or Frame Relay attachment circuit to an L2TPv3 pseudowire for Xconnect service. The virtual circuit identifier that you configure creates the binding between a pseudowire configured on a PE router and an attachment circuit in a CE device. The virtual circuit identifier configured on the PE router at one end of the L2TPv3 control channel must also be configured on the peer PE router at the other end.

Summary Steps

1.   enable
2.   configure terminal
3.   interface type slot/port
4.   xconnect peer-ip-address vcid pseudowire-parameters [sequencing {transmit I receive I both}]

Manually Configuring L2TPv3 Session Parameters

When you bind an attachment circuit to an L2TPv3 pseudowire for Xconnect service using the xconnect l2tpv3 manual command because you do not want signaling, you must then configure L2TP-specific parameters to complete the L2TPv3 control channel configuration.

Summary Steps

1.   enable
2.   configure terminal
3.   interface type slot/port
4.   xconnect peer-ip-address vc-id encapsulation l2tpv3 manual pw-class pw-class-name
5.   l2tp id local-session-id remote-session-id
6.   l2tp cookie local size low-value [high-value]
7.   l2tp cookie remote size low-value [high-value]
8.   l2tp hello l2tp-class-name

2. THE POINT-TO-POINT TUNNELING PROTOCOL (PPTP)

PPTP is a network protocol used in the implementation of Virtual Private Networks (VPN). RFC 2637 is the PPTP technical specification.

PPTP works on a client server model. PPTP (Schneier & Mudge, n.d.) clients are included by default in Microsoft Windows and also available for both Linux and Mac OS X. Newer VPN technologies like L2TP and IPsec may replace PPTP someday, but PPTP remains a popular network protocol especially on Windows computers.

PPTP technology extends the Point to Point Protocol (PPP) standard for traditional dial-up networking. PPTP operates at Layer 2 of the OSI model. As a network protocol, PPTP is best suited for the remote access applications of VPNs, but it also supports LAN internetworking.

PPTP-based Internet remote access VPNs are by far the most common form of PPTP VPN. In this environment, VPN tunnels are created via the following two-step process:

1.   The PPTP client connects to their ISP using PPP dial-up networking (traditional modem or ISDN).
2.   via the broker device (described earlier), PPTP creates a TCP control connection between the VPN client and VPN server to establish a tunnel. PPTP uses TCP port 1723 for these connections.

PPTP also supports VPN connectivity via a LAN. ISP connections are not required in this case, so tunnels can be created directly as in Step 2 above.

Table 4. PPTP control connection

No.	Name	Description
1	StartControlConnectionRequest	Initiates setup of the VPN session; can be sent by either client or server.
2	StartControlConnectionReply	Sent in reply to the start connection request (1); contains result code indicating success or failure of the setup operation, and also the protocol version number.
3	StopControlConnectionRequest	Request to close the control connection.
4	StopControlConnectionReply	Sent in reply to the stop connection request (3); contains result code indicating success or failure of the close operation.
5	EchoRequest	Sent periodically by either client or server to "ping" the connection (keep alive).
6	EchoReply	Sent in response to the echo request (5) to keep the connection active.
7	OutgoingCallRequest	Request to create a VPN tunnel sent by the client.
8	OutgoingCallReply	Response to the call request (7); contains a unique identifier for that tunnel.
9	IncomingCallRequest	Request from a VPN client to receive an incoming call from the server.
10	IncomingCallReply	Response to the incoming call request (9), indicating whether the incoming call should be answered.
11	IncomingCallConnected	Response to the incoming call reply (10); provides additional call parameters to the VPN server.
12	CallClearRequest	Request to disconnect either an incoming or outgoing call, sent from the server to a client.
13	CallDisconnectNotify	Response to the disconnect request (12); sent back to the server.
14	WANErrorNotify	Notification periodically sent to the server of CRC, framing, hardware and buffer overruns, timeout and byte alignment errors.
15	SetLinkInfo	Notification of changes in the underlying PPP options.

Once the VPN tunnel is established, PPTP supports two types of information flow (see Table 4):

- **Control** messages for managing and eventually tearing down the VPN connection. Control messages pass directly between VPN client and server.
- **Data** packets that pass through the tunnel, to or from the VPN client

Once the TCP connection is established in Step 2 above, PPTP utilizes a series of control messages to maintain VPN connections. These messages are listed below.

With control messages, PPTP utilizes a so-called magic cookie. The PPTP magic cookie is hardwired to the hexadecimal number 0x1A2B3C4D. The purpose of this cookie is to ensure the receiver interprets the incoming data on the correct byte boundaries.

2.2. PPTP Security

PPTP supports authentication, encryption, and packet filtering. PPTP authentication (Schneier & Mudge, n.d.) uses PPP-based protocols like EAP, CHAP, and PAP. PPTP supports packet filtering on VPN servers. Intermediate routers and other firewalls can also be configured to selectively filter PPTP traffic.

PPTP and PPP

In general, PPTP relies on the functionality of PPP for these aspects of virtual private networking.

- Authenticating users and maintaining the remote dial-up connection
- Encapsulating and encrypting IP, IPX, or NetBEUI packets

PPTP directly handles maintaining the VPN tunnel and transmitting data through the tunnel. PPTP also supports some additional security features for VPN data beyond what PPP provides.

2.3. PPTP Pros and Cons

PPTP remains a popular choice for VPNs thanks to Microsoft. PPTP clients are freely available in all popular versions of Microsoft Windows. Windows servers also can function as PPTP-based VPN servers.

One drawback of PPTP is its failure to choose a single standard for authentication and encryption. Two products that both fully comply with the PPTP specification may be totally incompatible with each other if they encrypt data differently, for example. Concerns also persist over the questionable level of security PPTP provides compared to alternatives.

3. IP SECURITY (IPsec)

Internet Protocol security (IPSec) (Shue, 2007) is a framework of open standards for helping to ensure private, secure communications over Internet Protocol (IP) networks through the use of cryptographic security services. IPSec supports network-level data integrity, data confidentiality, data origin authentication, and replay protection. Because IPSec is integrated at the Internet layer (layer 3), it provides security for almost all protocols in the TCP/IP suite, and because IPSec is applied transparently to applications, there is no need to configure separate security for each application that uses TCP/IP.

IPSec helps provide defense-in-depth against:

- Network-based attacks from untrusted computers, attacks that can result in the denial-of-service of applications, services, or the network
- Data corruption
- Data theft
- User-credential theft
- Administrative control of servers, other computers, and the network.

You can use IPSec to defend against network-based attacks through a combination of host-based IPSec packet filtering and the enforcement of trusted communications.

IPSec is integrated with the Windows Server 2003 operating system and it can use the Active Directory directory service as a trust model. You can use Group Policy to configure Active Directory domains, sites, and organizational units (OUs), and then assign IPSec policies as required to Group Policy objects (GPOs). In this way, IPSec policies can be implemented to meet the security requirements of many different types of organizations. This section describes the solution that IPSec is intended to provide by providing information about core IPSec scenarios, IPSec dependencies, and related technologies.

The Figure 10 shows an Active Directory-based IPSec policy being distributed to two IPSec peers and IPSec-protected communications being established between those two peers.

Figure 10. IPSec peers using active directory-based IPSec policy

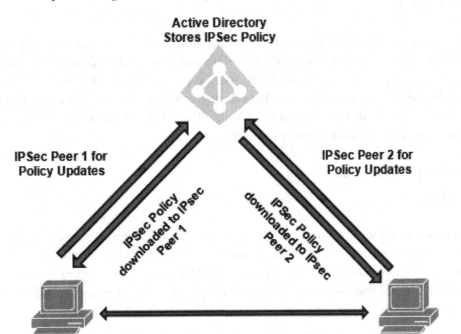

3.1. IPSec Scenarios

IPSec is a general-purpose security technology that can be used to help secure network traffic in many scenarios. However, you must balance the need for security with the complexity of configuring IPSec policies. Additionally, due to a lack of suitable standards, IPSec is not appropriate for some types of connectivity. This section describes IPSec scenarios (Treytl, 2010) that are recommended, IPSec scenarios that are not recommended, and IPSec scenarios that require special consideration.

RECOMMENDED SCENARIOS FOR IPSec

IPSec is recommended for the following scenarios:

Packet Filtering

- End-to-end security between specific hosts
- End-to-end traffic through a Microsoft Internet Security and Acceleration (ISA) Server-secured network
- address translator
- Secure server
- Layer Two Tunneling Protocol (L2TP) over IPSec (L2TP/IPSec) for remote access and site-to-site virtual private network (VPN) connections
- Site-to-site IPSec tunneling with non-Microsoft IPSec gateways

3.1.1. Packet Filtering

IPSec can perform host-based packet filtering to provide limited firewall capabilities for end systems. You can configure IPSec to permit or block specific types of unicast IP traffic based on source and destination address combinations and specific protocols and specific ports. For example, nearly all the systems illustrated in the Figure 11 can benefit from packet filtering to restrict communication to only specific addresses and ports. You can strengthen security by using IPSec packet filtering to control exactly the type of communication that is allowed between systems.

Filtering Packets by Using IPSec

As illustrated in Figure 11:

- The internal network domain administrator can assign an Active Directory-based IPSec policy (a collection of security settings that determines IPSec behavior) to block all traffic from the perimeter network (also known as a demilitarized zone [DMZ], demilitarized zone, or screened subnet).
- The perimeter network domain administrator can assign an Active Directory-based IPSec policy to block all traffic to the internal network.

Figure 11. Filtering packets by using IPSec

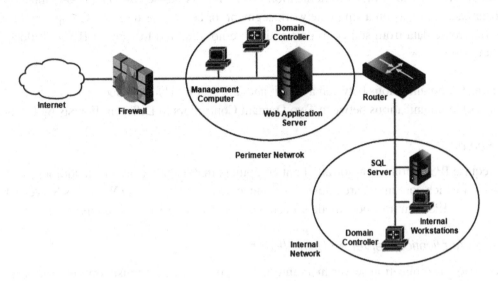

- The administrator of the computer running Microsoft SQL Server on the internal network can create an exception in the Active Directory-based IPSec policy to permit structured query language (SQL) protocol traffic to the Web application server on the perimeter network.
- The administrator of the Web application server on the perimeter network can create an exception in the Active Directory-based policy to permit SQL traffic to the computer running SQL Server on the internal network.
- The administrator of the Web application server on the perimeter network can also block all traffic from the Internet, except requests to TCP port 80 for the Hypertext Transfer Protocol (HTTP) and TCP port 443 for HTTPS (HTTP over Secure Sockets Layer/Transport Layer Protocol [SSL/TLS]), which are used by Web services. This provides additional security for traffic allowed from the Internet in case the firewall was misconfigured or compromised by an attacker.
- The domain administrator can block all traffic to the management computer, but allow traffic to the perimeter network.

You can also use IPSec with the IP packet-filtering capability or NAT/Basic Firewall component of the Routing and Remote Access service to permit or block inbound or outbound traffic, or you can use IPSec with the Internet Connection Firewall (ICF) (Cisco, 2013) component of Network Connections, which provides stateful packet filtering. However, to ensure proper Internet Key Exchange (IKE) management of IPSec security associations (SAs), you must configure ICF to permit UDP port 500 and port 4500 traffic needed for IKE messages.

End-to-End Security between Specific Hosts

IPSec establishes trust and security from a unicast source IP address to a unicast destination IP address (end-to-end). For example, IPSec can help secure traffic between Web servers and database servers or domain controllers in different sites. As shown in the following figure, only the sending and receiving computers need to be aware of IPSec. Each computer handles security at its respective end and assumes that the medium over which the communication takes place is not secure. The two computers can be located near each other, as on a single network segment, or across the Internet. Computers or network elements that route data from source to destination are not required to support IPSec. It does the following things too.

- Secures Communications between a Client and a Server by Using IPSec
- Secures Communications between Two Domain Controllers in Different Forests by Using IPSec

Secure Server

You can require IPSec protection for all client computers that access a server. In addition, you can set restrictions on which computers are allowed to connect to a server running Windows Server 2003. The Figure 13 shows IPSec in transport mode securing a line of business (LOB) application server.

Securing an Application Server by Using IPSec

In this scenario, an application server in an internal corporate network must communicate with clients running Windows 2000 or Windows XP Professional; a Windows Internet Name Service (WINS) server, Domain Name System (DNS) server, and Dynamic Host Configuration Protocol (DHCP) server; Active Directory domain controllers; and a non-Microsoft data backup server. The users on the client computers are company employees who access the application server to view their personal payroll information and performance review scores. Because the traffic between the clients and the application server involves highly sensitive data, and because the server should only communicate with other domain members, the network administrator uses an IPSec policy that requires ESP encryption and communication only with trusted computers in the Active Directory domain.

Other traffic is permitted as follows:

- Traffic between the WINS server, DNS server, DHCP server, and the application server is permitted because WINS servers, DNS servers, and DHCP servers must typically communicate with computers that run on a wide range of operating systems, some of which might not support IPSec. Traffic between Active Directory domain controllers and the application server is permitted, because using IPSec to secure communication between domain members and their domain controllers is not a recommended usage.
- Traffic between the non-Microsoft data backup server and the application server is permitted because the non-Microsoft backup server does not support IPSec.

Figure 13. SSL signs in an IE11 browser

L2TP/IPSec for Remote Access and Site-to-Site VPN Connections

You can use L2TP/IPSec for all VPN scenarios. This does not require the configuration and deployment of IPSec policies. Two common scenarios for L2TP/IPSec are securing communications between remote access clients and the corporate network across the Internet and securing communications between branch offices. Windows IPSec supports both IPSec transport mode and tunnel mode. Although VPN connections are commonly referred to as "tunnels," IPSec transport mode is used for L2TP/IPSec VPN connections. IPSec tunnel mode is most commonly used to help protect site-to-site traffic between networks, such as site-to-site networking through the Internet.

L2TP/IPSec for Remote Access Connections

A common requirement for organizations is to secure communications between remote access clients and the corporate network across the Internet. Such a client might be a sales consultant who spends most of the time traveling, or an employee working from a home office. In the Figure 12, the remote gateway is a server that provides edge security for the corporate intranet. The remote client represents a roaming user who requires regular access to network resources and information. An ISP is used as an example to demonstrate the path of communication when the client uses an ISP to access the Internet. L2TP/IPSec provides a simple, efficient way to build a VPN tunnel and help protect the data across the Internet.

L2TP/IPSec for Site-to-Site VPN Connections

A large corporation often has multiple sites that require communication — for example, a corporate office in New York and a sales office in Washington. In this case, L2TP/IPSec provides the VPN connection and helps protect the data between the sites. In the Figure 12, the router running Windows Server 2003 provides edge security. The routers might have a leased line, dial-up, or other type of Internet connection. The L2TP/IPSec VPN tunnel runs between the routers only and provides protected communication across the Internet.

Figure 12. Establishing an IPSec gateway-to-gateway tunnel between sites

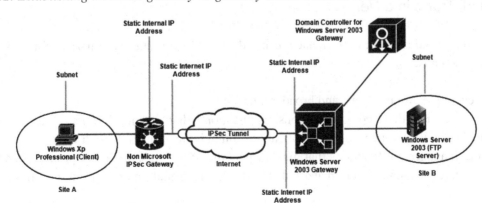

Site-to-Site IPSec Tunneling with Non-Microsoft Gateways

For interoperability with gateways or end systems that do not support L2TP/IPSec or Point-to-Point Tunneling Protocol (PPTP) VPN site-to-site connections, you can use IPSec in tunnel mode. When IPSec tunnel mode is used, the sending gateway encapsulates the entire IP datagram by creating a new IP packet that is then protected by one of the IPSec protocols. Figure 12 illustrates site-to-site IPSec tunneling.

In the Figure 12, traffic is being sent between a client computer in a vendor site (Site A) and a File Transfer Protocol (FTP) server at the corporate headquarters site (Site B). Although an FTP server is used for this scenario, the traffic can be any unicast IP traffic. The vendor uses a non-Microsoft IPSec-enabled gateway, while corporate headquarters uses a gateway running Windows Server 2003. An IPSec tunnel is used to secure traffic between the non-Microsoft gateway and the gateway running Windows Server 2003.

Scenarios for Which IPSec Is Not Recommended

- Securing communication between domain members and their domain controllers
- Securing all traffic in a network
- Securing traffic for remote access VPN connections using IPSec tunnel mode

Securing Communication between Domain Members and their Domain Controllers

Using IPSec to help secure traffic between domain members (either clients or servers) and their domain controllers is not recommended because:

- If domain members were to use IPSec-secured communication with domain controllers, increased latency might occur, causing authentication and the process of locating a domain controller to fail.
- Complex IPSec policy configuration and management is required.
- Increased load is placed on the domain controller CPU to maintain SAs with all domain members. Depending on the number of domain members in the domain controller's domain, such a load might overburden the domain controller.

Securing All Traffic in a Network

In addition to reduced network performance, using IPSec to help secure all traffic in a network is not recommended because:

- IPSec cannot secure multicast and broadcast traffic.
- Traffic from real-time communications, applications that require Internet Control Message Protocol (ICMP), and peer-to-peer applications might be incompatible with IPSec.
- Network management functions that must inspect the TCP, UDP, and other protocol headers are less effective, or cannot function at all, due to IPSec encapsulation or encryption of IP payloads.

Securing Traffic for Remote Access VPN Connections by Using IPSec Tunnel Mode

IPSec tunnel mode is not a recommended technology for remote access VPN connections, because there are no standard methods for user authentication, IP address assignment, and name server address assignment. Using IPSec tunnel mode for gateway-to-gateway VPN connections is possible using computers running Windows Server 2003. But because the IPSec tunnel is not represented as a logical interface over which packets can be forwarded and received, routes cannot be assigned to use the IPSec tunnel and routing protocols do not operate over IPSec tunnels. Therefore, the use of IPSec tunnel mode is only recommended as a VPN solution for site-to-site VPN connections in which one end of the tunnel is a non-Microsoft VPN server or security gateway that does not support L2TP/IPSec. Instead, use L2TP/IPSec or PPTP for remote access VPN connections.

Points to Remember

- In some cases, non-Microsoft VPN or firewall clients might disable the IPSec service, which is required for IPSec to function. If you encounter this problem, it is recommended that you contact the VPN or firewall vendor. IPSec is not recommended for end users in general home networking scenarios for the following reasons:
- The IPSec policy configuration user interface (IP Security Policy Management) is intended for professional network security administrators, rather than for end users. Improper policy configuration can result in blocked communications, and if problems occur, built-in support tools are not yet available to aid end users in troubleshooting.
- Some home networking applications use broadcast and multicast traffic, for which IPSec cannot negotiate security.
- Many home networking scenarios use a wide range of dynamic IP addresses.
- Many home networking scenarios involve the use of a network address translator. To use IPSec across a NAT, both IPSec peers must support IPSec NAT-T.

4. SECURE SOCKETS LAYER (SSL) AND TRANSPORT LAYER SECURITY (TLS)

The Secure Socket Layer (SSL) and Transport Layer Security (TLS) (Jain, n.d.) is the most widely deployed security protocol used today. It is essentially a protocol that provides a secure channel between two machines operating over the Internet or an internal network. In today's Internet focused world, the SSL protocol is typically used when a web browser needs to securely connect to a web server over the inherently insecure Internet.

Technically, SSL (Jain, n.d.) is a transparent protocol which requires little interaction from the end user when establishing a secure session. In the case of a browser for instance, users are alerted to the presence of SSL when the browser displays a padlock, or, in the case of Extended Validation SSL, when the address bar displays both a padlock and a green bar. This is the key to the success of SSL – it is an incredibly simple experience for end users (see Figure 13).

As opposed to unsecured HTTP URLs which begin with "http://" and use port 80 by default, secure HTTPS URLs begin with "https://" and use port 443 by default.

HTTP is insecure and is subject to eavesdropping attacks which, if critical information like credit card details and account logins is transmitted and picked up, can let attackers gain access to online accounts and sensitive information. Ensuring data is either sent or posted through the browser using HTTPS is ensuring that such information is encrypted and secure.

In practice, how is SSL used in today's modern e-commerce enabled / online workflow and service society?

- To secure online credit card transactions.
- To secure system logins and any sensitive information exchanged online.
- To secure webmail and applications like Outlook Web Access, Exchange and Office Communications Server.
- To secure workflow and virtualization applications like Citrix Delivery Platforms or cloud-based computing platforms.
- To secure the connection between an email client such as Microsoft Outlook and an email server such as Microsoft Exchange.
- To secure the transfer of files over https and FTP(s) services such as website owners updating new pages to their websites or transferring large files.
- To secure hosting control panel logins and activity like Parallels, cPanel, and others.
- To secure intranet based traffic such as internal networks, file sharing, extranets, and database connections.
- To secure network logins and other network traffic with SSL VPNs such as VPN Access Servers or applications like the Citrix Access Gateway.

SSL VPN

SSL VPN (Secure Sockets Layer Virtual Private Network) allows users to remotely access restricted network resources via a secure and authenticated pathway by encrypting all network traffic and giving the appearance that the user is on the local network, regardless of geographic location. This protocol achieves a higher level of compatibility with client platforms and configurations for remote networks and firewalls, providing a more reliable connection.

There are two major types of SSL VPNs:

SSL Portal VPN

This type of SSL VPN allows for a single SSL connection to a Web site so the end user can securely access multiple network services. The site is called a portal because it is one door (a single page) that leads to many other resources. The remote user accesses the SSL VPN gateway using any modern Web browser, identifies himself or herself to the gateway using an authentication method supported by the gateway and is then presented with a Web page that acts as the portal to the other services.

SSL Tunnel VPN

This type of SSL VPN allows a Web browser to securely access multiple network services, including applications and protocols that are not Web-based, through a tunnel that is running under SSL. SSL

Figure 14. SoftLayer SSL VPN portal login screen

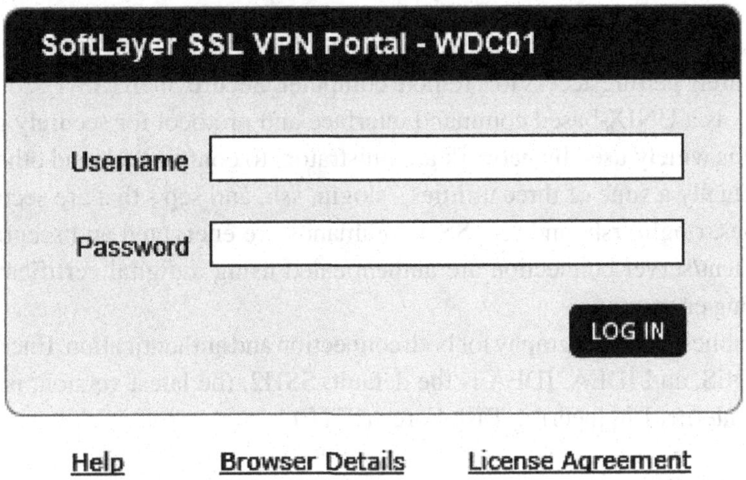

tunnel VPNs require that the Web browser be able to handle active content, which allows them to provide functionality that is not accessible to SSL portal VPNs. Examples of active content include Java, JavaScript, Active X, or Flash applications or plug-ins.

For Example: Softlayer

SoftLayer gives you the highest performing cloud infrastructure available. One platform that takes data centers around the world that are full of the widest range of cloud computing options, and then integrates and automates everything (see Figure 14).

It provides the secure hosted cloud environment for managing the hosted web applications and services. It's easy to manage and maintain in case of any issue which may be caused accidently.

SSL vs. TLS: What is the Difference?

TLS (Transport Layer Security) and SSL (Secure Sockets Layer) are protocols that provide data encryption and authentication between applications and servers in scenarios where that data is being sent across an insecure network, such as checking your email. The terms SSL and TLS are often used interchangeably or in conjunction with each other (TLS/SSL), but one is in fact the predecessor of the other — SSL 3.0 served as the basis for TLS 1.0 which, as a result, is sometimes referred to as SSL 3.1.

SSL means a "by port" connection to a port that expects to the session to start with security negotiation

TLS means a "by protocol" connection where the program will connect "insecurely" first and use special commands to enable encryption Use of either could result in a connection encrypted with either SSL or TLS of any version based on what is installed on the sever and what is supported by your program. Both methods of connection result in equally secure communications.

5. SECURE SHELL (SSH)

Secure Shell (SSH), sometimes known as Secure Socket Shell, is a UNIX-based command interface and protocol for securely getting access to a remote computer. Secure Shell (SSH), sometimes known as Secure Socket Shell, is a UNIX-based command interface and protocol for securely getting access to a remote computer. It is widely used by network administrators to control Web and other kinds of servers remotely. SSH is actually a suite of three utilities - slogin, ssh, and scp - that are secure versions of the earlier UNIX utilities, rlogin, rsh, and rcp. SSH commands are encrypted and secure in several ways. Both ends of the client/server connection are authenticated using a digital certificate, and passwords are protected by being encrypted.

SSH uses RSA public key cryptography for both connection and authentication. Encryption algorithms include Blowfish, DES, and IDEA. IDEA is the default. SSH2, the latest version, is a proposed set of standards from the Internet Engineering Task Force (IETF).

Common SSH Use Cases

There are three common use cases for SSH:

- **Interactive use**. SSH is used by system administrators for manually managing and configuring UNIX and Linux computers, networking equipment, and various other types of hosts remotely. SSH is also used for running applications remotely (particularly text-based legacy applications).
- **File transfers.** SSH is used as the foundation of the Secure Copy (scp) and Secure File Transfer Protocol (SFTP) protocols. These protocols are used to transfer files between hosts while leveraging the security capabilities built into SSH.
- **Point-to-point tunneling.** SSH can be used to implement a virtual private network (VPN) tunnel to protect data transmitted between two hosts. One or both of these hosts may be acting as a gateway for other hosts behind it.

Vulnerable SSH Implementation

An SSH server or client implementation could have vulnerabilities that allow it to be exploited in order to gain unauthorized access to communications or systems. These vulnerabilities could be any of the following types:

- Software flaws in the SSH implementation (i.e., coding errors)
- Configuration weaknesses (for example, allowing the use of weak encryption algorithms)
- Protocol weaknesses (for example, supporting the use of SSH version 1)

OpenSSH

OpenSSH is a FREE version of the SSH connectivity tools that technical users of the Internet rely on. Users of telnet, rlogin, and ftp may not realize that their password is transmitted across the Internet unencrypted, but it is. OpenSSH encrypts all traffic (including passwords) to effectively eliminate eavesdropping, connection hijacking, and other attacks. Additionally, OpenSSH provides secure tunneling capabilities and several authentication methods, and supports all SSH protocol versions.

The OpenSSH suite replaces rlogin and telnet with the ssh program, rcp with scp, and ftp with sftp. Also included is sshd (the server side of the package), and the other utilities like ssh-add, ssh-agent, ssh-keysign, ssh-keyscan, ssh-keygen and sftp-server.

How an SSH Tunnel Works?

SSH, which stands for "secure shell," isn't designed solely for forwarding network traffic. Generally, SSH is used to securely acquire and use a remote terminal session – but SSH has other uses. SSH also uses strong encryption, and you can set your SSH client to act as a SOCKS proxy. Once you have, you can configure applications on your computer – such as your web browser – to use the SOCKS proxy. The traffic enters the SOCKS proxy running on your local system and the SSH client forwards it through the SSH connection – this is known as SSH tunneling. This works similarly to browsing the web over a VPN – from the web server's perspective, your traffic appears to be coming from the SSH server. The traffic between your computer and the SSH server is encrypted, so you can browse over an encrypted connection as you could with a VPN (see Figure 15).

However, an SSH tunnel doesn't offer all the benefits of a VPN. Unlike with a VPN, you must configure each application to use the SSH tunnel's proxy. With a VPN, you're assured that all traffic will be sent through the VPN – but you don't have this assurance with an SSH tunnel. With a VPN, your operating system will behave as though you're on the remote network – which means connecting to Windows networked file shares would be easy. It's considerably more difficult with an SSH tunnel (see Figure 16).

Which Is More Secure?

If you're worried about which is more secure for business use, the answer is clearly a VPN — you can force all network traffic on the system through it. However, if you just want an encrypted connection to browse the web with from public Wi-Fi networks in coffee shops and airports, a VPN and SSH server both have strong encryption that will serve you well.

There are other considerations, too. Novice users can easily connect to a VPN, but setting up a VPN server is a more complex process. SSH tunnels are more daunting to novice users, but setting up an SSH server is simpler – in fact, many people will already have an SSH server that they access remotely. If you already have access to an SSH server, it's much easier to use it as an SSH tunnel than it is to set up a VPN server. For this reason, SSH tunnels have been dubbed a "poor man's VPN."

Businesses looking for more robust networking will want to invest in a VPN. On the other hand, if you're a geek with access to an SSH server, an SSH tunnel is an easy way to encrypt and tunnel network traffic – and the encryption is just as good as a VPN's encryption.

SOLUTIONS AND RECOMMENDATIONS

Tips to secure client VPNs:

1.   Secure remote wireless networks.

Figure 15. SSH tunneling

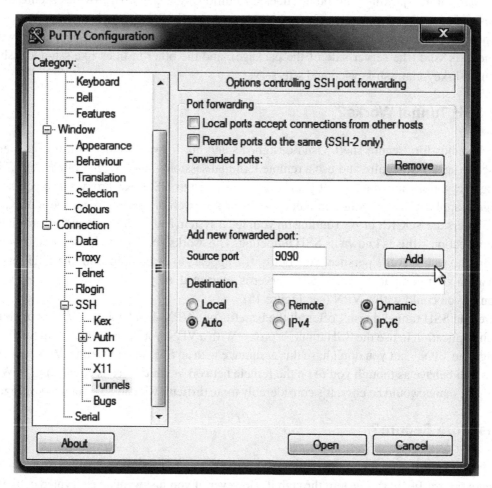

2. Use the strongest possible authentication method for VPN access.
3. Enable e-mail access without requiring VPN access.
4. Use the strongest possible encryption method for VPN access.
5. Provide strong antivirus, antispam and personal firewall protection to your remote users, and require that they use it.
6. Limit VPN access to those with a valid business reason, and only when necessary.
7. Provide access to selected files through intranets or extranets rather than VPNs.
8. Forbid the use of other VPNs and remote-control software while connected to your VPN.
9. Implement and enforce a strong password policy.
10. Quarantine users from the time to they connect to the VPN until their computer has been verified as safe.

VPN Security: Firewalls

Configuring VPN connections to pass through firewalls, proxy servers, and routers continues to bring many network administrators to their knees in exasperation and submission to the gods of the network

Figure 16. SSH tunneling configuration settings

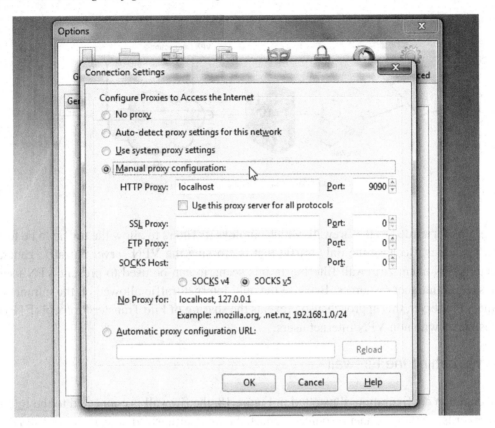

cloud. Thus, we are going to review how to configure VPN servers to make connections in concert with your stoic network defenders.

VPN Server Geography

One of the first decisions a network engineer has to make when configuring a VPN server is where to place it in relation to the network's firewall. As Figure A shows, there are essentially three options for placing a VPN server.

There are two approaches to using a firewall with a VPN server:

- The VPN server is attached to the Internet and the firewall is between the VPN server and the intranet.
- The firewall is attached to the Internet and the VPN server is between the firewall and the intranet.

VPN Server in Front of the Firewall

With the VPN server in front of the firewall attached to the Internet, as shown in Figure 17, you need to add packet filters to the Internet interface that only allow VPN traffic to and from the IP address of the VPN server's interface on the Internet. For inbound traffic, when the tunneled data is decrypted by the

Figure 17. VPN in front of the Firewall

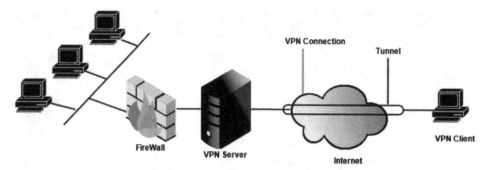

VPN server it is forwarded to the firewall, which employs its filters to allow the traffic to be forwarded to intranet resources. Because the only traffic that is crossing the VPN server is traffic generated by authenticated VPN clients, firewall filtering in this scenario can be used to prevent VPN users from accessing specific intranet resources. Because the only Internet traffic allowed on the intranet must go through the VPN server, this approach also prevents the sharing of File Transfer Protocol (FTP) or Web intranet resources with non-VPN Internet users.

VPN Server behind the Firewall

In a more common configuration, illustrated in Figure 18, the firewall is connected to the Internet and the VPN server is another intranet resource connected to a demilitarized zone (DMZ). The DMZ is an IP network segment that typically contains resources available to Internet users such as Web servers and FTP servers. The VPN server has an interface on the DMZ and an interface on the intranet.

In this approach, the firewall must be configured with input and output filters on its Internet interface to allow the passing of tunnel maintenance traffic and tunneled data to the VPN server. Additional filters can allow the passing of traffic to Web servers, FTP servers, and other types of servers on the DMZ.

Figure 18. VPN server behind the Firewall on the internet

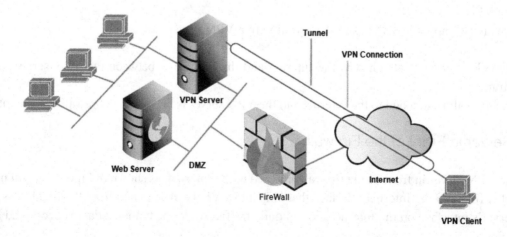

Because the firewall does not have the encryption keys for each VPN connection, it can only filter on the plaintext headers of the tunneled data, meaning that all tunneled data passes through the firewall. However, this is not a security concern because the VPN connection requires an authentication process that prevents unauthorized access beyond the VPN server.

VPN Security: Encryption

Data Encryption between VPN Server and Client

You must use data encryption to provide data confidentiality for the data that is sent between the VPN client and the VPN server across a shared or public network, where there is always a risk of unauthorized interception. You can configure the VPN server to force encrypted communications. Users who connect to that server must encrypt their data or a connection is not allowed. For VPN connections, the Windows Server 2003 family uses Microsoft Point-to-Point Encryption (MPPE) with the Point-to-Point Tunneling Protocol (PPTP) and Internet Protocol security (IPSec) encryption with the Layer Two Tunneling Protocol (L2TP).

Because data encryption is performed between the VPN client and VPN server, data encryption is not necessary on the communication link between a dial-up client and its Internet service provider (ISP). For example, a mobile user uses a dial-up connection to dial in to a local ISP. Once the Internet connection is made, the user creates a VPN connection with the corporate VPN server. If the VPN connection is encrypted, encryption is not needed on the dial-up connection between the user and the ISP.

Points to Remember

- Data encryption for Point-to-Point Protocol (PPP) or PPTP connections is available only if you use MS-CHAP, MS-CHAP v2, or EAP-TLS as the user-level authentication method. Data encryption for L2TP connections relies on IPSec computer-level authentication, which does not require any specific user-level authentication method.
- VPN data encryption does not provide end-to-end data encryption. End-to-end encryption is data encryption between the client application and the server hosting the resource or service that is accessed by the client application. To get end-to-end data encryption, you can use IPSec to create a secure connection after the VPN connection is made.

OpenVPN has many options when it comes to encryption. Our users are able to choose what level of encryption they want on their VPN sessions. Some of them as below mentioned.

Presets

- **Default Recommended Protection:** AES-128 / SHA1 / RSA-2048
- **All Speed No Safety:** None / None / ECC-256k1
- **Maximum Protection:** AES-256 / SHA256 / RSA-4096
- **Risky Business:** AES-128 / None / RSA-2048

Data Encryption

This is the symmetric cipher algorithm with which all of your data is encrypted and decrypted. The symmetric cipher is used with an ephemeral secret key shared between you and the server. This secret key is exchanged with the Handshake Encryption.

- **AES-128:** Advanced Encryption Standard (128bit) in CBC mode. For most people this is the fastest encryption mode.
- **AES-256:** Advanced Encryption Standard (256bit) in CBC mode.
- **Blowfish:** Blowfish (128bit) in CBC mode.
- **None:** No encryption. None of your data will be encrypted. Your login details will be encrypted. Your IP will still be hidden. This may be a viable option if you want the best performance possible while only hiding your IP address. This would be similar to a SOCKS proxy but with the benefit of not leaking your username and password.

Data Authentication

This is the message authentication algorithm with which all of your data is authenticated. This is only used to protect you from active attacks. If you are not worried about active attackers you can turn off Data Authentication.

- **SHA1:** HMAC using Secure Hash Algorithm (160bit). This is the fastest authentication mode.
- **SHA256:** HMAC using Secure Hash Algorithm (256bit)
- **None:** No authentication. None of your encrypted data will be authenticated. An active attacker could potentially modify or decrypt your data. This would not give any opportunities to a passive attacker.

Handshake Encryption

This is the encryption used to establish a secure connection and verify you are really talking to a Private Internet Access VPN server and not being tricked into connecting to an attacker's server. We use TLS v1.2 to establish this connection. All our certificates use SHA512 for signing.

- **RSA-2048:** 2048bit Ephemeral Diffie-Helman (DH) key exchange and 2048bit RSA certificate for verification that the key exchange really happened with a Private Internet Access server.
- **RSA-3072:** Like above but 3072bit for both key exchange and certificate.
- **RSA-4096:** Like above but 4096bit for both key exchange and certificate.
- **[!] ECC-256k1:** Ephemeral Elliptic Curve DH key exchange and an ECDSA certificate for verification that the key exchange really happened with a Private Internet Access server. Curve secp256k1 (256bit) is used for both. This is the same curve that Bitcoin uses to sign its transactions.
- **[!] ECC-256r1:** Like above but using curve prime256v1 (256bit, also known as secp256r1) is used for both key exchange and certificate.
- **[!] ECC-521:** Like above but using curve secp521r1 (521bit) is used for both key exchange and certificate.

AAA Servers

AAA stands for Authentication, Authorization and Accounting. An AAA server (Cisco Security, n.d.) checks the following information when a session is requested; who is sending the request, what they are authorized to do and what they are actually doing. Mobile VPN's are integral to certain fields. For example, they allow for public safety and emergency services to access resources on their home network from anywhere; if a police officer needs to access a criminal database during a traffic stop, he can do so as he is connected to the database through a VPN. While certain sectors have been using mobile VPN services for quite some time, they are currently gaining popularity in more fields.

Authentication

Authentication controls access by requiring valid user credentials, which are usually a username and password. You can configure the ASA to authenticate the following items:

All administrative connections to the ASA, including the following sessions:

- Telnet
- SSH
- Serial console
- ASDM using HTTPS
- VPN management access
- The enable command
- Network access
- VPN access

Authorization

Authorization controls access per user after users are authenticated. You can configure the ASA to authorize the following items:

- Management commands
- Network access
- VPN access

Authorization controls the services and commands that are available to each authenticated user. If you did not enable authorization, authentication alone would provide the same access to services for all authenticated users.

If you need the control that authorization provides, you can configure a broad authentication rule, and then have a detailed authorization configuration. For example, you can authenticate inside users who try to access any server on the outside network and then limit the outside servers that a particular user can access using authorization. The ASA caches the first 16 authorization requests per user, so if the user accesses the same services during the current authentication session, the ASA does not resend the request to the authorization server.

Accounting

Accounting tracks traffic that passes through the ASA, enabling you to have a record of user activity. If you enable authentication for that traffic, you can account for traffic per user. If you do not authenticate the traffic, you can account for traffic per IP address. Accounting information includes session start and stop times, username, the number of bytes that pass through the ASA for the session, the service used, and the duration of each session.

Configuring AAA Server Groups

If you want to use an external AAA server for authentication, authorization, or accounting, you must first create at least one AAA server group per AAA protocol and add one or more servers to each group. You identify AAA server groups by name. Each server group is specific to one type of server: Kerberos, LDAP, NT, RADIUS, SDI, or TACACS+.

Guidelines

You can have up to 100 server groups in single mode or 4 server groups per context in multiple mode.

Each group can have up to 16 servers in single mode or 4 servers in multiple mode. When a user logs in, the servers are accessed one at a time, starting with the first server you specify in the configuration, until a server responds. If all servers in the group are unavailable, the ASA tries the local database if you configured it as a fallback method (management authentication and authorization only). If you do not have a fallback method, the ASA continues to try the AAA servers.

Figure 19. AAA servers and VPN in EB automation process

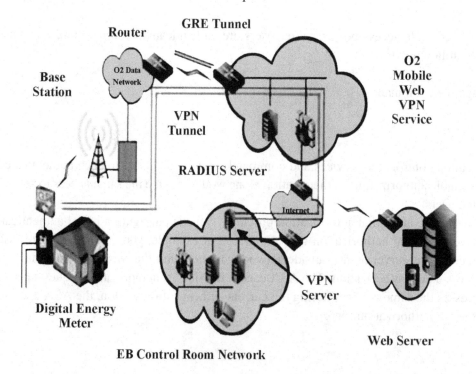

FUTURE RESEARCH DIRECTIONS

VPN contains several challenges since its more over to deal with providing the secure access to an Organizations resource. The Resources which are highly confidential. Due to the flexibility and ease of access it's getting more popular in IT Industry. Firewalls and AAA Servers are conventional options for the security but we can design new Encryption Algorithms and Techniques which will enhance the security features in future. ECC Crypto-Stegano Scheme (Narayanan & Vishwakarma, 2011) is one of the new way of Encryption used before sending the data over the network via VPN which has been published in *International Journal of Computer Applications*. Figure 19 shows the overall Functional Network diagram which uses AAA server and VPN for secure data access and data collection from remote sites.

There are many other possible research area which includes new method of Authentication and Authorization, Data Encryption and Network Protocols which can help in improving the VPN Security. Different Security Attacks can be taken into account while designing a new security protocols or authentication mechanism including DDoS over the entire system.

REFERENCES

Berger, T. (2006). Analysis of current VPN technologies. In *Proceedings of the First IEEE International Conference on Availability, Reliability and Security*. IEEE. doi:10.1109/ARES.2006.30

Cisco. (2013, August). *Firewall and IPS, Technology Design Guide*. Cisco Networks Inc.

Cisco. (n.d.). Understanding Pseudowire. In *Cisco MWR 2941 Mobile Wireless Edge Router Software Configuration Guide, Release 15.0(1) MR*. Author.

Cisco Security. (n.d.). Configuring AAA Servers and the Local Database. In *Cisco Security Appliance Command Line Configuration Guide*. Author.

Dialed Number Identification Service (DNIS). (n.d.). *Patton Tech Notes*.

Doverspike, R. D., Ramakrishnan, K. K., & Chase, C. (n.d.). *Structural Overview of ISP Networks*. AT&T Labs Research.

Government of the Hong Kong Special Administrative Region. (2008, February). *VPN Security*. Author.

Hätönen, S., & Nyrhine, A., et al.. (n.d.). An Experimental Study of Home Gateway Characteristics. *University of Helsinki*.

Hossain, M. A., Islam, M. K., Das, S. K., & Nashiry, M. A. (n.d.). *Cryptanalyzing of Message Digest Algorithms MD4 AND MD5*. Department of Computer Science & Engineering, *Jessore Science & Technology University*.

IMEX. (n.d.). *SAS, NAS, SAN Past, Present and Future*. IMEX Research White Paper.

Jain, R. (n.d.). Secure Socket Layer (SSL) Secure Socket Layer (SSL) and Transport Layer and Transport Layer Security (TLS) Security (TLS). *Washington University*.

Leduc, G. (n.d.). *Verification of two versions of the Challenge Handshake Authentication Protocol (CHAP)*. Research Unit in Networking (RUN), *Université de Liège*.

Microsoft Corporation. (2014). *Point-to-Point Tunneling Protocol (PPTP) Profile*. Microsoft Corporation.

Miltchev, S., Ioannidis, S., & Keromytis, A. D. (n.d.). *A Study of the Relative Costs of Network Security Protocols*. University of Pennsylvania.

Narayanan, A. E., & Vishwakarma, A. K. (2011). Cloud Automation: New Era of Electricity Bill Automation using GPRS and Web Interface. *International Journal of Computers and Applications*, 11.

SANS Institute. (n.d.). *Global Information Assurance Certification Paper*. White Paper. SANS Institute.

Schneier, B., & Mudge. (n.d.). Cryptanalysis of Microsoft's Point-to-Point Tunneling Protocol (PPTP). *Counterpane Systems*.

Seada, K., & Helmy, A. (n.d.). Geographic Services for Wireless Networks. Electrical Engineering Department, *University of Southern California*.

Shue, C. A. (2007). *IPSec: Performance Analysis and Enhancements*. IEEE.

Treytl, A. (2010). *Securing IEEE 1588 by IPsec tunnels - An analysis*. IEEE. doi:10.1109/ISPCS.2010.5609765

Valencia, A., Littlewood, M., & Kolar, T. (1998, May). *Cisco Layer Two Forwarding (Protocol) "L2F"*. Cisco Systems.

Vanguard Managed Solutions. (n.d.). *Vanguard Applications Ware Basic Protocols, Serial Line IP*. Author.

Web ProForum Tutorials. (n.d.). *Intelligent Network*. Paper presented at the International Engineering Consortium.

Chapter 4
Classification of Network Attacks and Countermeasures of Different Attacks

C. V. Anchugam
Government Arts College (Autonomous), India

K. Thangadurai
Government Arts College (Autonomous), India

ABSTRACT

Network security has become more important and the growing rate of network attacks together with hacker, cracker, and criminal enterprises are increasing, that impact to the availability, confidentiality, and integrity of vital information data. In order to understand and defend against network attacks, it is necessary to understand the kind of attack. This chapter focuses on the provisioning of a method for the analysis and categorization of both computer and network attacks, thus providing assistance in combating new attacks, improving computer and network security as well as providing consistency in language when describing attacks. Attacks are thus attempts by unauthorized individuals to access or modify information, to deceive the system so that an unauthorized individual can take over an authorized session, or to disrupt service to authorized users. During this chapter we tend to area unit providing the elucidation against black hole attack that relies on fuzzy rule in case study section.

INTRODUCTION

In today's information age, information sharing and transfer has increased exponentially. The information should be vulnerable and guarded to unauthorized access and interception. With the event of network techniques the problem of network security becomes a lot of and a lot of necessary throughout storage and transmission of information. With the rapid development of computer network and information technology, the Internet has been suffering from a variety of security attacks over the past few years. Fast Internet growth and increase in number of users make network security essential in recent decades.

DOI: 10.4018/978-1-4666-8761-5.ch004

Network security has become more important to personal computer users, organizations, and also the military., security became a significant concern and also the history of security permits a higher understanding of the emergence of security technology. The growing rate of network attacks together with hacker, cracker, and criminal enterprises are increasing, that impact to the availability, confidentiality, and integrity of vital information data. Attacks over the years have become both progressively numerous and sophisticated, and the defender cannot understand. In order to understand and defend against network attacks, it is necessary to understand the kind of attack.

Taxonomy of network attacks is designed to be useful to information bodies such as CERTs (Computer Emergency Response Teams) who have to handle and categorize an ever increasing number of attacks on a day to day. Information bodies could use the taxonomy to communicate more effectively because the taxonomy would supply a common classification scheme.

BASIC SECURITY CONCEPTS

It seems that every other day there is a story in the newspapers about a computer network being compromised by hackers. In fact, not too long ago the United States Department of Defense (DoD) was the victim of a successful hacker raid; hackers were able to penetrate DoD computers during a two-week period before they were detected. Fortunately, the computers contained only non-classified personnel and payroll information, so national security was not threatened. More recently, Yahoo, Amazon.com, eBay, and some other popular World Wide Web (WWW) sites were targets of what appears to have been a coordinated "denial-of-service" attack. During a three- or four-day period, the sites were overwhelmed with massive bombardments of false traffic from multiple sites. As a result, the sites were shut down for hours at a time. These attacks illustrate how pervasive the threat from outside hackers has become.

At the same time, every organization that uses computers faces the threat of hacking from individuals within the organization. Employees or former employees with malicious intent or who want to obtain information such as employee salaries or view other employee's files are also a threat to an organization's computers and networks. Computerworld recently ran a story about a programmer employee of a company who allegedly launched a denial-of-service attack against his own company, a provider of on-line stock trading services. Apparently, this programmer was in negotiations with the company for more compensation.

He became frustrated with the progress of the negotiations and decided to demonstrate to the company its vulnerability by launching an attack on its systems from the Internet. He was intimately familiar with the company's systems and software, and his inside knowledge enabled him to hit the firm in a manner that shut it down. In fact, the attack disrupted stock trading services at the company for three days. The U.S. Secret Service was eventually employed, and the attack was traced to the employee, who was subsequently arrested. Every organization should monitor its systems for possible unauthorized intrusion and other attacks. This needs to be part of the daily routine of every organization's IT unit, as it is essential to safeguarding a company's information assets.

The most reliable way to ensure the safety of a company's computers is to refrain from putting them on a network and to keep them behind locked doors. Unfortunately, however, that is not a very practical solution. Today, computers are most useful if they are networked together to share information and resources, and companies that put their computers on a network need to take some simple precautions to reduce the risk of unauthorized access. Every year, corporations, governments, and other organizations spend billions of dollars on expenditures related to network security. The rate at which these organizations are expending funds seems to be increasing. However, when companies need to find areas in which they can decrease spending, budget items such as security and business resumption planning have historically been some of the first to be cut.

What Is Network Security?

A "network" has been defined as "any set of interlinking lines resembling a net, *a network of roads* an interconnected system, *a network of alliances*" (*Network*, n.d.). This definition suits our purpose well: a computer network is simply a system of interconnected computers. System and network technology is a key technology for a wide variety of applications. Security is crucial to networks and applications. Although, network security is a critical requirement in emerging networks, there is a significant lack of security methods that can be easily implemented.

There exists a "communication gap" between the developers of security technology and developers of networks. Network design is a well-developed process that is based on the Open Systems Interface (OSI) model. The OSI model has several advantages when designing networks. It offers modularity, flexibility, ease-of-use, and standardization of protocols. The protocols of different layers can be easily combined to create stacks which allow modular development. The implementation of individual layers can be changed later without making other adjustments, allowing flexibility in development. In contrast to network design, secure network design is not a well developed process. There isn't a methodology to manage the complexity of security requirements. Secure network design does not contain the same advantages as network design.

When considering network security, it must be emphasized that the whole network is secure. Network security does not only concern the security in the computers at each end of the communication chain. When transmitting data the communication channel should not be vulnerable to attack. A possible hacker could target the communication channel, obtain the data, and decrypt it and re-insert a false message. Securing the network is just as important as securing the computers and encrypting the message.

When developing a secure network, the following need to be considered (Dowd & McHenry, 1998):

1. **Access:** Authorized users are provided the means to communicate to and from a particular network
2. **Confidentiality:** Information in the network remains private
3. **Authentication:** Ensure the users of the network are who they say they are
4. **Integrity:** Ensure the message has not been modified in transit
5. **Non-Repudiation:** Ensure the user does not refute that he used the network

An effective network security plan is developed with the understanding of security issues, potential attackers, needed level of security, and factors that make a network vulnerable to attack (Dowd & McHenry, 1998). The steps involved in understanding the composition of a secure network, internet or otherwise, is followed throughout this research endeavor.

To lessen the vulnerability of the computer to the network there are many products available. These tools are encryption, authentication mechanisms, intrusion-detection, security management and firewalls. Businesses throughout the world are using a combination of some of these tools. "Intranets" are both connected to the internet and reasonably protected from it. The internet architecture itself leads to vulnerabilities in the network. Understanding the security issues of the internet greatly assists in developing new security technologies and approaches for networks with internet access and internet security itself. The types of attacks through the internet need to also be studied to be able to detect and guard against them. Intrusion detection systems are established based on the types of attacks most commonly used. Network intrusions consist of packets that are introduced to cause problems for the following reasons:

- To consume resources uselessly
- To interfere with any system resource's intended function
- To gain system knowledge that can be exploited in later attacks

The last reason for a network intrusion is most commonly guarded against and considered by most as the only intrusion motive. The other reasons mentioned need to be thwarted as well.

Typical security currently exists on the computers connected to the network. Security protocols sometimes usually appear as part of a single layer of the OSI network reference model. Current work is being performed in using a layered approach to secure network design. The layers of the security model correspond to the OSI model layers. This security approach leads to an effective and efficient design which circumvents some of the common security problems.

HISTORY OF NETWORK SECURITY

Recent interest in security was fueled by the crime committed by Kevin Mitnick. Kevin Mitnick committed the largest computer-related crime in U.S. history (Security Overview, n.d.). The losses were eighty million dollars in U.S. intellectual property and source code from a variety of companies (Security Overview, n.d.). Since then, information security came into the spotlight.

Public networks are being relied upon to deliver financial and personal information. Due to the evolution of information that is made available through the internet, information security is also required to evolve. Due to Kevin Mitnick's offense, companies are emphasizing security for the intellectual property. Internet has been a driving force for data security improvement.

Internet protocols in the past were not developed to secure themselves. Within the TCP/IP communication stack, security protocols are not implemented. This leaves the internet open to attacks. Modern developments in the internet architecture have made communication more secure.

Why Is Network Security Important?

The good neighbor policy. Your mistakes can be someone else's headaches. If your network is insecure and someone takes control of one of your computers, they can use that machine to launch denial of service attacks on innocent third parties. They can also flood the Web with spam.

Patron privacy. Obviously, patron records are of paramount importance. Trust between the library and its clients can be irreparably harmed if these records are compromised.

Money and time. Tracking down a virus or a worm and eliminating it from your network is frustrating and time-consuming. You often have to rebuild your machines from the ground up, reinstalling the operating system and software and restoring data from backup tapes. Lax security can lead to weeks of wasted time spent patching your network and fixing the wreckage.

DATA SECURITY VS. NETWORK SECURITY

Data security is the aspect of security that allows a client's data to be transformed into unintelligible data for transmission. Even if this unintelligible data is intercepted, a key is needed to decode the message. This method of security is effective to a certain degree. Strong cryptography in the past can be easily broken today. Cryptographic methods have to continue to advance due to the advancement of the hackers as well.

When transferring cipher text over a network, it is helpful to have a secure network. This will allow for the cipher text to be protected, so that it is less likely for many people to even attempt to break the code. A secure network will also prevent someone from inserting unauthorized messages into the network. Therefore, hard ciphers are needed as well as attack-hard networks (Kartalopoulos, 2008).

The relationship of network security and data security to the OSI model is shown in Figure 1. It can be seen that the cryptography occurs at the application layer; therefore the application writers are aware of its existence. The user can possibly choose different methods of data security. Network security is mostly contained within the physical layer. Layers above the physical layers are also used to accomplish the network security required (Kartalopoulos, 2008). Authentication is performed on a layer above the physical layer. Network security in the physical layer requires failure detection, attack detection mechanisms, and intelligent countermeasure strategies (Kartalopoulos, 2008).

Ten Steps to Data and Network Security

Much of the information stored electronically at the University is sensitive financial, personal, medical and otherwise private information. Unauthorized dissemination or access to data and the University

Figure 1. Data security and network security have a different security function

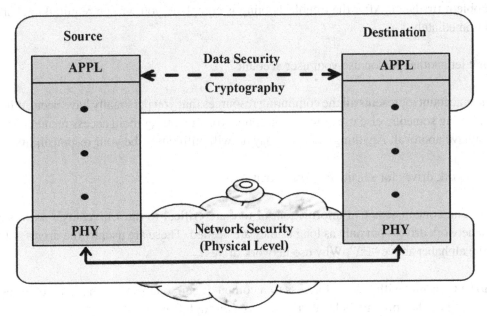

network is unethical and, possibly, illegal. Personal liability can be incurred whether either is compromised intentionally or inadvertently.

There are several statutory privacy requirements we must follow to prevent the unauthorized dissemination of this information. While following the suggestions below will not guarantee full compliance, they will help by providing affirmative evidence of our compliance efforts. The responsibility rests with the design and administration of the University Network and relies upon you to adhere to best security practices. There are ten simple changes in work behavior that would go a long way in limiting our vulnerability to unauthorized access and dissemination of confidential data (http://usm.maine.edu/computing/10-steps-data-and-network-security).

1.   Use a strong password and keep it a secret

The key to accessing the network is your password. In order to reduce the chance of a computer or another person guessing your password, you should choose a strong one. A strong password is a combination of letters, numbers, and symbols that is NOT a word or common phrase. Your password should not be a word from the dictionary or one that someone with a little personal knowledge of you might guess (i.e. your child's name or your phone number). As well, the password you use to access University resources should be unique from those you use to access resources outside the University, and, most importantly, you should never share your password with anyone or write it down anywhere.

University support technicians, including those at the USM HelpDesk, will NEVER ask you what your password is. One of the most common password-stealing tricks employed by hackers and information thieves is to call on the phone and impersonate a company's help desk staff or network administrator. Don't fall for it. If you receive a call or email requesting your password, you should refuse to provide it and immediately report the incident to the HelpDesk.

In situations where you initiated a call to the USM HelpDesk, the technician assisting you may set a temporary password on your account for their use. They will only do that with your approval, and only if other troubleshooting measures have failed and using your credentials will allow the technician to test the problem firsthand. After the troubleshooting is complete, you will be required to change your password immediately.

2.   Do not let another person use your user account

Your user account represents all the computing resources that you personally have been authorized to access. By letting someone else use your user account, you are letting them access resources for which they do not have approval. Anything that they may do will, ultimately, be your responsibility.

3.   Use network drives for sensitive or important files

All files that contain sensitive information, or that are critical to the University's work should be stored on a network drive – but only as long as they are needed. These are usually the drives with higher letters in the alphabet above "F:\". Why use network drives?

- **Security:** Anyone with physical access to a computer can, one way or another, get access to the files stored on the computer's local drives — A:\ through E:\.

- **Data Protection:** If a computer "crashes," then all data on the local drives might be lost. Files stored on the network drives are backed up on a nightly basis. In the event data is lost due to some disaster, there is a much greater chance that the data can be restored to a relatively recent state.

4. Lock your computer when away from your desk during the day

The world's strongest password won't matter at all if you walk away from your desk, even for a few minutes, and leave your computer on and unlocked. For computers running Windows 2000 and Windows XP, press Ctrl-Alt-Del keys simultaneously and select Lock Workstation. When you return to your desk, you will have to enter your Novell password to unlock the computer. For Mac workstations using OS X, you can password-protect your account under "System Preferences" to be activated every time the computer goes into Sleep mode. While you are at your computer you should arrange your work area so that your screen cannot be viewed by casual visitors. This can alleviate a lot of inadvertent viewing of personal or confidential information.

5. Shutdown your computer when you leave for the day

When you leave the office each night, turn off your computer. A computer that is off cannot be infected or compromised by attacks from other computers.

6. Use encryption for viewing and exchanging sensitive data

You should always use encryption to view web sites containing sensitive data. You can tell if a web site is using encryption if the web address begins with "https". If you have created a web site that collects sensitive data, you should be sure that the site forces users to use encryption when submitting data and that the data, once submitted, is being stored securely.

Remember, email is not encrypted and therefore should not be used to exchange sensitive data. If you have needed to transfer sensitive data via email, the information should be sent in a password-protected zip file attachment. Tell the recipient the password in person or via telephone, not via email. For a corollary caution see #8.

Finally, remember that when using wireless connections, they are not secure. Any data you may be accessing can be captured someone using similar technology. When accessing data and information that is confidential, you should only use a connection that is hardwired to your machine.

7. Do not install unapproved software

Only the programs found in Start > USM Apps > Install have been approved for installation on University computers. If you feel you need to install a piece of software not found there, you must get the approval of DoIT staff first.

Do not install free software found on the Internet. These programs often present a great security risk. To avoid this, be very wary, when surfing the Internet, of pages that offer anything for free by just "clicking here". If unexpected pop up messages are displayed while surfing the Internet, use the "X" in the upper right corner of the message to close it.

8. Think before opening email attachments

Be suspicious of emails with attachments that you were not expecting to receive, even if they appear to be from someone you know. If it appears to be from someone you know, before you open it, contact them and confirm that they intended to send you the attachment.

9.   Schedule an antivirus scan of your computer

Most of us have a weekly staff meeting. At these times your computer is usually sitting idle in your office. That is a perfect time to schedule an antivirus scan of your computer to run. These can run while your computer is locked. If any viruses are detected, please report them to the HelpDesk.

10.   Be careful using Internet Explorer

We feel it is best to only use Internet Explorer for those websites that require it (i.e., PeopleSoft) and use a different browser for all other web activity. The Internet Explorer web browser that comes with Microsoft Windows seems to have a new security flaw almost every month. While we apply patches for these flaws as quickly as possible, DoIT recommends the use of Mozilla's Firefox, available via Start > USM Apps > Install > Firefox Web Browser. You need to get approval before installing any other browser.

COMPUTER AND NETWORK ATTACKS

Before examining the types of attacks that can be launched against a computer or network, it is necessary to explain what network and computer attacks are. Figure 2 shows the relationship between them. Network attacks are almost a subset of computer attacks, but some network attacks are outside the computer attack domain. Computer attacks are attacks aimed at attacking a computer system in some way. This attack may involve destroying or accessing data, subverting the computer or degrading its performance. Traditionally attacks on computers have included methods such as viruses, worms, buffer-overflow exploits and denial of service attacks.

Network attacks are mostly attacks on computers that use a network in some way. A network could be used to send the attack (such as a worm), or it could be the means of attack (such as Distributed De-

Figure 2. The relationship between computer and network attacks

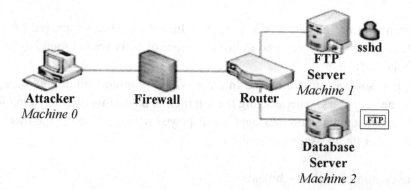

nial of Service attack). An attack on a computer that requires a network is a network attack. In general, network attacks are a subset of computer attacks.

However, there are several types of network attacks that do not attack computers, but rather the network they are attached to. Flooding a network with packets does not attack an individual computer, but clogs up the network. Although a computer may be used to initiate the attack, both the target and the means of attacking the target are network related. For the purposes of this research, the term attack (both for network and computer attacks) is broad enough to cover a wide range of attacks, ranging from viruses to physical attacks. The range of attacks is discussed in the next chapter.

A Brief History of Attacks

Computer and network attacks have evolved greatly over the last few decades. Since computers and networks were invented, there has always been the opportunity to attack them. However, over the last 25 years attacks have split into distinct categories. New attacks, such as worms and viruses have been developed and attacks have become increasingly complicated. Figure 3 shows this trend and shows some of the trends in the history of attacks. Some of the more important developments in the history of computer and network attacks are discussed below.

In 1978, the concept of a worm (Xerox, 2003) was invented by researchers at the Xerox Palo Alto Research Center. Although the original worm was designed to promote efficient use of computers by searching a network for idle computers, the concept was used by Robert Morris to release the first Internet worm: The Morris Worm (Spafford, 1988). The first viruses were released in 1981, among them Apple Viruses 1, 2 and 3 which targeted the Apple II operating system. In 1983, Fred Cohen was the first person to formally introduce the term "computer virus"2 in his thesis (Cohen, 1985), which was published in 1985. Over the next decade viruses became more common and prompted the development of anti-virus tools.

More recently, new attacks such as Denial Of Service (DoS) and Distributed DoS (DDoS) attacks have been developed. While DoS attacks such as pulling out the power cord of a computer have been around since computers have been invented, new forms using networks and processes on computers were

Figure 3. Attack sophistication vs. intruder technical knowledge

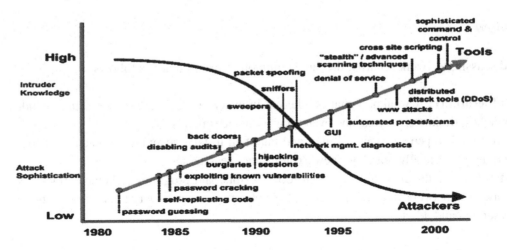

developed in the mid 1990s. DDoS attacks were first seen in 1999 with the introduction of a number of tools to automate the attack. Two major recent developments in computer and network attacks are blended attacks and information warfare. Both have influenced the way in which new attacks are being created and both will shape the future of attacks.

In 2001 a new wave of attacks began where existing attack techniques were blended together. The first of the new wave of blended attacks was seen on June 18th 2001 with the release of Code Red (Chien & Szor, 2002). Blended attacks contain two or more attacks merged together to produce a more potent attack. The deadliness of blended attacks soon became apparent, with the damage caused by Code Red, Nimda [6, Slammer (CERT Coordination Center, 2003a) and Blaster (CERT Coordination Center, 2003b). Slammer became the fastest worm in history and dramatically reduced network performance across the Internet.

However, blended attacks are not a new form of attack. The original Morris worm [12, 13], released in 1988, was a blended attack. The Morris worm used multiple UNIX vulnerabilities to spread. While blended attacks have been around since 1988, the new wave of blended attacks is far more damaging and more effective than previous blended attacks. Since Code Red, the number of blended attacks has increased. Symantec's Internet Security Threat Report Volume III (Symantec, 2003a) released in February 2003 found that blended threats are the greatest risk to the Internet community and that the potential existed for even more damaging blended threats. Months later, Slammer and Blaster wrecked havoc on the Internet. In the following volume (Symantec, 2003b), Symantec found that blended threats had increased 20% from the last half of 2002.

The new wave of blended attacks is still gathering momentum. As more vulnerability is discovered, blended attacks become more common and more damaging. Information warfare is a new and developing area of research. No common consensus has yet been reached on what information warfare is precisely. It is apparent that information warfare is an evolution in the way war is waged. Information warfare is essentially a country using relevant information to attack another country or defend itself. Instead of just waging war with bullets, information is used as a weapon. The attacks used in information warfare are varied. Traditional computer and network attacks are used, as well as less traditional attacks such as Electromagnetic Pulse (EMP) weapons.

INTRODUCTION TO VULNERABILITIES, THREATS AND ATTACKS

Overview

When discussing network security, the three common terms used are as follows:

- **Vulnerability:** A weakness that is inherent in every network and device. This includes routers, switches, desktops, servers, and even security devices themselves.
- **Threats:** The people eager, willing, and qualified to take advantage of each security weakness, and they continually search for new exploits and weaknesses.
- **Attacks:** The threats use a variety of tools, scripts, and programs to launch attacks against networks and network devices. Typically, the network devices under attack are the endpoints, such as servers and desktops.

The sections that follow discuss vulnerabilities, threats, and attacks in further detail.

Vulnerabilities

Vulnerabilities in network security can be summed up as the "soft spots" that are present in every network. The vulnerabilities are present in the network and individual devices that make up the network.

Networks are typically plagued by one or all of three primary vulnerabilities or weaknesses:

- Technology weaknesses
- Configuration weaknesses
- Security policy weaknesses

The sections that follow examine each of these weaknesses in more detail.

Technological Weaknesses

Computer and network technologies have intrinsic security weaknesses. These include TCP/IP protocol weaknesses, operating system weaknesses, and network equipment weaknesses. Table 1 describes these three weaknesses.

Configuration Weaknesses

Network administrators or network engineers need to learn what the configuration weaknesses are and correctly configure their computing and network devices to compensate. Table 2 lists some common configuration weaknesses.

Security Policy Weaknesses

Security policy weaknesses can create unforeseen security threats. The network can pose security risks to the network if users do not follow the security policy. Table 3 lists some common security policy weaknesses and how those weaknesses are exploited.

Table 1. Network security weaknesses

Weakness	Description
TCP/IP protocol	HTTP, FTP, and ICMP are inherently insecure. Simple Network Management Protocol (SNMP), Simple Mail Transfer Protocol (SMTP), and SYN floods are related to the inherently insecure structure upon which TCP was designed.
Operating system	The UNIX, Linux, Macintosh, Windows NT, 9x, 2K, XP, and OS/2 operating systems all have security problems that must be addressed. These are documented in the CERT archives at http://www.cert.org.
Network equipment	Various types of network equipment, such as routers, firewalls, and switches, have security weaknesses that must be recognized and protected against. These weaknesses include the following: Password protection, Lack of authentication, Routing protocols, Firewall holes

Table 2. Configuration weaknesses

Weakness	How the Weakness Is Exploited
Unsecured user accounts	User account information might be transmitted insecurely across the network, exposing usernames and passwords to snoopers.
System accounts with easily guessed passwords	This common problem is the result of poorly selected and easily guessed user passwords.
Misconfigured Internet services	A common problem is to turn on JavaScript in web browsers, enabling attacks by way of hostile JavaScript when accessing Untrusted sites. IIS, Apache, FTP, and Terminal Services also pose problems.
Unsecured default settings within products	Many products have default settings that enable security holes.
Misconfigured network equipment	Misconfigurations of the equipment itself can cause significant security problems. For example, Misconfigured access lists, routing protocols, or SNMP community strings can open up large security holes. Misconfigured or lack of encryption and remote-access controls can also cause significant security issues, as can the practice of leaving ports open on a switch (which could allow the introduction of noncompany computing equipment).

Vulnerability Analysis

Before adding new security solutions to an existing network, you need to identify the current state of the network and organizational practices to verify their current compliance with the requirements. This analysis also provides you with the opportunity to identify possible improvements and the potential need to redesign a part of the system or to rebuild a part of the system from scratch to satisfy the requirements. This analysis can be broken down into the following steps:

Table 3. Security policy weaknesses

Weakness	How the Weakness Is Exploited
Lack of written security policy	An unwritten policy cannot be consistently applied or enforced.
Politics	Political battles and turf wars can make it difficult to implement a consistent security policy.
Lack of continuity	Poorly chosen, easily cracked, or default passwords can allow unauthorized access to the network.
Logical access controls. not applied	Inadequate monitoring and auditing allow attacks and unauthorized use to continue, wasting company resources. This could result in legal action or termination against IT technicians, IT management, or even company leadership that allows these unsafe conditions to persist. Lack of careful and controlled auditing can also make it hard to enforce policy and to stand up to legal challenges for "wrongful termination" and suits against the organization.
Software and hardware installation and changes do not follow policy.	Unauthorized changes to the network topology or installation of unapproved applications create security holes.
Disaster recovery plan nonexistent	The lack of a disaster recovery plan allows chaos, panic, and is confusion to occur when someone attacks the enterprise.

1. Policy identification
2. Network analysis
3. Host analysis

The remainder of this section looks at each of these steps in more depth and at some analysis tools.

Policy Identification

If a security policy exists, the designer should analyze it to identify the security requirements, which will influence the design of the perimeter solution. Initially, the designer should examine two basic areas of the policy:

- The policy should identify the assets that require protection. This helps the designer provide the correct level of protection for sensitive computing resources and to identify the flow of sensitive data in the network.
- The policy should identify possible attackers. This gives the designer insight into the level of trust assigned to internal and external users, ideally identified by more-specific categories such as business partners, customers of an organization, and outsourcing IT partners.

The designer should also be able to evaluate whether the policy was developed using correct risk-assessment procedures. For example, did the policy development include all relevant risks for the organization and not overlook important threats? The designer should also reevaluate the policy mitigation procedures to determine whether they satisfactorily mitigate expected threats. This ensures that the policy, which the designer will work with, is current and complete. Organizations that need a high level of security assurance will require defense-in-depth mechanisms to be deployed to avoid single points of failure. The designer also needs to work with the organization to determine how much investment in security measures is acceptable for the resources that require protection. The result of policy analysis will be as follows:

- The evaluation of policy correctness and completeness
- Identification of possible policy improvements, which need to be made before the security implementation stage.

Network Analysis

Many industry best practices, tools, guides, and training are available to help secure network devices. These include tools from Cisco, such as AutoSecure and Cisco Output Interpreter, and from numerous web resources. Third-party resources include the U.S. National Security Agency (NSA) Cisco Router Security Recommendation Guides and the Center for Internet Security (CIS) Router Audit Tool (RAT) for auditing Cisco router and PIX Security Appliance configuration files.

Host Analysis

The hosts that are on the network need to be considered when designing a network security solution. Determining the role in the network of each host will help to decide the steps that will be taken to secure it. The network could have many user workstations, and multiple servers that need to be accessed from both inside and outside of the network.

The types of applications and services that are running on the hosts need to be identified, and any network services and ports that are not necessary should be disabled or blocked. All operating systems should be patched as needed. Antivirus software should be installed and kept current. Some servers may be assigned static routable IP addresses to be accessible from the Internet. These hosts in particular should be monitored for signs of malicious activity.

Many tools are available to test host security. Most tools have been developed on a UNIX or Linux platform, and some of them have now been ported to other operating systems. Two of the most common tools are as follows:

- **Network Mapper (Nmap):** Nmap is a popular free tool used for security scanning and auditing. It can rapidly perform a port scan of a single host or a range of hosts. Nmap was originally written to be run on UNIX systems, and it is now available for use on Microsoft Windows platforms.
- **Nessus:** Nessus is a vulnerability scanner that is available for UNIX and Microsoft Windows platforms. New vulnerability testing capabilities can be added to Nessus through the installation of modular plug-ins. Nessus includes a built-in port scanner, or it can be used along with Nmap. When the Nessus scan is finished, a report is created. This report displays the results of the scan and provides steps to mitigate vulnerabilities.

Threats

There are four primary classes of threats to network security, as Figure 4 depicts. The list that follows describes each class of threat in more detail.

1. **Unstructured Threats:** Unstructured threats consist of mostly inexperienced individuals using easily available hacking tools such as shell scripts and password crackers. Even unstructured threats that are only executed with the intent of testing and challenging a hacker's skills can still do serious damage to a company. For example, if an external company website is hacked, the integrity of the company is damaged. Even if the external website is separate from the internal information that sits behind a protective firewall, the public does not know that. All the public knows is that the site is not a safe environment to conduct business.
2. **Structured Threats:** Structured threats come from hackers who are more highly motivated and technically competent. These people know system vulnerabilities and can understand and develop exploit code and scripts. They understand, develop, and use sophisticated hacking techniques to penetrate unsuspecting businesses. These groups are often involved with the major fraud and theft cases reported to law enforcement agencies.
3. **External Threats:** External threats can arise from individuals or organizations working outside of a company. They do not have authorized access to the computer systems or network. They work their way into a network mainly from the Internet or dialup access servers.

Figure 4. Variety of threats

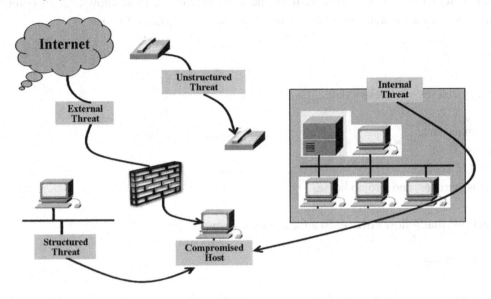

4. **Internal Threats:** Internal threats occur when someone has authorized access to the network with either an account on a server or physical access to the network. According to the FBI, internal access and misuse account for 60 percent to 80 percent of reported incidents.

As the types of threats, attacks, and exploits have evolved, various terms have been coined to describe different groups of individuals. Some of the most common terms are as follows:

*   **Hacker:** Hacker is a general term that has historically been used to describe a computer programming expert. More recently, this term is commonly used in a negative way to describe an individual who attempts to gain unauthorized access to network resources with malicious intent.
*   **Cracker:** Cracker is the term that is generally regarded as the more accurate word that is used to describe an individual who attempts to gain unauthorized access to network resources with malicious intent.
*   **Phreaker:** A phreaker is an individual who manipulates the phone network to cause it to perform a function that is normally not allowed. A common goal of phreaking is breaking into the phone network, usually through a payphone, to make free long-distance calls.
*   **Spammer:** A spammer is an individual who sends large numbers of unsolicited e-mail messages. Spammers often use viruses to take control of home computers to use these computers to send out their bulk messages.
*   **Phisher:** A phisher uses e-mail or other means in an attempt to trick others into providing sensitive information, such as credit card numbers or passwords. The phisher masquerades as a trusted party that would have a legitimate need for the sensitive information.
*   **White Hat:** White hat is a term used to describe individuals who use their abilities to find vulnerabilities in systems or networks and then report these vulnerabilities to the owners of the system so that they can be fixed.

- **Black Hat:** Black hat is another term for individuals who use their knowledge of computer systems to break into systems or networks that they are not authorized to use.

Attacks

Four primary classes of attacks exist:

1. Reconnaissance
2. Access
3. Denial of service
4. Worms, viruses, and Trojan horses

The sections that follow cover each attack class in more detail.

Reconnaissance

Reconnaissance is the unauthorized discovery and mapping of systems, services, or vulnerabilities. It is also known as information gathering and, in most cases, it precedes an actual access or denial-of-service (DoS) attack. Reconnaissance is somewhat analogous to a thief casing a neighborhood for vulnerable homes to break into, such as an unoccupied residence, easy-to-open doors, or open windows.

Reconnaissance attacks can consist of:

- Internet information lookup
- Ping sweeps
- Port scans
- Packet sniffers

Access Attacks

System access is the ability for an unauthorized intruder to gain access to a device for which the intruder does not have an account or a password. Entering or accessing systems to which one does not have authority to access usually involves running a hack, script, or tool that exploits a known vulnerability of the system or application being attacked. Access attacks exploit known vulnerabilities in authentication services, FTP services, and web services to gain entry to web accounts, confidential databases, and other sensitive information. Access attacks can consist of the following:

- Password attacks
- Trust exploitation
- Port redirection
- Man-in-the-middle attacks
- Social engineering
- Phishing

Denial of Service (DoS)

Denial of service implies that an attacker disables or corrupts networks, systems, or services with the intent to deny services to intended users. DoS attacks involve either crashing the system or slowing it down to the point that it is unusable. But DoS can also be as simple as deleting or corrupting information. In most cases, performing the attack simply involves running a hack or script. The attacker does not need prior access to the target because a way to access it is all that is usually required. For these reasons, DoS attacks are the most feared.

Worms, Viruses, and Trojan Horses

Malicious software is inserted onto a host to damage a system; corrupt a system; replicate itself; or deny services or access to networks, systems or services. They can also allow sensitive information to be copied or echoed to other systems.

Trojan horses can be used to ask the user to enter sensitive information in a commonly trusted screen. For example, an attacker might log in to a Windows box and run a program that looks like the true Windows logon screen, prompting a user to type his username and password. The program would then send the information to the attacker and then give the Windows error for bad password. The user would then log out, and the correct Windows logon screen would appear; the user is none the wiser that his password has just been stolen.

Even worse, the nature of all these threats is changing—from the relatively simple viruses of the 1980s to the more complex and damaging viruses, DoS attacks, and hacking tools in recent years. Today, these hacking tools are powerful and widespread, with the new dangers of self spreading blended worms such as Slammer and Blaster and network DoS attacks. Also, the old days of attacks that take days or weeks to spread are over. Threats now spread worldwide in a matter of minutes. The Slammer worm of January 2003 spread around the world in less than 10 minutes.

The next generations of attacks are expected to spread in just seconds. These worms and viruses could do more than just wreak havoc by overloading network resources with the amount of traffic they generate, they could also be used to deploy damaging payloads that steal vital information or erase hard drives. Also, there is a strong concern that the threats of tomorrow will be directed at the very infrastructure of the Internet.

LAYERS OF ATTACKS

The attacks in MANET can roughly be classified into two major categories, namely passive attacks and active attacks, according to the attack means [16, 17]. A passive attack obtains data exchanged in the network without disrupting the operation of the communications, while an active attack involves information interruption, modification, or fabrication, thereby disrupting the normal functionality of a MANET. Table 4 shows the general taxonomy of security attacks against MANET. Examples of passive attacks are eavesdropping, traffic analysis, and traffic monitoring. Examples of active attacks include jamming, impersonating, modification, denial of service (DoS), and message replay.

The attacks can also be classified into two categories, namely external attacks and internal attacks, according the domain of the attacks. Some papers refer to outsider and insider attacks (Cardenas, Bena-

Table 4. Security attacks classification

Passive Attacks	Eavesdropping, traffic analysis, monitoring
Active Attacks	Jamming, spoofing, modification, replaying, DoS

mmar, Papageorgious, & Baras, 2004). External attacks are carried out by nodes that do not belong to the domain of the network. Internal attacks are from compromised nodes, which are actually part of the network. Internal attacks are more severe when compared with outside attacks since the insider knows valuable and secret information, and possesses privileged access rights.

Attacks can also be classified according to network protocol stacks. Table 5 shows an example of a classification of security attacks based on protocol stack; some attacks could be launched at multiple layers. Some security attacks use stealth (Jakobsson, Wetzel, & Yenger, 2003), whereby the attackers try to hide their actions from either an individual who is monitoring the system or an intrusion detection system (IDS). But other attacks such as DoS cannot be made stealth. Some attacks are non-cryptography related, and others are cryptography primitive attacks. Table 6 shows cryptography primitive attacks and some examples.

Physical Layer Attacks

Eavesdropping is the intercepting and reading of messages and conversations by unintended receivers. The mobile hosts in mobile ad hoc networks share a wireless medium. The majorities of wireless communications use the RF spectrum and broadcast by nature. Signals broadcast over airwaves can be easily intercepted with receivers tuned to the proper frequency [20, 21]. Thus, messages transmitted can be eavesdropped, and fake messages can be injected into network. Moreover, a radio signal can be jammed or interfered, which causes the message to be corrupted or lost [20, 21]. If the attacker has a powerful transmitter, a signal can be generated that will be strong enough to overwhelm the targeted signals and disrupt communications. The most common types of this form of signal jamming are random noise and

Table 5. Security attacks on protocol stacks

Layer	Attacks
Application layer	Repudiation, data corruption
Transport layer	Session hijacking, SYN flooding
Network layer	Wormhole, black hole, Byzantine, flooding, resource consumption, location disclosure attacks
Data link layer	Traffic analysis, monitoring, disruption MAC (802.11), WEP weakness
Physical layer	Jamming, interceptions, eavesdropping
Multi-layer attacks	DoS, impersonation, replay, man-in-the middle

Table 6. Cryptography primitive attacks

Cryptography Primitive Examples	Attacks
Pseudorandom number attack	Nonce, timestamp, initialization vector (IV)
Digital signature attack	RSA signature, ElGamal signature, digital signature standard (DSS)
Hash collision attack	SHA-0, MD4, MD5, HAVAL-128, RIPEMD
Security handshake attacks	Diffie-Hellman key exchange protocol, Needham-Schroeder protocol

pulse. Jamming equipment is readily available. In addition, jamming attacks can be mounted from a location remote to the target networks.

Link Layer Attacks

The MANET is an open multipoint peer-to-peer network architecture. Specifically, one-hop connectivity among neighbors is maintained by the link layer protocols, and the network layer protocols extend the connectivity to other nodes in the network. Attacks may target the link layer by disrupting the cooperation of the layer's protocols.

Network Layer Attacks

Network layer protocols extend connectivity from neighboring 1-hops nodes to all other nodes in MANET. The connectivity between mobile hosts over a potentially multi-hop wireless link strongly relies on cooperative reactions among all network nodes.

A variety of attacks targeting the network layer have been identified and heavily studied in research papers. By attacking the routing protocols, attackers can absorb network traffic, inject themselves into the path between the source and destination, and thus control the network traffic flow, as shown in Figure 5 (a) and (b), where a malicious node M can inject itself into the routing path between sender S and receiver D.

The traffic packets could be forwarded to a non-optimal path, which could introduce significant delay. In addition, the packets could be forwarded to a nonexistent path and get lost. The attackers can create routing loops, introduce severe network congestion, and channel contention into certain areas. Multiple colluding attackers may even prevent a source node from finding any route to the destination, causing the network to partition, which triggers excessive network control traffic, and further intensifies network congestion and performance degradation.

Transport Layer Attacks

The objectives of TCP-like Transport layer protocols in MANET include setting up of end-to-end connection, end-to-end reliable delivery of packets, flow control, congestion control, clearing of end-to-end

Figure 5. Routing attack

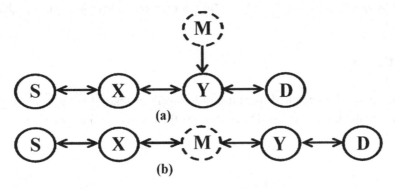

connection. Similar to TCP protocols in the Internet, the mobile node is vulnerable to the classic SYN flooding attack or session hijacking attacks. However, a MANET has a higher channel error rate when compared with wired networks. Because TCP does not have any mechanism to distinguish between whether a loss was caused by congestion, random error, or malicious attacks, TCP multiplicatively decreases its congestion window upon experiencing losses, which degrades network performance significantly (Hsieh & Sivakumar, 2002).

Application Layer Attacks

Application layer attacks can be mobile viruses, worm attacks, and repudiation attacks.

Mobile Virus and Worm Attacks

The application layer contains user data, and it normally supports many protocols such as HTTP, SMTP, and FTP. Malicious code, which includes viruses and worms, is applicable across operating systems and applications.

As we know, malicious programs are widely spread in networks. There are a number of techniques by which a worm can discover new machines to exploit. One example is IP address scanning used by Internet worms. That technique consists of generating probe packets to a vulnerable UDP/TCP port at many different IP addresses. Hosts that are hit by the scan respond, receive a copy of the worm, and hence get infected. The Code Red worm (Weaver, Paxson, Staniford, & Cunningham, 2003) is one of the scanning worms.

Some worms use a loophole of the system. For example, Worm Blaster and Worm Sasser (Weaver, Paxson, Staniford, & Cunningham, 2003) each use a different loophole: Worm Blaster uses a system RPC DCOM loophole, and Worm Sasser uses the system LSASS (local security authentication subsystem service). In MANET, an attacker can also produce a worm attack using any loophole of the system of the mobile ad hoc network.

Repudiation Attack

In the network layer, firewalls can be installed to keep packets in or keep packets out. In the transport layer, entire connections can be encrypted, end-to-end. But these solutions do not solve the authentication or non-repudiation problems in general. Repudiation refers to a denial of participation in all or part of the communications. For example, a selfish person could deny conducting an operation on a credit card purchase, or deny any on-line bank transaction, which is the prototypical repudiation attack on a commercial system.

Multi-Layer Attacks

Some security attacks can be launched from multiple layers instead of a particular layer. Examples of multi-layer attacks are denial of service (DoS), man-in-the middle, and impersonation attacks.

Denial of Service

Denial of service (DoS) attacks could be launched from several layers. An attacker can employ signal jamming at the physical layer, which disrupts normal communications. At the link layer, malicious nodes can occupy channels through the capture effect, which takes advantage of the binary exponential scheme in MAC protocols and prevents other nodes from channel access. At the network layer, the routing process can be interrupted through routing control packet modification, selective dropping, table overflow, or poisoning. At the transport and application layers, SYN flooding, session hijacking, and malicious programs can cause DoS attacks.

Impersonation Attacks

Impersonation attacks are just the first step for most attacks, and are used to launch further sophisticated attacks. For example, a malicious node can precede an attack by altering its MAC or IP address.

Man-in-the-Middle Attacks

An attacker sits between the sender and the receiver and sniffs any information being sent between two ends. In some cases the attacker may impersonate the sender to communicate with the receiver, or impersonate the receiver to reply to the sender.

Network Layer Attacks

In the past few years there is a rapid development in the area of mobile computing. Significant examples include establishing survivable, efficient, dynamic communication for emergency/rescue operations, disaster relief efforts, and military networks. Such network scenarios cannot rely on centralized and organized connectivity, and can be conceived as applications of Mobile Ad Hoc Networks. A MANET is an autonomous collection of mobile nodes that can change locations dynamically. Since the nodes are mobile, the network topology changes rapidly and randomly. The MANET network is decentralized. The examples can be a standard Wi-Fi connection, or another medium, such as a cellular or satellite transmission. As MANETs are dynamic in nature, they are typically not very secure, so it is important to be cautious what data is sent over a MANET .Security is the aspect not to be treated lightly. This is the most desired feature of communication. According to layered architecture there are different attacks on each layer of MANET but this section insight the network layer attacks in MANET and their countermeasures to prevent those attacks for security purpose. Network layer is affected by various security threats. These attacks may be passive or active. Various network layer attacks are listed below in the Figure 6.

Black Hole Attack

Security in MANETs can be often usually classified into route security and information security. In information security, information is protected against any form of unauthorized speech act, disruption and destruction. In route security, routing (packet forwarding) is protected against any form of deception. Solving all vulnerabilities associated with each route and information securities notice each information integrity and confidentiality. Typical attacks that may be simply performed against MANETs include:

Figure 6. Network layer attacks

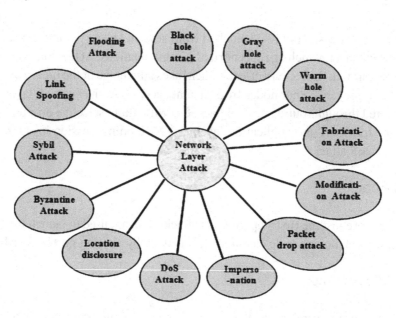

region, Denial of Service (DoS), Impersonation, Disclosure, Spoofing, and Sleep deprivation attacks (Luo, Fan, & Ye, 2008), (Deng, Li, & Agrawal, 2002), (Sarkar, Basavaraju, & Puttamadappa, n.d.), and (Kong, Yun, & Lee, 2006).

A single part attack is definitely happened within the mobile ad hoc networks (Deng, Li, & Agrawal, 2002). It's a nature of denial of service attack wherever a malicious node offers false data of getting shortest route to the destination so as to induce all the information packets and drop it (Deng, Li, & Agrawal, 2002). In black hole attack, (Bhalaji & Shanmugam, 2011), (Tamilselvan & Snakaranarayanan, 2007) a malicious node (or stingy node) takes advantage of route discovery procedure of routing protocol, to point out itself as having the shortest path to the destination node or to the node whose packet it desires to intercept. This hostile node advertises its convenience of recent routes regardless of checking its routing table. During this manner assaulter node can perpetually have the supply in replying to the route request and so intercept the information packet and retain it (Biswas & Ali, 2007). Therefore, all traffics are routed through the assaulter, and thus, the assaulter will misuse or discard the traffic (Rehman, 2010).

There are unit varied mechanisms are projected for finding single part attack in recent years. However, several detection schemes are unit unsuccessful in discussing the cooperative part issues. Some malicious nodes collaborate along so as to beguile the conventional into their unreal routing data, moreover, hide from the present detection theme. As a result, many cooperative detection schemes area unit projected preventing the collaborative black hole attacks (Oliveira, Bhargava, Azarmi, Ferreira, Wang, & Lindermann, 2009). The part attack has two properties. First property is, the node exploits the painter protocol, like AODV (Ad hoc On-demand Distance Vector) to advertise itself as having a legitimate path to a destination node, even if the path is invalid, with the intention of intercepting packets. Second property is, the assaulter consumes the intercepted packets while not forwarding to the other node (Al-Shurman & Yoo, 2004). Some major destruction generated by part is listed below:

1.   It will increase network overhead; thanks to unwanted transmission.

2.   It decreases the network's time period by boosting energy consumption unnecessarily.

3.   It destroys the network by dropping the crucial knowledge packets over the present communication.

Single Black Hole Attack

In single part attack solely single node behaves as malicious node inside a network. It's conjointly called part attack with single malicious node. An example is shown as Figure 7, node 1 stands for the source node and node 4 represents the destination node. Node 3 may be a misconduct node who replies the RREQ packet sent from source node, and makes a false response that it's the fastest route to the destination node. Thus node 1 mistakenly judges the route discovery method with completion, and starts to send knowledge packets to node 3. As what mentioned above, a malicious node in all probability drops or consumes the packets. This suspicious node is thought to be a black hole node in MANETs. As a result, node 3 is ready to misroute the packets simply, and also the network operation is suffered from this downside. The foremost important influence is that the PDR diminished severely.

Collaborative Black Hole Attack

In collaborative black hole attack multiple nodes within a network behave as malicious node within a network. It is also known as black hole attack with multiple malicious nodes. Here node 1 is the source node and 6 is the destination node. Nodes are 2, 3, 4, 5 and 7 acts as the intermediate nodes. Nodes are 3 and 5 acts as the cooperative Black holes. When the source node wishes to transmit a data packet to the destination, it first sends out the RREQ packet to the neighboring nodes. The malicious nodes being part of the network, also receive the RREQ. Since the Black hole nodes have the characteristic of responding first to any RREQ, it immediately sends out the RREP. The RREP from the Black hole node 3 reaches the source node, well ahead of the other RREPs, as it can be seen from the Figure 8. Now on receiving the RREP from node 3, the source starts transmitting the data packets. On the receipt of data packets, node 3 simply drops them, instead of forwarding to the destination or node 3 forwards all the data to node 5. Node 5 simply drops it instead of forwarding to the destination. Thus the data packets get lost and hence never reach the intended destination.

Figure 7. Single black hole attack

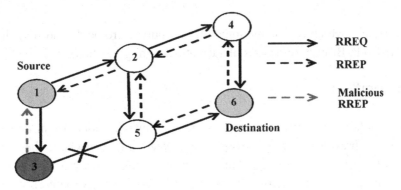

Figure 8. Collaborative black hole attack

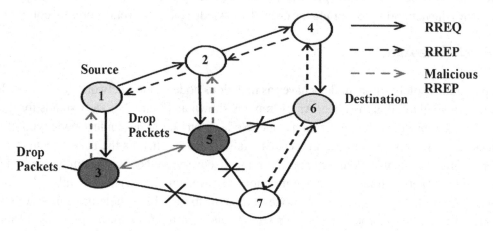

Defense against Black Hole Attack

There square measure three defense levels to counter act associate degree attack, namely, preventive, incentive and detective-corrective (Biswas & Ali, 2007). The preventive level forbids the malicious nodes from taking part in packet forwarding. The inducement level seeks to stimulate the cooperation among the router nodes via associate degree economic model. The detective-corrective level aims to reveal the identity of the malicious node and to exclude it from the network.

Byzantine Attack

In this attack, a compromised intermediate node or a set of compromised intermediate nodes works in collusion and carries out attacks such as creating routing loops, forwarding packets on non-optimal paths and selectively dropping packets (Awerbuch, Holmer, Rotaru, & Rubens, 2002) which results in disruption or degradation of the routing services. It is hard to detect byzantine failures. The network would seem to be operating normally in the viewpoint of the nodes, though it may actually be showing byzantine behavior.

Routing Attack

There are several attacks which can be mounted on the routing protocols and may disrupt the proper operation of the network. Brief descriptions of such attacks are given below:

Routing Table Overflow

In the case of routing table overflow, the attacker creates routes to nonexistent nodes. The goal is to create enough routes to prevent new routes from being created or to overwhelm the protocol implementation. In the case of proactive routing algorithms we need to discover routing information even before it is needed, while in the case of reactive algorithms we need to find a route only when it is needed.

Thus main objective of such an attack is to cause an overflow of the routing tables, which would in turn prevent the creation of entries corresponding to new routes to authorized nodes.

Routing Table Poisoning

In routing table poisoning, the compromised nodes present in the networks send fictitious routing updates or modify genuine route update packets sent to other authorized nodes.

Routing table poisoning may result in sub-optimal routing, congestion in portions of the network, or even make some parts of the network inaccessible.

Packet Replication

In the case of packet replication, an attacker replicates stale packets. This consumes additional bandwidth and battery power resources available to the nodes and also causes unnecessary confusion in the routing process.

Route Cache Poisoning

In the case of on-demand routing protocols (such as the AODV protocol (Perkins & Royer, 1999)), each node maintains a route cache which holds information regarding routes that have become known to the node in the recent past. Similar to routing table poisoning, an adversary can also poison the route cache to achieve similar objectives.

Rushing Attack

On-demand routing protocols that use duplicate suppression during the route discovery process are vulnerable to this attack (Hu, Perrig, & Johnson, 2003). An attacker which receives a route request packet from the initiating node floods the packet quickly throughout the network before other nodes which also receive the same route request packet can react. Nodes that receive the legitimate route request packets assume those packets to be duplicates of the packet already received through the attacker and hence discard those packets. Any route discovered by the source node would contain the attacker as one of the intermediate nodes. Hence, the source node would not be able to find secure routes, that is, routes that do not include the attacker. It is extremely difficult to detect such attacks in ad hoc wireless networks.

Resource Consumption Attack

In this attack, an attacker tries to consume or waste away resources of other nodes present in the network. The resources that are targeted are battery power, bandwidth, and computational power, which are only limitedly available in ad hoc wireless networks. The attacks could be in the form of unnecessary requests for routes, very frequent generation of beacon packets, or forwarding of stale packets to nodes. Using up the battery power of another node by keeping that node always busy by continuously pumping packets to that node is known as a sleep deprivation attack.

IP Spoofing Attack

A spoofing attack is when a malicious party impersonates another device or user on a network in order to launch attacks against network hosts, steal data, spread malware, or bypass access controls (http://www.veracode.com/security/spoofing-attack). There are several different types of spoofing attacks that malicious parties can use to accomplish this. Some of the most common methods include IP address spoofing attacks, ARP spoofing attacks, and DNS server spoofing attacks.

IP Address Spoofing Attacks

IP address spoofing is one of the most frequently used spoofing attack methods. In an IP address spoofing attack, an attacker sends IP packets from a false (or "spoofed") source address in order to disguise it. Denial-of-service attacks often use IP spoofing to overload networks and devices with packets that appear to be from legitimate source IP addresses.

There are two ways that IP spoofing attacks can be used to overload targets with traffic. One method is to simply flood a selected target with packets from multiple spoofed addresses. This method works by directly sending a victim more data than it can handle. The other method is to spoof the target's IP address and send packets from that address to many different recipients on the network. When another machine receives a packet, it will automatically transmit a packet to the sender in response. Since the spoofed packets appear to be sent from the target's IP address, all responses to the spoofed packets will be sent to (and flood) the target's IP address.

IP spoofing attacks can also be used to bypass IP address-based authentication. This process can be very difficult and is primarily used when trust relationships are in place between machines on a network and internal systems. Trust relationships use IP addresses (rather than user logins) to verify machines' identities when attempting to access systems. This enables malicious parties to use spoofing attacks to impersonate machines with access permissions and bypass trust-based network security measures.

ARP Spoofing Attacks

ARP is short for Address Resolution Protocol, a protocol that is used to resolve IP addresses to *MAC (Media Access Control)* addresses for transmitting data. In an ARP spoofing attack, a malicious party sends spoofed ARP messages across a Local Area Network in order to link the attacker's MAC address with the IP address of a legitimate member of the network. This type of spoofing attack results in data that is intended for the host's IP address getting sent to the attacker instead. Malicious parties commonly use ARP spoofing to steal information, modify data in-transit, or stop traffic on a LAN. ARP spoofing attacks can also be used to facilitate other types of attacks, including denial-of-service, session hijacking, and man-in-the-middle attacks. ARP spoofing only works on Local Area Networks that use the Address Resolution Protocol.

DNS Server Spoofing Attacks

The Domain Name System (DNS) is a system that associates domain names with IP addresses. Devices that connect to the internet or other private networks rely on the DNS for resolving URLs, email addresses, and other human-readable domain names into their corresponding IP addresses. In a DNS server spoofing attack, a malicious party modifies the DNS server in order to reroute a specific domain name to a different IP address. In many cases, the new IP address will be for a server that is actually controlled by the attacker and contains files infected with malware. DNS server spoofing attacks are often used to spread computer worms and viruses.

Sybil Attack

A faulty node or an adversary may present multiple identities to a network in order to appear and function as multiple distinct nodes. After becoming part of the network, the adversary may then overhear communications or act maliciously. By presenting multiple identities, the adversary can control the network substantially. In Figure 9, shows an example of Sybil attack.

Fabrication

In this type of attacks, where an attacker as a malicious node try to inject wrong messages or fake routing packets in order to disrupt the routing process. The fabrication attacks are very much difficult to detect in the mobile ad hoc network. Attacks using fabrication process are discussed very well in [40, 41]. In Figure 10, where fabrication attacks is explained by an example. In the example where the source node S wants to send data towards the destination node X, so therefore at start it sends broadcast message and request for route towards the destination node X. An attacker as a malicious node M try to pretends and modify route and returns route reply to the node (S). Furthermore, an attacker's nodes use to fabricate RERR requests and advertise a link break nodes in a mobile ad hoc network by using AODV routing protocols.

Figure 9. An example of sybil attack

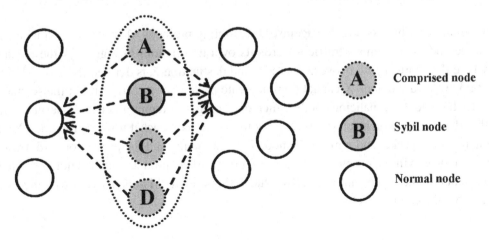

Figure 10. Fabrication attack example

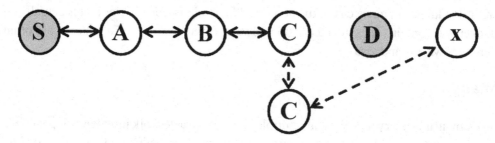

Modification

In case of modification type of attacks some of the messages in the protocol fields are modified and then these messages passed among the nodes, due to this way it become the cause of traffic subversion, as well as traffic redirection and also act as a Denial of Service (DoS) attacks. There are some of these types of attacks are given below:

Route Sequence Numbers Modification

In this type of attack which is mainly possible against the AODV protocol. In this case an attacker (i.e. malicious node) used to modify the sequence number in the route request packets.

Hop Count Modification Attack

In this type of attacks where it is also mainly possible against the routing protocol AODV, here attacker mostly change hope count value and due to this way it will become the cause of attract traffic. They are mainly used to include new routes in order to reset the value of hop count field to a lower value of a RREQ packet or sometime even it is used to set to zero.

Source Route Modification Attack

In this type of attack which is possible against DSR routing protocol where attacker (malicious node) modify source address and move traffic towards its own destination. In Figure 11 the mechanism is defined, where the shortest path between source S and destination X is defined (S-A-B-C-DX). Which shows that node S and the node X cannot communicate each other directly, and in the scenario where the node M which act as a malicious node which are going to attempt a denial-of-service attack. Let suppose that the node S which act as a source try to send a data packet towards the node X but if the node M intercept the packet and remove the node D from the list and the packet forward towards node C, where the node C will try to send the picket towards the distention X which is not possible because the node C can't communicate with X directly, Due to this way the M node has successfully established a DoS attack on X (see Figure 11).

Figure 11. An example of route modification attack

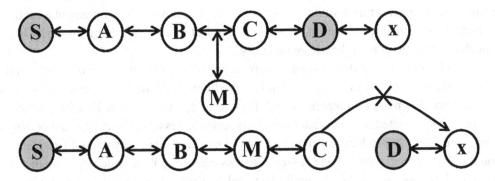

COUNTER MEASURE OF DIFFERENT ATTACKS

Security Attacks Countermeasures

Security is an essential service for wired and wireless network communications. The success of MANET strongly depends on whether its security can be trusted. However, the characteristics of MANET pose both challenges and opportunities in achieving the security goals, such as confidentiality, authentication, integrity, availability, access control, and non-repudiation.

The mobile hosts forming a MANET are normally mobile devices with limited physical protection and resources. Security modules, such as tokens and smart cards, can be used to protect against physical attacks. Cryptographic tools are widely used to provide powerful security services, such as confidentiality, authentication, integrity, and non-repudiation. Unfortunately, cryptography cannot guarantee availability; for example, it cannot prevent radio jamming. Meanwhile, strong cryptography often demands a heavy computation overhead and requires the auxiliary complicated key distribution and trust management services, which mostly are restricted by the capabilities of physical devices (e.g. CPU or battery).

The characteristics and nature of MANET require the strict cooperation of participating mobile hosts. A number of security techniques have been invented and a list of security protocols has been proposed to enforce cooperation and prevent misbehavior, such as 802.11 WEP, IPsec, SEAD, SAODV, SRP, ARAN, SSL, and so on. However, none of those preventive approaches is perfect or capable to defend against all attacks. A second line of defense called intrusion detection systems (IDS) is proposed and applied in MANET. IDS are some of the latest security tools in the battle against attacks. Distributed IDS were introduced in MANET to monitor either the misbehavior or selfishness of mobile hosts. Subsequent actions can be taken based on the information collected by IDS.

Security Attributes

Security is the combination of processes, procedures, and systems used to ensure confidentiality, authentication, integrity, availability, access control, and nonrepudiation.

Confidentiality is to keep the information sent unreadable to unauthorized users or nodes. MANET uses an open medium, so usually all nodes within the direct transmission range can obtain the data. One way to keep information confidential is to encrypt the data, and another technique is to use directional antennas.

Authentication is to be able to identify a node or a user, and to be able to prevent impersonation. In wired networks and infrastructure-based wireless networks, it is possible to implement a central authority at a point such as a router, base station, or access point. But there is no central authority in MANET, and it is much more difficult to authenticate an entity.

Integrity is to be able to keep the message sent from being illegally altered or destroyed in the transmission. When the data is sent through the wireless medium, the data can be modified or deleted by malicious attackers. The malicious attackers can also resend it, which is called a replay attack.

Non-repudiation is related to a fact that if an entity sends a message, the entity cannot deny that the message was sent by it. By producing a signature for the message, the entity cannot later deny the message. In public key cryptography, a node A signs the message using its private key. All other nodes can verify the signed message by using A's public key, and A cannot deny that its signature is attached to the message.

Availability is to keep the network service or resources available to legitimate users. It ensures the survivability of the network despite malicious incidents.

Access control is to prevent unauthorized use of network services and system resources. Obviously, access control is tied to authentication attributes.

In general, access control is the most commonly thought of service in both network communications and individual computer systems.

Security Mechanisms

A variety of security mechanisms have been invented to counter malicious attacks. The conventional approaches such as authentication, access control, encryption, and digital signature provide a first line of defense. As a second line of defense, intrusion detection systems and cooperation enforcement mechanisms implemented in MANET can also help to defend against attacks or enforce cooperation, reducing selfish node behavior.

Preventive Mechanism

The conventional authentication and encryption schemes are based on cryptography, which includes asymmetric and symmetric cryptography. Cryptographic primitives such as hash functions (message digests) can be used to enhance data integrity in transmission as well. Threshold cryptography can be used to hide data by dividing it into a number of shares. Digital signatures can be used to achieve data integrity and authentication services as well.

It is also necessary to consider the physical safety of mobile devices, since the hosts are normally small devices, which are physically vulnerable. For example, a device could easily be stolen, lost, or damaged. In the battlefield they are at risk of being hijacked. The protection of the sensitive data on a physical device can be enforced by some security modules, such as tokens or a smart card that is accessible through PIN, passphrases, or biometrics.

Although all of these cryptographic primitives combined can prevent most attacks in theory, in reality, due to the design, implementation, or selection of protocols and physical device restrictions, there are still a number of malicious attacks bypassing prevention mechanisms.

Reactive Mechanism

An intrusion detection system is a second line of defense. There are widely used to detect misuse and anomalies. A misuse detection system attempts to define improper behavior based on the patterns of well-known attacks, but it lacks the ability to detect any attacks that were not considered during the creation of the patterns; Anomaly detection attempts to define normal or expected behavior statistically. It collects data from legitimate user behavior over a period of time, and then statistical tests are applied to determine anomalous behavior with a high level of confidence. In practice, both approaches can be combined to be more effective against attacks. Some intrusion detection systems for MANET have been proposed in recent research papers.

COUNTER MEASURES FOR VARIOUS ATTACKS

Black Hole Attack

A DPRAODV (Detection, Prevention and Reactive AODV) (Raj & Swades, 2009) is designed as a countermeasure to the blackhole attack. Two authentication mechanisms (Min & Jiliu, 2009), based on the hash function is proposed to identify multiple black holes cooperating with each other. Wait and check the replies mechanism (Tamilselvan & Sankaranarayanan, 2007) is also proposed to find a safe route for packets. TOGBAD (Gerhards-Padilla, Aschenbruck, & Martini, 2007) a new centralized approach is proposed to identify nodes attempting to create a black hole. Security-aware ad hoc routing protocol (SAR) (http://usm.maine.edu/computing/10-steps-data-and-network-security), is also proposed which can be used to defend against blackhole attacks. Black hole is a type of routing attack where a malicious node advertise itself as having the shortest path to all nodes in the environment by sending fake route reply. By doing this, the malicious node can deprive the traffic from the source node.

A DPRAODV (Detection, Prevention and Reactive AODV) is designed to prevent security threats of blackhole by notifying other nodes in the network of the incident. The simulation results in ns2 demonstrate that this protocol not only prevents blackhole attack but consequently improves the overall performance of (normal) AODV in presence of black hole attack.

Two authentication mechanisms, based on the hash function, the Message Authentication Code (MAC) and the Pseudo Random Function (PRF), are proposed to provide fast message verification and group identification, identify multiple black holes cooperating with each other and to discover the safe routing avoiding cooperative black hole attack. To reduce the probability it is proposed to wait and check the replies from all the neighboring nodes to find a safe route.

Computer simulation using GLOMOSIM shows that this protocol provides better performance than the conventional AODV in the presence of Black holes with minimal additional delay and Overhead.

TOGBAD a new centralized approach, using topology graphs to identify nodes attempting to create a black hole. In this, use well-established techniques to gain knowledge about the network topology and use this knowledge to perform plausibility checks of the routing information propagated by the nodes in the network. In this approach, we have to consider a node generating fake routing information as malicious. Therefore, we have to trigger an alarm if the plausibility check fails.

Furthermore, there is a present promising first simulation result. With this new approach, it is possible to already detect the attempt to create a black hole before the actual impact occurs. Security-aware ad hoc routing protocol (SAR) can be used to defend against blackhole attacks. The security-aware ad hoc routing protocol is based on on-demand protocols, such as AODV or DSR. In SAR, a security metric is added into the RREQ packet, and a different route discovery procedure is used. Intermediate nodes receive an RREQ packet with a particular security metric or trust level. At intermediate nodes, if the security metric or trust level is satisfied, the node will process the RREQ packet, and it will propagate to its neighbors using controlled flooding. Otherwise, the RREQ is dropped. If an end-to-end path with the required security attributes can be found, the destination will generate a RREP packet with the specific security metric. If the destination node fails to find a route with the required security metric or trust level, it sends a notification to the sender and allows the sender to adjust the security level in order to find a route.

Byzantine Attack

A secure on-demand MANET routing protocol, named Robust Source Routing (RSR) (Crepeau, Davis, & Maheswaran, 2007) is proposed as countermeasure of Byzantine attacks. A Chord mechanism is proposed which is a distributed hash table (DHT).

A secure on-demand MANET routing protocol, named Robust Source Routing (RSR). In addition to providing data origin authentication services and integrity checks, RSR is able to mitigate against intelligent malicious agents which selectively drop or modify packets they agreed to forward. Simulation studies confirm that RSR is capable of maintaining high delivery ratio even when a majority of the MANET nodes are malicious. Chord is a distributed hash table (DHT) that requires only O(log n) links per node and performs searches with latency and message cost O(log n), where n is the number of peers in the network. Chord assumes all nodes behave according to protocol. We give a variant of Chord which is robust with high probability for any time period.

Sybil Attacks

A robust Sybil attack detection framework (Tangpong, Kesidis, Yuan, & Hurson, 2007) is proposed for MANETs based on cooperative monitoring of network activities.

In this mechanism, we do not require designated and honest monitors to perform the Sybil attack detection. Each mobile node in the network observes packets passing through it and periodically exchanges its observations in order to determine the presence of an attack. Malicious nodes fabricating false observations will be detected and rendered ineffective. Our framework requires no centralized authority and, thus, is scalable in expanding network size. Privacy of each mobile node is also a consideration of our framework. Our preliminary experimental results yield above 80% accuracy (true positives) and about 10% error rate (false positives).

Gray Hole Attacks

An aggregate signature algorithm (Xiaopeng & Wei, 2007) is proposed to trace packet dropping nodes.

In the proposed mechanism, firstly, DSR protocol, aggregate signature algorithm and network model were introduced. Secondly, we proposed to use aggregate signature algorithm to trace packet dropping nodes. The proposal was consisted of three related algorithms: the creating proof algorithm, the checkup algorithm and the diagnosis algorithm. The first was for creating proof, and the second was for checking up source route nodes, and the last was for locating the malicious nodes. Finally, the efficiency of the proposal was analyzed. The simulation results using ns-2 show that in a moderately changing network, most of the malicious nodes could be detected, the routing packet overhead was low, and the packet delivery rate has been improved.

Modification Attacks

A new key management scheme (Vaithiyanathan, Sheeba, Edna, & Radha, 2010) is implemented in NTP protocol. The security protocol SEAD (Spafford, 1988) is used here as an example of a defense against modification attacks.

A new key management scheme is implemented in NTP protocol, since Node Transition Probability (NTP) based algorithm provides maximum utilization of bandwidth during heavy traffic with less overhead. NTP determines stable routes using received power, but the packet delivery cannot be guaranteed since it is a non secured protocol. The proposal detects the modification, impersonation attacks and TTL attacks and, avoids the effects of malicious node and determines appropriate measures to discard such malicious nodes in dynamic condition.

The security protocol SEAD is used here as an example of a defense against modification attacks. Similar to a packet leash (Hu, Johnson, & Perrig, 2002), the SEAD protocol utilizes a one-way hash chain to prevent malicious nodes from increasing the sequence number or decreasing the hop count in routing advertisement packets. In SEAD, nodes need to authenticate neighbors by using TESLA broadcast authentication or a symmetric cryptographic mechanism. Specifically, in SEAD, a node generates a hash chain and organizes the chain into segments of m elements as $(h0, h1, ..., hm_i1), ..., (hkm, hkm+1, ..., hkm+m_i1), ..., hn$, where $k = n\ m - i$, m is the maximum network diameter, and i is the sequence number.

Packet Sniffing

Packet sniffing is a passive threat that does not alter the packets that are being transmitted. It is, therefore, quite difficult to know whether a specific system is running a packet sniffer or not. However, some techniques can be used to determine whether the NIC (Network Interface Card) on the suspect machine is running in promiscuous mode or not. The non-trusting assumption is that because it is in promiscuous mode, 7the machine must be running a sniffer. These tests assume that the sniffer detection tool and the suspect machine are both in the same Ethernet segment:

- **DNS Test:** Create numerous fake TCP connections expecting a poorly written sniffer to pick up on those connections and resolve the IP addresses of the nonexistent hosts. Some packet sniffers perform reverse DNS lookups for the packets it captures. When reverse DNS lookup occurs, the detection tool sniffs the lookup request to see if the target is the one requesting resolution of that nonexistent host (Spafford, 1988).
- **Ping Test:** This method relies on a problem in the target machine's kernel. One can build an ICMP echo request packet with the IP address of the machine suspected of hosting a sniffer but with a deliberately mismatched MAC address (Spafford, 1988). Send the ICMP packet to the target with the correct destination IP address, but a bogus destination hardware address. Most systems

will disregard this packet since its hardware address information is incorrect. But in some Linux, NetBSD and NT systems, since the NIC is in promiscuous mode, the sniffer will grab this packet off the network as a legitimate packet and respond accordingly. If the target in question replies to our request, we know it is in promiscuous mode. Clever attackers are of course aware of this and can update their sniffers to filter out such packets.

The above tests can be used to help detect machines that are running sniffers. To prevent such threats, the best solution is to use protocols that use strong cryptographic schemes to encrypt all the incoming and outgoing traffic.

IP Spoofing

If the spoofed address is for instance 127.0.0.1 or one of the IP addresses that are used for experimental or private purposes then one can detect such spoofing easily. Otherwise, it is quite difficult to know whether an address is spoofed or not. Consider for instance the following trace:

- The attacker sends the victim an echo request:
  IP spoofed-address > victim: icmp 64: echo request
- The victim sends the attacker an echo reply:
  IP victim > spoofed-address: icmp 64: echo reply

If the above trace was captured, then one might think that spoofed-address attempted to ping victim. Is it possible, however, to know whether the source IP address is a real IP or a spoofed one? The answer to this question is it depends. To be able to know whether a spoofed address was used or not, one needs to analyze more traces which show the given address and its related activities. Even then determining whether the used IP address is real or spoofed is still not guaranteed.

Buffer Overflow

Some techniques like monitoring the return address on the stack, making the stack nonexecutable, etc have been developed to help protect against buffer overflow. However, an effective countermeasure for this type of attack has not been implemented. Keeping 18your operating system and software up to date can sometimes help. The best solution, however, would be to write secure code in the first place by checking buffers size limits.

Trojan Horses

Do not download and execute code from untrusted websites. Keeping your anti-virus software up to date can help detect known Trojans. However, anti-virus software will not be able to detect Trojans whose code can be found in the wild (the Internet).

Viruses and Worms

Effective countermeasure against worms is still not yet found. However, keeping your operating system, softwares and anti-virus software up to date will help protect your system to some extent.

CASE STUDY: HOW TO DETECT AND PREVENT BLACK HOLE ATTACK IN MOBILE AD HOC NETWORK

Overview

MANET could be a dynamic network with sizable amount of mobile nodes. Devices in MANET be a part of and leave the network asynchronously. The Dynamic topology, decentralized management, mobile communications structure renders impromptu network susceptible to numerous kind of attacks. Because the traffic will increase over the MANET it'll results in range of issues i.e., congestion and packet loss. This congestion and packet loss issues happens owing to the attack in MANET. We tend to gift a fuzzy based mostly management technique to find and mitigate a kind of attack, particularly malicious packet dropping. A malicious node will promise to forward packets however drop or delay them. Each node within the MANET sends the request and waits for the acknowledgment. As a result some packet loss over the network and slows the communication method. During this section we tend to area unit providing the elucidation against black hole attack that relies on fuzzy rule. Fuzzy rule based mostly resolution determine the infected node further as offer the answer to scale back knowledge loss over network.

Introduction

Ad-hoc networks type form impulsively while not a necessity of an infrastructure or centralized controller. This kind of peer-to-peer system infers that every node, or user, within the network will act as a knowledge end or intermediate repeater. Thus, all users work beside to improve the consistency of network communications. These styles of networks also are popularly better-known to as "mesh networks" as a result of the topology of network communications resembles a mesh. The redundant communication methods provided by spontaneous mesh networks drastically improve fault tolerance for the network. In addition, the power for information packets to "hop" from one user to a different effectively extends the network coverage space and provides an answer to overcome non-Line Of Sight (LOS) problems.

Mobile applications gift further challenges for mesh networks as changes to the network topology are swift and widespread. Such eventualities need the utilization of Mobile Ad hoc Networking (MANET) technology to confirm communication routes are updated quickly and accurately. MANETs are self-forming, self-maintained, and self-healing, giving extreme network flexibility. Whereas MANETs is utterly self-contained, they'll even be tied to an IP-based world or native network (e.g. net or non-public networks). These are observed as Hybrid MANETs

A Mobile Ad-hoc NETwork (MANET) [51, 52] could be a self-configuring network of mobile routers (and associated hosts) connected by wireless links - the union of that type a random topology. The routers are unengaged to move at random and organize themselves at random; therefore, the network's wireless topology might amendment apace and erratically. Such a network might operate in an exceedingly standalone fashion, or is also connected to the larger network. Exposed configuration and fast deployment create spontaneous networks suitable for emergency things like natural or human induced disasters, military conflicts, emergency medical things etc.

Black Hole Attack in MANET

Security is one amongst the foremost primary considerations in MANET for the protection of communication and security of data. For network operation it's necessary to perform routing and packet forwarding. Hence numbers of security mechanisms has been created to counter live the malicious attacks. Mechanisms used for the protection of MANET area unit referred to as preventive and reactive mechanism. In preventive mechanism, authentications, access controls, and secret writing techniques area unit concerned. Whereas in Reactive mechanism, totally different schemes like intrusion detection systems (IDS) and cooperation mechanisms are unit used. Just in case of MANET intrusion is employed for detection of misuse. Black hole downside in MANETS (Rehman, 2010) could be a serious security downside to be resolved.

In black hole attack, a malicious node uses its routing protocol so as to advertise itself for having the shortest path to the destination node or to the packet it desires to intercept. This hostile node advertises its availableness of contemporary routes regardless of checking its routing table. During this means offender node can continually have the supply in replying to the route request and so intercept the information packet and retain it (Biswas & Ali, 2007). In protocol supported flooding, the malicious node reply are going to be received by the requesting node before the reception of reply from actual node; thence a malicious and cast route is formed. Once this route is established, currently it's up to the node whether or not to drop all the packets or forward it to the unknown address (Bhalaji & Shanmugam, 2011).

The method how malicious node fits in the data routes varies. Figure 12 shows how black hole problem arises, here node "S" wants to send data packets to node "D" and initiate the route discovery process. So if node "4" is a malicious node then it will claim that it has active route to the specified destination as soon as it receives Route REQuest (RREQ) packets. It will then send the response to node "S" before any other node. In this way node "S" will think that this is the active route and thus active route discovery is complete. Node "S" will ignore all other replies and will start seeding data packets to node "4". In this way all the data packet will be lost consumed or lost.

Figure 12. Black hole attack problem

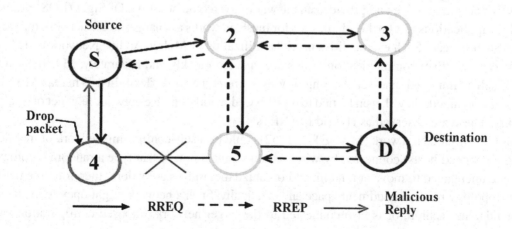

Black Hole Attack Caused by RREQ

An assaulter will send pretend RREQ messages to create Blackhole attack (Thangadurai & Anchugam, 2013). In RREQ Blackhole attack, the assaulter pretends to air a RREQ message with a non-existent node address. Different nodes can update their route to travel by the non-existent node to the destination node. As a result, the conventional route is going to be counteracted (see Figure 12).

The assaulter will generate Black hole attack by faked RREQ message as follows:

1.   Set the sort field to RREQ (1);
2.   Set the conceiver informatics address to the originating node's informatics address;
3.   Set the destination informatics address to the destination node's informatics address;
4.   Set the supply informatics address (in the informatics header) to a non-existent informatics address (Black hole);
5.   Increase the supply sequence range by a minimum of one, or decrease the hop count to one.

The assaulter forms a Black hole attack between the supply node and therefore the destination node by faked RREQ message because it is shown in Figure 13.

Black Hole Attack Caused by Route Reply (RREP) Message

The assaulter could generate a RREP message to create part as follows:

1.   Set the sort field to RREP (2);
2.   Set the hop count field to 1;
3.   Set the conceiver informatics address because the originating node of the route and therefore the destination informatics address because the destination node of the route;
4.   Increase the destination sequence range by a minimum of one;
5.   Set the supply informatics address (in the informatics header) to a non-existent informatics address (Black hole).

The assaulter unicasts the faked RREP message to the originating node. Once originating node receives the faked RREP message, it'll update its route to destination node through the non-existent node. Then RREP Black hole is made because it is shown in Figure 14.

Figure 13. Black hole node is formed by faked RREQ

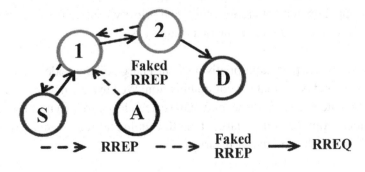

Figure 14. Black hole node is formed by faked RREP

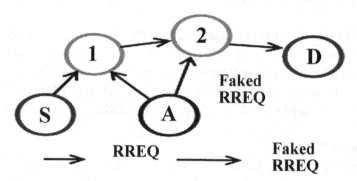

Proposed Work

Mobile ad hoc network is one in every of commonest unexpected network with lot of issues associated with congestion and routing. We have a tendency to area unit providing one in every of the solutions to secure the transmission over the network. Security aspects play a very important role in most of the appliance situations given the vulnerabilities inherent in unexpected networking from the actual fact that radio communication takes place to routing, man-in-the-middle and elaborate information injection attacks (Sonal, 2013). Security has become a primary concern so as to supply protected communication between mobile nodes in an exceedingly hostile setting. The planned system is near to style associate intrusion detection system to detect the region attack on painter. This detection system relies on symbolic logic. We have a tendency to propose a detection system during which improvement is by creating use of two factors i.e., Packet Loss Rate, Data Rate. We will use each factors victimization symbolic logic that is downside determination system.

Fuzzy logic provides a straightforward thanks to reach a precise conclusion based mostly upon obscure, ambiguous, shouting or missing information. We have a tendency to planned associate formula that relies on higher than factors. During this formula first off we have a tendency to outline the network with N range of nodes and we set supply node to S and destination node D and at that time we let current node is as supply node. We have a tendency to repeat the steps till current node isn't capable destination node. During this currently we discover the list of neighboring nodes of current node. We have a tendency to determine the parameter S of every neighbor node i.e., packet loss, data rate. During this planned formula we have a tendency to use the idea of priority, solely high priority nodes participate in communication. For priority we have a tendency to outline the three steps at sender aspect.

Step 1: Packet loss is low and data rate is high then priority is high
Step 2: packet loss is medium and data rate is high then priority is medium.
Step 3: Packet loss is low and data rate is low then priority is low.

We set priority at receiver aspect additionally once the energy of any node is low then set the priority of node is low and node don't participate in communication. We have a tendency to increase the priority of node that they participate in communication. We have a tendency to area unit providing the condition information Transmitted from the node is larger than threshold and Rate of node is additionally greater than threshold then increase the amount of priority.

Table 7.

Packet Loss Rate	Data Rate	Priority
Low	High	High
Medium	Medium	Medium
Low	Low	Low

Algorithm to Detect Black Hole Attack Using Fuzzy Logic

1. Define a Network with N number of nodes.
2. Define a Source Node(S) and Destination Node (D).
3. Set CN = S as Current Node
4. Check the node is current node or destination node
5. Identify the list of Neighboring Nodes to CN called NEN (1), NEN (2)… NEN (M)
6. Identifying the analysis parameter for each neighbor node called packet loss, data rate.
7. Source node enter into fuzzy logic system
8. Fuzzify there rules under the Fuzzification process
9. Check the each parameter is high or low
10. Parameters are low then set priority of neighboring node is low
11. Find the list of high priority received from the Neighbor node list called P(1), P(2)…P(K)
12. Find receiver level using fuzzy logic
13. Check energy of priority node
14. Energy is low then neighboring node is malicious node
15. Energy is high then transmitted a data
16. Again check priority node of data transmitted and rate to threshold value
17. Threshold value is high then node is malicious node

CONCLUSION

In this section we've got given fuzzy based mostly trust worth routing algorithmic program to single black-hole and cooperative black-hole attack that are measure caused by malicious nodes. The proposed algorithmic program can give the answer of packet loss and rate against the part attack in network. The proposed work can foremost notice the black hole attack exploitation the fuzzy logic. The fuzzy logic is enforced on packet loss and rate at time of node communication. Currently rather than transferring information on this node, it'll be passing on from the encompassing nodes; it'll solely handle the transmission that's directed to it solely.

SUMMARY

This chapter focuses on the provisioning of a method for the analysis and categorization of both computer and network attacks, thus providing assistance in combating new attacks, improving computer and network security as well as providing consistency in language when describing attacks. Attacks are thus attempts by unauthorized individuals to access or modify information, to deceive the system so that an unauthorized individual can take over an authorized session, or to disrupt service to authorized users.

This module introduced the needs, trends, and goals of network security. The exponential growth of networking has led to increased security risks. Many of these risks are due to hacking, device vulnerabilities, and improper uses of network resources. Awareness of the various weaknesses and vulnerabilities is critical to the success of modern networks. Security professionals who can deploy secure networks are in high demand. The four primary threats to network security include unstructured threats, structured threats, external threats, and internal threats. To defend against threats, an understanding of the common methods of attack must be established, including reconnaissance, access, DoS, and malicious code.

Case study section focused about how to detect and prevent black hole attack in network layer. This section analyzes the black hole attack which is one of the possible attacks in ad hoc networks. In a black hole attack, a malicious node impersonates a destination node by sending a spoofed route reply packet to a source node that initiates a route discovery. By doing this, the malicious node can deprive the traffic from the source node. During this section we tend to area unit providing the elucidation against black hole attack that relies on fuzzy rule. Fuzzy rule based mostly resolution determine the infected node further as offer the answer to scale back knowledge loss over network.

REFERENCES

Al-Shurman & Yoo. (2004). *Black Hole Attack in Mobile Ad Hoc Networks*. ACMSE'04.

Awerbuch, B., Holmer, D., Nita Rotaru, C., & Rubens, . (2002). An On-Demand Secure Routing Protocol Resilient to Byzantine Failures. *Proceedings of the ACM Workshop on Wireless Security 2002*. doi:10.1145/570681.570684

Bhalaji, N., & Shanmugam, A. (2011). A Trust Based Model to Mitigate Black Hole Attacks in DSR Based Manet. *European Journal of Scientific Research*, *50*(1), 6–15.

Biswas & Ali. (2007). *Security Threats in Mobile Ad-Hoc Network*. (Master Thesis). Blekinge Institute of Technology Sweden.

Cardenas, A., Benammar, N., Papageorgiou, G., & Baras, J. (2004). Cross-Layered Security Analysis of Wireless Ad Hoc Networks. *Proc. of 24th Army Science Conference*.

CERT Coordination Center. (2003a). *Advisory CA-2003-04 MS-SQL Server Worm*. Retrieved from http://www.cert.org/advisories/CA-2003-04.html

CERT Coordination Center. (2003b). *Advisory CA-2003-20 W32/Blaster Worm*. Retrieved from http://www.cert.org/advisories/CA-2003-20.html

Chien, E., & Szor, . (2002). *Blended Attacks Exploits, Vulnerabilities and Buffer-Overflow Techniques in Computer Viruses. Virus Bulletin Conference*.

Cohen, F. (1985). *Computer Viruses*. (PhD thesis). University of Southern California.

Crepeau, C., Davis, C. R., & Maheswaran, M. (2007). *A secure MANET routing protocol with resilience against byzantine behaviors of malicious or selfish nodes*. 21st International Conference on Advanced Information Networking and Applications Workshops (AINAW'07).

Deng, H., Li, W., & Agrawal, D. P. (2002). Routing Security in Wireless Ad hoc Networks. *IEEE Communications Magazine, 40*(10), 70–75. doi:10.1109/MCOM.2002.1039859

Dowd, P. W., & McHenry, J. T. (1998). Network security: It's time to take it seriously. [Sep.]. *Computer, 31*(9), 24–28. doi:10.1109/2.708446

Gerhards-Padilla, E., Aschenbruck, N., & Martini, P. (2007). *Detecting Black Hole Attacks in Tactical MANETs using Topology Graphs Networks*. 32nd IEEE Conference on Local Computer Networks.

Hsieh, H., & Sivakumar, R. (2002). *Transport over Wireless Networks. Handbook of Wireless Networks and Mobile Computing* (I. Stojmenovic, Ed.). John Wiley and Sons, Inc.

Hu, Y., Johnson, D., & Perrig, A. (2002). SEAD: Secure Efficient Distance Vector Routing in Mobile Wireless Ad-Hoc Networks. *Proc. of the 4th IEEE Workshop on Mobile Computing Systems and Applications (WMCSA'02)*.

Hu, Y., Perrig, A., & Johnson, D. B. (2003). Rushing Attacks and Defense in Wireless Ad Hoc Network Routing Protocols. *Proceedings of the ACM Workshop on Wireless Security 2003*. doi:10.1145/941311.941317

Jakobsson, M., Wetzel, S., & Yener, B. (2003). Stealth Attacks on Ad Hoc Wireless Networks. *Proc. of IEEE Vehicular Technology Conference (VTC)*. doi:10.1109/VETECF.2003.1285396

Kartalopoulos, S. V. (2008).Differentiating Data Security and Network Security. *Communications, ICC '08. IEEE International Conference on*. doi:10.1109/ICC.2008.284

Kong,, H., Yun, , & Lee, H. (2006). A Distributed Intrusion Detection. *Electrical Engineering*, 2–5.

Luo, J., Fan, M., & Ye, D. (2008). *Black hole Attack Prevention based on Authentication Mechanism*. Science and Technology.

Min, Z., & Jiliu, Z. (2009). *Cooperative Black Hole Attack Prevention for Mobile Ad Hoc Networks. International Symposium on Information Engineering and Electronic Commerce*. doi:10.1109/IEEC.2009.12

Network. (n.d.). In *The New Lexicon Webster's Encyclopedic Dictionary of the English Language*. New York: Lexicon.

Oliveira, R., Bhargava, B., Azarmi, M., Ferreira, E. W. T., Wang, W., & Lindermann, M. (2009). *Developing Attack Defense Ideas for Ad Hoc Wireless Networks*. Paper presented at the 2nd International Workshop on Dependable Network Computing and Mobile Systems (DNCMS 2009) (in Conjunction with IEEE SRDS 2009), New York, NY.

Perkins, C. E., & Royer, E. M. (1999). Ad Hoc On-Demand Distance Vector Routing. *Proceedings of IEEE Workshop on Mobile Computing Systems and Applications*.

Raj & Swades. (2009). DPRAODV: A Dynamic Learning System against Blackhole Attack in AODV based MANET. *International Journal of Computer Science Issues, 2*.

Rehman. (2010). *Analysis of Black Hole Attack on MANETs Using Different MANET Routing Protocols.* Academic Press.

Sarkar, Basavaraju, & Puttamadappa. (n.d.). *Ad hoc Mobile Wireless Networks Principles, protocols and Applications.* Academic Press.

Security Overview. (n.d.). Retrieved from www.redhat.com/docs/manuals/enterprise/RHEL-4-Manual/security-guide/ch-sgs-ov.html

Sonal. (2013). Black hole Attack Detection using Fuzzy Logic. *International Journal of Science and Research, 2*(8).

Spafford, E. (1988). *The Internet Worm Program: An Analysis. Technical report.* Department of Computer Sciences, Purdue University.

Symantec. (2003a). *Symantec Internet Security Threat Report Volume III.* Retrieved from http://enterprisesecurity.symantec.com/content.cfm?articleid=1539&EID=0%

Symantec. (2003b). *Symantec Internet Security Threat Report Volume IV.* Retrieved from http://enterprisesecurity.symantec.com/content.cfm?articleid=1539&EID=0%

Tamilselvan & Sankaranarayanan. (2007). *Prevention of Blackhole Attack in MANET.* The 2nd International Conference on Wireless Broadband and Ultra Wideband Communications (AusWireless).

Tangpong, Kesidis, Yuan, & Hurson. (2007). *Robust Sybil Detection for MANETs.* IEEE.

Thangadurai, K., & Anchugam, C. V. (2013). *Survey of routing Protocols in Mobile Ad hoc Network. ICIESMS.* Enathi, Madurai: Vickram Engineering College.

Vaithiyanathan, G. S. R., Edna, E. N., & Radha, S. (2010). *A Novel method for Detection and Elimination of Modification Attack and TTL attack in NTP based routing algorithm.* 2010 International Conference on Recent Trends in Information, Telecommunication and Computing. doi:10.1109/ITC.2010.23

Weaver, N., Paxson, V., Staniford, S., & Cunningham, R. (2003). *A taxonomy of Computer Worms. First Workshop on Rapid Malcode (WORM).*

Xerox Palo Alto Research Center. (2003). *Parc history.* Retrieved from http://www.parc.xerox.com/about/history/default.html

Xiaopeng & Wei. (2007). *A Novel Gray Hole Attack Detection Scheme for Mobile Ad-Hoc Networks.* 2007 IFIP International Conference on Network and Parallel Computing – Workshops.

Chapter 5
Attacks in Wireless Sensor Networks

George William Kibirige
Department of Informatics, Sokoine University of Agriculture, Tanzania

Camilius A. Sanga
Department of Informatics, Sokoine University of Agriculture, Tanzania

ABSTRACT

Wireless Sensor Networks (WSN) consists of large number of low-cost, resource-constrained sensor nodes. The constraints of the WSN which make it to be vulnerable to attacks are based on their characteristics which include: low memory, low computation power, they are deployed in hostile area and left unattended, small range of communication capability and low energy capabilities. Examples of attacks which can occur in a WSN are sinkhole attack, selective forwarding attack and wormhole attack. One of the impacts of these attacks is that, one attack can be used to launch other attacks. This book chapter presents an exploration of the analysis of the existing solutions which are used to detect and identify passive and active attack in WSN. The analysis is based on advantages and limitations of the proposed solutions.

1. INTRODUCTION

Wireless Sensor Networks (WSN) consists of small nodes with ability to sense and send data to base station (Rong, Eggen, & Cheng, 2011). WSN is used in different applications, for example in military activities, where there is a need of tracking movement of enemies. Also, it is used in fire detection and healthy service for monitoring heart beat (Chen, Song & Hsieh, 2010; Sharma & Ghose, 2010; Teng & Zhang, 2010). Unfortunately, most of WSN are deployed in unfriendly area and normally left unattended. Furthermore, many routing protocols used in WSN do not consider security aspect due to resource constraints which include: low computational power, low memory, low power supply and low communication range (Martins & Guyennet, 2010; Ngai, Liu, & Lyu, 2006). These constraints create chance for several attackers to easily attack WSN. There are two types of attacks, namely: passive and active attacks. In passive attack, a malicious node only eavesdrops upon the packet contents, while in

DOI: 10.4018/978-1-4666-8761-5.ch005

active attack; it may imitate, drop or modify legitimate packets (Sanzgiri, Dahill, Levine, Shields, & Belding-Royer, 2002). Examples of active attacks are sinkhole and selective forwarding attack. Example of passive attack is wormhole attack. In selective forwarding attack such attack adversary node creates their own path so attacker can drop the data packet and perform spy on those dropped data packet (Patel & Manoranjitham, 2013). This type of attack is difficult to detect (Tripathi, Gaur, Laxmi, & Jatav, 2012). Sinkhole attack is an active attack implemented in network layer where an adversary tries to attract many traffic with the aim of preventing base station from receiving a complete sensing data from nodes (Samundiswary, Sathian, & Dananjayan, 2010). Wormhole attack occurs when two or more adversary node create a higher level virtual tunnel between those two adversary nodes and advertise high link quality so that all other neighbors node transfer data packet through the virtual tunnel (Verma & Singh, 2011).

The purpose of this book chapter is to review existing solutions used to detect passive and active attack which include selective forwarding, wormhole, blackhole and sinkhole. Different solutions which are being used to detect and prevent attacks are suggested (Krontiris, Dimitriou, Giannetsos, & Mpasoukos, 2008; Tumrongwittayapak & Varakulsiripunth, 2009; Ngai, Liu & Lyu, 2007; BabuKaruppiah, Vidhya, & Rajaram, 2013; Sheela, Kumar, & Mahadevan, 2011; Kibirige & Sanga, 2015). Rule based detection solution as proposed by Krontiris, Giannetsos and Dimitriou (2008) to detect sinkhole attack. All the rules focus on node impersonation and are implanted in intrusion detection system. The intruder is easily detected when violate either of the rules. BabuKaruppiah, Vidhy and Rajaram (2013) proposed an energy efficient wormhole detection technique by traffic analysis in WSN. The technique use statistical method and involve base station in the detection process. Another centralized solution which involves base station in detection process is called a non cryptography scheme which use mobile agent in the network to prevent sinkhole attack (Sheela, Kumar, & Mahadevan, 2011).

This book chapter is organized into five sections. Section 2 presents the discussion of sinkhole, wormhole, blackhole and selective forwarding attacks and their mechanism. Section 3 presents the challenges in detecting attacks in WSN. Section 4 presents different approaches to detect wormhole, sinkhole, blackhole and selective forwarding attacks. Finally, section 5 concludes by proposing future work.

2. REVIEW OF WSN ATTACKS

2.1. Sinkhole Attack

Sinkhole attack is an insider attack where an intruder compromises a node inside the network and launches an attack (Ngai, Liu, & Lyu, 2007; Kibirige & Sanga, 2015). The compromised node try to attract all the traffic from neighbor nodes based on the routing metric in routing protocol. Due to communication pattern of WSN, there are many to one communication where each node sends data to base station. This makes WSN vulnerable to sinkhole attack (Ngai & Liu, 2007).

The following subsections present the techniques used in MintRoute protocol in launching sinkhole attack (Figure 1).

Sinkhole Attack in MintRoute Protocol

MintRoute protocol is a type of protocol which is commonly used in WSN. It was designed purposely for the WSN. It is suitable for sensor nodes which have minimum storage capacity, low computation power

Figure 1. Sinkhole attack in MintRoute protocol (Krontiris et al., 2008)

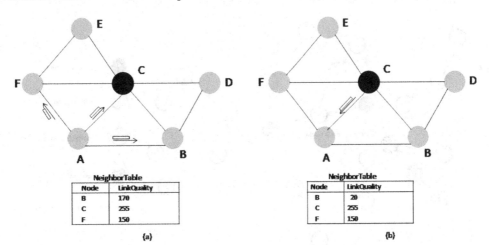

and limited power supply. MintRoute protocol uses link quality as a metric to choose the best route to send packet to the Base Station (Krontiris et al., 2008; Kibirige & Sanga, 2015).

Figure 1 show six sensor nodes A, B, C, D, E, and F. Node C is malicious, and it is used to launch a sinkhole attack. The Figure 1 shows a route table of node A with IDs of its neighbors with their corresponding link quality. The parent node is node B but node C advertises its link quality with a value of 255 which is maximum value. Node A does not change its parent node until the node B's link quality fall to 25 below the absolute value.

In Figure 1, the malicious node can send new update route packet that the link quality fall up to 20 and impersonate node B so that node A believe the packet come from node B. Node A will update its route table and change the parent node to node C (Krontiris et al., 2008). The attacker uses node impersonation to launch an attack.

2.2. Selective Forwarding Attack

Selective Forwarding attack is one of the type that malicious node drop packet instead of forwarding to the base station. Based on this behavior, the Selective Forwarding attack is smarter attacks than the Sinkhole attacks (Tumrongwittayapak & Varakulsiripunth, 2009). The attacker selectively drops packets based on some predefined criterion, which makes it even harder to detect. The adversary only needs to ensure the presence of one compromised node in each path to compromise the system. The attacker is selected either on the basis of the packets' contents or packets' source/origin address(s) (Tumrongwittayapak & Varakulsiripunth, 2009). The attackers have another advantage because in WSN the traditional transport layer protocol fail to guarantee that packets are not maliciously dropped (Wan, Campbell, & Krishnamurthy, 2002; Sankarasubramaniam, Akan, & Akyildiz, 2003). They are not designed to deal with malicious attacks. The critical mission application such as military surveillance and forest fire monitoring can be inactive by selective forward attack. They can also corrupt a number of existing routing protocols such as TinyOS beaconing and Directed Diffusion (Intanagonwiwat, Govindan, & Estrin, 2000).

Figure 2. Selective forwarding attacks (Tumrongwittayapak & Varakulsiripunth, 2009)

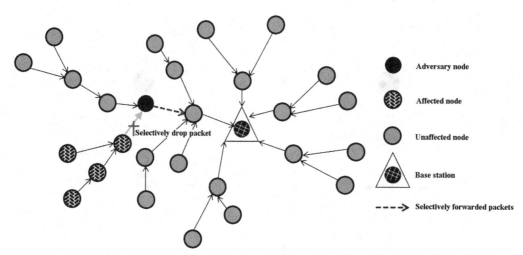

Figure 2 shows a selective forwarding attack where attack drops the packet based on the source address. In Figure 2, the adversary node drops all the packets from source nodes and forwards the packet from other nodes.

2.3. Wormhole Attack

Wormhole attack is one of the passive attacks in network layer in WSN which causes severe threat inside network or between networks (Verma & Singh, 2011). The passive attack malicious nodes do not change or interfere the packet content, it eavesdrops the packet content. It is considered as one of the deadlier attack based on its behavior of disrupting the packets' route which reduces the network performance. In this attack, two or more attacker creates a virtual tunnel (Wormhole link) between those two attacker nodes. Then, they advertise high link quality so that all other nodes transfer data packet through the virtual tunnel (Verma & Singh, 2011). This kind of attack puts the adversary in powerful position compared to other attacks because the attack does not need any knowledge of cryptograph. Even if the WSN infrastructure provides confidentiality, integrity and authenticity (CIA) still wormhole attack is possible and an adversary does not have cryptographic keys (Xu, Chen, Ford, & Makedon, 2007).

Figure 3 shows an example of wormhole attack. Two adversary nodes near to the base station create a powerful link between themselves. All the nodes that close to adversary nodes will use this link to forward their packet instead of their normal multi-hop routing. All traffic in the target area will channel through the wormhole.

2.4. Blackhole Attack

Blackhole attack is one of the types of denial of services attack in WSN (Figure 4). It is similar to selective forwarding attack but can change the content of the packet before transmitting or dropping the packets from the neighbor nodes. This type of attack happens with the help from adversary node which is outside the WSN network. It normally attacks several nodes in the network then reprogram them. It changes affected nodes in such a way instead of receiving and forwarding packets to their neighbor nodes, they

Figure 3. Wormhole attack using two powerful adversary nodes (Chen, Song, & Hsieh, 2010)

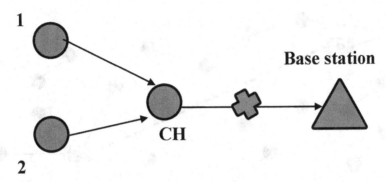

just drop those packets or selective forward the packet based on the malicious filtering process. They can also change the content of packets before transmitting to their neighbor. Blackhole attack achieves this goal using the following strategy: (i) it attracts all the traffic to itself by advertising the powerful and attractive route to the base station (Singh, & Singh, 2013). (ii) it also have more energy than other nodes and end up becoming cluster head of other nodes because they are not using energy in packet transmission (Iqbal, Srinivas, Sudarshan, & Kashyap, 2014).

3. CHALLENGES ON DETECTION OF WSN ATTACKS

Based on the literature review for detection and prevention of WSN attacks (Table 1), the following are the main challenges.

3.1. Communication Pattern in WSN

All the messages from sensor nodes in WSN are destined to base station. The transmission range of the nodes is generally limited and so each node seeks the assistance of its neighboring nodes in forwarding packets. This created opportunity to different attacks. For example, sinkhole attacks normally occur when compromised node send fake routing information to other nodes in the network with aim of attracting as many traffic as possible. Based on this communication pattern, the intruder will only compromise the nodes which are close to base station instead of targeting all nodes in the network. Also wormhole attack uses this advantage because the nodes need assistant in transmitting their packets. A malicious node in wormhole attack will act like normal nodes and participate in multi-hop communication. Those malicious nodes will advertise their powerful link to base station and attract all the packets from the nodes. Selective forwarding attack also uses this behavior to launch attack. This is a challenge because the communication pattern itself provides opportunity for attack.

3.2. WSN Attacks is Unpredictable

Selective forwarding attacks are very smart. They normally drop packets based in certain criteria. Sometimes they drop packets based on content or base on the node sender address. While the sinkhole attack change based on type of routing protocol. In WSN, the packets are transmitted based on routing

Figure 4. Blackhole attack (Singh, & Singh, 2013)

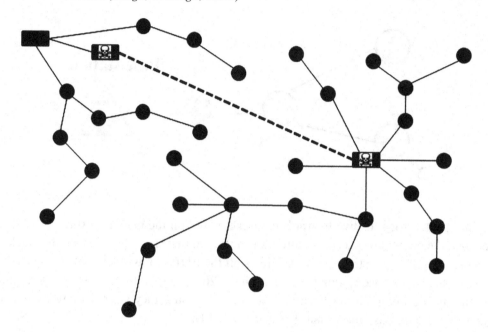

metric that are used by different routing protocols (El Kaissi, Kayssi, Chehab, & Dawy, 2005). The compromised node uses its routing metric that is based on routing protocol to lie to its neighbors in order to launch sinkhole attack. Then all the data from its neighbors to base station will pass through compromised node. Therefore, the sinkhole attack techniques change based on routing metric of routing protocol. Wormhole attack is passive attack which either drops the packets or selectively forwards the packet leading to network disruption. Wormhole attack does not require MAC protocol information as well as it is immune to cryptographic techniques (El Kaissi, Kayssi, Chehab, & Dawy, 2005). This makes it very difficult to detect.

3.3. Insider Attack

Insider attack and outsider attack are two categories of WSN attack. Outside attack is when intruder is not part of network. In inside attack, the intruder compromises one of the legitimate node through node tempering or through weakness in its system software then compromised node inject false information in network after listening to secret information. Inside attack can disrupt the network by modifying routing packet. Through compromised node sinkhole attack, wormhole attack and selective attack can be launched. The compromised node possesses adequate access privilege in the network and has knowledge pertaining to valuable information about the network topology this creates a challenge in detecting it. Based to this situation even cryptographic method cannot defend against insider attack although it provides integrity, confidentiality and authentication (Pathan & Al-S, 2011). Therefore, the internal attack has more serious impact on victim system compared to outsider attack.

Table 1. Existing works on detection and prevention of attacks in WSN

Type of approach and attack detected	Proposed Solution	Results	Limitations/Advantages
Rule Based. Krontiris et al. (2007) Sinkhole attack	Extended intrusion detection system (IDS) which can detect sinkhole attack.	-the success of IDS depend on the increase number of watchdog -When the network density increase the false negative rate decrease.	**Limitations** -Memory and network overhead was created. -They used MintRoute protocol -Node impersonation was the focus of the rules. **Advantages** -More secure and robust measure can be developed based on valuable principle they develop.
Rule Based. Krontiris et al. (2008) Sinkhole attack	Proposed detection rules that identify legitimate node in case there attack.	-They showed how vulnerabilities of Multihope can be exploited by sinkhole node and suggest the rules which make the protocol more resilient.	**Limitation** -They did not show practically how those rules can prevent attack. -All the rules are only detecting attack but cannot give ID of sinkhole node. -They assume attacker has the same power as normal node and can capture sensor node and change the internal state.
Trusted based model Pirzada and McDonald (2005) Wormhole	They implemented detection system in WSN that uses DSR protocol -Each node participates in detection. The node uses its trust information to compute the most trustworthy path to a particular destination	- the packet loss in nodes executing the DSR-mod protocol was 30% lower than those executing the standard DSR or GPSR protocol - there was increase in the packet latency and deviation from the optimal paths - Multiple colluding nodes may not be detected if they located along the path of the data connections	**Limitation-** Model uses features of the DSR protocol - Node transceivers are omni directional and that they can receive and transmit in all directions -Multiple colluding were not detected, they suggest using of IDS
Anomaly based. Tumrongwittayapak and Varakulsiripunth (2009) Selective Forwarding attack	-They proposed detection solution based on monitoring traffic packet -Their proposed solution required support from extra monitor node	-False positive rate decrease when threshold increased -False negative rate increase when threshold increased -shows percentage of detecting is equal 128Bytes	**Limitation** - A BS is placed at the center of the network to collect data from the sensors -They assumed no packet drop during simulated.
Anomaly based. Tumrongwittayapak, and Varakulsiripunth (2009) Sinkhole attack	-They proposed detection solution based on received signal strength indicator(RSSI) -Their proposed solution required support from extra monitor node	-For 0 to 40% percentage of message drop the detection rate is 100% -False positive rate was 0 for 0-40% of message drop but increase when percentage drop increase -The same applied to false negative rate with the more message drop the more negative rate.	**Limitation** -They assume sensor network are static -No instant attack -Base station remain 0,0 position -Base station and extra monitor node are physically protected. -Their proposed solution cannot detect attack if it happened instantly after network deployment.
Anomaly based. Choi et al. (2009) Sinkhole attack	They proposed method that can detect sinkhole attack that used LQI(link quality indicator).	-The probability of detection increase when number of detector nodes increase -detection rate increase when detector node increase -The false positive rate depend on extent of tolerance value (constant value which will show if changes is beyond abnormal)	**Limitations** -All sensor node have no mobility -The detection of sinkhole occurs when detector node is between sinkhole node and source node and sinkhole and base station -The detector nodes have high source of energy than sensor nodes **Advantage** -Detector node communicate themselves through exclusive channel

continued on following page

Table 1. Continued

Type of approach and attack detected	Proposed Solution	Results	Limitations/Advantages
Anomaly based. Yurong Xu et al. (2008) (Wormhole attack)	-Proposed algorithm uses a hop counting technique as a probe procedure -The proposed algorithm uses a diameter of local map feature to detect abnormalities caused by wormholes.	- They introduce to increase detection. When the value is decreased, the accuracy of detecting wormhole attacks is increased at the same time false alarms is increased -Under simulation overall detection rate of nearly 100% - in case of shorter wormholes that are less than three hops long the detection rate was over 80%	**Limitations** -they used uniform placement nodes. - The location of the wormhole was randomized within the network. -they assume that a wormhole is bi-directional with two endpoints -they assume wormhole node does not send a message without receiving an inbound message. -Wormhole is passive and static -the algorithm cannot detect multi-end wormholes
Anomaly based. Sharmila, and Umamaheswari, (2011) Sinkhole attack	-They proposed message digest algorithm to detect sinkhole node.	-The results show the algorithm worked well when malicious nodes are below 50% -False positive rate was 20% (due to packet drop) that figure obtained when malicious node reach 50 -False negative error was 10% but was increasing when malicious node reach above 40	**Limitations** -Network throughput, overhead and communication cost was not calculated -The performance was not good when there is node collision, limited transmitted power and packet drops -Only one advertisement is considered at a time, after computation another take place **Advantage** -The algorithm achieve data integrity and authenticity
Anomaly based. Patel and Manoranjitham (2008) Wormhole	-They proposed a techniques of detecting wormhole attack WSN that used MintRoute protocol -the proposed technique is used to analyzed the packet received ratio, packet drop ratio and throughput to detect wormhole attack.	-There is no data on false negative or false positive -The graph show changes in drop packet ratio, throughput and packet reception ratio when wormhole attack in	**Limitations** -Detection done on base on data packet flow -They used MintRoute protocol -The data show wormhole was detected.
Key Management Papadimitriou et al. (2009) Sinkhole attack	-They proposed two RESIST protocols which increase resilience to sinkhole attack in WSN	-Results show that RESIST-0 has high resilience to sinkhole attack (it does not allow node to lie about their distance to base station) than other protocol	**Limitations** -Resist-0 is very expensive it require two additional message to a packet -In their simulation message losses and collusion were not considered -Collusion node has impact on RESIST-0 not in RESIST-1 -Their routing algorithm relying on tree-based topology construction -Route tree is build by hop distance **Advantage** -RESIST-1 prevent malicious nodes from changing their advertised distance to the sink more than one hop -RESIST-0 completely stops any lying about distance.

continued on following page

Table 1. Continued

Type of approach and attack detected	Proposed Solution	Results	Limitations/Advantages
Statistical based Roghui et al. (2009) wormhole attack	- They developed system that used beacon nodes to detect and locate wormhole nodes in WSN	-The detection algorithm was successful with zero false tolerance rate.	**Limitation** - they assume that the beacon-to-sensor communication range is the same with the sensor-to-sensor communication range - they assume that all beacon nodes are uniquely identified - they assume that a wormhole link is bidirectional with two end points and network nodes are not compromised by attackers. **Disadvantages** - The communication cost is relatively high because of the flood-based approach for the hop counting procedure -Their algorithm is very expensive
Statistical based Chen et al. (2010) Sinkhole attack	They developed an algorithm which detect sinkhole attack and identified intruder.	-From first simulation the detection time increase when threshold (CPU value) become bigger -Also the false positive rate decrease when threshold become bigger. -From the second simulation the detection time did not change too much but the false positive rate increase due to increase in traffic	**Limitations** -Base station makes the final decision on which node is malicious -No results on the network overhead -The scheme will not detect attack if it launch instantly after deployed -Assumption-base station is trustworthy and it participates in detection system. **Advantages** .Their algorithm showed that it can detect malicious node in short time with low false positive rate
Statistical based BabuKaruppiah et al. (2002) (Wormhole attack)	-they proposed an energy efficient wormhole detection techniques by traffic analysis in WSN	- The wormhole in the network was detected successfully - From the simulated results it is inferred that the savings in power consumed of a wireless sensor node is 5% which is considered to be a great reduction when a WSN is considered -No data on false negative rate, false positive rate and throughput	**Limitation** -The network is static
Hybrid base Coppolino et al. (2007) Sinkhole attack	They proposed IDS which is able to protect critical information from attacks directs from its WSN.	-Detection rate was 95-97% when malicious node modified sensor packet. -Detection rate was 93-96% when malicious node modified the received and control packets -False positive rate is 3% -IDS usage in real sensor network was 734bytes (RAM) and 3208bytes (ROM)	**Advantages** -Their solution satisfied the available resource in sensor nodes -Their solution proved to detect sinkhole attack -They used both anomaly and misuse based method

continued on following page

Table 1. Continued

Type of approach and attack detected	Proposed Solution	Results	Limitations/Advantages
Hybrid base Yu and Xiao (2006) selective forwarding attack	- They developed a light multi-hope Acknowledgement based detection scheme. - the developed scheme uses both anomaly and key management detection approach	- when the channel error rate is less than 10%, detection alarm is close to 100% - detection alarm falls when channel error rate increases over 10% - On the whole, the detection scheme works well to achieve over 80% even when the channel error rate is 15% - when the channel error rate increases, relative communication overhead increases very little. - The number of malicious nodes also impact the relative communication overhead	**Limitations** - detection scheme is appropriate to use in a mission-critical application such as military reconnaissance -they assume during the deployment phase each sensor can acquire its geographical position and loosely synchronize its time with the base station. - their scheme does not rely on geographic routing - adversary cannot successfully compromise a node during the short deployment phase - each node shares a master secret key with the base station and a node can establish a pairwise key with another node
A non cryptographic Sheela et al. (2011) Sinkhole attack	They proposed scheme which uses mobile agent to defend against this attack	-Probability of detecting sinkhole is decrease when nodes increase -Node average energy decrease as time goes up because of storage information. -The algorithm create high network overheads	**Limitations** -Mobile wireless sensor network -No specification of exactly number of MA (mobile agent) in network -Matrix method is very complex with relate to available resources -MA communicate with sensor nodes at active mode only **Advantages** -MA used dummy data to detect modification -MA has sufficient power to run its activities
symmetric key cryptographic Singh and Singh (2013) Black-hole attack	-They used IPsec (Internet protocol security) protocol that uses symmetric key cryptography to secure data in WSN - It works in IP packet level - They used two security services authentication and confidentiality of packet	-The throughput increase in small amount when IPsec was implemented in WSN -The delay in end to end data packet decreased when IPsec protocol was implemented in WSN. -The value of jitter decreased when IPsec protocol implemented in WSN. -The packet received in WSN increased from 15 to 21 out of 48 when IPSec protocol received	**Limitations** -Mobile node used in WSN -They use four metrics to evaluate their proposed protocol include throughput, delay on end to end packet transmitted, jitter and total packet received **Advantages** -The proposed solution efficiently prevent blackhole attack

3.4. Resource Constraints

The limited power supply, low communication range, low memory capacity and low computational power are the main constraints in WSN that hinder implementation of strong security mechanism. The strong cryptographic method that is used in other network cannot be implemented in network with limited resources due to low computational power and low memory capacity. Therefore cryptographic algorithms which require less strong key are considered to be viable in an environment with limited available resources.

3.5. Physical Attack

A WSN normally is deployed in hostile environment and left unattended. This provides an opportunity for an intruder to attack a node physically and get access to all necessary information (Jaydip Sen, 2009).

4. APPROACHES FOR SECURING WSN

Many researchers are working on wireless sensor network field to provide security mechanisms to match the resource constrained due to growing demand of applications in sensitive areas (Krontiris, Dimitriou, Giannetsos, & Mpasoukos, 2008; Özdemir et al., 2008; Roghui et al., 2009; Coppolino, D'Antonio, Romano, & Spagnuolo, 2010; Papadimitriou et al., 2009) . Approaches that are used to detect and identify different types of attacks such as wormhole attack, selective forwarding attack and sinkhole attack are classified into rules based, key management, anomaly based, trust base-model, statistical method and hybrid based.

4.1. Rule Based Approach

The rules are designed based on the behavior or technique used to launch sinkhole attack. Normally rules are imbedded in intrusion detection system (IDS) which runs on each sensor nodes. In a sensor node, rules are applied to the packet transmitted through the network nodes. If any node violates the rules it is considered as adversary and isolated from the network. Among the existing researches which used rules based approach include Krontiris et al. (2008). Krontiris used rule based approach to detect sinkhole attack. They create two rules and implanted in IDS. When one of the rules is violated by one of the nodes, the IDS trigger an alarm but it does not provide node ID of compromised node. The first rule "for each overhead route update packet the ID of the sender must be different from your node ID". The second rule "for each overhead route update packet the ID of the sender must be one of the node ID in its neighbors". Also Krontiris et al. (2008) used the same approaches using two rules. The first rule "rule for each overhead route update packet the ID of the sender must be one of node ID in your neighbors". The second rule "for each pair of parent and child node their link quality they advertise for the link between them, the difference cannot exceed 50''.

4.2. Trust Based Model

Trusted based model is the detection model which uses trust information to select safest path. In this model, each node generates its trust information and use it to calculate the most reliable path to the destination by avoiding intermediate malicious node. Pirzada and McDonald (2005) presented a trust-based scheme to detect and avoid wormhole attack. The scheme uses Dynamic Source Routing Protocol (DSR) and it allows each node to participate in detection process by execute trust mode. Each node privately evaluates other nodes and maintains that information. Each node, based upon its own experience, rewards collaborating nodes for their behavior and punishes malicious nodes for their nasty conduct. Based on this mode of communication, each source node uses its trust information to compute the most trustworthy path to a particular destination by circumventing intermediary malicious nodes. Özdemir et al. (2008) also developed a trusted based approach to detect wormhole attack. A wormhole node have the least trust level that drops all the packets and if all the packets sent reach the destination then the neighboring node of a source node will have the highest trust level. The system combines both time and trust model.

4.3. Anomaly-Based Detection

In anomaly based detection, the normal user behavior is defined and intrusion detection is done through searching for anything that is anomalous in the network. In this method, intrusion is considered as anomalous activity because it looks abnormal compare to normal behavior. The rule based and statistical approaches are also included under anomaly based detection approach. Tumrongwittayapak and Varakulsiripunth (2009) proposed light detection scheme called Traffic Monitor Based Selective Forwarding (TMBSF) attacks, which is one of the anomaly based approach. In brief, the scheme uses EM (Extra Monitor) nodes to eavesdrop and monitor all traffic of the network. Tumrongwittayapak and Varakulsiripunth (2009) proposed another system that used RSSI (Received Signal Strength Indicator) value with the help of EM nodes to detect sinkhole attack. The EM had high communication range and one of their functions is to calculate RSSI of node and send to base station with ID of source and next hop. This process happens instantly when node are deployed. Base station uses that RSSI value to calculate VGM (visual geographical map). The VGM shows the position of each node, then later when EM send updated RSSI value and base station identify there is change in packet flow from previous data this indicate there is sinkhole attack. The compromised node is identified and isolated from the network by base station using VGM value. However, if attack is launched immediately after network deployment, the system will not be able to detect that attack (Tumrongwittaya & Varakulsiripunth, 2009).

Xu, Chen, Ford and Makedon (2008) proposed an algorithm to detect wormhole attack in WSN using hop counting techniques as probe procedure. Using this technique, each node calculates the local map for its neighbors based on hop coordination that obtained through hop counting. Xu et al. (2008) developed a formula to calculate the diameter of local map. The diameter is used to detect wormhole attack. The existence of wormhole in local maps causes the diameter to increase compared to the diameters for the same nodes in the network without wormhole.

Patel and Manoranjitham (2013) proposed a technique of detecting wormhole attack in WSN that uses MintRoute protocol. The technique is used to analyze the packet received ratio, packet drop ratio and throughput to detect wormhole attack. These packet received ratio, packet drop ratio and throughput generated in MintRoute protocol is based on received packet and total generated packet of the nodes. The throughput after launching wormhole attack decreased compare before the attack. The packet drop ratio is increased during wormhole attack than before attack. Also, the number of packet reception ratio decreased in wormhole attack than before attack.

4.4. Statistical Method

In statistical approaches, the data associated with certain activities of the nodes in network is studied and recorded. For example, monitoring the normal packet transmitted between the nodes or monitoring resource depletion of the nodes like CPU usage is done using statistical method. Then, the adversary or compromised node is detected by comparing the actual behavior with the threshold value which used as reference, if any nodes exceed that value is considered as an intruder. He Roghui et al. (2009) proposed a system that uses beacon nodes to detect and locate wormhole nodes in WSN. Every beacon nodes are able to know the number of hop to other beacon nodes and their coordinate using counting hop techniques. The presence of worm link may reduce the hop distance significantly while the corresponding straight line distance calculated by beacons remains unchanged. When the difference between straight line distance and hop distance is large than threshold this indicate that there is a wormhole attack.

Chen et al. (2010) proposed statistical GRSh (Girshick-RubinShyriaev)–based algorithm for detecting malicious nodes in WSN. Base station calculates the difference of CPU usage of each node after monitoring the CPU usage of each node in fixed time. Base station identifies whether a node is malicious or not after comparing the difference of CPU usage with the threshold.

Dynamic trust management system developed to detect and eliminate multiple attacks such as sinkhole attack (Roy et al., 2008). Each node calculates the trust of its neighbor node based on experience of interaction; recommendation and knowledge then sends to base station. The base station decides which node is sinkhole after it receives several trust values from other nodes. Therefore, the trust value of the node which falls beyond the normal value 0.5 is considered as sinkhole attack (Roy, Singh, & Choudhury, 2008).

BabuKaruppiah et al. (2013) proposed an energy efficient wormhole detection technique by traffic analysis in WSN. The techniques involve base station in the process. At the beginning the base station saved the entire node IDS of network. The distance between the individual node and its neighboring nodes is calculated when the individual node create the route with his neighbor nodes. Through this the neighbor list is identified and saved in the base station, this happens to every node. This approach assumes that each node has a counter and it increments automatically when a node process data. A maximum threshold counter was set for the counter and saved to base station. If the counter is greater than threshold the alert message raised to base station and that node is included in the suspicions set. Then later the base station sent 'an hello' message to suspicions node and its neighbor nodes. If the suspicions node and its neighbor reply to base station then that node is not wormhole. The suspicions node is considered wormhole attack if the reply doesn't come from the neighbors.

4.5. Hybrid Based Intrusion Detection

The combination of both anomaly and signature based or misused based is used in this approach. The false positive rate which is produced by anomaly based is reduced in this approach due to the use of both methods. Also the advantage of this approach is to be able to catch any suspicious nodes which their signature is not included in detection database.

Coppolino and Spagnuolo (2010) proposed hybrid Intrusion detection system (HIDS) to detect sinkhole attack and other attacks. They used detection agent which was responsible for identifying sinkhole attack. The hybrid intrusion detection was attached to sensor node and share resource of that node. The suspicious nodes were inserted to the blacklist based on anomalous behavior after analyzed the collected data from neighbors. Then the list is sent to central agent to make final decision based on feature of attack pattern (misused based). Similar to solution proposed by Tumrongwittayapak and Varakulsiripunth (2009), it is designed for static WSN.

Yu and Xiao (2006) developed a light multi-hope Acknowledgement based detection scheme to detect selective forwarding attack in WSN. The scheme used both anomaly and key management detection approach. One application of this scheme is on military application where sensor networks for reconnaissance of opposing forces need to be determined before attack. The scheme allows both the base station and source nodes to collect attack alarm information from intermediate nodes. The scheme obtains those alarm information whenever intermediate nodes in a packet forwarding path detect any malicious packet dropping. The scheme uses both public key and symmetric key. The key server loads the unique secret key to the every node. The key is shared with each node and base station and used to encrypt sensor report and generate MACs (Message Authentication Codes) for the report. The scheme also used OHC (One way Hash Chain) to establish one-to-many authentication among sensor nodes, which might be multiple hops. However the scheme focuses on an inside attacks where an adversary compromise a legitimate node.

4.6. Key Management

In key management approach, the integrity and authenticity of packet travels within the network is protected by using encryption and decryption key. Any packet transmitted in the network is added with another message in a way that to access the message which requires a key and any small modification of the message can be easily detected (Papadimitriou et al., 2009). Those keys also help nodes to check if the message comes from base station and check the authenticity of the message.

Papadimitriou et al. (2009) proposed a cryptographic approach in routing protocol to address the problem of sinkhole attack. Each node obtain public key which is used to verify if the message comes from base station. They also used pair of public and private keys for authentication and sign data message. Fessant et al. (2011) proposed two protocols which use cryptographic method to increase the resilience of sinkhole attack. Both protocols prevent malicious node from lying about their advertised distances to base station. However, they did not show the memory usage of their protocols and message size.

Singh and Singh (2013) proposed IPsec protocols that use a symmetric key cryptographic method to prevent of black-hole attack. The protocols prevent the launching of black-hole attack in mobile WSN. The protocol includes two protocols Encapsulating Security Protocol (ESP) and Authentication Header (AH) to accomplish their objectives. The proposed protocol managed to prevent black-hole attack in WSN.

5. DISCUSSIONS

This book chapter has shown that most approaches detect and prevent passive and active attacks in WSN. Rule based approach is capable to detect sinkhole attack but it creates memory and network overhead.

Trusted base model approach also is used in detection of wormhole attack. The approach uses DSR protocol and is able to detect wormhole attack but multiple colluding may not be detected by this approach.

Anomaly based approach also is used to detect selective forwarding attack, wormhole attack and sinkhole attack but it deals only with static WSN. This approach created high false positive rate when there is high message dropping and cannot detect multi-end wormholes.

Key management is another approach which focuses on resistance to sinkhole attack but not does not detect or eliminate the attack.

Statistical based approach is capable to detect wormhole attack and sinkhole attack but it does not give result of the network overhead. Also, this approach cannot detect an instant attack after WSN is deployed. False positive rate is the main drawback to this approach.

Hybrid approach uses the combination of both anomaly and signature-based. This approach can detect sinkhole attack and selective forwarding attack but is designed for static WSN. A non cryptographic is another approach which detect sinkhole attack but it creates high network overhead.

IPsec protocol that uses symmetric key encryption is an alternative approach which is used for detecting blackhole attack in WSN. The approach works well with consideration of limited resource constraints of WSN node such as energy consumption, low memory and processing power and communication bandwidth.

All the reviewed approaches have the capability of detecting, identifying and providing resistance to selective forwarding attack, wormhole attack and sinkhole attack. The major drawbacks of the reviewed approaches includes high network and memory overhead, create high false positive rate and some are not able to work on mobile WSN (i.e. dynamic WSN).

6. CONCLUSION AND FUTURE WORK

Based on literature review from this book chapter, researchers are trying to look for information security technology solutions for detecting, identifying and providing prevention solutions to sinkhole attack, wormhole attack and selective forwarding attack in WSN. Some researchers use anomaly detection method, other use trusted based- model, rule based, hybrid method and key management to detect and identify passive and active attacks. Security challenges corresponding with availability of resources and mobility of wireless sensor nodes is a researchable topic. Some researchers provide solutions for only static and on mobile network which are dynamic. Few researchers managed to validate their security system using real/actual WSN. Also some of results showed low detection rate, high network overhead and high communication cost. The future solutions should focus on reducing high network and memory overhead, increase detection rate and must be validated in real/actual WSN environment. Using real time validation, it will be easy to check if the proposed solutions meet the available resources of mobile WSN.

REFERENCES

BabuKaruppiah, A., Vidhya, G. S., & Rajaram, S. (2013). An Energy Efficient Wormhole Detection Technique by Traffic Analysis in Wireless Sensor Networks. *International Journal of Engineering and Computer Science*.

Chen, C., Song, M., & Hsieh, G. (2010). Intrusion detection of sinkhole attacks in large-scale wireless sensor networks. In *Wireless Communications, Networking and Information Security (WCNIS), 2010 IEEE International Conference on* (pp. 711-716). IEEE.

Choi, B. G., Cho, E. J., Kim, J. H., Hong, C. S., & Kim, J. H. (2009). *A sinkhole attack detection mechanism for LQI based mesh routing in WSN*. ICOIN.

Coppolino, L., D'Antonio, S., Romano, L., & Spagnuolo, G. (2010). An intrusion detection system for critical information infrastructures using wireless sensor network technologies. In *Critical Infrastructure (CRIS), 2010 5th International Conference on* (pp. 1-8). IEEE. doi:10.1109/CRIS.2010.5617547

Dallas, D., Leckie, C., & Ramamohanarao, K. (2007). Hop-count monitoring: Detecting sinkhole attacks in wireless sensor networks. In *Networks, 2007. ICON 2007. 15th IEEE International Conference on* (pp. 176-181). IEEE.

El Kaissi, R. Z., Kayssi, A., Chehab, A., & Dawy, Z. (2005). *DAWWSEN: A defense mechanism against wormhole attacks in wireless sensor networks* (Doctoral dissertation). American University of Beirut, Department of Electrical and Computer Engineering.

Intanagonwiwat, C., Govindan, R., & Estrin, D. (2000). Directed diffusion: a scalable and robust communication paradigm for sensor networks. In *Proceedings of the 6th annual international conference on Mobile computing and networking* (pp. 56-67). ACM. doi:10.1145/345910.345920

Ioannis, K., Dimitriou, T., & Freiling, F. C. (2007). Towards intrusion detection in wireless sensor networks. In *Proc. of the 13th European Wireless Conference*.

Iqbal, S., Srinivas, S. P. A., Sudarshan, G., & Kashyap, S. (2014). Comparison of Different Attacks on Leach Protocol In WSN. *International Journal of Electrical. Electronics and Data Communication, 2,* 16–19.

Jatav, V. K., Tripathi, M., Gaur, M. S., & Laxmi, V. (2012). Wireless sensor networks: Attack models and detection. In *Proceedings of the IACSIT Hong Kong conferences IPCSIT 30,* 144-149.

Kibirige, G. W., & Sanga, C. A. (2015). A Survey on Detection of Sinkhole Attack in Wireless Sensor Network. *International Journal of Computer Science and Information Security, 13*(5), 1–9.

Krontiris, I., Dimitriou, T., Giannetsos, T., & Mpasoukos, M. (2008). Intrusion detection of sinkhole attacks in wireless sensor networks. In *Algorithmic Aspects of Wireless Sensor Networks* (pp. 150–161). Springer Berlin Heidelberg. doi:10.1007/978-3-540-77871-4_14

Krontiris, I., Giannetsos, T., & Dimitriou, T. (2008). Launching a sinkhole attack in wireless sensor networks; the intruder side. In *Networking and Communications, 2008. WIMOB'08. IEEE International Conference on Wireless and Mobile Computing,* (pp. 526-531). IEEE.

Le Fessant, F., Papadimitriou, A., Viana, A. C., Sengul, C., & Palomar, E. (2012). A sinkhole resilient protocol for wireless sensor networks: Performance and security analysis. *Computer Communications, 35*(2), 234–248. doi:10.1016/j.comcom.2011.09.005

Martins, D., & Guyennet, H. (2010). Wireless sensor network attacks and security mechanisms: A short survey. In *Network-Based Information Systems (NBiS), 2010 13th International Conference on* (pp. 313-320). IEEE. doi:10.1109/NBiS.2010.11

Ngai, E. C., Liu, J., & Lyu, M. R. (2006). On the intruder detection for sinkhole attack in wireless sensor networks. In *Communications, 2006. ICC'06. IEEE International Conference on*. IEEE.

Ngai, E. C., Liu, J., & Lyu, M. R. (2007). An efficient intruder detection algorithm against sinkhole attacks in wireless sensor networks. *Computer Communications, 30*(11), 2353–2364. doi:10.1016/j.comcom.2007.04.025

Özdemir, S., Meghdadi, M., & Güler, Ý. (2008). A time and trust based wormhole detection algorithm for wireless sensor networks. In *3rd Information Security and Cryptology Conference (ISC'08)*.

Pandey, A., & Tripathi, R. C. (2010). A survey on wireless sensor networks security. *International Journal of Computers and Applications, 3*(2), 43–49. doi:10.5120/705-989

Papadimitriou, A., Le Fessant, F., Viana, A. C., & Sengul, C. (2009). Cryptographic protocols to fight sinkhole attacks on tree-based routing in wireless sensor networks. In *Secure Network Protocols, 2009. NPSec 2009. 5th IEEE Workshop on* (pp. 43-48). IEEE. doi:10.1109/NPSEC.2009.5342246

Patel, K., & Manoranjitham, M. T. (2013). Detection of wormhole attack in wireless sensor network. *International Journal of Engineering Research and Technology, 2(5)*.

Pathan, A. S. K. (Ed.). (2010). Security of self-organizing networks: MANET, WSN, WMN, VANET. CRC Press. doi:10.1201/EBK1439819197

Pirzada, A. A., & McDonald, C. (2005, May). Circumventing sinkholes and wormholes in wireless sensor networks. In *IWWAN'05: Proceedings of International Workshop on Wireless Ad-hoc Networks 71*.

Raghunandan, G. H., & Lakshmi, B. N. (2011). A comparative analysis of routing techniques for Wireless Sensor Networks. In *Innovations in Emerging Technology (NCOIET), 2011 National Conference on* (pp. 17-22). IEEE. doi:10.1109/NCOIET.2011.5738826

Rong, C. M., Eggen, S., & Cheng, H. B. (2011). A novel intrusion detection algorithm for wireless sensor networks. In *Wireless Communication, Vehicular Technology, Information Theory and Aerospace & Electronic Systems Technology (Wireless VITAE), 2011 2nd International Conference on* (pp. 1-7). IEEE. doi:10.1109/WIRELESSVITAE.2011.5940938

Ronghui, H., Guoqing, M., Chunlei, W., & Lan, F. (2009). Detecting and locating wormhole attacks in wireless sensor networks using beacon nodes. World Academy of Science, Engineering and Technology.

Roy, S. D., Singh, S. A., Choudhury, S., & Debnath, N. C. (2008). Countering sinkhole and black hole attacks on sensor networks using dynamic trust management. In *Computers and Communications, 2008. ISCC 2008. IEEE Symposium on* (pp. 537-542). IEEE. doi:10.1109/ISCC.2008.4625768

Samundiswary, P., Sathian, D., & Dananjayan, P. (2010). Secured greedy perimeter stateless routing for wireless sensor networks. *International Journal of Ad Hoc, Sensor & Ubiquitous Computing, 1(2)*.

Sankarasubramaniam, Y., Akan, Ö. B., & Akyildiz, I. F. (2003). ESRT: event-to-sink reliable transport in wireless sensor networks. In *Proceedings of the 4th ACM international symposium on Mobile ad hoc networking & computing* (pp. 177-188). ACM. doi:10.1145/778415.778437

Sanzgiri, K., Dahill, B., Levine, B. N., Shields, C., & Royer, E. M. B. (2002). A secure routing protocol for ad hoc networks. In *Network Protocols, 2002. Proceedings. 10th IEEE International Conference on* (pp. 78-87). IEEE. doi:10.1109/ICNP.2002.1181388

Sen, J. (2010). A survey on wireless sensor network security. *International Journal of Communication Networks and Information Security, 1(2)*, 55–78.

Sharma, K., & Ghose, M. K. (2010). Wireless sensor networks: An overview on its security threats. *IJCA*, 42-45.

Sharmila, S., & Umamaheswari, G. (2011). Detection of sinkhole attack in wireless sensor networks using message digest algorithms. In *Process Automation, Control and Computing (PACC), 2011 International Conference on* (pp. 1-6). IEEE. doi:10.1109/PACC.2011.5978973

Sheela, D., Naveen, K. C., & Mahadevan, G. (2011). A non cryptographic method of sink hole attack detection in wireless sensor networks. In *Recent Trends in Information Technology (ICRTIT), 2011 International Conference on* (pp. 527-532). IEEE. doi:10.1109/ICRTIT.2011.5972397

Singh, G., & Singh, J. (2013). Prevention of Blackhole Attack in Wireless Sensor Network using IPSec Protocol. *International Journal of Advanced Research in Computer Science, 4*(11), 45–49.

Singh, S., & Verma, H. K. (2011). Security for Wireless Sensor Network. *International Journal on Computer Science and Engineering, 3*(6), 2393–2399.

Teng, L., & Zhang, Y. (2010). SeRA: a secure routing algorithm against sinkhole attacks for mobile wireless sensor networks. In *Computer Modeling and Simulation, 2010. ICCMS'10. Second International Conference on*. IEEE. doi:10.1109/ICCMS.2010.95

Tumrongwittayapak, C., & Varakulsiripunth, R. (2009). Detecting Sinkhole attacks in wireless sensor networks. In ICCAS-SICE, 2009 (pp. 1966-1971). IEEE.

Tumrongwittayapak, C., & Varakulsiripunth, R. (2009). Detecting sinkhole attack and selective forwarding attack in wireless sensor networks. In *Information, Communications and Signal Processing, 2009. ICICS 2009. 7th International Conference on* (pp. 1-5). IEEE. doi:10.1109/ICICS.2009.5397594

Wan, C. Y., Campbell, A. T., & Krishnamurthy, L. (2002). PSFQ: a reliable transport protocol for wireless sensor networks. In *Proceedings of the 1st ACM international workshop on Wireless sensor networks and applications* (pp. 1-11). ACM. doi:10.1145/570738.570740

Xu, Y., Chen, G., Ford, J., & Makedon, F. (2008). Detecting wormhole attacks in wireless sensor networks. In Critical infrastructure protection (pp. 267-279). Springer US.

Yu, B., & Xiao, B. (2006). Detecting selective forwarding attacks in wireless sensor networks. In *Parallel and Distributed Processing Symposium, 2006. IPDPS 2006. 20th International*. IEEE.

ADDITIONAL READING

Akyildiz, I. F., Su, W., Sankarasubramaniam, Y., & Cayirci, E. (2002). Wireless sensor networks: A survey. *Computer Networks, 38*(4), 393–422. doi:10.1016/S1389-1286(01)00302-4

KEY TERMS AND DEFINITIONS

Active Attack: It is kind of security attack which try to modify the content of the message and they are normally interact with the system.

Attack: In computer science attack is any action of breaking either of three goals of security which includes confidentiality, integrity and availability.

Passive Attack: It is kind of security attack which does not modify the content of the message, does not interact with the system and they are difficult to detect.

Selective Forwarding Attack: This is kind of attack in Wireless Sensor Network where adversary node stay between the legitimate nodes and drop some packets instead of forward to the base station.

Sinkhole attack: This attack focus on deviate the data traffic from base station to the adversary node in Wireless Sensor Network.

Wireless Sensor Network: One of the categories of wireless network that consist of very small nodes that sense information within their diameter and send to the base station.

Wormhole Attack: It is kind of attack where attacker attract traffic in Wireless Network with the aim of snooping the data.

Chapter 6
Sensors Network:
In Regard with the Security Aspect and Counter Measures

Mamta Bachani
Mehran University of Engineering and Technology, Pakistan

Ahsan Memon
Mehran University of Engineering and Technology, Pakistan

Faisal Karim Shaikh
Mehran University of Engineering and Technology, Pakistan & Umm Al-Qura University, Saudi Arabia

ABSTRACT

This chapter aims to develop an understanding of sensor networks and the security threats posed to them, owing to the inherently insecure wireless nature. It also highlights the current security issues associated with the exchange of information and presents respective countermeasures that can be used to secure the network of malevolent behavior. It builds the reader's understanding of security threats by presenting an idealistic security mechanism and comparing it to currently practiced security mechanisms. Doing so, it identifies the security flaws in each mechanism, henceforth, enumerating a list of well-known security attacks that are connected to the respective security flaws. To provide a better understanding of security threats, the security attacks, in general, are discussed in the perspective of a network administrator, and an adversary. Their impact is also considered from the side of a network administrator and its respective benefits to the adversary. The chapter is later concluded along with future directives and an insight on requirements of forthcoming technologies.

INTRODUCTION

This chapter aims to construct a fundamental understanding of sensors, the respective wireless sensor networks formed with these sensors and the security concerns that arise from such networks along with the classical countermeasures that can be put into effect to detect, prevent and counter the security

DOI: 10.4018/978-1-4666-8761-5.ch006

fissures. The text in this chapter is hence, mainly consistent of: 1) Sensors, 2) Security Attacks and 3) Respective countermeasures. We begin the chapter with the introduction to the scenario which we will be using to construct viability for the aim of chapter.

Sensors have had great impact on our everyday lifestyle with the list of implementations from personal gadgets to commercial applications. When in swarms, sensors have demonstrated even better results and displayed tremendous potential of monitoring and analyzing an area under surveillance especially when the networks of wireless nodes are formulated to being. Such wireless networks are broadly categorized under the umbrella of Wireless Networks However, we will be discussing a subset of this category, named Wireless Sensor Networks (WSNs) that consist of battery powered sensing nodes comprised deployed in an environment to perform a task mainly relating to surveillance. While wireless medium presents many advantages over wired medium, its wireless nature inherently offers challenges to the security of transmitted data. The increased use of wireless channels increases the risk of being spoofed and attacked by an introduction of a third person who can easily overhear the wireless traffic if it is not adequately protected. It poses a considerable threat to the flow of information. This threat evolves a possibility of corruption of authentication, integrity and privacy. The main aim of this chapter is make the reader aware of the sensor network security and its usage in modern technology. Also to highlight the current security issues associated with the sensors installment and the transfer of data among multiple nodes in a network. We discuss some of the techniques that can be used to overcome these issues and provide secure ways that can be used for exchange of information throughout the sensor network.

Researchers from around the world have used wireless sensor networks in various sets of applications. Some of the commercial applications include smart parking (S. Lee, D. Yoon & A. Ghosh, 2008), security of intra car (K. P. Shih, S. S. Wang, H. C. Chen & P. H. Yang, 2008), event detection (E. Hussain, G. Chow, V. C. M. Leung, R. D. McLeod, J. Misic, V. W. S.Wong & O. Yang, 2010), health monitoring (R. Tan, G. Xing, J. Wang, &H.C.So, 2008), vehicle telematics (G. Y. Ming & J. Rencheng, 2008) etc. Environmental applications such as greenhouse monitoring (J. F. Martinez, M. S. I. Familiar, Corredor, A. B. Garcia, S. Bravo & L. Lopez, 2011), habitat surveillance (Q. Wang, S. Zhang, Y. Yang & L. Tang, 2011) and variety of applications in military (L. Cao, J. Tian, & Y. Liu, 2008) and industries (N. Alsharabi, L. R. Fa, F. Zing & M. Ghurab, 2008). Most of the applications are based on wireless networks or at least, tend to be wireless due to the easier deployment and cost effectiveness. With regards to some of these applications, later in this chapter, we analyze the security threats and then discuss relevant counter measures.

We also focus on the security challenges posed to the transfer of information in a Wireless Sensor Networks (WSNs). We notice that there are number of routing protocols designed to serve the application goals like sensing data in a particular fashion and triggering events on specified conditions. In addition to which, the routing protocols serve the general requirements of keeping the application low cost and low power consuming, but few of the applications regard security as its major requirement. The advancements in the field WSN are also leading to insecurity with conventional techniques, as there are powerful decoders available to flaw security of such networks. Nonetheless, in majority of the applications, security is handled by key cryptography, which provides security to the network but is expensive in terms of processing and power constraint and can be cracked (Karlof, 2003). Based on the network description provided in the preceding text, we try to develop an understanding about the security concerns in a WSN. A background summary of the mentioned network is illustrated in the following network assumptions.

We assume that the communication channel used by devices in a WSN can be eavesdropped, replicated and controlled by a hacker using a similar device. We also assume that sensor nodes can be replicated and malicious nodes be added to the network while they seem normally functional to the network administrator. Since sensor networks are power constrained devices, we assume that the devices do not use wide bandwidth for data transmission. Also, the nodes cannot use long encryption keys as lots of processing power is required for the signal to be decoded. We do not assume that sensor nodes are tamper resistant. They can be physically tampered with, stolen and replaced with new or malicious nodes. We assume that an adversary may have mote-class nodes or laptop-class nodes (Karlof, 2003). Mote class nodes are inexpensive nodes with similar specifications to the deployed network nodes, while the laptop-class nodes possess sensitive antennas and high-end processors enabling the adversary eavesdrop far fledged wireless information transfer. A laptop-class attacker can also affectively transmit data over a higher distance and hence, it can also jam the signals. Unlike inexpensive sensor nodes deployed by the network administrator, a laptop-class adversary can have the capability to spoof signals transmitted by a distant mote. It is also assumed that it has cutting edge processing equipment, allowing it to process and decode the received data much quicker than that a conventional node can do.

SENSORS

Instrument Society of America defines a sensor "as a device which provides a usage output in response to a specified measurand "where the output is an electric quantity which is measured as a physical quantity, property or condition (John Wilson, 2005). This definition can be concisely articulated as "The sensor is a device that measures and converts a physical quantity to a form that is understandable to a digital device". Once sensor measures the quantity, it has to generate a machine understandable output. After generating the machine output, the information is transferred to the respective recipient and then again, it is processed into the digital device and decoded to human understandable information. This information can now be stored, manipulated and destroyed. While, this tiny little sensor information is valuable, it alone is not suitable for real-time applications. For real-time applications spanning over multiple geographically isolated regions, we need networks of sensors. Hence, a collection of sensors is manifested and linked to their respective base stations, also called sinks. Base stations are simply collection points and are responsible to relay the information from one network to the other. Whereas, the sensors, also called "sensor nodes" are the information sources. The networks formed by sensor nodes and base stations are scalable to thousands of sensor nodes that can reliably exchange information. The information exchange linked to the base station can be available to a human by a serial interface to a computing device such as a laptop.

A sensor can be optical (Tao Wei, XinweiLan, Hai Xiao, Yukun Han & Hai-Lung Tsai, 2011), thermal (Li Shu-jun, Zhao Cun-hu, Yang You-song &JiaXiu-min, 2011), chemical, infrared (Liu Hongfei&Chen Zhong,2009), ultrasonic (Chris Gearhart, Alex Herold, Brian Self, Charles Birdsong & Lynne Slivovsky, 2009), light etc. The exchange of information among the sensor nodes can be wired or wireless. Wired sensors are bulky and do not support mobility and deployment in remote areas, while wireless sensors have the limitation of using portable batteries inside them severely limiting them by available power. Moreover, the sensors also exhibit a variety of power requirements with regards to its type, purpose and frequency of information gathering. Also, the working principle of every sensor relates to its requirements and architecture. For some cases such as temperature measurement, sensors are required to react to the surrounding they are placed in. For example, a common temperature sensor also known as a resistance temperature detector (RTD) contains a platinum wire which changes its resistance with the temperature and thus a reading of the temperature is acquired relative to resistance of the wire.

WIRELESS SENSOR NETWORKS

A wireless sensor network (WSN) is a wireless network consisting of spatially distributed autonomous devices using sensors to monitor physical or environmental conditions. It has been emerged as one of the most promising technologies for the future. It is enabled by advances in technology and availability of small, inexpensive, and smart sensors resulting in cost effective and easily deployable WSNs. The wireless sensor devices can automatically organize themselves to form an ad-hoc multi hop network. Wireless sensor networks (WSNs), may be comprised by hundred or may be thousands of wireless sensors, working together to accomplish a common task. Wireless sensor network consists of three layer architecture: network layer- where the sensor nodes are deployed to form a network, server layer-here the data from the sensor nodes gather at the base-station which acts as a gate-way between the sensor node and end user, client layer-the output is displayed to the client at this layer.

Security Goals of Wireless Sensor Networks

The idealistic security goals in any wireless sensor network would be the protection of data integrity, authenticity, confidentiality and continuous availability(Karlof, 2003). However, since the data in wireless networks is available to the surroundings, the inherently unsecure nature of wireless medium presents challenges to the integrity of transmitted data. Furthermore, the power constraints make complex encryption impractical for use, making it difficult to attain an idealistic security goal. The best possible scenario is determined by the notion 'effectiveness of a routing protocol in achieving the above goals should degrade no faster than a rate approximately proportional to the ratio of compromised nodes to total nodes in the network(Karlof, 2003). This sentence can be shortly termed as 'graceful degradation' of performance. To make the most of available power, we assume the security concerns depend on application type. Since, security concerns vary from one application to another, security goals can be minimized using a tradeoff between power and compromises i.e. some compromises need to be made to cut the power costs. Applications such as an environmental monitoring would require data integrity to be guaranteed whereas, an audio streaming application would want its latency requirements to be satisfied, suggesting that application type also needs consideration for power constrained devices. For the sake of conciseness, we have developed Table 1 by incorporating the application types against their goal requirements.

Application based sensor network security planning is a common practice with power and bandwidth constrained nodes(Akyildiz, 2010; Puccinelli & Haenggi, 2005; Wassim Znaidi, Marine Minier, 2008). As an example, we construct the security goals according to the intent of attacker for two applications that are fundamentally different from each other in terms of network requirements and data secrecy, i.e. environmental monitoring and audio streaming. We assume that the former application of environmental monitoring collects humidity and temperature from a crop field, the network administrator has a graphical overview of crop field incorporating readings from all the sensors. Having stated the scenario, we

Table 1. Application based goal splitting in wireless sensor networks (Karlof, 2003)

Application	Basic Requirement of Goals			
	Data Integrity	Authenticity	Continuous Availability	Confidentiality
Pollution Monitoring	Yes	No	Yes	No
Forest Fire Detection	No	No	Yes	No
Landslide Detection	No	No	Yes	No
Water Quality Monitoring	Yes	No	No	No
Natural Disaster Prevention	Yes	No	Yes	No
Structural Health Monitoring	Yes	No	No	Yes
Water Waste Monitoring	No	No	No	No
Machine Health Monitoring	Yes	Yes	No	Yes
Warfare	Yes	Yes	Yes	Yes
Micro-surgery	Yes	No	Yes	Yes
Vital Signs Monitoring	Yes	No	No	Yes
Process Management	No	Yes	Yes	Yes
Security Surveillance	Yes	Yes	Yes	Yes
Child Education	Yes	No	No	No

construct our security goals by judging the goals of an adversary. The data of a particular area of a crop field would not be of much importance to an adversary, however, an intruder can plot a routing hack that would draw routing packets to itself by increasing its 'interest' to the neighbors, hence drawing crop field data into itself. Once it has created a hotspot, it can gather whatever data it wants. Hence, the security goal for this application would be the protection of routing updates and the attack can be minimized by eliminating attractive nodes that draw much of traffic. For the latter application of voice transmission, it is possible that sensor network constructs a static route for transmission of data. However, if the intruder manages to find a HOTSPOT (place of concentration of traffic) and eavesdrops the signal, the whole of data can be compromised. Hence, for such applications, the network security goals can be set to the protection of data in the network. It can be achieved by: 1) encrypting the transmitted data2) avoiding hotspots or 3) dynamically changing the routing topology.

Security Attacks in Wireless Sensor Network

Traffic in sensor networks is comprised of sensor readings or routing update information. With regards to the type of application, both these information can be very useful for the intruder for various reasons. Considering the broadcast nature of a WSN, there can be various ways of hacking into a network. We categorize those challenges on the basis of two measures: Radius of Compromise and Intended Goal of Attacker. Subject to these two metrics, we try to develop an understanding of security attacks in wireless sensor networks in the latter part of this topic.

Security breach in a network is sometimes a result of carefully planned attack. At other times it can be unintentional, where two sensor networks sharing same content overlap its data and generate erroneous data. For the former case, the adversary (usually equipped with more powerful antenna and processing power) can make use of collected data to feed itself or to use it to hemorrhage communication within network. It can do so by compromising individual nodes and making them attractive to neighbors, or this can be done by hacking multiple nodes to form a network of malicious nodes to serve a malevolent purpose.

Owing to the nature of the attack in a wireless sensor network, the security attacks have been categorized into two areas: Active Attacks and Passive Attacks(Padmavathi, 2009). Active attacks are those attacks in which an adversary monitors information and alters the data stream in communication. Whereas, in passive attacks the adversary listens to the communication pattern and doesn't take part in data transmission at all. Based on the understanding of these two criterions, we present a classification of security attack dynamics and their respective security attacks in Figure 1. Later, in Table 2, we analyze the intention and span of attack for the respective security attacks.

With the emerging trends in sensor network security, there also exist along lists of security attacks that can be planned to disrupt normal communication of a network. We describe and compare some of them in Table 2 that we believe, will cover majority of categories mentioned in Figure 1. Security

Figure 1. Classification of security attacks in WSN (adapted from Padmavathi, 2009)

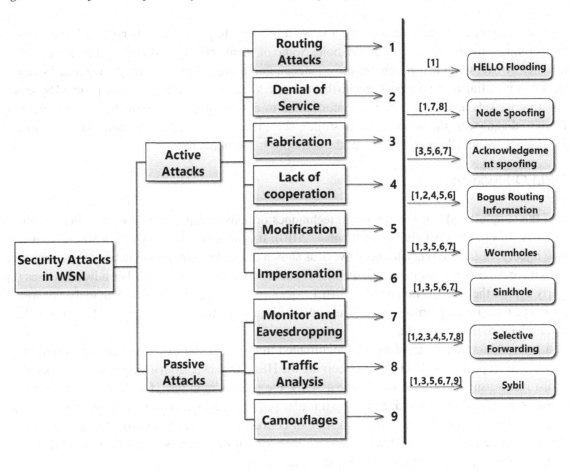

Table 2. Some well-known security attacks (adapted from Karlof, 2003)

Security Attack	Radius of Compromise	Compromised Entity	Goal of Attacker/ Aftermath
HELLO Flooding	Extended Neighborhood / Network Wide	None	state of confusion, increased latency, retransmissions
Node Spoofing	Neighborhood	Routing Packets and Data Packets	network information leak
Acknowledgement spoofing	Neighborhood	Acknowledgement Packets	distrustful link, increased latency
Bogus Routing Information	Extended Neighborhood	Routing Packets	distrustful link
Wormholes	Extended Neighborhood / Network Wide	Routing and Information Packets	compromise of all information within network
Sinkhole	Neighborhood/Extended Neighborhood	Routing Information	Compromise of Neighborhood information.
Selective Forwarding	Neighborhood/Extended Neighborhood	Information Packets	suppress warnings, data corruption
Sybil	Neighborhood	None	data corruption, selective data forwarding

attacks can vary in complexity from being a very simple flooding technique using HELLO packets to a more complex routing hack such as sinkhole. Some of them actively participate in an attack, while others merely eavesdrop using their sensitive antenna and powerful processors. Active attacks can be launched by injecting malicious packets into the network. While passive attacks can be planned by spoofing routing packets and relaying routing information to adversary nodes. These attacks are relatively difficult to diagnose by the network administrator, since the inserted malicious nodes do not announce their presence by not taking part in any of the activities in the network

1. HELLO Flooding

One of the simplest and yet, very powerful techniques of hemorrhaging the network using individual nodes is Hello Flooding(Singh, Jain,& Singhai, 2010). It is an active security attack where a intruder tries to inject HELLO packets into the network as shown in Figure 2. In a usual network, a sensor node notifies its 'isAlive' state by broadcasting HELLO packets as shown in Figure 3. The adversary uses this property against the cause by broadcasting HELLO packets for a node that is inexistent in the network. It needs not be done by a legitimate traffic. The node needs just to retransmit the previously heard HELLO packet exchanged in the network.

If a laptop-class transmitter is used as highlighted in Figure 4, the link dynamics are usually high enough to attract packets from the nodes receiving the HELLO packet from a long distance. Since there is a trust relationship between nodes inside a WSN, the neighbors in turn, forward routing packets to oblivion as portrayed in Figure 5. Since the intruder possesses a high power transmitter, it can reach farther into many tiers of nodes, creating a state of confusion and hence, a havoc inside the network. Hello flooding can also be used if the adversary intends to attract neighborhood packets while having the network discard the packet exchange in other parts of network.

Figure 2. Mote Class attacker injecting HELLO packets into network (adapted from Singh et al., 2010)

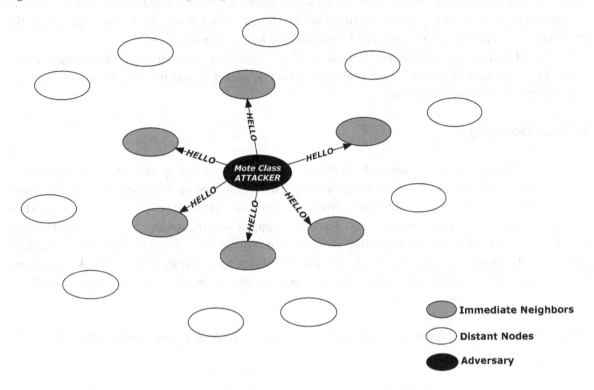

Figure 3. Network nodes replying with network information (adapted from Singh et al., 2010)

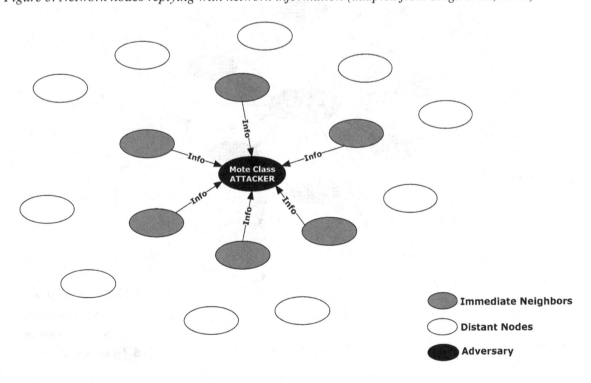

HELLO flooding can be prevented by using a key management system, where each link on a network is maintained by a secret key, as shown in Figure 6 (Hamid, 2006). Since the key is unknown to the adversary, hence the HELLO floods aren't authenticated by the network.

HELLO flooding is especially problematic for delay intolerant applications of the wireless sensor networks. These attacks usually cause jitter and delays in packet forwarding due to retransmissions, sometimes even dropping the packets.

2. Node Spoofing

A simple technique for an intruder to hack into a network is to eavesdrop and impersonate an existing node from the network. Eavesdropping the information exchange on a WSN is hence called Node Spoofing and can be depicted as in Figure 7. Since the attack is performed passively into the network, it is very difficult to detect the possible hack. The eavesdropped information can be used against routing and access techniques for an air. A spoofing node can also actively participate into the network attack by replicating the information sequentially. Doing so, it confirms its ingenuity to the network administrator and extract out valuable information. Due to power constraints in WSN, the listening intervals are

Figure 4. Laptop class attacker injecting packets into network (adapted from Hamid, 2006)

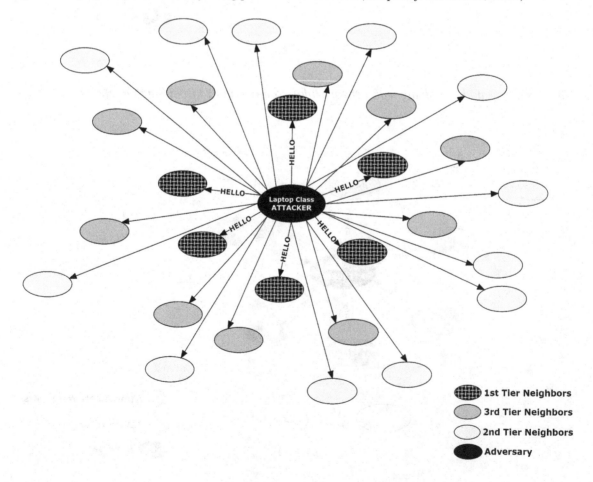

Figure 5. Network nodes sending packets into oblivion (adapted from Hamid, 2006)

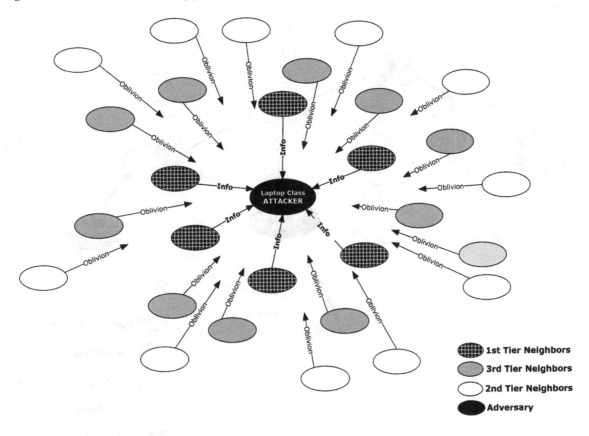

Figure 6. Preventing HELLO flooding using secret keys (adapted from Hamid, 2006)

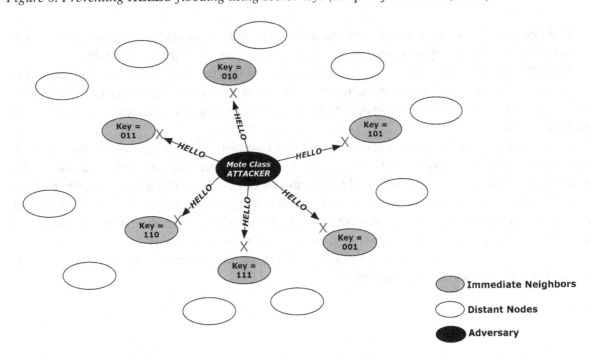

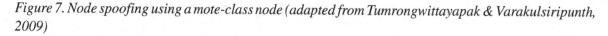

Figure 7. Node spoofing using a mote-class node (adapted from Tumrongwittayapak & Varakulsiripunth, 2009)

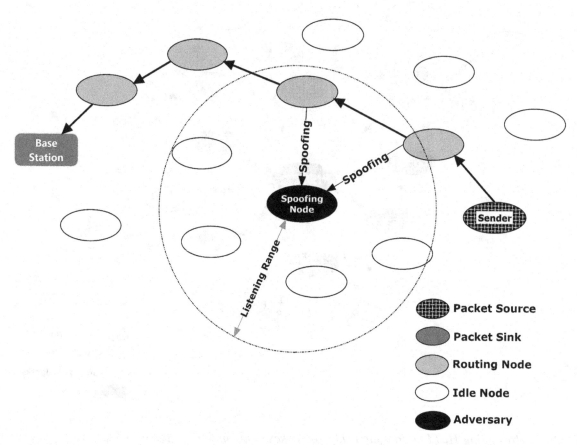

divided into duty cycles, hence the replicate transmission must be performed by sending messages at an expected time of listening by using the periodic data eavesdropped from the victim node.

Since the network information is broadcasted onto the air interface, hence node spoofing cannot be prevented if passive. However, if a node plays an active part in the network disruption using the spoofed packets, there is a possibility for authenticating messages via encrypted communication as described in (Hamid, 2006).

Node spoofing can be used by an adversary to trigger false alarms by altering the information within transmitted packets(Padmavathi, 2009). It can also be used to impersonate another node from within the network, confusing the administrator of two genuine nodes. Additionally, it can be used to relay the network packets onto another network of malicious nodes using private and out of band channels, such data can be used to compromise the entire network security upon proper decoding of information. Node spoofing can also lead to selective forwarding, as discussed in its respective text.

For simplicity, we relate the node spoofing OSI layers. Hence we further categorize it into attacks on the data link layer and the network layer as:

Layer 2: Acknowledgement Spoofing

Acknowledgement spoofing is a hack, plot for inducing latency into the network. It inherits its behavior from the basic mechanism of node-to-node communications that use acknowledgements to inform the sender for received packets. The acknowledgements also serve to discover the node state and link viability of the destination. An adversary can in turn, eavesdrop and replicate such acknowledgements and transmit them to unintentional recipients, invoking confusion between nodes inside the network. It can do so by overhearing the genuine acknowledgement and iterating it for a period of time(Karlof, 2003). It can also retransmit a previously sent acknowledgement, making the network believe that the packet has been received multiple times, causing changes in routing topology.

Acknowledgement spoofing gives an attacker the ability to induce latency in the network. Since the network will be busy in determining the origin of problem. The injection of new packets can be delayed by a certain amount of time, causing problems for real-time applications.

Layer 3: Bogus Routing

A very important aspect in any communication system is the routing of data. It can be performed by selecting proper routes for the packet traversal. Packets reach the destination by either pre-defined or dynamic routes. To do so, the nodes send routing updates to update dynamics of an established route. Though very useful, this information can be used against the network to serve a malevolent intention. Routing information can be altered, selectively increasing the use of a route or diminishing the use of another. In such an attack, the compromised node sends false routing information, hence the word 'Bogus Routing'. Bogus routing can have a prominent effect on network security if combined with Wormholes and Sinkholes. Both of which are discussed in the following text.

3. Sinkholes

Since most of routing protocols in wireless sensor networks use link metrics for the selection of next hop. One can advertise bogus link metrics to contend for gaining the "preferred neighbor" status on its neighboring nodes, subsequently, attracting significant traffic from neighbors. Such practices, when used against the system form a sinkhole attack as shown in Figure 8. One such metric for planting a sinkhole attack is Received Signal Strength Indicator (RSSI). It is conventionally used to register the signal strength of a packet received from another node. Sinkhole can also be plotted using Link Quality Indicator (LQI), where LQI represents the quality of packet received and is based principally on the number of errors in the packet at arrival time. Another important parameter to judge a link's efficiency is the Link Latency. It is the expected time that a packet will take to reach the destination. Residual Energy, Bandwidth and Throughput are some additional metrics that can also be used similarly. These link metrics are used by the routing protocols, hence, depending upon the type of protocol there can be various link parameters that can also be used to plot a sinkhole attack. A readily tested deployment of sinkhole formed through link information can be found in (Krontiris, Giannetsos, & Dimitriou, 2008).

Sinkholes are used in conjunction with wormholes where, nodes are provided by sinkhole and the tunnel is created by wormhole. The combination of these two techniques can result in erroneous data exchange, data alteration, false alarms network-wide confusion and many other mishaps.

Figure 8. Node creating a sinkhole (adapted from Tumrongwittayapak & Varakulsiripunth, 2009)

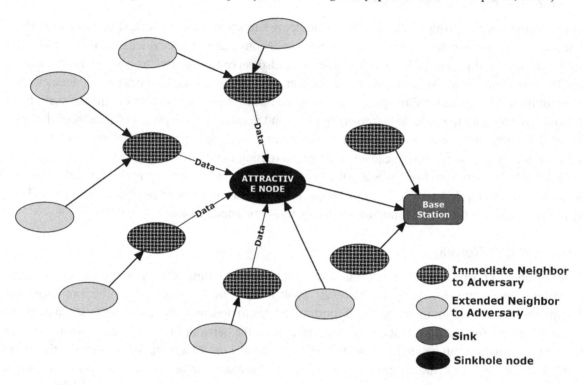

The routing information that is used by a malicious node to make it 'attractive' can be used against the attack to detect the possible hack. There are ways to accomplish a counter to sinkholes. One of the renowned techniques by Krontiris et al. is described as a collection of four rules (Krontiris et al., 2008).

Rule 1: For each overheard route update packet, check the sender field, which must belong to one of your neighbors.

Rule 2: For each [parent, child] pair of your neighbors, compare the link quality estimate they advertise for the link between them. Their difference cannot exceed 50.

Rule 3: For each beacon, check that the advertised path cost of the node is bigger than the path cost of its father.

Rule 4: For each [parent, child] pair of your neighbors, compare the LQI they advertise for the link between them. Their difference cannot exceed 10.

As pointed out by Soni et al. (Soni, Modi,& Chaudhri, 2013), Sinkholes can also be prevented and detected by the use of cryptography, processing power monitoring, use of mobile agent, and hash chains. These approaches can be enumerated as Data Consistency & Network Flow Information Approach (Ngai, Liu, & Lyu, 2006), Hop Count Monitoring Scheme(Dallas, Leckie, & Ramamohanarao, 2007), RSSI Based Scheme(Tumrongwittayapak & Varakulsiripunth, 2009), Monitoring node's CPU usage(Song& Hsieh, 2010), Mobile Agent Based Approach(Sheela, 2011) and the Usage of Message Digest Algorithm(Sharmila & Umamaheswari, 2011).

4. Wormholes

One of the most challenging attacks in a WSN is a Wormhole attack. In this attack, an adversary uses laptop-class motes to create attractive nodes so it could attract more packets to itself for manipulating it as shown in Figure 9. A mote is labeled attractive if it has a low hop count to base station, provides lower latency, greater bandwidth and a better link quality. Depending upon the protocol that is used, these dynamics can be used intuitively to prepare a preferred route to the base station. Wormhole attacks make use of these link dynamics to create a tunnel from its laptop-class sensitive antenna and powerful transmitter. Thus, the wormhole tunnel would have lower hop count, lower latency and better link dynamics, which is ideal for a routing protocol in selecting its next hop. In other words, the malicious nodes in this network create a shortcut leading directly to the sink; hence the term 'Wormhole' is used. Wormhole attacks require two or more compromised nodes to build a virtual tunnel. The nodes in this case can be formed by an approach called 'sinkhole'. As discussed in greater detail later, the sinkhole nodes are attractive nodes within a network, compromised to drive most of network traffic through themselves.

Two strategies can be applied in creating wormholes, hidden-mode and participation-mode(Sharif & Ahmed, 2010). Hidden-mode relays information packets to the network without wanting to change the contents of information packet. This approach is relatively simple due to the reason that there is no need for adversary to decrypt information. On the contrary, the participation-mode is very difficult to mount. If successful, the adversary commands the power to change whatever information it wants and ignore any security mechanisms placed to provide hindrance to an attack. Generally, since these attacks are mounted using the link information, it's difficult for a base station to differentiate the malicious packets from the genuine packets with true link dynamics due to the trust relationship between parent and its child nodes. Wormholes are particularly difficult to troubleshoot since they can use out of band channels for data transmission, transparent to the network administrator. Difficult to launch, wormholes are considered one of the most dangerous attacks on WSN.

Wormholes can be used to extract sensitive information from a deployed wireless sensor network. While the network is fooled to aggregate data at a malicious aggregation point near base station, all of the data exchange in the network becomes transparent to the adversary. Wormholes can also be used to generate false alarms and create glitches on-demand in the network. These attacks are particularly

Figure 9. A Wormhole attack in WSN forming a tunnel (adapted from Sharif & Ahmed, 2010)

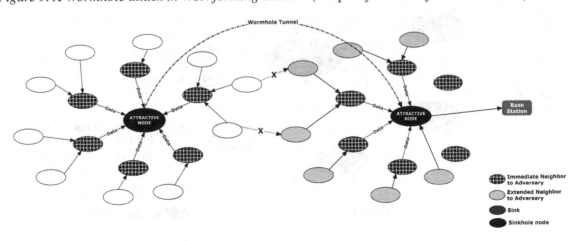

difficult to defend due to their capability of combining the power of Node Spoofing and Alteration to serve a malicious intent. Wormhole attacks are similar to sinkhole attacks with only few characteristic differences, these differences are discussed in the pertaining text for sinkhole attacks.

Wormholes are particularly famous for their notorious data compromise techniques. They are equally difficult to counter in a practical environment. However, this attack seems to be ineffective in geographic routing algorithms where the actual geographic location is used for routing through the shortest path instead of node information (Havinga, 2005). Various other techniques have also been specified to counter wormholes (Jen, Laih, & Kuo, 2009; Wassim Znaidi, Marine Minier, 2008) but they suffer from high cost of reliability and limited scalability.

5. Selective Forwarding

In a sensor network, it is often important to report any sudden changes in the sensor readings. However, if these readings are suppressed, there is a less use of such a system. On the contrary, an adversary can take command of few sensor nodes in a network, taking control of the sensor readings passing through those nodes. Once an attacker succeeds in impersonating a node, it acquires control of all information passing through that node. Be it any information, the node can decrypt and process the contents of information for evaluation. Sometimes, an adversary would want to conceal sensitive information from network administrator as shown in Figure 10. However, hemorrhaging the entire node communication can result in suspicion. Hence, decisive and useful information such as alarm triggers or critical updates can be effectively blocked by selective forwarding mechanisms. If need be, the attacker can selectively stop forwarding any information that might reveal the attack.

Figure 10. A compromised node selectively forwarding sensor readings (adapted from Yu, 2006)

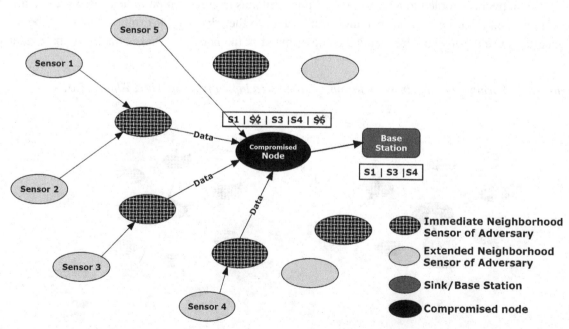

Selective forwarding can be used in conjunction with node spoofing and wormhole to create 'attractive' nodes. After successful operation and sufficient nodes, this mechanism can build an attack strategy that can be used to selectively suppress warnings in a sensor field, hence it can compromise the purpose of an entire network.

Selective forwarding mechanisms can be countered using end-to-end acknowledgement mechanisms, where a sensor node demands acknowledgement from the base station. But this approach is very costly in terms of energy. Since every sensor reading traverses multiple hops, it could create plenty of traffic in the network. However, this technique can be modified to form intermediary acknowledgement nodes (cutting down the cost of transportation to base station) which acknowledge the sensor data and report any suspicious activity on the path to base station. One such scheme is defined in the work of Bo Yu et al(Yu, 2006). Various other techniques have been used to counter selective forwarding such as the "Using Support Vector Machines"(Kaplantzis, Shilton, Mani, & Sekercioglu, 2007), "Lightweight Defense scheme Using Neighbor Nodes as Monitor Nodes"(Xin-sheng, Yong-zhao, Shu-ming, & Liang-min, 2009), "Multi Data Flow Scheme" (Sun, Chen,& Hsiao, 2007), "Data Loss Detection in Cluster based Heterogeneous Systems" (Brown & Du, 2008) and "Detection Using Two hop Neighborhood Information" (Hai & Huh, 2008). The reader is encouraged to read the details of these techniques provided in aforementioned references.

6. Sybil

Every node in a network is assigned a locally unique identification named as 'Node ID'. These IDs may be assigned from a pool of available IDs at the base station, or chosen arbitrarily from a range of a given integer value. Node IDs can be used for constructing routing tables, transmitting information or sending acknowledgements. But these IDs can be tampered with, and it is possible for an attacker to plan an attack by assigning each node a set of multiple IDs. This kind of attack is called "Sybil Attack" and the fake IDs used are called "Sybil IDs". If successful, the attacker is able to impersonate multiple nodes, or create an additional set of nodes that are physically absent inside the network. Such a situation can be illustrated using Figure 11.

Research suggests that Sybil can be used in multipath or disparity routing where seemingly disjoint paths could in fact go through a single malicious node presenting several Sybil identities(Newsome, Song,& Perrig, 2004).Another vulnerable mechanism is geographic routing (Karp & Kung, 2000; Ko & Vaidya, 1998) where instead of having one set of coordinates, a Sybil node could appear in more than one place at once. Sybil attacks can also be used for influencing a data corruption sequence by using multiple Sybil IDs such that one Sybil node is actually many nodes. So it can be used as many nodes giving the wrong readings. Furthermore, extended applications include voting, resource allocation and misbehavior detection(Newsome et al, 2004). In order to have an ID, a Sybil node will either look for a legitimate ID, or it can choose a random ID for itself. In the latter case, if there is a pool of network IDs that a network administrator assigns, it can counter the effect of Sybil node by declaring it malicious. If a Sybil node uses legitimate ID stolen from another node or the pool of network IDs, the ID can be verified by the base station. It can be done so by registering the node within the network or by Position Verification(Sastry, Shankar, & Wagner, 2003), where a node's location will be known to the network. In case of a Sybil node, if it uses another ID, the network will know that multiple IDs are being transmitted from the same location.

Figure 11. Sybil node collecting data packets via multiple Sybil IDs

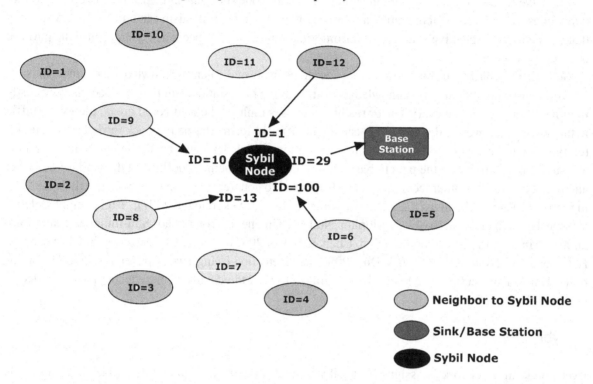

Newsome et al. suggests that security goals for Sybil nodes can be achieved by linking the node IDs with cryptographic keys. In addition to that, there must exist a key validation scheme that prevents a Sybil node from getting into the networks without valid authentication of its key and its node ID (Newsome et al., 2004).

FUTURE RESEARCH DIRECTION

Research in the field of WSN has been carried out for many years. Numerous issues have been addressed and resolved but there still exist a list of challenges that need careful addressing. We have observed extensive use of application layer in securing conventional networks, but for WSNs and the inherent wireless insecure nature, there arises a need for security mechanisms on each hop. For the security to be guaranteed hop-by-hop we require first three layers of a wireless sensor network, i.e. physical, data link and network layer. While there has been substantial amount of research on these layers, there exist numerous challenges that haven't been resolved yet. In this chapter, we have presented security mechanisms suitable for a basic systems but there still exist security holes for large scale network due to which we aim to design security mechanisms based on the application requirements only. In practice, there doesn't exist a security mechanism for a wireless sensor network which would feasibly guarantee all of the four security goals in a network i.e. Confidentiality, Data Integrity, Data Authenticity and Continuous Availability. On the other hand, while a single application may only require the fulfillment of one or two of these goals, it doesn't guarantee the same security in scalable or heterogeneous networks. This tradeoff between security and scalability and heterogeneity is a very potential research area for future networks. Also, the existing encryption techniques are expensive in terms of energy. Hence, we cannot rely on encryption techniques alone to secure the network. There is a need of equally efficient physical layer encoding schemes that would work in conjunction with other layers to form a proficient security mechanism. Such network security can be achieved by cognitive, self-learning and a self-healing wireless sensor network but it doesn't exist due to its complexity and cost. Hence, this tradeoff between power consumption and network security also remains an active research issue for wireless sensor networks.

CONCLUSION

In this chapter, we described the security challenges posed to a wireless sensor network in real-time deployment scenarios. We also discussed respective countermeasures that can be put into effect for an efficient detection and prevention of a security attack that might create a security hole in the network. We observed that most of the security attacks take advantage of broadcast nature insecurity in a wireless link as a result of which, the information inside a network is vulnerable to security threats. Link layer encryption and authentication may be a first step towards the achievement of improved security in WSN. Even so, sensitive applications might require additional layers of security mechanisms on their chips. Eventually, there is always going to be a tradeoff between energy consumption and security level that one cannot escape.

REFERENCES

Akyildiz, I. F. (2010). *Wireless Sensor Networks* (1st ed.). Wiley. doi:10.1002/9780470515181

Brown, J., & Du, X. (2008). Detection of Selective Forwarding Attacks in Heterogeneous Sensor Networks. *2008 IEEE International Conference on Communications*. doi:10.1109/ICC.2008.306

Dallas, D., Leckie, C., & Ramamohanarao, K. (2007). Hop-Count Monitoring: Detecting Sinkhole Attacks in Wireless Sensor Networks. *2007 15th IEEE International Conference on Networks*. doi:10.1109/ICON.2007.4444082

Gearhart, C., Herold, A., Self, B., Birdsong, C., & Slivovsky, L. (2009). *Use of Ultrasonic Sensors in the Development of an Electronic Travel Aid*. IEEE Sensors Applications Symposium, New Orleans, LA.

Hai, T. H., & Huh, E.-N. (2008). Detecting Selective Forwarding Attacks in Wireless Sensor Networks Using Two-hops Neighbor Knowledge. *2008 Seventh IEEE International Symposium on Network Computing and Applications*. doi:10.1109/NCA.2008.13

Hamid, A. (2006). Defense against lap-top class attacker in wireless sensor network. *2006 8th International Conference Advanced Communication Technology*. doi:10.1109/ICACT.2006.205976

Havinga, P. J. M. (2005). How to Secure a Wireless Sensor Network. *2005 International Conference on Intelligent Sensors, Sensor Networks and Information Processing*. doi:10.1109/ISSNIP.2005.1595561

Hongfei, L., & Zhong, C. (2009). An Infusing Infrared-Sensor Simulator Design Based on USB2.0. *Computer Network and Multimedia Technology, 2009. CNMT 2009. International Symposium on.* doi:10.1109/CNMT.2009.5374680

Jen, S.-M., Laih, C.-S., & Kuo, W.-C. (2009). A Hop-Count Analysis Scheme for Avoiding Wormhole Attacks in MANET. *Sensors (Basel, Switzerland), 9*(6), 5022–5039. doi:10.3390/s90605022 PMID:22408566

Kaplantzis, S., Shilton, A., Mani, N., & Sekercioglu, Y. A. (2007). Detecting Selective Forwarding Attacks in Wireless Sensor Networks using Support Vector Machines. *2007 3rd International Conference on Intelligent Sensors, Sensor Networks and Information.* doi:10.1109/ISSNIP.2007.4496866

Karlof, C., & Wagner, D. (2003). Secure routing in wireless sensor networks: Attacks and countermeasures. *Ad Hoc Networks, 1*(2-3), 293–315. doi:10.1016/S1570-8705(03)00008-8

Karp, B., & Kung, H. T. (2000). *GPSR: Greedy Perimeter Stateless Routing for Wireless Networks.* Academic Press.

Ko, Y.-B., & Vaidya, N. H. (1998). Location-aided routing (LAR) in mobile ad hoc networks. *Proceedings of the 4th Annual ACM/IEEE International Conference on Mobile Computing and Networking - MobiCom '98.* doi:10.1145/288235.288252

Krontiris, I., Giannetsos, T., & Dimitriou, T. (2008). Launching a Sinkhole Attack in Wireless Sensor Networks; The Intruder Side. *2008 IEEE International Conference on Wireless and Mobile Computing, Networking and Communications.* doi:10.1109/WiMob.2008.83

Newsome, J., Song, D., & Perrig, A. (2004). *The Sybil Attack in Sensor Networks : Analysis & Defenses.* Academic Press.

Ngai, E. C. H., Liu, J., & Lyu, M. R. (2006). *On the Intruder Detection for Sinkhole Attack in Wireless Sensor Networks.* Academic Press.

Padmavathi, G. (2009). A Survey of Attacks. *Security Mechanisms and Challenges in Wireless Sensor Networks, 4*(1), 1–9.

Puccinelli, D., & Haenggi, M. (2005). Wireless sensor networks: Applications and challenges of ubiquitous sensing. *IEEE Circuits and Systems Magazine, 5*(3), 19–31. doi:10.1109/MCAS.2005.1507522

Sastry, N., Shankar, U., & Wagner, D. (2003). Secure verification of location claims. *Proceedings of the 2nd ACM Workshop.* Retrieved from http://dl.acm.org/citation.cfm?id=941313

Sharif, L., & Ahmed, M. (2010). The Wormhole Routing Attack in Wireless Sensor Networks (WSN). *Journal of Information Processing Systems, 6*(2), 177–184. doi:10.3745/JIPS.2010.6.2.177

Sharmila, S., & Umamaheswari, G. (2011). Detection of Sinkhole Attack in Wireless Sensor Networks Using Message Digest Algorithms. *2011 International Conference on Process Automation, Control and Computing.* doi:10.1109/PACC.2011.5978973

Sheela, D. (2011). A non cryptographic method of sink hole attack detection in wireless sensor networks. *IEEE-International Conference on Recent Trends in Information Technology.*

Shu-Jun, L., Cun-Hu, Z., You-Song, Y., & Jia, X-M. (2011). Design research on the temperature sensor in hot iron based on ANSYS emulation. *Mechanic Automation and Control Engineering (MACE), 2011 Second International Conference on.*

Singh, V. P., Jain, S., & Singhai, J. (2010). *Hello Flood Attack and its Countermeasures in Wireless Sensor Networks.* Academic Press.

Song, M., & Hsieh, G. (2010). Intrusion detection of sinkhole attacks in large-scale wireless sensor networks. *2010 IEEE International Conference on Wireless Communications, Networking and Information Security.* doi:10.1109/WCINS.2010.5541872

Soni, V., Modi, P., & Chaudhri, V. (2013). *Detecting Sinkhole Attack in Wireless Sensor Network.* Academic Press.

Sun, H., Chen, C., & Hsiao, Y. (2007). An efficient countermeasure to the selective forwarding attack in wireless sensor networks. *TENCON 2007 - 2007 IEEE Region 10 Conference.* doi:10.1109/TENCON.2007.4428866

Tumrongwittayapak, C., & Varakulsiripunth, R. (2009). Detecting Sinkhole attacks in wireless sensor networks. *ICCAS-SICE, 2009.* Retrieved from http://ieeexplore.ieee.org/xpls/abs_all.jsp?arnumber=5334764

Wei, Lan, Xiao, Han, & Tsai. (2011). Optical fiber sensors for high temperature harsh environment sensing. *Instrumentation and Measurement Technology Conference (I2MTC).* IEEE.

Wilson, J. (2005). *Sensor Technology – Handbook.* Academic Press.

Xin-sheng, W., Yong-zhao, Z., Shu-ming, X., & Liang-min, W. (2009). Lightweight defense scheme against selective forwarding attacks in wireless sensor networks. *2009 International Conference on Cyber-Enabled Distributed Computing and Knowledge Discovery.* doi:10.1109/CYBERC.2009.5342206

Yu, B. (2006). Detecting selective forwarding attacks in wireless sensor networks. *Proceedings 20th IEEE International Parallel & Distributed Processing Symposium.* doi:10.1109/IPDPS.2006.1639675

Znaidi, , & Minier, . (2008). An Ontology for Attacks in Wireless Sensor Networks. *Society of General Physiologists Series, 32,* 1–13.

KEY TERMS AND DEFINITIONS

Ad-Hoc Network: A network where devices connect spontaneously.

Adversary Node: A node which serves a malevolent purpose in opposition to that original purpose of the networks, also known as intruder.

Authentication: Authentication is the process of determining whether someone or something is, in fact, who or what it is declared to be.

Base Station: It is a transceiver connecting a number acting like a gateway to another network

Bogus Routing: Routing with false information.

Constraint Devices: Devices that are limited by their abilities of power and performance.

Deployment: It refers to the installation of sensor nodes in the network.

Extended Neighborhood: Nodes that can be reached up to three hops of communication by a mote-class node.

Genuine Node: A legitimate node serving the intended purpose.

Havoc: A state of urgency resulting in damage or destructions of data in the network.

Hop Count: The number of point-to-point links in a transmission path.

Hotspot: A node serving as a relay for traffic from many directions.

Integrity: It refers to maintaining and assuring the accuracy and consistency of data over its entire life-cycle.

Intruder: An intruder access the network through authorized network devices.

Link Latency: The delay exhibited by the data to traverse a link.

Link Quality: A measure of link efficiency characterized by signal strength and other link metrics.

Malicious: Desire to harm the information of the network.

Neighborhood: Range of nodes to which a mote-class node can communicate directly.

Network-Wide: All the reachable nodes in the network.

Public Key Cryptology: A public key cryptology is a method that uses two keys, a public key known to everyone and a *private* or secret key known only to the recipient of the message.

Residual Energy: The amount of energy that remains when most of it is consumed in the energy.

Routing Protocol: A routing protocol specifies how routers communicate with each other, disseminating information that enables them to select routes between any two nodes in the network.

Sensitivity: It statistical measures of the performance for the secured transmission of data in the network.

Sensor: A sensor is a device that detects events or changes in quantities and provides a corresponding output.

Sensor Node: A sensor node is a node in a wireless sensor network that is capable of performing some processing, gathering sensory information and communicating with other connected nodes in the network.

Symmetric Key Cryptology: An encryption system in which the sender and receiver of a message share a single, common key that is used to encrypt and decrypt the message.

Tampered: Interfere with (something) in order to cause damage or make unauthorized alterations.

Traffic: The packets of data in the network.

Wire Communication: Wire communication refers to the transmission of data over a wire-based technology.

Wireless Communication: It is transfer of information between two or more points that are not connected by an electrical conductor and usually use radio technology.

Chapter 7
DDoS Attacks and Their Types

Dileep Kumar
Adama Science and Technology University, Ethiopia

ABSTRACT

Billions of people rely on internet to discover and share ideas with the world. However, the websites are vulnerable to deliver the attacks, preventing people to access them. The recent study of global surveys showed that DDoS Attacks evolved in strategy and tactics. A Distributed Denial of Service (DDoS) attack is a new emerging bigger threat that target organization's business critical services such as e-commerce transactions, financial trading, email or web site access. A DDoS attack is a large-scale, coordinated attack on the availability of services of a victim system or network resource, launched indirectly through many compromised computers on the Internet. To create attacks, attackers first discover vulnerable sites or hosts on the network. Then vulnerable hosts are exploited by attackers who use their vulnerability to gain access to these hosts. This chapter deals with the introduction, architecture and classification of DDoS Attacks.

INTRODUCTION

The core concepts of cyber security are Availability, Integrity, and Confidentiality. In Computing, a Denial-of-Service (DoS) attack is an attempt to make a machine or network resource unavailable to its intended users. The attacker sends a large number of special requests to the server machine. When the load is too much for the server to cope up with, it will fail to respond to the requests. When a legitimate user tries to access the server, the requests will time out. In DoS attacks, the malicious packets are sent from single machine.

Today, DoS attacks are usually distributed, known as Distributed Denial of Service (DDoS) Attacks. A DDoS attack is a tactic to attack on the availability of services of a victim system or network resource launched indirectly from multiple compromised computers. Examples include

- Attempts to "flood" a network, thereby preventing legitimate network traffic
- Attempts to disrupt connections between two machines, thereby preventing access to a service
- Attempts to prevent a particular individual from accessing a service
- Attempts to disrupt service to a specific system or person

DOI: 10.4018/978-1-4666-8761-5.ch007

Massive Distributed Denial of Service (DDoS) attacks have the potential to severely decrease backbone availability and can virtually detach a network from the Internet. The DDoS attacks impact the availability of information resources by targeting organization's business critical services such as ecommerce transactions, financial trading, email or web site access.

There would be multiple victims in DDoS Attacks; the owner of the targeted system, the users of the targeted system and the users of the targeted systems. A computer used in the attack is known as a bot. A group of co-opted computers is known as botnet. Although the owner of the co-opted computer typically is unaware that their computer is compromised, they are nevertheless likely to suffer degradation of service and malfunction.

It is very difficult to identify, avoid and minimize impact of DDoS attack due to its many to one configuration. The Internet design raises several security issues concerning opportunities for DDoS attacks.

- **Highly Interdependent Internet Security:** DDoS attacks are commonly launched from systems that are subverted through security-related compromises. Regardless of how well secured the victim system may be, its susceptibility to DDoS attacks depends on the state of security in the rest of the global Internet.
- **Limited Internet Resources:** Each Internet entity (host, network, service) has limited resources that can be consumed by too many users.
- **Intelligence and Resources are not collocated:** A peer-to-peer communication paradigm led to storing most of the intelligence needed for service guarantees with end hosts, limiting the amount of processing in the intermediate network so that packets could be forwarded quickly and at minimal cost. At the same time, a desire for large throughput led to the design of high bandwidth pathways in the intermediate network, while the end networks invested in only as much bandwidth as they thought they might need. Thus, malicious clients can misuse the abundant resources of the unwitting intermediate network for delivery of numerous messages to a less provisioned victim.
- **Accountability is not enforced**: IP spoofing gives attackers a powerful mechanism to escape accountability for their actions, and sometimes even the means to perpetrate attacks (reflector attacks, such as the Smurf attack).
- **Control is distributed**: Internet management is distributed, and each network is run according to local policies defined by its owners. The implications of this are many. There is no way to enforce global deployment of a particular security

In addition to the internet design issues, the following are motives ranging from political extortion to random attacks by amateurs.

- **Hactivism or ideological and political differences:** Anonymous and LulzSec are two of the most publicized notorious hacktivist groups. They have brought down the websites of the world's largest and most prestigious brands and organizations. Often these groups send clear warning signals by openly discussing their targets, releasing their plans to news outlets and posting their intentions on social media and blogs before launching the attacks.
- **Extortion and other financial motivators:** A potential attacker will often email or call with a ransom demand, ranging from several hundred dollars to hundreds of thousands of dollars, depending on sophistication and the motives of the attacker. Paying the ransom is not good enough. Rather, have a proactive DDoS mitigation plan in place and be ready to deploy it.

- **Competitive and cyber hate crime:** While rare, DDoS attacks can be fueled by a competitor, a disgruntled customer or former employee, or hackers whose sole intent is cyber hate crimes. These attackers have been known to use social media, blogs and message boards to express negative comments and recruit participants before they attack. Online gaming sites and sites associated with specific religious, minority or alternative lifestyle groups are also common targets.
- **Hacker Experimentation:** Novice hackers hone their skills and gain prestige among their peers by launching DDoS attack tools on random sites in preparation for a future attack on their true target. Many hackers do this for personal satisfaction, while others may advance to active cyber criminal rings and hactivist groups.

The main objective of this chapter is to have an understanding of DDoS Attacks, presenting architecture and classifying DDoS Attacks.

BACKGROUND

Short History

The first DDoS attacks occurred in the summer of 1999 (K.J. Houle & G.M. Weaver, 2001). In February 2000, DDoS attacks were launched against major internet sites such as eBay, Amazon, CNN, Datek and Yahoo. This attack kept these off the Internet for about 2 hours and caused damage of 1.7 billion dollars. Another DDoS attack occurred on October 20, 2002 against the 13 root servers that provide the DNS service to Internet users around the world. If all 13 servers were to go down, there would be disastrous problems accessing the Web. Although the attack only lasted for an hour and the effects were hardly noticeable to the average Internet user, it caused 7 of the 13 root servers to shut down. If unchecked, more powerful DDoS attacks could potentially cripple or disable essential Internet services in minutes (M. Ritchel, 2000).

In December 2010, a group calling themselves "Anonymous" orchestrated DDoS flooding attacks on organizations such as Mastercard.com, PayPal, Visa.com and PostFinance. The attack brought down the Mastercard, PostFinance, and Visa websites. In September 2012, the Operation Ababil campaign launched by "Izz ad-Din al-Qassam Cyber Fighters" foreign hactivist group attacked online banking sites of 9 major U.S. banks (i.e., Bank of America, Citigroup, Wells Fargo, U.S. Bancorp, PNC, Capital One, Fifth Third Bank, BB&T, and HSBC) continuously with DDoS flooding attacks. Consequently, banking sites have slowed or grounded to a halt before they get recovered several minutes later.

According NSFOCUS, of the 90 major multiple DDoS attacks that occurred worldwide in the first half of 2013, 39 (43%) targeted banks, mainly resulting from the Operation Ababil campaign. Government and enterprises were assaulted in 26 (29%) and 19 (21%) major DDoS events, respectively. Non-profit organizations (NPOs) and Internet service providers (ISPs) also fell victim to these attacks. Beginning on March 18, 2013, Spamhaus suffered a DDoS attack in which hackers exploited botnet and DNS reflection technologies. The attack traffic continuously rose from 10Gbps to an astonishing 300Gbps on March 27, recording it as the largest scale DDoS attack (traffic-wise) aimed at a single target in history. Spamhaus is an anti-spam NGO based in London and Geneva, and it maintains a colossal spam blacklist that is widely used by numerous universities, research institutions, ISPs, militaries and commercial enterprises.

According to Neustar's Survey 2014, criminals used DDoS attacks to distract IT staff while inserting malware to breach bank accounts and customer data. More than half of attacked companies reported theft of funds, data or intellectual property. The survey reveals further evidence that the DDoS attack landscape is changing. The number of companies attacked is up, but attack duration is down. Larger attacks are more common, but most attacks are still less than 1 Gbps. Companies report a greater financial risk during a DDoS outage; however, most still rely on traditional defenses like firewalls, not purpose-built solutions like DDoS mitigation hardware or cloud services.

The smokescreening is a new growing trend in DDoS Attack crime. While IT and security teams are fully distracted by a DDoS attack, criminals grab and clone private data to siphon off funds, intellectual property and more. In one case, crooks used DDoS to help steal bank customers' credentials and drain $9 million from ATMs in just 48 hours. Such incidents have caused the FDIC to warn about DDoS as "a diversionary tactic."

Methodology

To launch a DDoS attack, an attacker will often start by building a botnet, which is network of infected machines that they will use to produce the volume of traffic needed to deny services to computer users. To create attacks, attackers first discover vulnerable hosts or sites on the network. Vulnerable hosts are usually those that are either running no antivirus software or out-of-date antivirus software, or those that have not been properly patched. Then vulnerable hosts are exploited by attackers who use their vulnerability to gain access to these hosts. The next step for the attacker is to install malicious code (attack tools) on the compromised hosts of the attack network. The hosts that are running these attack tools are known as *Masters* or *Handlers*, and they can carry out any attack under the control of the attacker(J. Mirkovic & P. Reiher, 2004).

After that, the systems that have been infected by the malicious code look for other vulnerable computers and install on them the same malicious code. Because of that widespread scanning to identify victim systems, it is possible that large attack networks can be built very quickly. The result of this automated process is the creation of a DDoS attack network that consists of masters and slaves machines. It can be inferred from this process that another DDoS attack takes place while the attack network is being built, because the process itself creates a significant amount of traffic.

Typical victims of such attacks are the servers of e-commerce websites, news websites, corporate networks, banks and governmental websites.

A DDoS Attack is composed of four important elements, as shown in Figure 1:

- The Attacker or Client, who is typically a person who launches the attacks.
- The Masters or Handlers, which are compromised hosts with a attacker program running on them, capable of controlling multiple Slaves or Agents.
- The Slaves or Daemon or Agents or Zombie hosts, who are compromised hosts that are running a attacker program and are responsible for generating a stream of packets towards the intended victim.
- A Victim or Target host.

Therefore, the attackers could take the following steps in order to launch DDoS attacks:

Figure 1. Architecture of DDoS Attacks

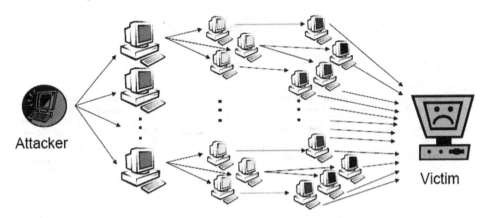

1. **The Recruit Phase:** It involves scanning network looking for vulnerable hosts. Scanning tools helps to identify the victims. Examples include Nmap, Nessus etc.
2. **The Exploit Phase:** After the discovery of vulnerable hosts, exploit the vulnerability to gain access to the victims.
3. **The Inject Phase:** The insertion of malicious code to control these hosts.
4. **The Propagation Phase:** The infected machines are used recursively to infect other machines in the network.

DDOS ATTACK TYPES

It is beneficial to understand the various types of that are being used today in order to implement an efficient strategy to mitigate them. Now a day, the attackers are using over twenty seven types of DDoS methods. This chapter classifies DDoS attacks based on exploited vulnerability as shown in Figure 2 (J. Mirkovic & P. Reiher, 2004).

Flood Attacks

In a flood attack, the slaves send large volumes of IP traffic to a victim system in order to congest the victim system's bandwidth. The impact of packet streams sent by the slaves to the victim system varies from slowing it down or crashing the system to saturation of the network bandwidth. Some of the well-known flood attacks are UDP flood attacks and ICMP flood attacks (R.K.C. Chang, 2002).

User Datagram Protocol (UDP) is a connectionless protocol. When data packets are sent via UDP, there is no handshaking required between sender and receiver, and the receiving system will just receive packets and process it. A large number of UDP packets sent to a victim system can saturate the network, depleting the bandwidth available for legitimate service requests to the victim system (Puneet Zaroo, 2003).

In a DDoS UDP Flood attack, the UDP packets are sent to either random or specified ports on the victim system. Typically, UDP flood attacks are designed to attack random victim ports. This causes the victim system to process the incoming data to try to determine which applications have requested data. If the victim system is not running any applications on the targeted port, then the victim system will

Figure 2. Classification of DDoS Attacks

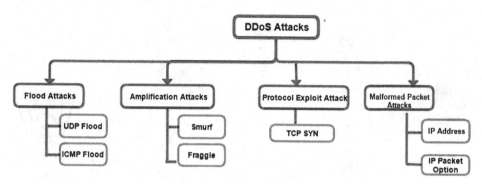

send out an ICMP packet to the sending system indicating a "destination port unreachable" message to the forged source address. If enough UDP packets are delivered to ports of the victim, the system will go down. By the use of a DDoS tool the source IP address of the attacking packets can be spoofed and this way the true identity of the secondary victims is prevented from exposure and the return packets from the victim system are not sent back to the zombies.

ICMP Flood attacks exploit the Internet Control Message Protocol (ICMP), which enables users to send an echo packet to a remote host to check whether it's alive. More specifically during a DDoS ICMP flood attack, the Slaves send large volumes of ICMP_ECHO_REPLY packets ("ping") to the victim. These packets request reply from the victim and this has as a result the saturation of the bandwidth of the victim's network connection. During an ICMP flood attack, the source IP address may be spoofed.

Amplification Attacks

In amplification attacks, the attacker or the Slaves exploit the broadcast IP address feature found on most routers to amplify and reflect the attack and send messages to a broadcast IP address. This instructs the routers servicing the packets within the network to send them to all the IP addresses within the broadcast address range. This way the malicious traffic that is produced reduces the victim system's bandwidth. In this type of DDoS attack, the attacker can send the broadcast message directly, or by the use of slaves to send the broadcast message in order to increase the volume of attacking traffic. If the broadcast message is sent directly, the attacker can use the systems within the broadcast network as slaves without needing to infiltrate them or install any agent software. Some well known amplification attacks are Smurf and Fraggle attacks (Puneet Zaroo, 2003).

The intermediary nodes that are used as attack launchers in amplification attacks are called reflectors. A reflector is any IP host that will return a packet if sent a packet. So, web servers, DNS servers, and routers are reflectors, since they return SYN ACKs or RSTs in response to SYN or other TCP packets (R.B. Lee, 2003).

An attacker sends packets that require responses to the reflectors. The packets are address-spoofed with source addresses set to a victim's address. The reflectors return response packets to the victim according to the types of the attack packets. The attack packets are essentially reflected in the normal packets towards the victim. The reflected packets can flood the victim's link if the number of reflectors is large enough. Note that the reflectors are readily identified as the source addresses in the flooding packets received by the victim. The operator of a reflector on the other hand, cannot easily locate the slave that is pumping the reflector, because the traffic sent to the reflector does not have the slave's source address, but rather the source address of the victim.

The attack architecture of reflector attacks is very similar to the one used for direct ones. However, there are several important differences.

- A reflector attack requires a set of predetermined reflectors.
- The reflectors could also be dispersed on the Internet, because the attacker does not need to install any agent software
- The reflected packets are normal packets with legitimate source addresses and cannot be filtered based on route-based mechanisms.

Smurf attacks send ICMP echo request traffic with a spoofed source address of the target victim to a number of IP broadcast addresses. Most hosts on an IP network will accept ICMP echo requests and reply to the source address, in this case, the target victim. On a broadcast network, there could potentially be hundreds of machines to reply to each ICMP packet. The use of a network in order to elicit many responses to a single packet has been labeled as ''amplifier''. In this type of attack the party that is hurt is not only the spoofed source address target (the victim) but also the intermediate broadcast devices (amplifiers).

The Fraggle attacks are a similar to the Smurf except that they use UDP echo packets instead of ICMP echoes. Fraggle attacks generate even more bad traffic and can create even more damaging effects than just a Smurf attack.

The Simple Service Discovery Protocol (SSDP) Attack is a new reflection and amplification DDoS Attack. This SSDP protocol is part of the Universal Plug and Play (UPnP) Protocol standard. SSDP comes enabled on millions of home and network devices – including personal computers, routers, Wi-Fi access points, media servers, mobile devices, web cams, smart TVs and printers – to allow them to discover each other on a network, establish communication and carry out their functional services. Attackers have been abusing these protocols to launch DDoS attacks that amplify and reflect network traffic to their targets. The Simple Object Access Protocol (SOAP) is used to deliver control messages to UPnP devices and pass information back from the devices. Attackers have discovered that SOAP requests can be crafted to elicit a response that reflects and amplifies a packet, which can be redirected towards a target. By employing a great number of devices, attackers create large quantities of attack traffic that can be aimed at selected targets.

Protocol Exploit Attacks

Protocol Exploit attacks exploit a specific feature or implementation bug of some protocol installed at the victim in order to consume excess amounts of its resources. A representative example of protocol exploit attacks is TCP SYN attacks (R.B Lee, 2003).

TCP SYN attacks exploit the inherent weakness of the three-way handshake involved in the TCP connection setup. A server, upon receiving an initial SYN (synchronize/start) request from a client, sends back a SYN/ACK (synchronize/acknowledge) packet and waits for the client to send the final ACK (acknowledge). An attacker initiates an SYN flooding attack by sending a large number of SYN packets and never acknowledges any of the replies, essentially leaving the server waiting for the nonexistent

ACK's. Considering that the server only has a limited buffer queue for new connections, SYN Flood results in the server being unable to process other incoming connections as the queue gets overloaded.

Malformed Packet Attacks

Malformed packet attacks rely on incorrectly formed IP packets that are sent from slaves to the victim in order to crash the victim system. The malformed packet attacks can be divided in two types of attacks: IP address attack and IP packet options attack.

In an IP address attack, the packet contains the same source and destination IP addresses. This has as a result the confusion of the operating system of the victim system and the crash of the victim system.

In an IP packet options attack, a malformed packet may randomize the optional fields within an IP packet and set all quality of service bits to one. This would have as a result the use of additional processing time by the victim in order to analyze the traffic. If this attack is combined with the use of multiple agents, it could lead to the crash of the victim system.

FUTURE RESEARCH DIRECTIONS

DDoS attacks have been changing their strategies and tactics. So, there is a need for continuously monitoring DDoS attacks in the near future and classifying them according to their impact.

REFERENCES

Chang, R. K. C. (2002). Defending against flooding-based, Distributed Denial of Service attacks: A tutorial. *IEEE Communications Magazine, 40*(10), 42–51. doi:10.1109/MCOM.2002.1039856

Houle, K. J., & Weaver, G. M. (2001). *Trends in Denial of Service Attack Technology, CERT and CERT coordination center(CERT/CC)*. Carnegie Mellon University. Available from http://www.cert.org/archive/pdf/DoS_trends.pdf

Lee, R. B. (2003). *Taxonomies of Distributed Denial of Service networks, attacks, tools and countermeasures*. Princeton University. Available: http://www.ee.princeton.edu/rblee

Mirkovic, & Reiher. (2004). A Taxonomy of DDoS Attack and DDoS defense Mechanisms. *ACM SIGCOMM Computer Communications Review, 34*(2), 39-53.

Richtel, M. (2000). Yahoo Attributes a Lengthy Service Failure to an Attack. *NY Times*. Retrieved from http://www.nytimes.com/library/tech/00/02/biztech/articles/08yahoo.html

Zaroo. (2003). *A Survey of DDoS attacks and some DDoS defense mechanisms*. Advanced Information Assurance (CS 626).

KEY TERMS AND DEFINITIONS

Attack: An Attack is an intentional attempt to bypass computer security measures in some fashion. In computer and computer networks an attack is any attempt to destroy, expose, alter, disable, steal or gain unauthorized access to or make unauthorized use of an asset.

Attacker: An attacker is the person who launches the attack.

Botnet: A large swarm of computer acts under the control of a single attacker is called botnet.

Master: A master is a compromised host with an attacker program running on it.

Slave: A is slave is a compromised host that is running an attacker program and is responsible for generating a stream of packets towards the intended victim.

Threat: A threat is any situation or event that has the potential to harm a system.

Victim: A targeted host.

Vulnerability: A weakness in a system that can be exploited in a way that violates security policy.

Chapter 8
Cluster–Based Countermeasures for DDoS Attacks

Mohammad Jabed Morshed Chowdhury
Daffodil International University, Bangladesh

Dileep Kumar G
Adama Science and Technology University, Ethiopia

ABSTRACT

Distributed Denial of Service (DDoS) attack is considered one of the major security threats in the current Internet. Although many solutions have been suggested for the DDoS defense, real progress in fighting those attacks is still missing. In this chapter, the authors analyze and experiment with cluster-based filtering for DDoS defense. In cluster-based filtering, unsupervised learning is used to create profile of the network traffic. Then the profiled traffic is passed through the filters of different capacity to the servers. After applying this mechanism, the legitimate traffic will get better bandwidth capacity than the malicious traffic. Thus the effect of bad or malicious traffic will be lesser in the network. Before describing the proposed solutions, a detail survey of the different DDoS countermeasures have been presented in the chapter.

INTRODUCTION

Among the many security threats in the current Internet, Distributed Denial of Service (DDoS) attacks are considered to be one of the most serious. Denials of Service (DoS) attacks aim to make the resources of the computer system of the victim unavailable or unreliable in providing their intended services. In the context of this work, DoS attacks try to consume and exhaust the victim's bandwidth or the server capacity. In DDoS attacks, the attacker compromises a large number of hosts in Internet and instructs them to conduct a coordinated attack. The network of the compromised hosts is called a botnet. In recent years, a sharp increase in large DDoS attacks has been reported (Figure 1).

While progress has been made in preventing or at least significantly lessening the impact of various security vulnerabilities, real progress in fighting DDoS is still missing. While automated software updates and antivirus programs can limit the number of compromised computers, there are still botnets compris-

DOI: 10.4018/978-1-4666-8761-5.ch008

Figure 1. Size of largest reported DDoS Attack (Gbps)[1]

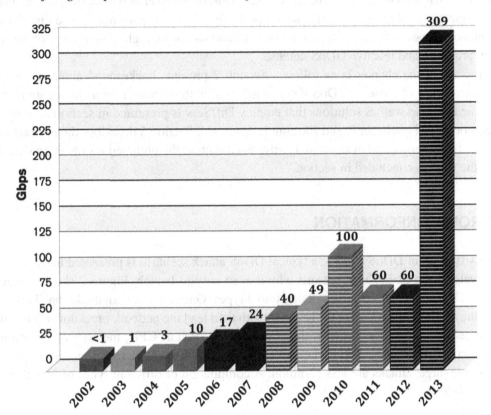

ing of millions of nodes. Another potential defence is to filter the packets sent by the DDoS attacker at a firewall after detecting the attack with and intrusion detection system (IDS). These rule-based detection and filtering techniques have not been successful in filtering DDoS attack because the DDoS attacker can send seemingly legitimate traffic. In the case of open services, such as web servers, the DDoS attacker only needs to send large quantities of useless service requests. Thus, there might be no specific features of DDoS attack traffic that the rule-based filters can be instructed to filter. With such malicious but legitimate traffic, DDoS attackers are able to relatively easily bypass most means of DDoS defence.

This work analyzes and experiment with cluster-based filtering for DDoS defense. In cluster-based filtering, unsupervised learning is used to create a normal profile of the network traffic. Then the filter for DDoS attacks is based on this normal profile. This work focuses on the scenario in which the cluster-based filter is deployed at the target network and serves for proactive or reactive defense.

A game-theoretic model is created for the scenario, making it possible to model the defender and attacker strategies as mathematical optimization tasks. The obtained optimal strategies are then experimentally evaluated. In the test bed setup, the hierarchical heavy hitters (HHH) algorithm is applied to traffic clustering and the Differentiated Services (DiffServ) quality-of-service (QoS) architecture is used for deploying the cluster-based filter on a Linux router.

The theoretical results suggest that the cluster-based filtering is an effective method for DDoS defense, unless the attacker is able to send traffic which perfectly imitates the normal traffic distribution. The experimental outcome confirms the theoretical results and shows the high effectiveness of cluster-based filtering in proactive and reactive DDoS defense.

The structure of the chapter is as follows. Section 2 presents background about different DDoS attacks. An overview of existing DDoS defense methods with particular focus on solutions based on clustering the traffic as well as solutions that employ DiffServ is presented in section 3. In section 4, a game-theoretic model of cluster-based filtering is described. Section 5 describes the test bed setup and the results of the experimental evaluation. Lastly, discussion of the obtained results is presented in section 6 and the work is concluded in section 7.

BACKGROUND INFORMATION

Before classification of DDoS attacks, a typical DDoS attack scenario is presented here. It shows why it is so prevalent, and its intrinsic reasons why it is so easy to launch. Figure 2 shows a hierarchical model of a DDoS attack. DDoS attack divide into 2 types. One is bandwidth depletion. This method is to congest the network, massive use of the bandwidth then lead the network breakdown. The other type is resource depletion. Attacker depletes the key resources such as CPU, memory and so on and then breaks the server (Mittal et al., 2011). The attack usually starts from numerous sources to aim at a single target. Multiple target attacks are less common. A compilation of different types of DDoS attacks are presented as follows:

SYN Flood Attack

Any system providing TCP-based network services is potentially subject to this attack. The attackers use half-open connections to cause the server exhaust its resource to keep the information describing all pending connections. The result would be system crash or system inoperative (Khattab, 2003).

TCP Reset Attack

TCP reset also utilize the characteristics of TCP protocol. By listening the TCP connections to the victim, the attacker sends a fake TCP RESET packet to the victim. Then it causes the victim to inadvertently terminate its TCP connection.

ICMP Attack

Smurf attack sends forged ICMP echo request packets to IP broadcast addresses. These attacks lead large amounts of ICMP echo reply packets being sent from an intermediary site to a victim, accordingly cause network congestion or outages. ICMP datagram can also be used to start an attack via ping. Attackers use the ping Command to construct oversized ICMP datagram to launch the attack.

Figure 2. A common DDoS Attack scenario

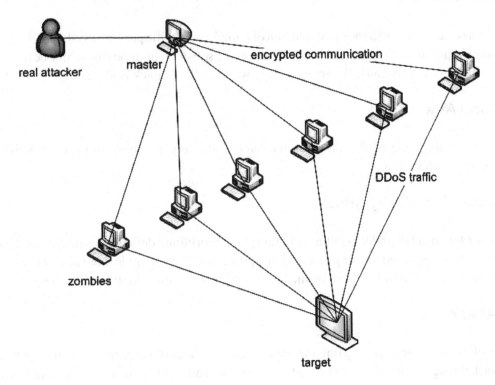

UDP Storm Attack

This kind of attack can not only impair the hosts. Services, but also congest or slow down the prevailing network. When a connection is established between two UDP services, each of which produces a very huge number of packets, thus cause an attack.

DNS Request Attack

In this attack scenario, the attack sends a large number of UDP-based DNS requests to a name server using a spoofed source IP address. Then the name server, acting as an intermediate party in the attack, responds by sending back to the spoofed IP address as the victim destination. Because of the amplification effect of DNS response, it can cause serious bandwidth attack (Yaar, 2003).

CGI Request Attack

By simply sending multiple CGI request to the target server, the attacker consumes the CPU resource of the victim. Then the server is forced to terminate its services.

Mail Bomb Attack

A mail bomb is the sending of a enormous amount of e-mail to a specific person or system. A huge amount of mail may simply fill up the recipient's disk space on the server or, in some cases, may be too much for a server to handle and may cause the server to stop working. This attack is also a kind of flood attack.

ARP Storm Attack

During a DDoS attack, the ARP request volume can become very massive, and then the victim system can be negatively affected

Algorithmic Complexity Attack

It's a class of low-bandwidth DDoS attacks that exploit algorithmic deficiencies in the worst case performance of algorithms used in many mainstream applications. For example, both binary trees and hash tables with carefully chosen input can be the attack targets to consume system resources greatly.

Spam Attack

This type of attack is used for targeting the various mail services of corporate as well as public users. DDoS attack through spam has increased and disturbed the mail services of various organizations. Spam penetrate through all the fifilters to create DDoS attacks, which causes serious trouble to users and the data. But these mail services are frequent target of hackers and spammers (Nagamalai, 2007)

TAXONOMY OF COURTER MEASURES

DDoS defense mechanisms can be classified according to the main role they take in the process of defense as, i) detection mechanisms, ii) source identification techniques, and iii) prevention and reaction mechanisms.

The distinction between DDoS prevention and reaction is not always clear, since often one mechanism serves for the both of the functions, depending on its location in the network. That is the case with the method focus on, the cluster-based traffic filtering, as it will be discussed later. A fully exemplified version of the taxonomy presented below can be found in Figure 3. All the countermeasures have been categorized into three broad categories namely i) Mitigation ii) Prevention and iii) Deterrence.

A. Mitigation

DDoS countermeasures can be classified as separate techniques for server, network or client based mitigation.

Figure 3. A fully exemplified version of the taxonomy

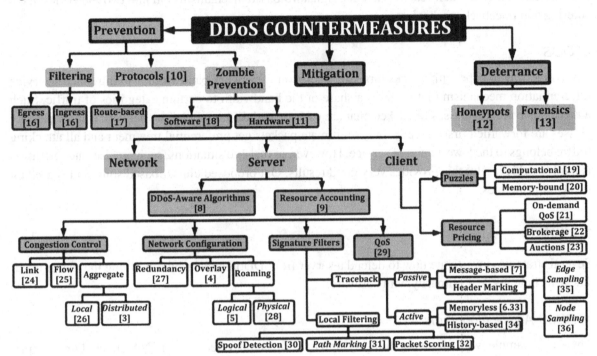

1. Network

In network-based mitigation techniques involves the intermediate network as well as some mitigation methods assisted by client or server subnets.

a. Congestion Control

Mitigating the effects of a DDoS attack does not necessarily require detection of the attack. A defense mechanism can be effective without knowing whether there is an ongoing attack or not. Applying policies that isolate certain portions of traffic from others can limit the impact of malicious behavior without the need for an attack detection mechanism.

b. Network Configuration

Several schemes provide protection from DDoS attacks by modifying the physical or logical configuration of a network and its servers. In (Keromytis, 2002), a Secure Overlay Service (SOS) is provided by an overlay network of routers which use a hash-based algorithm to route packets to a server. An outside host wishing to communicate with that server must first contact a Secure Overlay Access Point (SOAP), a designated router that lets a packet enter the overlay only after authenticating its source.

c. Signature Filters

Signature-based strategies maintain the traditional best-effort routing model of the Internet in normal conditions. The defense system reacts only when an attack detection mechanism flags certain packets as malicious. Based on their reactive actions, signature-based mechanisms fall into two categories: local filtering and traceback mechanisms.

d. QOS

A possible way to cope with attacks targeting depletion of network bandwidth is to introduce a service differentiation mechanism that reserves a share of the bandwidth to certain categories of traffic. Such a mechanism creates classes of packets that are each treated differently by the network (higher priority classes are forwarded first). Ideally, only legitimate packets get preferential treatment and all attacking traffic belongs to the lowest class of service. However, in real-life situations, such precise categorization is hard to achieve. But this provides very good results. Out proposed cluster based solution is based on this QoS principles.

2. Server

Several strategies investigate how to defend a server from DDoS attacks by modifying the server itself. These techniques deal primarily with software.

a. DDoS-Aware Algorithms

There exist simple ways for an operating system to mitigate the effects of a DDoS attack. For example, an OS can periodically scan the TCP connection queue and drop half-open connections. By doing so, the OS prevents a TCP SYN attack from hogging memory resources.

b. Resource Accounting

Some OS-level resource accounting schemes like Escort (Spatscheck, 1999) are more elaborate than simple DDoS-aware algorithms. They enforce policies which control allocation of time multiplexed resources such as CPU time or network bandwidth.

3. Client

Puzzles and Resource Pricing schemes are client-centric classes of countermeasures that take advantage of the limited computational and monetary resources of client hosts in order to force them to regulate their traffic. With Puzzles, every client requesting access to services must commit a certain amount of resources determined by the network or server. Resource Pricing strategies establish different market-like schemes in which resources are available for purchase by the clients.

B. DDoS Prevention

Reactive measures protecting critical services during an ongoing attack – e.g. the majority of measures in section A – undoubtedly are important, but ultimately, proactive measures need to be implemented to prevent the occurrence of an attack in the first place. Such preventive measures should either eliminate exploitable flaws on a network or work towards complicating the task of a potential attacker.

1. Filtering

When internetworking protocols such as TCP and IP were initially designed, functionality was of greater concern than security. As a result, malicious parties can generate invalid information or send harmful commands without being detected by those protocols. Filtering packets with such contents is a first step towards reducing an eventual enemy's perniciousness.

2. Protocols

How to design protocols that do not offer opportunities for DoS attacks is still an unsolved research problem. However, there are some desirable properties known to prevent specific types of attacks. For example, the goal of some attacks is to deplete a server's resources by establishing a large number of bogus TCP connections. That way, the TCP buffers are saturated with connection status and incoming connection requests must be ignored. A remedy to this problem involves designing stateless protocols which shift the burden of state holding from the server to the clients. SYN cookies partially reach this goal by remaining stateless in the first steps of a TCP connection establishment.

3. Zombie Prevention

An important step towards solving the DDoS problem consists in preventing the attacker from constituting an army of zombie computers in the first place. To attain this goal, it is necessary to remediate the weaknesses attackers exploit to gain control of hosts connected to the public Internet. One of the most important weaknesses, buffer overflow (Lee, 2004), can be mitigated using either software or hardware mechanisms.

C. Deterrence

Even though some techniques allow the tracing of an attack back to the attacking hosts, a victim will rarely be able to identify and prosecute the attacker controlling those zombies.

1. Honeypots

Honeypots are computer systems placed on a network for the sole purpose of being abused by unsuspecting attackers (Spitzner, 2003). Since a honeypot does not offer any useful service, nearly all activity detected on it is malicious. It is thus simple to use such a computer as an intrusion detection system. In regular operating systems, rootkits can be used to cover the attacker's traces. In advanced honeypot systems, the OS is encapsulated in a logging framework so all attacker activity is recorded, regardless of attempts to filter the audit trail

2. Forensics

With the use of custom-made "sniffers" and scripts, skilled programmers can manually trace the activity of malicious software back to the IRC channel used by the master attacker for controlling the bot network. Such forensic activity could ultimately lead to the discovery of the attacker's identity.

LITERATURE REVIEW

Today's data networks carry lots of traffic and it is getting more difficult day by day to correctly identify the malicious traffic. Another challenge is that the malicious hackers are also getting smarter and changes their strategies from time to time. They evolve their attack methods to bypass the tradition countermeasures. A new line of research is getting immersed to address these new security requirements, clustering based traffic filtering.

Cluster-based traffic filtering, when implemented close to the attack sources is a DDoS prevention mechanism, while it is deployed at the target network, serves as a target bandwidth management scheme in DDoS reaction. The method conceptually belongs to the history based prevention since it relies on finding clusters in the normal traffic, and using them as filters when the malicious traffic appears.

Clustering of traffic as a DDoS prevention or reaction has one important advantage over the other filtering methods. While the previously described filtering methods need to distinguish is some way between the normal and the attack packets, the cluster-based filtering does not need such distinction. Filtering based on clusters prioritizes some traffic classes over others, thus increasing normal packet survival ratio (NPSR), but inside each of the classes it is not necessary to know which packets are malicious.

In the scenario, a cluster-based filter is placed on a router between the web server, which is the target, and the Internet. The filter is used for the bandwidth management by setting different reservations of bandwidth for the traffic classes corresponding to the different clusters. This paper is focused on the question how to create the bandwidth management policy using clusters so that the DDoS attack impact is maximally reduced.

Clustering Algorithms for Network Traffic

As discussed in the previous section, the important factor in DDoS defense that uses cluster-based filtering is to find the "good set of clusters" in the traffic. Thus many academic solutions are focused solely on the question how to cluster network traffic into qualitatively good classes.

Erman et al. (2003) examined existing data mining algorithms: density-based spatial clustering of applications with noise (DBSCAN) (Ester et al., 1996), K-Means (Li et al., 2002) and AutoClass (Fayyad et al., 1996). The algorithms are evaluated and compared from the point of accuracy of clustering traffic into known traffic classes, then from the point of algorithm speed and number of clusters that is produced. McGregor et al. (2004) also applied machine learning techniques to cluster network packet header traces. The authors showed appropriate correspondence between known traffic types in the traces, such as HTTP, SMTP, IMAP or TCP DNS, and the traffic classes obtained by the clustering.

However, the common data mining algorithms are not the best choice for the network traffic data. Firstly, the traffic datasets have larger size compared to the common datasets in data mining. Secondly, for the purpose of DDoS defense, network traffic often needs to be examined in real time, meaning that clustering should be applied to the data stream. Common data mining algorithms are slow for such task, or would require so high computing resources that are not available in networking devices. Third, the traffic features such as IP addresses and URLs, have the specific hierarchical structure. Thus researchers developed specific algorithms for clustering the network traffic.

Cormode et al. (2008) developed the hierarchical heavy hitters algorithm (HHH) which is an extension to the heavy hitters algorithm and takes into account the hierarchical structure of the network traffic. The authors also provide approximate versions of the HHH algorithm that are fast enough to cluster the data stream. Theoretical proofs on the error bounds for the approximate algorithms are provided. An implementation of the HHH algorithm is done in the evaluation phase. Hijazi et al. (2008) developed another algorithm which takes into account specific features of the network traffic. The algorithm is named approximate divisive hierarchical clustering (ADHIC). ADHIC is an adaptive algorithm since the features used during the clustering, called (p,n)-grams, are chosen depending on the structure of the particular dataset. (p,n)-grams are defined as "a byte strings of length n located at an a set p in a packet within a data stream. The authors of ADHIC also developed a fast and lightweight algorithm implementation intended for the streaming data which is called netADICT.

Traffic Clustering as a DDoS Detection Technique

Most of the prior work involving traffic clustering focuses on anomaly and, particularly, DDoS detection. Lakhina et al. (2005) describe an anomaly detection method that relies on changes in the feature distributions of traffic. In the case of DDoS, the authors find that features that are affected are source and destination addresses. Entropy is used as a metric when detecting changes in traffic distributions induced by anomalies. The main advantage of using entropy over volume-based metrics is that entropy can detect and classify low-volume anomalies, such as port scan, which stay undetected, or it is not possible to distinguish their structure by volume-based methods. However, entropy cannot distinguish between different distributions having the same amount of uncertainty. Gu et al. (2005) create a detection model that uses relative entropy that avoids such problem in detection. Relative entropy or Kullback-Leibler divergence (KL-divergence) (Kullback, 1997), is a measure of the difference between two probability distributions and is often interpreted as non-symmetric metric. The authors first decide on a certain number of packet classes, precisely 2348 two-dimensional classes induced by the protocol and port numbers. Second, the maximum-entropy configuration is calculated by feature selection and parameter estimation giving an initial, normal traffic, configuration. This configuration is then used as a reference point to compare the monitored traffic to it. If the KL-divergence from the maximum-entropy distribution is found to be greater than a threshold value on any packet class, then an alarm for that packet class is raised. Stoecklin (2006) suggests improving the work of Gu by using symmetrical KL divergence as the deviation measure. The author provides experimental evidence that such detection is resilient to periodical changes in normal traffic which reduces false positives.

Kang et alo. (2013) have proposed a DDoS avoidance strategy to provide service availability to those preregistered important users. In the proposed strategy, the attack scenarios are divided into different time points and provide alternative access channels to already authenticated and other valid users. Oldmeadow et al. (2004) present a time-varying adaptive clustering algorithm that is based on the fixed-width clustering (Eskin, 2002). Fixed-width clustering is a clustering algorithm that is based on a geometric framework and can be applied to unlabeled data. The authors improve the detection based on fixed-width clustering by traffic feature weighting. Zhong et al. (2010) apply two existing clustering algorithms to DDoS detection. The algorithms used are: fuzzy c-means (FCM) algorithm (Bezdek, 1973) and apriori association algorithm (Agrawal & Srikant, 1994). After creating the normal traffic profile, the authors developed the model to discern abnormal traffic and measure its duration. The evaluation in LAN network showed that the DDoS detection reaches up to 97% accuracy. Ming-Yang (2011) applied to DDoS detection the k-nearest neighbor (KNN) algorithm (Hastie & Tibshirani, 1996) improved by feature weighting and selection based on a genetic algorithm (Holland, 1975). Overall accuracy over 97% for known DDoS attacks is achieved and over 78% in the case of unknown attacks. In (Petiz et al. 2014), have propose a novel and more efficient methodology to detect DDoS attacks at the source that relies on the inherent periodicity of the traffic generated by DDoS attack sources. Detecting and quantifying the traffic periodic components using multiscaling traffic analysis based on wavelet scalograms allows an efficient detection of DDoS attacks at the source, even when the attacks are performed using encrypted channels or are embedded within licit traffic.

Traffic Clustering in the Role of DDoS Prevention and Reaction

As discussed before, filters based on clustered traffic are often used for both functions, for the DDoS prevention and reaction. Muhai et al. (2010) present a mathematical nonlinear defense model against DDoS. They involve the victim, a router and an additional application server in the defense process. Using the model it is possible to control how much of the attacker and regular user traffic is served. The main weakness is in the assumption that the regular user traffic and the attacker traffic can be distinguished. However, depending on how well is the attack adapted to the normal traffic patterns (for example by spoofing addresses so that they appear legitimate) such distinction might not be possible. The authors also describe DDoS detection by the traffic analysis. After the attack is detected, the application server sends the signal to the router to start the nonlinear traffic control system.

Similarly to this approach, Matrawy et al. (2005) do not explicitly distinguish between malicious and regular traffic, but rather filter disruptive traffic according to its membership in clusters. The authors deploy traffic clustering as a reaction technique in DDoS defense in the following way. Adaptive traffic management based on traffic shapers is applied after establishing the baselines. In this work, different clustering algorithm is used, HHH algorithm, and the implementation of bandwidth management which is based on DiffServ is different. DiffServ enables more possibilities in DDoS defense, since among other traffic provisioning features it can, in particular, provide the traffic shaping. In (Iyengar et al. 2014), have proposed a fuzzy logic based defense mechanism that can be set with predefined rules by which it can detect the malicious packets and takes proper counter measures to mitigate the DDoS attack. Also a detailed study of different kind of DDoS attack and existing defense strategies has been carried out.

Even though not employing a classical clustering mechanism, the approach by Li et al. (2008) is similar to this work in building a mathematical model based on traffic classes and bandwidth measurements. After creating the model, the bandwidth reservations decided by the model are allocated to the specific classes. The similar procedure is maintained here. However, unlike in this approach, the traffic is classified into only two classes: normal and anomalous. The traffic feature used to distinguish those two classes is the ratio of the number of common, i.e., users that have been already recorded, to the number of users that have been recorded for the first time. Instead, the similar ratio of normal traffic rate is applied to the one observed during the congestion, on each of the traffic cluster.

DiffServ in DDoS Defense

DiffServ is a quality-of-service provisioning framework that is used in evaluation phase for creating filtering policy based on clusters. The DiffServ environment with CBQ algorithm is used for reducing disruption of normal traffic during the attack. After deciding whether the incoming packet is normal or not, it is passed to the high priority queue or low priority queue, following the queuing discipline (Figure 4). The decision about the packet type is based on the difference from the harmonic mean of the intervals of transmission times of incoming packets. Differing from the mentioned approach, HTB

Figure 4. Different levels of queue based on the quality of traffic

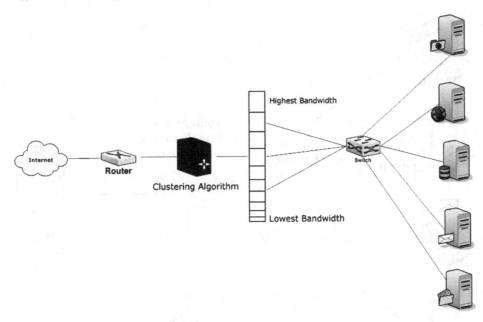

queuing discipline is used, which is an advancement of CBQ. One of the early papers with similar idea (Lau et al., 2000) describes implementing CBQ mechanism as a prevention technique against DDoS on a router. CBQ and RED queuing disciplines were shown to be successful in providing fixed bandwidth to legitimate users and reducing the impact of DDoS. This work differs from the described proposals since this combines DiffServ with traffic clustering. Thus it effectively uses the DiffServ capability of provisioning many different traffic classes, instead of having only two classes (normal and anomalys).

THEORETICAL MODEL

In order to model and analyze traffic clustering as a DDoS defense mechanism, a particular scenario is used in which traffic clustering is deployed. Since the focus is on traffic clustering as a DDoS reaction mechanism, the mechanism close to the target in the scenario is deployed. Secondly, a theoretical model for traffic clustering is created by abstracting only relevant elements from the scenario. The results of the analysis provide an insight into the effectiveness of traffic clustering as a DDoS reaction technique.

Many solutions based on traffic clustering use two versions of the clustering algorithm, which are often called the offline and online algorithm. The offline algorithm is applied to recorded normal traffic to obtaining the normal traffic clusters. The online algorithm is an approximation of the offline algorithm. It is faster and less demanding, so that it can be applied to the live data stream. Clustering of streaming data is necessary in DDoS detection and also for the adaptive DDoS reaction.

A traffic cluster is defined by ranges of traffic feature values. All the packets in which the feature values are inside these ranges forms a traffic class. The terms traffic class and traffic cluster are often used interchangeably. Additionally, as a part of the cluster definition the amount of the recorded traffic belonging to the class is taken.

Figure 5. Scenario with clustering mechanism deployed

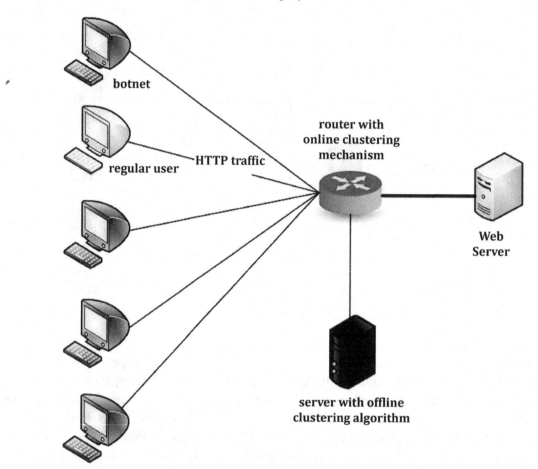

Scenario

In this scenario, the target is a web server, as shown in Figure 5. The web server has exposed its services through a router. To make this model as general as possible, in the start, algorithm as is considered as a black box that outputs clusters from the network traffic.

In the scenario, the normal traffic is observed over a certain period of time. Afterwards, some offline algorithm is applied to the traffic records. The offline algorithm outputs a cluster set which represents the normal traffic profile. A filtering policy on the router is created using that profile. When the attack happens, a predefined action using the filtering policy is taken on the router as a DDoS defense reaction. The heavy task of the initial cluster computation may be allocated to a separate server which executes the offline algorithm. In that case, such a server may instruct the router about the filtering policy that the router should deploy. The online algorithm might be employed on the router to cluster the traffic stream passing through the router. In the case of an attack, the online algorithm provides information about the distribution of the attack traffic. Using the output of the online algorithm, the filter reservations may be adapted so that the DDoS reaction is improved. The success of this method, however, depends on the particular clustering algorithm used. If successfully employed, this method can be also used for DDoS detection. Different possibilities are analyzed when only the offline algorithm is used.

Depending whether the attacker or defender is more agile in changing its attack or defense strategy, the following cases in this scenario are distinguished:

1. In scenario 1, the defender 'makes the first move', meaning that it start from a fixed defender strategy and analyze what is the best strategy for the attacker, who is the more agile party.
2. In scenario 2, the defender is the less agile party and decides to use the filtering policy that will serve as the optimal proactive defense against the more adaptive attack. It is observed that such optimal filtering policy should allocate cluster reservations proportionally to the normal traffic cluster sizes.
3. In scenario 3, the attacker 'makes the first move'. When the attack is launched, the changes in the amounts of traffic recorded per class will be observed by the filtering mechanism on the router. Using the data about new traffic amounts, the defender can adapt its filtering policy for the optimal reactive defense. Thus, in this case, the defender is the more agile party.

Problem Classification and Preliminaries

As stated in the definition of DDoS attacks, the focus is on capacity exhaustion attacks. Thus the capacity of the server is the main resource to model. The filtering policy on the router will be based on different bandwidth allocations to traffic classes corresponding to different clusters. The aim is to find the optimal filtering policies that will serve for DDoS defense in the different scenarios that is described above. The class of mathematical problems which deal with allocating resources in an economic way is called resource allocation or knapsack problems. Thus, the problems that will arise during the analysis of the model, it can be classified as knapsack problems.

The knapsack problem has two distinct variants, depending on the variable that is optimized: discrete knapsack problems, and continuous knapsack problems. However, in this model, a less well known variant of the knapsack problem is used, the continuous knapsack problem. In the continuous knapsack problem, a fraction of an item can be taken, i.e., the variable values are not constrained only to the integers, but can take the real values.

Another categorization of knapsack problems is done depending on the objective function that is optimized: linear knapsack problems, and nonlinear knapsack problems. The knapsack problem as described above has the feature that the objective function in the problem is linear. A class of more complex resource allocation problems appears in the case when the objective function is nonlinear and they are called nonlinear knapsack problems.

A continuous form of the linear knapsack problem is solvable more easily compared to the discrete knapsack case since the solution can be given in the form of a simple greedy approximation algorithm, as proposed by Dantzig (1998). According to the algorithm, the items are sorted depending on the item value, and take the most valuable item as long as it is available. Then the following most valuable item is being consumed and so on, until we reach the price limit or exhaust all the items available.

The server bandwidth in this model is normalized to 1, corresponding to 100% utilization. We also need to model the cluster set and corresponding cluster sizes which are the output of the clustering algorithm. Finally, the filtering policy on the router needs to be modeled. The policy uses the knowledge about the clusters and allocates reservations to the corresponding traffic classes according to a predefined algorithm. This work is aimed to find out the best algorithm for each of the different scenarios described in the previous section.

RESEARCH METHODOLOGY

In this section, an experimental test bed is created for evaluating the proposed solution. The experiments have been conducted to follow the scenario. Three virtual machines are set up in a virtual network in order to serve for the router, the server and the user in the scenario, respectively. Using the real data from a web server at Daffodil University, normal traffic is simulated, and different types of attack traffic are generated for different attack scenarios. The clustering algorithm applied to the web server traffic records in this experiments is the hierarchical heavy hitters algorithm (HHH). Using the output from the clustering algorithm, the filters for the Differentiated Services (DiffServ) environment are created, particularly using its HTB queuing discipline. The cluster-based filter is deployed on the router in this experiments. DiffServ is a quality-of-service (QoS) provisioning environment and, for the task, it is used for defining the bandwidth management policy and for filtering the traffic according to the policy.

Hierarchical Heavy Hitters Algorithm

In the heavy hitters data mining algorithm, the data are grouped into clusters based on the frequency of data items having common values on a certain subset of features. A threshold is defined, and all the feature combinations having a frequency over the threshold define clusters in the dataset. For instance, having the client IP address as the only feature in the feature set, heavy hitters would be defined as all the individual addresses that are found in the number of packets that is not smaller than the threshold value. Since the algorithm is based on finding high-frequency features, it is called heavy hitters.

In data mining traffic datasets deals with large, some-times live data streams, and also, as with the example of the IP address, the features of the data have a hierarchical structure. That is why Cormode at el. (2008) adapted the heavy hitters approach to the traffic data (or any other type of data having the hierarchical structure in features). The idea behind the hierarchical heavy hitters (HHH) approach is that when using individual features, such as single IP addresses, it is not always possible to define well the heavy hitters in the dataset. It can happen that there are many users from the campus subnet who are accessing the web server of the university. Each of the individual users is not having a number of requests to the server high enough to account his address for a heavy hitter. But all the campus users together form a subset of the requests which exceeds the threshold value and it is obviously useful to consider such a subset as a cluster since it describes a meaningful structure in the dataset. In such example, it is useful to consider the frequency of the IP address feature on the higher level of the hierarchy, i.e., on the level of subnets.

This examples focus on the IP address as a feature because that is the feature used for clustering the datasets. Examples of other traffic features that have a hierarchical structure are URLs, protocol types, port numbers (here the hierarchical structure can be defined in different ways, more or less artificially chosen according to the needs of the particular clustering).

Without the need, however, to consider multi-dimensional feature spaces, and thinking only of the IP address feature, it is still possible to realize that the task of HHH clustering is complex. Namely, at the fine-grained level, the IP address feature can be considered to have 32 levels of hierarchical structure, each level being defined by one bit in the 32-bit binary representation of the IP address. A smaller number of levels inside IP addresses can be defined, for example 4 levels, each corresponding to eight bits. The decision about defining the granularity of the hierarchy is up to the implementers of HHH, and they need to decide depending on the specific application of the algorithm. A more granular hierarchy will enable finding more precise heavy hitters in the dataset, but it has the disadvantage of making the clustering algorithm computationally intensive.

For the purpose of clustering the streaming data, different solutions are proposed in order to make the HHH algorithm less computationally demanding and faster. In those approaches a common idea is approximating the quality of the cluster output, with certain error guaranties.

Since the traffic records, in this scenario, are clustered offline, high computational requirements as well as the algorithm taking long time to compute the clusters can be affored. For that reason, in this implementation of HHH, the IP address feature is divided into full 32 levels of hierarchy.

DiffServ Environment

DiffServ is a networking architecture for QoS provisioning proposed by the IETF (Internet Engineering Task Force). The architecture of DiffServ is described by the RFC document (Blake et al., 1998), while other relevant RFC documents describe PHBs (per hop behaviors), DSCP (differentiated services code point) in IPv4 and IPv6, framework for Integrated Services operation using DiffServ environment etc. Kilkki, in his book (Kilkki, 1999), gives an overview of the RFC doc-uments related to DiffServ and the applications of DiffServ. DiffServ receives special attention as nowadays many applications have emerged that require assurances of provisioning and monitoring of QoS that cannot be provided by the existing network architecture. DiffSerf is a promising architecture to support the critical requirements of the new generation applications. DiffServ also enables providing different levels of service according to service level agreement (SLA) profiles between different domains such as ISPs, companies and users.

The idea behind the DiffServ is that the differentiation of services should be based on the essential service features, such as throughput, jitter, delay, packet loss, relative priority etc. Per-hop behaviors (PHBs) are DiffServ functional units that make such differentiation possible by classifying packets into different queues in the routers. The classification is based on the bits in the differentiated services (DSCP) field or uses some other features of the traffic for differentiation, which are supported by Dif-fServ. The architecture document specifies three types of DiffServ forwarding nodes (corresponding to the network routers in practice): interior nodes, ingress nodes and egress nodes. The functions of the nodes are separated according to one of the main principles of the current Internet that is keeping the core of the network simple and scalable, and moving intelligence and computational burden to the edges of the network. This means that the edge nodes do the tasks of classification, metering and marking of packets, while the core nodes are usually only classifying and forwarding or delaying and possibly dropping the packets according to the DSCP field and the respective PHBs. The DiffServ architecture fulfills the requirements for a DDoS defense mechanism since it is simple and complies with the current Internet model.

A QoS provisioning environment such as DiffServ may be used in the DDoS defense mechanism thanks to the PHB as means of resource allocation. DiffServ provides coarse-grained QoS provisioning, and PHB provides the means of resource allocation to aggregate streams. Thus, PHBs is used for the bandwidth allocation to the different classes of traffic (corresponding to the clusters).

DiffServ Queuing Disciplines (qdiscs)

The DiffServ forwarding nodes need to implement queues in which the packets are buffered in order to get delayed and prioritized according to different PHBs before being transmitted. Thus, a very important part in the implementation of DiffServ is queuing disciplines (qdiscs).

HTB Queuing Discipline

HTB defines a hierarchical structure of classes, and by default, each of the classes contains a PFIFO qdisc attached. When a packet is received, the HTB qdisc starts from the root class and examines whether it should enqueue the packet by consulting the filter that is attached to the class. If not, the classes attached to the root class are examined, and soon recursively. If the process comes to examining a leaf class and the filter accepts it, the packet is enqueued there. If no class filter is found to accept the packet, it is possible that a default class is defined, in which case such packet gets enqueued in the default class, or otherwise it stays enqueued in the last examined class. Such rules ensure that each packet gets enqueued into some of the classes. The DiffServ traffic polycing is depicted in Figure 6. HTB has with each of the classes associated the following set of parameters:

RESULTS AND DISCUSSION

Talking in the terms of game theory, the cases when one of the parties in the DDoS scenario "makes the first move" is analyzed. This means that either the defender or the attacker is clearly more agile than the other and can adapt his strategy to the slowly changing strategy of the other party. This corresponds to standard game-theoretic models. Quite different modeling techniques would be needed if both parties were equally adaptive or if they competed on the speed of the adaptation.

The quality of the DDoS defense in this analysis is measured by the amount of the normal traffic served during the attack, or NPSR. That is one limitation of this study, since traffic flows neither the different requirements that some types of flows might demand are considered. Namely, as described by Mirkovic et al. (2009) the DDoS defense quality is not only measured by the NPSR or similar quantitative measures of traffic, but different requirements for different protocols and applications should be considered.

The traffic clustering can be done offline, by clustering the offline traffic records as in the experiments, or it can be done online. In the second case, the normal traffic profile is created by clustering a live data stream and such a clustering is more demanding in computational resources and time. At highest speed links, it is often necessary to sample the traffic stream in order to apply the online clustering. However, the filtering method that is used in this work with both of the described clustering types, and itself is a lightweight process that can filter live data streams.

Figure 6. Schema representing DiffServ traffic filtering with HTB qdiscs

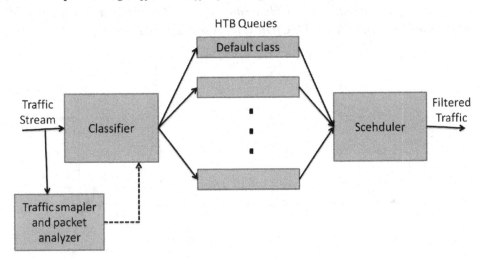

In this work, the hierarchical heavy hitter (HHH) is used. The tests are conducted with the HHH clustering algorithm and based only on one traffic feature, the client IP address. If the clustering was based on more features, for instance port numbers, it can be expected that the results in the DDoS defense would be improved.

The results of preserving the normal traffic packets during DDoS attack using DiffServ show promising results. Using the largest number of clusters, with 1% threshold clustering, highest NPSR is obtained. With such clustering, the NPSR corresponding to the Apache log les from January 2014 and from June 2014, respectively, equals 63% and 89%. Without the filter the NPSR rates were between 12% and 35%. We analyze how the significant increase in NPSR is achieved. According to the filtering policy, the dropped traffic mostly belongs to the default class, since that is the class in which the most of the attack packets are queued. That means, the normal traffic belonging to the default class is the most damaged, as shown in Figure 7.

The normal traffic was generated with source IP addresses based on the real traffic logs, but at a fixed rate which is many times higher than in real scenarios. Two types of synthetic attack traffic were generated: randomly spoofed attack traffic and the attack traffic having a certain number of fixed sources. It might be relevant to test different traffic distributions in future experiments.

Although in this test bed environment, many real parameters are omitted or could not be tested, the results suggest possibilities of using the existing DiffServ implementation embedded in standalone routers and also in the Linux kernel for cluster-based filtering in DDoS prevention. Thus, this experiments can be taken as a starting point for implementing the cluster-based filtering for real network services.

CONCLUSION

Cluster-based traffic filtering as a DDoS defense technique has received attention in the academia since the first such approaches were described a decade ago. Different kind of DDoS attack methods are discussed in section 2. Solutions can be obtained from different perspective that is shown in section 3. Due to the current pattern of traffic and attack methods, clustering based methods are getting attention

Figure 7. Classes inside the normal traffic that is served under randomly spoofed attack. The filter created by HHH using 10% threshold. The black line shows the total normal traffic rate. The default class is represented by the blue bars. Class with CIDR is represented by the green line.

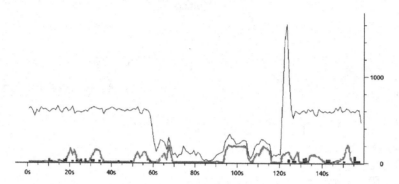

among research community. However, after surveying the literature and readings on different solutions that involve clustering of network traffic in DDoS defense, it was not possible to find a general analysis on the method. Developing such an analysis is the main contribution of this work.

This work focused on solutions that use unsupervised learning to cluster normal traffic and create filters for DDoS prevention or reaction based on the clusters. Particularly, a scenario was chosen in which the cluster-based filter is deployed at the target or at a router near the target. In such a scenario, the cluster-based filter can serve as a proactive or reactive DDoS defense.

The central part of this study involves creating a game-theoretic model for cluster-based filtering in the described scenario. The generality of the model makes this analysis applicable in different DDoS defense scenarios. Optimal filtering policies are modeled for the defense in the cases when the attacker is adaptive or when he uses a fixed strategy. Also, the best attack strategy is evaluated when the defender is using a fixed cluster-based filter. This theoretical results give insight into the applicability of filters based on traffic clusters to DDoS defense. The only case when the method does not provide any benefit is when the attack traffic perfectly imitates the normal traffic distribution. However, such attacker capability is unlikely in reality, for example, for the IP address distribution.

A test bed was developed in order to experimentally evaluate the cluster-based filtering. We applied the HHH algorithm to model normal traffic as set of clusters and implemented the cluster-based filter using a standard quality-of-service architecture, DiffServ. Particularly, experiments are conducted to evaluate the theoretical model. The experiments confirm the theoretical results. Additionally, the experimental results suggest high effectiveness of cluster-based filtering, with NPSR reaching above 97% with the most fine-grained clustering.

The results suggest that the cluster-based filtering can be applied for practical DDoS defense. In particular, a rather simple approach such as DiffServ would be useful in DDoS defense for a small web server because it would not require a large investment in hardware or software. Also, in cooperation with ISPs, this method could protect against bandwidth-band DDoS attacks on the ISP links for the specific domain.

As a first step in the future work is to conduct the similar experiments in a real network with DiffServ filter implementation at a real router. Such experiments would provide accurate quantitative performance results. As a second step, generating and testing additional attack traffic profiles would provide more confidence about the quality of the DDoS defense results.

REFERENCES

Agrawal, R., & Srikant, R. (1994). Fast algorithms for mining association rules. In *Proc. 20th int. conf. very large data bases, VLDB 1215*, 487-499.

Bezdek, J. C. (1973). *Fuzzy mathematics in pattern classification*. Academic Press.

Blake, S., Black, D., Carlson, M., Davies, E., Wang, Z., & Weiss, W. (1998). *An architecture for differentiated services*. Academic Press.

Cormode, G., Korn, F., Muthukrishnan, S., & Srivastava, D. (2008). Finding hierarchical heavy hitters in streaming data. *ACM Transactions on Knowledge Discovery from Data*, *1*(4), 2. doi:10.1145/1324172.1324174

Dantzig, G. B. (1998). *Linear programming and extensions*. Princeton University Press.

Erman, J., Arlitt, M., & Mahanti, A. (2006). Traffic classification using clustering algorithms. In *Proceedings of the 2006 SIGCOMM workshop on Mining network data* (pp. 281-286). ACM. doi:10.1145/1162678.1162679

Eskin, E., Arnold, A., Prerau, M., Portnoy, L., & Stolfo, S. (2002). A geometric framework for unsupervised anomaly detection. In Applications of data mining in computer security (pp. 77-101). Springer US. doi:10.1007/978-1-4615-0953-0_4

Ester, M., Kriegel, H. P., Sander, J., & Xu, X. (1996). A density-based algorithm for discovering clusters in large spatial databases with noise. In Kdd 96.

Fayyad, U., Piatetsky-Shapiro, G., & Smyth, P. (1996). From data mining to knowledge discovery in databases. *AI Magazine*, *17*(3), 37.

Gu, Y., McCallum, A., & Towsley, D. (2005). Detecting anomalies in network traffic using maximum entropy estimation. In *Proceedings of the 5th ACM SIGCOMM conference on Internet Measurement* (pp. 32-32). USENIX Association. doi:10.1145/1330107.1330148

Hastie, T., & Tibshirani, R. (1996). Discriminant adaptive nearest neighbor classification. *Pattern Analysis and Machine Intelligence. IEEE Transactions on*, *18*(6), 607–616.

Hijazi, A., Inoue, H., Matrawy, A., Van Oorschot, P., & Somayaji, A. (2008). Discovering packet structure through lightweight hierarchical clustering. In *Communications, 2008. ICC'08. IEEE International Conference on* (pp. 33-39). IEEE. doi:10.1109/ICC.2008.15

Holland, J. H. (1975). *Adaptation in natural and artificial systems: An introductory analysis with applications to biology, control, and artificial intelligence*. U Michigan Press.

Iyengar, N. C. S., Banerjee, A., & Ganapathy, G. (2014). A Fuzzy Logic Based Defense Mechanism against Distributed Denial of Services Attack in Cloud Environment. *International Journal of Communication Networks and Information Security*, *6*(3).

Kang, S. H., Park, K. Y., Yoo, S. G., & Kim, J. (2013). DDoS avoidance strategy for service availability. *Cluster Computing*, *16*(2), 241–248. doi:10.1007/s10586-011-0185-4

Keromytis, A. D., Misra, V., & Rubenstein, D. (2002). SOS: Secure overlay services. *Computer Communication Review, 32*(4), 61–72. doi:10.1145/964725.633032

Khattab, S. M., Sangpachatanaruk, C., Melhem, R., Mossé, D., & Znati, T. (2003). Proactive server roaming for mitigating denial-of-service attacks. In *Information Technology: Research and Education, 2003. Proceedings. ITRE2003. International Conference on* (pp. 286-290). IEEE. doi:10.1109/ITRE.2003.1270623

Kilkki, K. (1999). *Differentiated services for the Internet.* Macmillan Publishing Co., Inc.

Kullback, S. (1997). *Information theory and statistics.* Courier Dover Publications.

Lakhina, A., Crovella, M., & Diot, C. (2005). Mining anomalies using traffic feature distributions. *Computer Communication Review, 35*(4), 217–228. doi:10.1145/1090191.1080118

Lau, F., Rubin, S. H., Smith, M. H., & Trajkovic, L. (2000). Distributed denial of service attacks. In *Systems, Man, and Cybernetics, 2000 IEEE International Conference on.* IEEE. doi:10.1109/ICSMC.2000.886455

Lee, R. B., Karig, D. K., McGregor, J. P., & Shi, Z. (2004). Enlisting hardware architecture to thwart malicious code injection. In *Security in Pervasive Computing* (pp. 237–252). Springer Berlin Heidelberg. doi:10.1007/978-3-540-39881-3_21

Li, J., Mirkovic, J., Wang, M., Reiher, P., & Zhang, L. (2002). SAVE: Source address validity enforcement protocol. *Proceedings of the IEEE, 3,* 1557–1566.

Li, M., & Li, M. (2010). An adaptive approach for defending against DDoS attacks. *Mathematical Problems in Engineering,* 2010.

Li, M., Li, M., & Jiang, X. (2008). DDoS attacks detection model and its application. *WSEAS Transactions on Computers, 7*(8), 1159–1168.

Matrawy, A., van Oorschot, P. C., & Somayaji, A. (2005). Mitigating network denial-of-service through diversity-based traffic management. In *Applied Cryptography and Network Security* (pp. 104–121). Springer Berlin Heidelberg. doi:10.1007/11496137_8

McGregor, A., Hall, M., Lorier, P., & Brunskill, J. (2004). Flow clustering using machine learning techniques. In *Passive and Active Network Measurement* (pp. 205–214). Springer Berlin Heidelberg. doi:10.1007/978-3-540-24668-8_21

Mirkovic, J., Hussain, A., Fahmy, S., Reiher, P., & Thomas, R. K. (2009). Accurately measuring denial of service in simulation and testbed experiments. *Dependable and Secure Computing. IEEE Transactions on, 6*(2), 81–95.

Mittal, A., Shrivastava, A. K., & Manoria, M. (2011). A Review of DDOS Attack and its Countermeasures in TCP Based Networks. *International Journal of Computer Science & Engineering Survey, 2,* 4.

Nagamalai, D., Dhinakaran, C., & Lee, J. K. (2007). Multi layer approach to defend DDoS attacks caused by spam. In *Multimedia and Ubiquitous Engineering, 2007. MUE'07. International Conference on* (pp. 97-102). IEEE. doi:10.1109/MUE.2007.157

Oldmeadow, J., Ravinutala, S., & Leckie, C. (2004). Adaptive clustering for network intrusion detection. In *Advances in Knowledge Discovery and Data Mining* (pp. 255–259). Springer Berlin Heidelberg. doi:10.1007/978-3-540-24775-3_33

Petiz, I., Salvador, P., Nogueira, A., & Rocha, E. (2014, September). Detecting DDoS attacks at the source using multiscaling analysis. In *Telecommunications Network Strategy and Planning Symposium (Networks), 2014 16th International* (pp. 1-5). IEEE. doi:10.1109/NETWKS.2014.6959267

Spatscheck, O., & Peterson, L. L. (1999). Defending against denial of service attacks in Scout. In OSDI.

Spitzner, L. (2003). *Honeypots: tracking hackers* (Vol. 1). Reading: Addison-Wesley.

Stoecklin, M. (2006). Anomaly detection by finding feature distribution outliers. In *Proceedings of the 2006 ACM CoNEXT conference* (p. 32). ACM. doi:10.1145/1368436.1368476

Su, M. Y. (2011). Real-time anomaly detection systems for Denial-of-Service attacks by weighted k-nearest-neighbor classifiers. *Expert Systems with Applications, 38*(4), 3492–3498. doi:10.1016/j.eswa.2010.08.137

Yaar, A., Perrig, A., & Song, D. (2003). Pi: A path identification mechanism to defend against DDoS attacks. In *Security and Privacy, 2003. Proceedings. 2003 Symposium on* (pp. 93-107). IEEE. doi:10.1109/SECPRI.2003.1199330

Zhong, R., & Yue, G. (2010). DDoS detection system based on data mining. In *Proceedings of the Second International Symposium on Networking and Network Security*.

ENDNOTE

[1]   Worldwide Infrastructure Security Report, Arbor Networks, Inc, http://pages.arbornetworks.com/rs/arbor/images/WISR2014.pdf

Chapter 9
Intrusion Detection System (IDS) and Their Types

Manoranjan Pradhan
GITA, India

Chinmaya Kumar Nayak
GITA, India

Sateesh Kumar Pradhan
Utkal University, India

ABSTRACT

Over the last two decades, computer and network security has become a main issue, especially with the increase number of intruders and hackers, therefore systems were designed to detect and prevent intruders. This chapter per the authors investigated the most important design approaches, by mainly focusing on their collecting, analysis, responding capabilities and types of current IDS products. For the collecting capability, there were two main approaches, namely host- and network-based IDSs. Therefore, a combination of the two approaches in a hybrid implementation is ideal, as it will offer the highest level of protection at all levels of system functions. The analysis capability of an IDS can be characterised by the misuse and anomaly detection approaches. Therefore, a combination of the two approaches should improve the analysis capability of an IDS i.e. hybrid of misuse and anomaly detection.

INTRODUCTION

Organizations usually wish to preserve the confidentiality of their data which is very vital to an organization.. With the widespread use of the internet, it has become a key challenge to maintain the secrecy and integrity of organizations' vital data. Network security has been an issue almost since computers have been networked together. Since the evolution of the internet, there has been an increasing need for security systems. Conventional techniques for network security include security mechanisms like user authentication, cryptography and intrusion prevention systems like firewalls.

DOI: 10.4018/978-1-4666-8761-5.ch009

Figure 1. A computer network with intrusion detection system

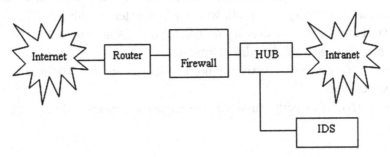

One important type of security software that has emerged since the evolution of the internet is intrusion detection systems. Intuitively, intrusions in an information system are the activities that violate the security policy of the system, and intrusion detection is the process used to identify intrusions. Intrusion detection, is the attempt to monitor and possibly prevent attempts to intrude into or otherwise compromise your system and network resources. Simply put, it works like this: You have a computer system. It is attached to a network, and perhaps even to the internet. You are willing to allow access to that computer system from the network, by authorized people, for acceptable reasons. Consider a real life scenario: you have a web server, attached to the internet, and you are willing to allow your clients, staff, and potential clients, to access the web pages stored on that web server. You are, however, not willing to allow unauthorized access to that system by anyone, be that staff, customers, or unknown third parties. For example, you do not want people (other than the web designers that your company has employed) to be able to change the web pages on that computer. Typically, a firewall or authentication system of some kind will be employed to prevent unauthorized access. Sometimes, however, simple firewalling or authentication systems can be broken. Intrusion detection is the set of mechanisms that you put in place to warn of attempted unauthorized access to the computer. Intrusion detection systems can also take some steps to deny access to would-be intruders. Intrusion detection systems (IDS) address problems that are not solved by firewall techniques, as a firewalls simply act like a fence around a network. IDS is capable of recognizing these attacks which firewalls are not able to prevent. Also, newer attacks are being developed that are able to penetrate through firewalls. IDS provides a solution to this problem. As a result, IDSs, as originally introduced by Anderson (Anderson, 1980) and later formalized by Denning (Denning, 1987), have received increasing attention in the recent years. The IDS along with the firewall form the fundamental technologies for network security which is in the Figure 1.

BACKGROUND

Definitions and Terminology

Intrusion detection is the process of monitoring and analyzing events that occur in a computer or networked computer system to detect behaviour of users that conflict with the intended use of the system. An intrusion detection system (IDS) employs techniques for modeling and recognizing intrusive behaviour in a computer system. When referring to the performance of IDSs, the following terms are often used when discussing their capabilities:

- **True positive (TP):** classifying an intrusion as an intrusion. The true positive rate is synonymous with detection rate, sensitivity and recall, which are other terms often used in the literature.
- **False positive (FP):** incorrectly classifying normal data as an intrusion. Also known as a false alarm. False positives measure the false alarm rate.
- **True negative (TN):** correctly classifying normal data as normal. The true negative rate is also referred to as specificity.
- **False negative (FN):** incorrectly classifying an intrusion as normal. False negatives measure the detection rate.

The performance metrics calculated from these are:

- True positive rate (TPR) $= \dfrac{TP}{TP + FN} = \dfrac{\text{No. of correct intrusions}}{\text{No.of intusions}}$

- False positive rate(FPR) $= \dfrac{FP}{TN + FP} = \dfrac{\text{No.of normal as intrusions}}{\text{No.of normal}}$

- True negative rate(TNR) $= \dfrac{TN}{TN + FP} = \dfrac{\text{No.of correct normal}}{\text{No.of normal}}$

- False negative rate(FNR) $= \dfrac{FN}{TP + FN} = \dfrac{\text{No.of intrusions as normal}}{\text{No.of intusions}}$

Two additional performance metrics also commonly used, referred to as accuracy and precision:

- Accuracy $= \dfrac{TP + TN}{TP + FP + TN + FN} = \dfrac{\text{No.of correct classifications}}{\text{No.of all instances}}$

- Precision $= \dfrac{TP}{TP + FP} = \dfrac{\text{No.of correct intrusions}}{\text{No.of instances classified as intusion}}$

Accuracy is also referred to as an overall classification rate, and according to Wu and Yen (Wu and Yen, 2009), precision is also referred to as recall. Due to the direct nature of many intrusions, the terms 'intrusion' and 'attack' are used interchangeably.

Components of Intrusion Detection Systems

An intrusion detection system typically consists of three sub systems or components which are given in Figure 2:

- **Information Sources:** It is responsible for collecting and providing the audit data (in a specified form) that will be used by the next component (analysis engine) to make a decision. Information sources is, thus, concerned with collecting the data from the desired source and converting it into a format that is comprehensible by the analysis engine. This gathers data that may contain evidence of intrusion. All modern IDS monitor host computers, networks, routers or application links to capture intrusion-relevant data. Also, it is based upon *where* data analysis is done.
- **Analysis Engine:** It is the core component which analyzes the audit patterns to detect attacks. This is a critical component and one of the most researched. Various pattern matching, machine

Figure 2. IDS architecture

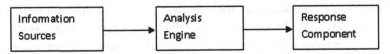

learning, data mining and statistical techniques can be used as intrusion detectors. The capability of the analyzer to detect an attack often determines the strength of the overall system. This can also categorize three types of detections: misuse detection, anomaly detection, and hybrid detection. Also, it is based upon *how* data analysis is done.

- **Response Component:** It controls the reaction mechanism and determines how to respond when the analysis engine detects an attack. The system may decide either to raise an alert without taking any action against the source i.e. "passive response" or may decide to block the source for a predefined period of time i.e. "active response". Such an action depends upon the predefined security policy of the network. This reports intrusions and takes other responses such as isolation, changing logging or disconnection, etc.

OVERVIEW OF INTRUSION DETECTION SYSTEM

Many intrusion detection systems have been employed. These systems differ primarily *where, when and how* the data analysis has been carried out. Based on *where* data analysis is done, intrusion detection systems can be classified into the following two broad categories:

Network-Based Intrusion Detection Systems

This type of systems are placed on the network, near the system or systems being monitored and analyze network traffic for attacks that exploit the connections between computers and the data that can be accessed via a network connection by examining the individual packets flowing through a network. Unlike firewalls, which typically only look at IP addresses, ports and ICMP types, network based intrusion detection systems (NIDS) are able to understand all the different flags and options that can exist within a network packet. The role of the network intrusion detection systems (IDS) is to flag and sometimes stop an attack before it gets to information assets or causes damage. A NIDS can therefore detect maliciously crafted packets that are designed to be overlooked by a firewall's relatively simplistic filtering rules. Hackers often craft such traffic in order to "map out" a network, as a form of preattack reconnaissance. NIDS are also able to look at the "payload" within a packet, i.e. to see which particular web server program is being accessed, and with what options, and to raise alerts when an attacker tries to exploit a bug in such code. Most firewalls are unable to do this. NIDS can detect the broadest range of attacks on corporate information assets. NIDS are effective for monitoring both inbound and outbound network traffic. Network sniffers are an effective means for gathering information about events that occur on the network architecture. Capturing packets before they enter the server is an effective means of monitoring data on the network. If the analysis is on the lower level of analyzing the content of the TCP or IP packet, then the system can perform quickly. However, if the system analyses each packet with respect to the application or protocol, this could be time consuming and raises several issues. Detection of network specific attacks cannot be determined in a timely fashion. Also, is it difficult to identify the user how submitted the packets. Another problem that arises is that the encryption makes it hard to analyze the payload of the packets. Therefore, a skillful attacker could still get past these intrusion detection systems.

Advantages of Network-Based Intrusion Detection Systems

- The deployment of network-based IDSs is usually easy with minimal effort.
- Network-based IDSs can be made very secure and is often invisible to most attackers.
- They can monitor a heterogeneous set of hosts and operating systems simultaneously, due to the fact that standard network protocols (e.g. TCP, UDP and IP) are supported and used by most major operating systems.

Disadvantages of Network-Based Intrusion Detection Systems

- Network-based IDSs cannot analyze encrypted information. This problem is increasing as more organizations and attackers use virtual private networks, which normally utilize encrypted information.
- The processing load in a large or busy network may cause significant difficulties to the analysis engine part of the IDS. This condition (high processing load) can seriously limit an IDS's ability to detect attacks when the network load is above a specific amount of network traffic. Although some vendors have adopted hardware-based solutions for IDSs, to increase the speed of their processing capability (and the cost of implementation), the limitation still remains.
- The need to analyze packets as fast as possible, force developers to detect fewer attacks. Thus, the detection effectiveness is often compromised for the sake of cost effectiveness.

Host-Based Intrusion Detection System

This type of systems monitor specific files, logs and registry settings on a single individual computer or "host" and can alert on any access, modification, deletion and copying of the monitored object. The role of a HIDS is to flag any tampering with a specific host and can automatically replace the altered files when changed to ensure data integrity. They are able to detect such things as repeated failed access attempts or changes to critical system files. A derivation of HIDS is centralized-host-based intrusion detection (CHIDS) that serves the same purpose but does the analysis centrally by sending monitored files, logs and registry settings to the manager for analysis. The primary difference between these systems is as follows. CHIDS is more secure because it sends all the needed information off the host so that if the host is compromised, the alerting and forensic analysis can still take place. The tradeoff is that centralized analysis requires substantially more network bandwidth to move the data to the manager. HIDS makes policy compliance decisions locally and only sends alerts to the manager when warranted. This uses substantially less network bandwidth. The shortcoming of HIDS is that if the host is compromised there is no alert or forensic data to determine what happened or what was lost. Information about the activities are gathered by the host audit. However, while the host based intrusion detection system is processing the audit trail and setting off alarms, the attacker can sabotage the audit trail or the entire system. There are other audit sources that are used in host based intrusion detection systems to gather information. The operating system can obtain a snapshot of the information about the events occurring. Accounting, another method, provides information on the consumption of the shared resources, such a processor time, memory, etc. Syslog is another audit service that is provided by the operating system to the applications. The service receives a text string from the application and prefixes it with a time stamp and the name of the system, then it is archived. C2 security audits are required on all computers systems. It records the crossing of instructions executed by the processor in the user space and instructions executed in the kernel. This contains information about the events, and user identification. There are many advantages to this because it identifies the user and login information. It repartitions the audit events into classes to facilitate the configuration of the audit system.

Advantages of Host-Based Intrusion Detection System

- Host-based IDSs can analyze intrusion activities with greater reliability and precision, because of the vast amount of input data collected from an individual computer system.
- Host-based IDSs can operate in an encrypted network environment, because audit and system logs are generated before and after data packets are encrypted.
- Host-based IDSs are unaffected by switched networks.
- Trojan horse or other attacks that involve software integrity breaches can be detected by host-based IDSs. These breaches appear as a result of inconsistencies in process execution (Bace, 2000).

Disadvantages of Host-Based Intrusion Detection System

- Host-based IDSs are harder to manage, as information must be configured and managed for every host monitored.
- Since sensors for host-based IDSs reside on the host targeted by attacks, the IDS may be attacked and disabled as part of the attack.
- Host-based IDSs are not well suited for detecting network scans or other such surveillance that targets an entire network, because the IDS only analyses those network packets received by its host.
- Host-based IDSs can be disabled by certain denial-of-service attacks. The amount of information included in operating system audit trails can be immense, which can result in the need for additional local storage on the system.

Hybrid Intrusion Detection System

Hybrid Intrusion Detection Systems complement HIDS technology with the ability to monitor the network traffic coming in or out of a specific host. This is very different than NIDS technology that monitors all network traffic management and alert notification from network and host based intrusion detection devices can be done with Hybrid intrusion detection systems.

Classification of Intrusion Detection System

The task of intrusion detection systems is to monitor and detect any misuse of the system. In today's computerized world, commercial tools for intrusion detection systems are becoming easily available. A generic intrusion detection system is essentially a detector that processors information received from a system (server, mainframe, firewall etc.). The detector processes the following information: knowledge of attacks, configuration information of the current state of the system, and audit information (information about the inner workings and behaviour of the system). The detector evaluates all this data to determine if there is indeed an intrusion. Evaluating efficiency is essential in intrusion detection systems. Different measures need to be considered such as accuracy, performance, such as the rate at which audit events are processed. Completeness is also important as well as fault tolerance. The intrusion detection system should be resistant to attacks. Finally, timeliness to perform and propagate the analysis as soon as possible so that it can be handled. There are many characteristics of intrusion detection systems. The analyzer has two functionality's: it can be behaviour based, using information about the normal behaviour, or knowledge based where the system uses information about the attacks. Another functional characteristic is the behaviour on detection, how it reacts. It can react passively, generating alarms, or actively for example logging out attackers. The audit source location distinguishes amongst systems based on the kind of information they analyze (logs, packets etc.). Finally, there is a usage frequency concept, either running real-time or periodically. In real-time analysis information about the environment is acquired immediately after an event occurs, but with a static intrusion detection tool a snapshot of the environment is taken periodically.

Based on *how* data analysis is done, intrusion detection can be classified into the following two types.

Misuse Detection

The system learns patterns from already known attacks. These learned patterns are searched through the incoming data to find intrusions of the already known types. This method is not capable in detecting new attacks that do not follow pre-defined patterns. Since this approach searches for patterns known to cause security problems, it is called a "misuse" or "attack signature" detection approach. Attack patterns that correspond to known attacks are called signatures (Bace, 2000; Mosses, 2001; Sundaram, 1996). A block diagram of typical misuse detection system is given in Figure 3.

The misuse detection approach is particularly suited to detecting external penetrators that produce repeated login attempts or exploit known security vulnerabilities in order to break into a system. However, the definition of attack signatures may not be comprehensive enough to cover all existing and future intrusion patterns, thus certain variations of intrusive behaviour may not be detected, resulting in a false negative (Bace, 2000).

It is useful to consider the following example to understand the key ideas behind this approach of IDS. Consider a security guard present at an entrance who is responsible for allowing only valid persons to pass through the gate. In this approach, the guard can check each coming person with the database and find out if the person is one of those culprits. If so, the guard prevents the culprit from passing through

Figure 3. Block diagram of a typical misuse detection system

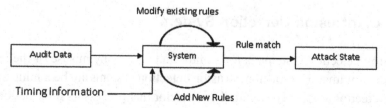

the entrance. The problem here is that a culprit whose photograph is not in the database will be allowed entry. This approach corresponds to the misuse detection technique.

Advantages of Misuse Detection

- It detects the intrusions and also identifying the type of the particular intrusion.
- It is very effective at detecting attacks without generating an overwhelming number of false positive alarms.

Disadvantages of Misuse Detection

- It can only detect those attacks that are known to the system. Therefore, systems utilizing this approach must be constantly updated with signatures of new attacks.
- The process of developing a new attack signature is time consuming.

Anomaly Detection

Here patterns are learned from normal data. The unseen data is checked and searched to find deviations from these learned patterns. These deviations are "anomalies" or possible intrusions. So anomaly detection approaches must first baseline the normal behaviour of the object being monitored, and then detect possible intrusions by using deviations from this baseline. These profiles are constructed from historical data collected over a period of time of normal operation. Anomaly detection typically creates knowledge bases containing the profiles of the monitored users, programs or systems. Threshold detection, statistical measures, neural networks and rule-based measures are the techniques used in anomaly detection. A block diagram of a typical anomaly detection system is given in Figure 4.

It is useful to consider the following example to understand the key ideas behind in this approach of IDS. Consider a security guard present at an entrance who is responsible for allowing only valid persons to pass through the gate. In this approach that the guard may follow is to maintain a database of photographs of all the valid persons to be allowed entry. The guard allows entry to the incoming person, only if his photograph is found in the database. This way, all persons whose photographs are not found in the database are identified as culprits and not allowed entry. This approach corresponds to the anomaly detection technique.

Advantages of Anomaly Detection

- It has the advantages of not being able to find the type of the intrusion but new or unknown intrusions can be detected using this method.

Figure 4. Block diagram of a typical anomaly detection system

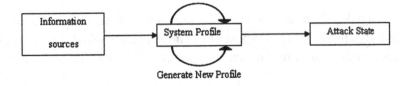

- Anomaly detectors do not require constant updating of rules or signatures of novel intrusion.

Disadvantages of Anomaly Detection

- It usually has difficulty in determining whether unpredictable behaviour of users or objects of a system is indeed abnormal, thus they may produce a large number of false positive alarms.
- It often requires extensive training periods in order to characterize normal behaviour of users and system objects.

A combined approach of both these methods may be more helpful. One such approach is to first apply anomaly detection to find possible intrusions, then the type of intrusions can be identified using misuse detection.

Hybrid of Misuse and Anomaly IDS

There are systems out now that combines the two types of intrusion detection systems. Hybrid systems can use a rules base to check for known attacks against a system, and an anomaly algorithm to protect against new types of attacks(Herringshaw, 1997). This type of intrusion detection system takes the advantages from both systems, but unfortunately it also takes some of the disadvantages. Misuse detection could be used in combination with anomaly detection to name the attacks. This will shorten the response time the system administrator needs as he can see what type of attack the system are under.

Intrusion detection systems differs from on-line to off-line systems (J. Ryan et al., 1998). Depending on *when* audit data analysis is done, two situations are possible:

Offline Intrusion Detection System

Although off line analysis permits greater depth of coverage because processing of audit information can be shifted to non-peak times. It can only detect intrusions after the event has occurred. Offline intrusion detection systems are run periodically and they detect intrusions after the fact based on system logs.

Online Intrusion Detection System

Online systems are designed to detect intrusions while they are happening, thereby allowing for quicker intervention. Online intrusion detection systems are computationally very expensive because they require continuous monitoring. Decisions need to be made quickly with less data and therefore they are not as reliable.

CURRENT INTRUSION DETECTION PRODUCTS

Having defined intrusion detection architecture in the previous section, it might be useful to investigate current intrusion detection products. The purpose of this investigation is firstly to determine which architectures are more commonly used by the current intrusion detection products and secondly to determine which detection approaches are mostly utilized and what responses are provided. Intrusion detection products can basically be categorized into two main groups (Hart et al., 1999) and they are:

- Commercial intrusion detection products; and
- Research intrusion detection products.

In the rest of this section each of these groups will be investigated.

Commercial Intrusion Detection Products

An extensive investigation revealed that there are a multitude of commercial intrusion detection products available today. The list is increasing daily and Price, (1998) provides an extensive list of commercial as well as "public" products, for instance, Axent Technologies NetProwler, Axent Technologies Intruder Alert, CentraxICE, Cisco Secure IDS, SessionWall and ISS RealSecure (Hart et al., 1999; Network Computing, 2000; Hugh, 2001; Yocom et al., 2001). The following is a discussion of a variety of commercial products. The purpose of this section is only to illustrate each product's detection methods, the advantages and disadvantages. It is worth mentioning that Network Computing (2000) utilized a comprehensive testing environment and they spent several months in a lab to test these products, using an assortment of attacks tools, utilities and load-generation mechanisms. The goal was to measure how accurately the systems detected hostile activity and how well they conveyed such activity to the user.

ISS RealSecure

RealSecure is a network based intrusion detection product from Internet Security Systems. It offers a secure, distributed architecture that consists of five components listed below:

- RealSecure Network Sensor;
- RealSecure Server Sensor;
- RealSecure OS Sensor;
- RealSecure for Nokia; and
- RealSecure Workgroup Manager.

The intrusion detection is done through multiple detection engines. Each engine can be distributed to various networks and reports back to a central management console. The engines can be set to detect a multitude of intrusions by using technical controls and a technique called pattern matching (it is a form of misuse detection). Pattern matching is a technique where the system looks for a signature that identifies an intruder. This signature is usually in the form of a pattern of events. When the intrusion engine detects a suspicious activity, it notifies the system administrator. All events are logged and a complete record of the intrusion can be viewed. (Clure et al., 1998; Yocom et al., 2001).

Advantages

- "Accurate Attack Identification" – the product accurately identifies known intrusions;

- "Flexible, Secure Distributed Management" – the product offers a secure distributed environment;
- "Easy to use GUI"; and
- "Quality Reporting with interesting session-recording tools".

Disadvantages

- "Cannot create custom attacks"- the product cannot identify new types of intrusions (McClure et al., 1998).

SessionWall

SessionWall is a product from Abirnet. The SessionWall product is similar to a firewall. It also utilizes the pattern matching technique and allows the system administrator to define rules for monitoring, filtering and blocking network traffic. Thus, its action is very similar to a firewall except that it captures the TCP/IP session from a LAN segment and applies the defined rules accordingly. SessionWall does not offer distributed management and it can only be monitored on the host that is watching the LAN segment. SessionWall does offer a variety of methods for reporting intrusions and will alert the local console, e-mail, page, and log data depending on configuration. It does also offer many other reporting features and it consists of a report scheduler that allows report generation as often as every fifteen minutes. The report contains a variety of LAN data including data on the attack (McClure et al., 1998).

Advantages

- "Easy to use GUI";
- "Granular session filtering and blocking";
- "Simple to administer"; and
- "Low cost".

Disadvantages

- "No Distributed Management" – the product can only be monitored on the host that is watching the LAN segment;
- "No True Intrusion-Detection Reports" – the intrusion-detection report does not contain all the details of the intrusion attack; and Minor traffic-monitoring bugs" (McClure et al., 1998).

Cisco Secure IDS

Cisco Secure IDS is a large scale, real network IDS and formerly known as NetRanger. It uses various different detection techniques and these include stateful pattern recognition, protocol parsing, heuristic detection, and anomaly detection. It comes with two components, the sensor and director. The sensor component detects the misuse in real time and forwards an alert to the director. The director component can then take the appropriate action, such as, removing the offender off the network. The director provides a centralized management point for the sensors. The sensor has comprehensive intrusion detection capabilities and can detect many known intrusions (Yocom et al., 2001; Hart et al., 1999).

Advantages

- Uses a network vulnerability database that is updated with current threats on a regular basis;
- Ability to define own vulnerabilities; and
- "Centralized Management" through the director.

Disadvantage

- Only available for Sun Operating System (Hart et al., 1999).

Three commonly known commercial packages were briefly described in this sub-section. These packages offer various detection and management functions. The detection function detects attacks through analysing network traffic. The management component usually allows for event managing and reporting, and incorporates a response component with a varying level of functionality. Most of these packages have numerous drawbacks which lead to the increase in the amount of new research projects conducted on intrusion detection. A few of these projects will be discussed in the following subsection.

Research Intrusion Detection Products

Currently, there is a significant amount of active research performed in the intrusion detection domain. The most commonly known research projects will be investigated theoretically, in order to determine whether these projects developed new advanced approaches that can be used to overcome the shortcomings of the commercial products.

Emerald

Event Monitoring Enabling Responses to Anomalous Live Disturbances (EMERALD) is an intrusion detection project, being pursued within the Systems Design Laboratory at SRI International, which has been actively involved in the intrusion detection domain since 1983. Their first effort was the development of the Intrusion Detection Expert System (IDES), followed by the Next-Generation IDES (NIDES). Emerald is the current research focus of SRI, an IDS that is expected to detect and respond to modern network attacks. The Emerald environment is a distributed scalable tool suite for tracking malicious activities through and across large networks. Emerald introduces a highly distributed, building-block approach to network surveillance, attack isolation and automated response. The central concept of this project is its distributed, lightweight monitors, diverse with respect to both the monitored event streams and to analysis techniques. expert-BSM (a Host-based intrusion detection solution for sun solaris) represents one example of an Emerald monitor that can stand alone as an important host protection service and can also be easily configured to fit into a distributed framework of surveillance, correlation and response. The Emerald monitor architecture consists of three computational units, and they are as follows:

- A signature-based engine;
- A statistic-based engine; and
- Countermeasure unit called the resolver.

Emerald implements the misuse detection approach through the signature based engine and the anomaly detection approach through the statistic based engine. The resolver is the response module in the architecture and performs countermeasure activities according to the incident. The resolver is an expert system that receives the intrusion and suspicion report from the two engines. Based on these reports, it decides what response to invoke and how to invoke it. Possible responses include:

- Closing connections;
- Terminating processes; or
- Dispatching integrity-checking handlers to verify the operating state of the analysis target.

Finally, the monitor also incorporates versatile interfaces that enhance the monitor's ability to be interoperated with other third-party intrusion detection tool suites (Porras et al., 1997; Lindqvist et al., 2001). Emerald provides an interesting architectural approach to combat intrusions and focuses on the operation of distributed response elements. It is already defined at a conceptual level and an initial system (expert-BSM) based on this architectural approach is developed and is currently being tested as a production system.

Intrusion Monitoring System

Intrusion Monitoring System (IMS) is a research prototype conducted by the Network Research Group at the University of Plymouth. The prototype is developed for intrusion monitoring and activity supervision, based on the concept of a centralised console handling the monitoring of a number of networked client systems. Intrusion detection in the system is based on the comparison of current user activity against both historical profiles of "normal" behaviour for legitimate users (anomaly detection) and intrusion specifications of recognised attack patterns (misuse detection). The architecture comprises a number of functional modules, addressing data collection and response on the client side and data analysis and recording at the console. The eight modules of the architecture are as follows:

- Anomaly Detector (Detection Engine);
- Profile Refiner;
- Recorder;
- Archiver;
- Collector;
- Responder;
- Communicator; and
- Controller (Furnell et al., 2001).

The IMS research prototype is an interesting research project which provides an alternative architecture to build an IDS. More research is currently being performed on this architecture, especially the response module.

Characteristics of an Intrusion Detection System

Cramer (Cramer et al., 1996) has described several important characteristics and they are as follows:

- **Timeliness:** The IDS must detect intrusion activities while they are occurring. If it is not possible to detect an intrusion in real time (near real-time), the time between the attack and its detection, must be as short as possible.
- **High Probability of Detection:** The IDS observes a computer system and must distinguish any deviation from normal behaviour. Therefore, all possible intrusions must be detected.
- Low false alarm rate

There are three main types of errors that can occur in an IDS (Price, 1997) and they are:

- **False Positive Errors:** These errors occur when the IDS classifies a certain action as a possible intrusion when it is a perfectly legitimate action.
- **False Negative Errors:** An actual intrusion has occurred, but the IDS identifies these intrusive actions as legitimate.
- **Subversion Errors:** These errors are more complex and occur when an intruder modifies the operation of the IDS, forcing false negative errors to occur.

The number of false alarms caused by the three types of errors, must be as low as possible.

- **Specificity:** If an attack is identified, sufficient information such as, the time and place, must be supplied by the IDS in order to support an effective response.
- **Scalability:** The IDS must be applicable to any size of networks.
- **Low A Priori Information:** The IDS must be able to detect intrusions with a minimum amount of applicable information regarding the intruder and intrusion methods.

FUTURE RESEARCH DIRECTIONS

Three most commonly known commercial intrusion detection products and three well-known research projects on intrusion detection were investigated. The most noticeable difference between the two groups is that most commercial products opt for the misuse detection approach and that the research projects attempt to improve the anomaly detection approach so that it can be used in conjunction with the misuse detection approach. Most of these products make use of technical controls and in most cases, if not all, these controls are used in a reactive manner. Authors of this chapter are also in the process of developing hybrid of misuse and anomaly detection approach in research projects.

CONCLUSION

This chapter has discussed the most important design approaches, by mainly focusing on their collecting, analysis, responding capabilities, types of current IDS products and its characteristics. For the collecting capability, there were two main approaches, namely host- and network-based IDSs. Host-based IDSs can detect with great reliability and precision, when an intrusion is directed against a single host. However, these systems are harder to manage and cannot protect multiple hosts simultaneously. On the contrary, network-based IDSs can protect multiple hosts connected to the monitored network, they are very easy to manage, but can only detect network-based attacks. Therefore, a combination of the two approaches in a hybrid implementation is ideal, as it will offer the highest level of protection at all levels of system functions. The analysis capability of an IDS can be characterised by the misuse and anomaly detection approaches. The misuse detection approach searches for well known patterns of intrusions. The main limitation of this approach is that it can only detect those intrusions known to the system. The anomaly detection approach overcomes this limitation by searching for abnormalities caused by intrusions. However, the anomaly detection approach normally cannot provide the same level of reliability as misuse detection approach. Therefore, a combination of the two approaches should improve the analysis capability of an IDS i.e. hybrid of misuse and anomaly detection.

REFERENCES

Anderson, J. P. (1980). *Computer security threat monitoring and surveillance*. Anderson Co.

Bace, R.G. (2000). *Intrusion Detection*. Macmillan Technical Publishing.

Clure, M., Hart, R., Morgan, D., & Tran, H. (1999). An Introduction to Automated Intrusion Detection Approaches. *Information Management and Computer Security, 7*(1), 76-81.

Cramer, M. L., Cannady, J., & Harrell, J. (1996). New Methods of Intrusion Detection Using Control-loop Measurement. In *Fourth Technology for Information Security Conference*, Houston, TX.

Denning, D. E. (1987). An Intrusion Detection Model. *IEEE Transactions on Software Engineering, SE-13*(2), 222–232. doi:10.1109/TSE.1987.232894

Furnell, S. M., Magklaras, G. B., Papadaki, M., & Dowland, P.S. (2001). A Generic system for Intrusion Specification and Response. *Proceedings of Euromedia 2001*.

Hart, R., Morgan, D., & Tran, H. (1999). An introduction to automated Intrusion Detection Approach. *Information Management & Computer Security, 7*(1), 76–81. doi:10.1108/09685229910265501

Herringshaw, C. (1997). Detecting Attacks on Networks. *IEEE Computer, 30*(12), 16–17. doi:10.1109/2.642762

Lindqvist, U., & Jonsson, E. (2001). How to Systematically Classify Computer Security Intrusions. *IEEE Symposium on Security and Privacy*. Oakland, CA: IEEE Computer Society Press.

Mc Hugh, J. (2001). Intrusion and Intrusion Detection. *International Journal of Information Security, 1*(1), 14–35. doi:10.1007/s102070100001

Mosses, R. (2001). *Information Technology – Security Techniques*. ISO /IECJTC 1/SC 27 N 3011. Available at http:// www.din.de/ni/sc27

Porras, P. A., & Neumann, P. G. (1997). *EMERALD: Event Monitoring Enabling Responses to Anomalous Live Disturbances*. Retrieved from http://www.sdi.sri.com/projects/emerald-niss97.html

Price, K. (1997). *Intrusion Classification*. COAST Library. Available at http://www.cs.purdue.edu/coast/intrusion-detection

Ryan, J., Lin, M. J., & Miikkulainen, R. (1998). Advances in Neural Information Processing Systems: Vol. 10. *Intrusion Detection with Neural Networks* (pp. 943–949). Cambridge, MA: MIT Press.

Sundaram, A. (1996). *An Introduction to Intrusion Detection*. ACM. Available from http://www.acm.org/crossroads/xrds2-4/ intrus.html

Wu, S-Y. & Yen, E. (2009). Data mining-based intrusion detectors. *Expert Systems with Application, 36*, 5605-5612.

Yocom, B., Brown, K., & Van Der Veer, D. (2001). Review: Intrusion-Detection Products Grow Up. *Network World*. Retrieved 27 May 2002 from http://www.nwfusion.com/reviews/2001/1008rev.html

KEY TERMS AND DEFINITIONS

Attack: In computing environment, attack is an attempt to disrupt, destroy, theft or unauthorized access to or unauthorized use of a computing resource.

Cryptography: It is a method of storing and transmitting data into an unreadable or unintelligible form so that only intended recipients can read and process it.

Detection Rate: The number of intrusion instances detected by the system divided by the total number of intrusion instances present in the test set is called detection rate.

Firewall: It is a network device located at a network gateway server to protect the resources of a private network from users from other networks. The purpose is to allow or block traffic into and out of a private network or the user's computer.

GUI: It refers to the graphical interface of a computer that allows users to perform various activities by means of clicking and dragging objects with a mouse instead of entering text at a command line.

HIDS: This type of systems monitor specific files, logs and registry settings on a single individual computer or "host" and can alert on any access, modification, deletion and copying of the monitored object.

Internet Control Message Protocol (ICMP): Is used by network devices, like routers, to send error messages indicating, for example, that a requested service is not available or that a host or router could not be reached.

Internet Protocol (IP): The method or protocol used by Internet to send data from one computer to another that uses IP address to recognize computers in Internet.

Intrusion Detection System (IDS): Employs techniques for modeling and recognizing intrusive behaviour in a computer system.

Local Area Network (LAN): An interconnection of computers within a limited area such as premises of a home, school, computer laboratory, or office building, using network media.

Network Security: It is the mechanism to protect computer files and directories in a computer network against hacking, misuse and unauthorized changes to the system.

NIDS: This type of systems are placed on the network, near the system or systems being monitored and analyze network traffic for attacks that exploit the connections between computers and the data that can be accessed via a network connection by examining the individual packets flowing through a network.

TCP: It is a connection-oriented protocol which is responsible to establish and maintain connection until the application programs at each end have completed exchange of messages.

User Datagram Protocol (UDP): A communications protocol used to provide limited service when two computers in a network exchange messages by using Internet Protocol (IP).

Chapter 10
Intrusion Prevention System

Bijaya Kumar Panda
GITA, India

Manoranjan Pradhan
GITA, India

Sateesh Kumar Pradhan
Utkal University, India

ABSTRACT

In the last decade, there is a rapid growth in the use of Internet by the organization for information sharing. As information is very vital to the organizations, it should be preserved and insulated from any unauthorized access or alternation. In last few years, attacks on the computer infrastructures have increased exponentially. Several information security techniques are available now a days like firewalls, anti-virus software and Intrusion prevention systems (IPSs), which are important tools for protecting an organization from intrusions. Now most attacks are impossible to defend with firewalls and anti-virus software alone. Without an IPS, such attacks are difficult to detect and prevent. This chapter presents different definitions of intrusion prevention system with meaningful explanation; compare network IPS with Host IPS, common and the advanced detection methods, common IPS components, coverage of attacks by IPS and criteria to select right IPS. Finally, this chapter concludes with an analysis of the challenges that still remain to be resolved.

INTRODUCTION

In the last decade, there is rapid growth of communication networks through computers and Internet. The numbers of Internet users are also rapidly increasing for business applications, other online applications and services. With the rapid growth of internet communication and availability of tools to intrude the network, network security has become indispensable. Security threat comes not only from external intruder but also from internal misuse.

Security and protection of computer networks and their resources is one of the most important IT activities today. Most organizations no longer take for granted that their deployed networks and appli-

DOI: 10.4018/978-1-4666-8761-5.ch010

cations are secure and therefore use all kind of protection tools and products. But, even after installing various protection mechanisms, performing continuous monitoring of security logs, and running extensive penetration tests, network and hosting security personnel spend considerable time chasing incidents, preventing penetrations or solving problems after intrusions and damages. More or less everybody has already realized that the "secure the perimeter" approach does not prevent the tide of incidents, intrusions and damages, because current techniques and products do not provide effective solutions. Over the last several years, the trends and styles of intrusions have been changing (CERT, 2007). Intrusion profiles have enhanced from simple methods like tracing passwords, social engineering attacks (Bishop, 2005), and exploiting simple software vulnerabilities to more sophisticated methods, like exploiting protocol flaws, defacing web servers, installing snifter programs, denial of service attacks, distributed denial–of–service attacks, or developing command and control networks using compromised computer to launch attacks. CERT Coordination Center confirmed in the "Recent CERT/CC Experiences Vulnerability Report" (CERT, 2008) that there has been significant exponential increase in discovered vulnerabilities: 171 in 1997 to 7236 in 2007. This increase in vulnerabilities and intrusion profiles has also dramatically increased the number of security incidents in past few years. These statistics show an alarming situation in which expertise of intruders is increasing, complexity of network and system administration is increasing, ability to react fast enough is declining significantly and along this, vendors continue to produce software with inherent vulnerabilities. In addition to direct attacks and penetrations by humans (hackers or insiders), one of the additional rising problems in today's networks is the existence of malicious bots and bot networks (Security, 2007). Most botnets are created to conduct malicious actions such as conducting Denial of Service (DoS) attacks, stealing user identities, installing keyboard loggers to record keystrokes, or generating e-mail spam.

The network security is to protect the networks and their services from unauthorized modification, destruction or disclosure. It is the process of preventing and detecting unauthorized access to data or resources across the network. It involves all activities that organization, enterprises and institutions undertake to protect the value of asset and the integrity and the continuity of operation. The security strategy requires identifying threats and then choosing the most effective set of tools to combat them. The security risks to be managed are unauthorized access to data and unauthorized use of system resource.

Current security policies do not sufficiently guard data stored in an information system against privileged users. Intruders who have gained super-user privileges can perform malicious operations and disable many resources in the information system. Many other mechanisms and technologies like firewalls, encryption, authorization, vulnerability checking and access control policies can offer security but they are still susceptible for attacks from hackers who take advantage of system flaws and social engineering tricks. In addition, computer systems with no connection to public networks remain vulnerable to disgruntled employees who misuse their privileges.

These observations result in the fact that much more emphasis has to be placed on Intrusion Detection and prevention System (IDPS) to protect the system from intruders

BACKGROUND

Stallings & Brown (2008)defined computer security that deals with computer related assets that are subjected to a variety of threats and for which various measures are taken to protect those assets.

Computer System Security is defined as the process of protecting the factors for any secure computer system. Those factors are: *Confidentiality, Integrity,* and *Availability*. These three concepts form what is often referred to as:

- **Confidentiality:** Is the concealment of information or resources. The need for keeping information secret arises from the use of computers in sensitive fields such as Government and industry. Confidentiality applies to the existence of data as well as Hiding resources.
- **Integrity:** Refers to the trustworthiness of data or resources, and it is usually phrased in terms of preventing improper or unauthorized change. Integrity includes data Integrity (the content of the information) and origin integrity (the source of the data, often called authentication). The source of the information may bear on its accuracy and Credibility and on the trust that people place in the information. Working with integrity is very different from working with confidentiality. With confidentiality, the data is either compromised or it is not, but integrity includes both the correctness and the trustworthiness of the data.
- **Availability:** Refers to the ability to use the information or resource desired. Availability is an important aspect of reliability as well as of system design because an unavailable system is as least bad as no system at all. The aspect of availability that is relevant to security is that someone may deliberately arrange to deny access to data or to a service by making it unavailable. Attempts to block availability, called Denial of Service attacks (DoS), can be the most difficult to detect, because the analyst must determine if the unusual access patterns are attributable to deliberate manipulation of resources or of environment.

The Intrusion Protection Systems (IPS) can be thought of as a proactive defense tool against active attacks on computers and networks. This network device monitors a network or system activities to find malicious or unwanted behavior and can react to block those activities. This system prevents attacks before entering the network by examining various data record and detects demeanor pattern recognition sensor. When an attack is identified, intrusion prevention blocks and logs the offending data.

NETWORK IPS AND HOST IPS

Intrusion prevention systems are classified into two categories

- Network-based
- Host-based.

Network-Based IPS

A Network based IPS is a dedicated computer or special hardware platform, with detection software installed. It is placed at a strategic point on a network (like a gateway or sub network) to analyze all network traffic on that particular segment. The network is configured to send a copy of all the traffic in the network through the IPS so that the IPS may examine it to identify possible intrusions. This system can detect attacks against multiple hosts on a single subnet, but it usually cannot monitor multiple subnets at one time.

A network based IDPS (NIDPS) monitors wired networks traffic for particular Network segments or devices and analyses network, transport and application protocols to identify suspicious activity. Most of analysis is done in application layer. Transport and network layers also analyzed to identify attacks at those layers and to help the analysis in application layer

Host-Based IPS

This is an intrusion prevention system that is installed on a host and is designed to block attacks against the host system.

Host based IDPS(HIDPS) are used to protect both servers and workstations through software that runs between your system's applications and OS kernel. The software is preconfigured to determine the protection rules based on intrusion and attack signatures. The HIPS will catch suspicious activity on the system and then, depending on the predefined rules, it will either block or allow the event to happen. HIPS monitors activities such as application or data requests, network connection attempts, and read or write attempts etc.

DIFFERENT TYPES OF ATTACKS

Worms

A worm is a program that is designed to replicate itself and send copies from computer to computer across network connections. Upon arrival, the worm may be activated to replicate and propagate again.
To replicate itself, a network worm uses facilities like:

- **E-Mail:** A worm mails a copy of itself to other systems, so that its code is run when the e-mail or an attachment is received or viewed.
- **Remote Execution Capability:** A worm executes a copy of itself on another system, either using an explicit remote execution facility or by exploiting a program flaw in a network service to subvert its operations.
- **Remote Login Capability:** A worm logs onto a remote system as a user and then uses commands to copy itself from one system to the other, where it then executes

In addition to propagation, the worm also performs many unwanted activities like:

- Flood networks with their probes for new victims
- Consume resources on the victim system through their propagation operations and
- Consume resources on adequately protected systems.
- Hunt for specific data on infected systems, implant other malware, or intentionally harm data.

The concept of a computer worm was introduced in John Brunner's 1975 SF novel The Shockwave Rider. The first known worm implementation was done in Xerox Palo Alto Labs in the early 1980s. It was non malicious, searching for idle systems to use to run a computationally intensive task

Trojan

Like worm a Trojan horse is another type of malware that is designed to propagate itself from system to system. A Trojan horse is a useful, or apparently useful, program or command procedure containing hidden code that, when invoked, performs some unwanted or harmful function. Trojan horse programs can be used to accomplish functions indirectly that an unauthorized user could not accomplish directly. For example, to gain access to the files of another user on a shared system, a user could create a Trojan horse program that, when executed, changes the invoking user's file permissions so that the files are readable by any user. Trojan requires human intervention to keep it moving. A Trojan horse is so named because it is disguised as something benign. For example, a Trojan may be embedded inside a computer program purported to be a game, screen saver, or other program. But once activated, a Trojan will do whatever harmful things that it was designed to do. When activated, a Trojan may scan nearby networks for neighboring systems that are potential victims. Or, the Trojan may scan the user's system to look for valuable data, or install other malware that it is carrying.

Buffer Overflows

A buffer overflow, or buffer overrun, is an anomaly where a program, while writing data to a buffer, overruns the buffer's boundary and overwrites adjacent memory. This is a special case of violation of memory safety.

Buffer overflows can be triggered by inputs that are designed to execute code, or alter the way the program operates. This may result in erratic program behavior, including memory access errors, incorrect results, a crash, or a breach of system security. Thus, they are the basis of many software vulnerabilities and can be maliciously exploited.

A buffer overflow is a specific type of attack against a system, where the attack is designed to confuse the system into executing the attacker's instructions. A buffer overflow attack works like this. An attacking program establishes a communications session with a specific component on the target system, and sends a specially crafted message to the target system. The message deliberately sends too much data into the target system's input buffer. In a program that is vulnerable to a buffer overflow attack, the excess data will overwrite program instructions in the vulnerable program, and eventually the program will execute those instructions (thinking that it is executing its original instructions). Those new instructions usually contain code to open the target system and permit a partial or complete takeover of the target system. A buffer overflow attack isn't easy to develop. It takes detailed knowledge of the target system's internal architecture (both software and hardware), as well as detailed knowledge of the program or service being attacked. That said, hackers who develop buffer overflow exploits often build a "kit" that makes it easy for others to exploit the same vulnerability.

Worms, Trojans, viruses, and other types of malware often use buffer overflows as a way of gaining a foothold in a new victim system. Buffer overflows account for a significant portion of the attacks against systems on the Internet.

Spyware

Spyware is a term ascribed to a wide range of techniques used to covertly obtain information from computers. Spyware most often takes on the form of computer code that is installed on a user's computer without his or her knowledge or consent, gathers specific information, and sends that information to a central source. Spyware may also alter the behavior of the victim's computer.

The activities performed by spyware include:

- Tracking sites visited with a browser
- Recording keystrokes and mouse clicks
- Changing browser settings (for instance, changing home page, default search engine, and so on)

Unlike other types of malware such as viruses and Trojans, spyware doesn't usually contain code for making copies of itself onto other computers.

Phishing

Phishing is the attempt to acquire sensitive information such as usernames, passwords, and credit card details (and sometimes, indirectly, money) by masquerading as a trustworthy entity in an electronic communication.

A typical phishing scam works like this:

- **The Bait:** The scammer sends out large quantities of genuine-looking e-mail messages to intended victims in an effort to entice them to open an attachment or click a URL.
- **The Hook:** Although most people ignore or don't receive (because of anti-spam) the message, a few believe it is legitimate, or they're just curious. They open the attachment or click on the link.

The attachment installs malware or spyware on the victim's computer, which may steal information, install a key logger, or perform some other harmful action. If the user clicks a URL, the website may trick the user into believing she is logging into a legitimate website (such as online banking). If she types in her user ID and password, the scam artist will use these credentials to log in later and steal money from the victim.

Botnets

A botnet is a collection of Internet-connected programs communicating with other similar programs in order to perform tasks. Creators of botnets are typically financially motivated. Here is how a botnet works. An individual or group will write a small software program — a bot — that will enable the computer it's running on to be remotely controlled. This bot will be packaged into a worm, malware program, or loaded on a malicious website, at which time a campaign of some sort (say, a phishing scam) will ensue to get the bot installed on as many computers as possible. The owner of these bots, usually known as a bot herder,has a centralized "command and control" program that can be used to control all the computers that are running his bots. This control program can then be used to perform work on behalf of the bot herder, such as:

- **Spam:** A bot army can be used to send millions of spam messages — which themselves may contain malware intended to grow the bot army.

- **Denial of Service Attacks:** The bot army can be used to remotely attack a computer or network of the bot herder's choosing. Denial of service attacks are discussed later in this chapter.

SYN Floods

A SYN flood is an attack on a target system, specifically an attack in a key design attribute of the TCP/IP networking protocol. In a SYN flood, the attacker sends thousands of SYN packets to a target system. A *SYN* packet is ordinarily a message sent from another computer that wants to establish a network connection with the target. Upon receiving the SYN, the target system will reply with a SYN/ACK, at which point the conversation will begin. An important fact to note is that the target computer will allocate resources (mainly, memory) in anticipation of the new connection. But in a SYN flood, the attacker sends thousands of SYNs and ignores all the SYN/ACKs. The purpose of this is to flood the target system until it is incapable of communicating on any legitimate channels. A SYN flood is a special type of a denial of service attack. These attacks are discussed in the next section.

Denial of Service

Denial of Service (DoS) is a class of attacks where an attacker makes some computing or memory resource too busy or too full to handle legitimate requests, thus denying legitimate users access to a machine(Paul Innella,2010). There are different ways to launch DoS attacks like:

- Abusing the computers legitimate features.
- Targeting the implementations bugs.
- Exploiting the system's misconfigurations.

DoS attacks are classified based on the services that an attacker renders unavailable to legitimate users. An attack used was Apache2, Back, Mail bomb, Neptune, Ping of death, Process table, Smurf, Syslogd and UDP storm.

There are two basic types of DoS attacks:

- **Flooding:** The most common form of DoS attack is one where the attacker sends such a high volume of messages to a target system that it either malfunctions or is otherwise unavailable for legitimate purposes.
- **Malfunction:** The other common form of DoS attack is one where a specially crafted message is sent to the target system; the message causes the target system to malfunction or crash. Another type of DoS attack is known as the Distributed Denial of Service (DDoS) attack. In a DDoS attack, the attacker causes many different systems to flood a target system simultaneously. Such an attack can be nearly impossible to block if there are hundreds or thousands of different sources.

User to Root Attacks

User to root exploits are a class of attacks where an attacker starts out with access to a normal user account on the system and is able to exploit vulnerability to gain root access to the system. Most common exploits in this class of attacks are regular buffer overflows, which are caused by regular programming mistakes and environment assumptions. Attacks used was Perl and Xterm.

Remote to User Attacks

A remote to user (R2L) attack is a class of attacks where an attacker sends packets to a machine over a network, then exploits machine's vulnerability to illegally gain local access as a user. There are different types of R2L attacks; the most common attack in this class is done using social engineering.

Attacks used was Dictionary, FTP-write, Guest, Imap, Named, Phf, Sendmail, Xlock and Xnsnoop.

Probing (Probe)

Probing is a class of attacks in which an attacker scans a network of computers togather information or find known vulnerabilities. An attacker tries to find information about the target host, such as scanning victims in order to get knowledge about available services, using Operating System. Examples are Mscan, Nmap, Saint, and Satan.

Zero-Day Attacks

A zero-day attack is a brand new attack on a previously unknown vulnerability, or a new type of an attack on an existing vulnerability. The term zero day comes from the number of days of warning between the time when the vulnerability is announced and when it is exploited. In other words, these are vulnerabilities for which no patches are available. Zero-day attacks are significant because signature-based(exploit-based) IPS devices are generally defenseless against them. However, IPSs that also use anomaly-based detection and leverage vulnerability-based rules (as opposed to exploit based signatures) can protect effectively against zero-day attacks.

Advanced Persistent Threats (APT)

An advanced persistent threat is information warfare, conducted by sophisticated adversaries who are determined to control information systems and gather intelligence on persons, organizations, and governments. Advanced persistent threats are malicious, and they certainly fall into the class of malware. For highly sophisticated threats, you won't find signatures in anti-virus products or intrusion detection systems. Advanced persistent threats do consist of attacks that are detectable. However, these attacks may be subtle and take place over a very long period of time. Traditional defenses such as anti-virus, IPS, and firewalls may not see anything a tall. The actors behind an advanced persistent threat don't want to set off any alarms.

COMMON COMPONENTS OF IPS

The most common components of IPS are shown in Figure 1 and are described below

Figure 1. Components of IPS

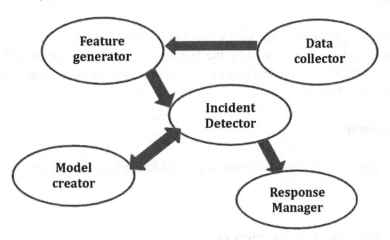

Data Collector Module

This module is used in the data collection phase. In the case of a Network Intrusion Detection System (NIDS), the source of the data can be the raw frames from the network or information from upper protocol layers such as the IP or UDP. In the case of host based detection system, source of data are the audit logs maintained by the operating system.

Feature Generator

This module is responsible for extracting a set of selected features from the data acquired by the acquisition module. Features can be classified as low-level and high-level features. A low-level feature can be directly extracted from captured data whereas some deductions are required to be performed to extract the high-level features. Considering the example of a network based IDS, the source IP and destination IP of network packets would be the low level features whereas information such as number of failed login attempts would be classified as high level features. Sometimes features are categorized based on the source of data as well.

Incident Detector

This is the core of an IDS. This is the module that processes the data generated by the Feature Generator and identifies intrusions. Intrusion detection methodologies are generally classified as misuse detection and anomaly detection. Misuse detection systems have definitions of attacks and they match the input data against those definitions. Upon a successful match, the activity is classified as intrusion. Anomaly detection systems are based on a definition of normal behavior of a system. Any deviations from this normal profile lead to the classification of the corresponding activity as suspicious. Irrespective of the detection methodology, upon detection of an intrusion, an alert is generated and sent to the Response Management module.

Model Generator

This module contains the reference data with which the Incident Detector compares the data acquired by the acquisition modules and processed by the feature generator. The source of data of the Traffic Model Generator could be non-automated (coming from human knowledge) or automated (coming from automated knowledge gathering process).

Response Manager

Upon receiving an alert from the incident detector, this module initiates actions in response to a possible intrusion.

COMMON DETECTION METHODOLOGIES

Intrusion Detection methods are generally classified as the following.

Misuse or Signature Detection

A signature is a sequence of bytes identifying an attack The IPS includes a collection of intrusion signatures, which are encapsulation of the identifying characteristics of specific intrusion techniques.

Signature detection involves matching intrusive behavior of malicious users/code or searching network traffic for a series of bytes or packet sequences known to be malicious Misuse detection based detection consists of comparing the traffic against a Model describing known intrusion event. This approach is quite effective at detecting known threats but its performance while detecting unknown threats is very poor. This method works well against attacks with a fixed behavioral pattern, but do not work well against the multitude of attack patterns created by a human or a worm with self-modifying behavioral characteristics. Because they only detect known attacks, a signature must be created for every attack, and novel attacks cannot be detected. Pattern recognition, Implication rules and Data mining techniques are some of the most commonly used techniques for misuse detection.

Anomaly Detection Based System

The assumption in anomaly detection is that an intrusion can be detected by observing a deviation from the normal or expected behavior of the system or network (Computer and Network IDS: Anomaly-Based - IDStutorial.com, 2010).

This method is based on the comparison of current traffic profile against the profiles representing normal traffic behavior. Normal system behavior is determined by observing the standard operation of the system or network. Initially an anomaly detector creates a baseline profile of the normal legitimate traffic activity. Thereafter, any new activity deviating from the normal profile is considered an anomaly. This detection methodology has the potential of detecting previously unknown attacks. Pattern recognition, Data mining technique and soft computing techniques are some of the most commonly used techniques for misuse detection. However, currently the major problem with this system is the high false alarm rate.

Statistical Methods

Machine learning and data mining techniques are among the most commonly used techniques for anomaly detection. Statefull Protocol Analysis Based System This methodology is based on the assumption that IDS could know and trace the protocol states. Though SPA process seems similar to the Anomaly Detection methodology, they are basically different. SPA depends on vendor-developed generic profiles to specific protocols whereas, Anomaly Detection uses preloaded network or host specific profiles. Generally, the network protocol models in SPA are based on protocol standards from international standard organizations, e.g., IETF. SPA is also known as Specification- based Detection.

Target Monitoring

These systems do not actively search for anomalies or signatures, but instead look for the modification of specified files. This is more of a corrective control, designed to uncover an unauthorized action after it occurs in order to reverse it. One way to check for the hidden editing of files is by computing a cryptographic hash beforehand and comparing this to new hashes of the file at regular intervals. This type of system is the easiest to implement, because it does not require constant monitoring by the administrator. Integrity checksum hashes can be computed at whatever intervals you wish, and on either all files or just the mission/system critical files (Paul Innella, 2010).

Stealth Probes

This technique attempts to detect any attackers that choose to carry out their mission over prolonged periods of time. Attackers, for example, will check for system vulnerabilities and open ports over a two-month period, and wait another two months to actually launch the attacks. Stealth probes collect a wide-variety of data throughout the system, checking for any methodical attacks over a long period of time. They take a wide-area sampling and attempt to discover any correlating attacks. In effect, this method combines anomaly detection and misuse detection in an attempt to uncover suspicious activity (Paul Innella, 2010)

Denial of Service (DoS) Detection

DoS detection compares current traffic behavior with acceptable normal behavior to detect DoS attacks, where normal traffic is characterized by a set of pre-programmed thresholds. This can lead to false alarms or attacks being missed because the attack traffic is below the configured threshold (Generation Intrusion Detection Systems (IDS) - McAfee Network Protection Solutions,2010).

Hybrid

Most existing IPSs use multiple methodologies to improve the accuracy of detection. For example, Signature Detection and Anomaly Detection are used as complementary methods as they provide a mixture of improved accuracy and ability to detect unknown attacks.

RELATED WORK

Ghosh and Schwartzbard used system behavior as input for the neural network in their experiment. They used 4 weeks of training data and 161 sessions with testing data. Out of these, they only had 22 attack sessions. The results from this experiment showed a detection rate of 77.3% and a false positive rate of 3.6%. In their experiments, they used software behavior for the input to the neural network, not user behavior (Ghosh et.al. 1999).

Lippmann and Cunningham have done some experiments using keyword selection and neural networks. The results from their experiments showed a detection rate of 80%, but they had roughly 10 false alarms per day. Unfortunately they did not calculate the false positive rate into percentage(R. P. Lippmann et.al.,2000).

Neural networks can successfully be used as a method for training and learning an Intrusion Detection System. Experimental results shows detection rate of 88% on 50 attacks, false positive rate of 0%. But there is need to regular update of the signature database, need to consider known and unknown attacks, only detect, cannot prevent the intrusions and it's an offline system(M. Pradhan et.al., 2012).

A. Abraham investigated the suitability of linear genetic programming (LGP) technique to model fast and efficient intrusion detection systems. Linear Genetic Programming examines the evolution of imperative computer programs written as linear sequences of instructions. In contrast to functional expressions or syntax trees used in traditional Genetic Programming (GP), Linear Genetic Programming (LGP) employs a linear program structure as genetic material whose primary characteristics are exploited to achieve acceleration of both execution time and evolutionary progress(A. Abraham,2004).

Ensafi R, Dehghanzadeh S, Mohammad R and Akbarzadeh T, used a hybrid swarm fuzzy K-means (SFK-means) approach with the DARPA Data Set in which each particle contained a constant number of clusters, resulting in a particle with the best fitness of clusters. The clusters in this particle were then used to classify anomalies when a distance was beyond a threshold. (Ensafi et al. 2008)

Fuzzy rule-based classifiers,decision trees, support vector machines, linear genetic programming have been used by A. Abraham and R.Jain to illustrate the importance of soft computing paradigm for modeling intrusion detection systems(A..Abraham et.al.,2007).

STEPS IN SELECTING AN IPS

The following things should be taken into account while selecting an IPS.

- Determine the Level of Security and Coverage requirement of the user
- Determine Performance Requirements of the users
- Determine whether the IPS can be Installed with ease or not
- Determine whether the IPS will provide flexible configurations for different networking needs or not.
- Determine whether a wide range of attacks can be covered the IPS or
- Meets enterprise architecture and management needs

CONCLUSION AND FUTURE WORK

This chapter has provided a comprehensive overview of intrusion prevention systems, different types of attack and different methods of intrusion detection used now days with explanation. There are some issues and challenges in this area. The major challenge is how to create a model of normal behavior of the system and distinguish between normal abnormal behaviors of the system. Another challenge is how to create and update signatures of new attacks. The size of the IPS is also another challenge. False positive alarms and false negative alarms are to be reduced. These are some issues that can be studied in the future.

REFERENCES

Abraham, A. (2004). Evolutionary Computation in Intelligent Network Management. In Evolutionary Computing in Data Mining. Springer.

Abraham, A. & Jain, R. (2007). Soft computing models for network intrusion detection systems. *Studies in Computational Intelligence*, 191–211.

Bishop, M. (2005). Malicious Logic. In Introduction to Computer Security. Addison Wesley.

CERT. (2007). *CERT/CC Statistics 1988-2007*. CERTCoordination Center. Retrieved from http://www.cert.org/stats/

Computer and Network IDS. (2010). *Anomaly-Based IDStutorial.com*. Retrieved from http://idstutorial.com/anomaly-detection.php

Ensafi, R., Dehghanzadeh, S., Mohammad, R., & Akbarzadeh, T. (2008). Optimizing fuzzy k-means for network anomaly detection using pso. ACS/IEEE international conference on computer systems and applications, Doha, Qatar. doi:10.1109/AICCSA.2008.4493603

Ghosh, A. K., & Schwartzbard, A. (1999). A Study in using Neural Networks for Anomaly and Misuse Detection. In *Proc. th USENIX Security Symposium*.

Innell, P. (2010). *An Introduction to IDS*. Retrieved from http://www.symantec.com/connect/articles/introduction-ids

Lippmann, R. P., & Cunningham, R. K. (2000). Improving Intrusion Detection Performance using Keyword Selection and Neural Networks. *Computer Networks*, *34*(4), 597–603. doi:10.1016/S1389-1286(00)00140-7

Next Generation Intrusion Detection Systems (IDS). (2010). *McAfee Network Protection Solutions*. Retrieved from http://www.mcafee.com/us/local_content/white_papers/wp_intruvertnextgenerationids.pdf

Pradhan, M., Pradhan, S. K., & Sahu, S. K. (2012). Anomaly Detection Using Different Artificial Neural Network Training Functions. *IJCSET*, *2*(4), 1155–1159.

Security Department of Homeland Cyber Security Research and Development. (2007). Department of Homeland Security, Science and Technologies Division.

KEY TERMS AND DEFINITIONS

Artificial Neural Network: (ANN): This is an information processing inspired by biological neural networks (the central nervous systems of animals, in particular the brain) and are used to estimate or approximate functions that can depend on a large number of inputs and are generally unknown. Artificial neural network is generally represented as systems of interconnected "neurons" which can compute values from inputs, and are capable of machine learning as well as pattern recognition.

Attack: In computing environment, attack is an attempt to disrupt, destroy, theft or unauthorized access to or unauthorized use of a computing resource.

Data Mining: Data Mining is an analytic process designed to explore data in search of consistent patterns and/or systematic relationships between variables, and then to validate the findings by applying the detected patterns to new subsets of data.

Firewall: It is a network device located at a network gateway server to protect the resources of a private network from users from other networks. The purpose is to allow or block traffic into and out of a private network or the user's computer.

Genetic Algorithm (GA): The genetic algorithm is a model of machine learning which derives its behavior from a metaphor of the processes of natural evolution. This is done by the creation of a population of individuals represented by chromosomes, which represents a possible solution. The individuals in the population then go through a process of evolution to produce next generation population. Only the fittest individuals are survived in the evolution.

Internet Protocol: (IP): The method or protocol used by Internet to send data from one computer to another that uses IP address to recognize computers in Internet.

Network Security: It is the mechanism to protect computer files and directories in a computer network against hacking, misuse and unauthorized changes to the system.

Chapter 11
AdaBoost Algorithm with Single Weak Classifier in Network Intrusion Detection

P. Natesan
Kongu Engineering College, India

P. Balasubramanie
Kongu Engineering College, India

G. Gowrison
Institute of Road and Transport Technology, India

ABSTRACT

Recently machine learning based intrusion detection system developments have been subjected to extensive researches because they can detect both misuse detection and anomaly detection. In this paper, we propose an AdaBoost based algorithm for network intrusion detection system with single weak classifier. In this algorithm, the classifiers such as Bayes Net, Naïve Bayes and Decision tree are used as weak classifiers. KDDCup99 dataset is used in these experiments to demonstrate that boosting algorithm can greatly improve the classification accuracy of weak classification algorithms. Our approach achieves higher detection rate with low false alarm rates and is scalable for large datasets, resulting in an effective intrusion detection system.

1. INTRODUCTION

Intrusion detection techniques have become an active area in the research of computer security field over the past ten years. The goals of network intrusion detection are to identify, classify and possibly respond to malicious or suspicious activities. There are basically two types of intrusion detection systems namely misuse detection and anomaly detection. Anomaly detection system first learns normal system activities and then alerts all system events that deviate from the learned model. The advantage of anomaly detection is the ability to detect the unknown attack types. The main drawback of anomaly detection system

DOI: 10.4018/978-1-4666-8761-5.ch011

is their high false positive rate (i.e) it mistakenly classify the normal behaviors as attacks. The misuse detection uses the signature of attacks to detect intrusions by modeling attacks. Misuse detection has higher detection rate than anomaly detection but it fails to detect unknown attacks.

1.1 Related Work

Kayacik et al and Heywood (2003)proposed a hierarchical SOM for intrusion detection. They utilized the classification capability of the SOM on selected dimensions and specific attention is given to the hierarchical development of abstractions. The reported results showed that there was an increase in attack detection rate. AnazidaZainal (2009) demonstrated the ensemble of different learning paradigms by assigning proper weight to the individual classifiers. They have observed that there was an improvement on attack detection and significant reduction on false alarm.

Several hybrid IDS have been proposed recently to deal with the complexity of the intrusion detection problem by combining different machine learning algorithms. Shi-Jinn Horng and Ming-Yang Su (2011),were developed a hybrid intelligent IDS by incorporating a hierarchical clustering and support vector machines. The SVM theory was slightly modified in this research in order to be used with standard network intrusions dataset that contains labels. Cheng Xiang and Png Chin Yong (2008) designed IDS by combining the supervised tree classifiers and unsupervised Bayesian Clustering to detect intrusions.

Jiang Zhang (2006) proposed a new framework of unsupervised anomaly NIDS based on the outlier detection technique in random forests algorithm. The framework builds the patterns of network services over datasets labeled by the services. With the built in patterns, the framework detects attacks in the datasets using the outlier detection algorithm. This approach reduced the time complexity and cost of memory to a larger extent.

Giacinto at al (2007) took a slightly different approach. Their anomaly IDS was based on modular multiple classifier system where each module was designed for each group of protocols and services. The reported results showed that this approach provides a better trade-off between generalization abilities and false alarm generation than that provided by an individual classifier trained on the overall feature set. MrudulaGudadhe and Prakash (2010) have demonstrated a new ensemble boosted decision tree for intrusion detection system. The underlying idea of this approach is to combine simple rules to form an ensemble such that the performance of the single ensemble is improved.

Yongiin Liu et al (2010) constructed a classifier by using a decision tree as its base learner. The classification accuracy this algorithm is little better than SOM algorithms. Weiming Hu (2008) has proposed an adaboost based algorithm for network intrusion detection which uses decision stump as a weak learner. The decision rules are provided for both categorical and continuous features and some provision was made for handling the overfitting.

1.2 Dataset Analysis

Under the sponsorship of Defense Advanced Research Projects Agency (DARPA) and Air Force Research Laboratory (AFRL), MIT Lincoln laboratory has collected and distributed the datasets for the evaluation of researches in computer network intrusion detection systems. The KDDCup99 dataset is a subset of the DARPA benchmark dataset.

Table 1. Number of samples in the KDDCup'99 training set

Normal	Attacks				Total
	Probe	Dos	R2L	U2R	
97278	4107	391458	1126	52	494021

KDDCup99 training dataset is about four giga bytes of compressed binary TCP dump data from seven weeks of network traffic, processed into about five million connections record each with about 100 bytes. The two weeks of test data have around two million connection records. Each KDDCup'99 training connection record contains 41 features and is labeled as either normal or an attack, with exactly one specific attack type.

The attack types are grouped into attack categories in order to combine similar attack types into a single category which could improve the detection rate. Tables 1 and 2 shows the number of records for each attack category in the 10% KDDCup99 training and testing datasets of respectively.

The rest of the paper is organized as follows. Section 2 gives the overview of AdaBoost algorithm, Bayesian Classifiers and Decision Tree algorithms. Section 3 gives a brief overview of our proposed work. Experimental analyses are performed in section 4. Section 5 concludes the paper with suggestions for future work.

2. OVERVIEW OF ALGORITHMS

2.1 AdaBoost Algorithm

AdaBoostis a machine learning algorithm, can be used in conjunction with many other learning algorithms to improve their performance. It calls a weak classifier repeatedly in a series of rounds. For each call a distribution of weights D_t is updated that indicates the importance of examples in the data set for the classification. On each round, the weights of each incorrectly classified example are increased so that the new classifier focuses more on those misclassified examples (Zan Xin et al.,2007).The pseudo code of adaboost algorithm is given in Table 3.

2.2 Bayesian Classifiers

Bayesian approaches are a fundamentally important Data Mining technique. Given the probability distribution, Bayes classifier can provably achieve the optimal result. Bayesian method is based on the

Table 2. Number of samples in the KDDCup'99 test set

Normal	Attacks				Total
	Probe	Dos	R2L	U2R	
60593	4107	391458	1126	52	311029

Table 3. Adaboost Algorithm

Input: Sequence of m training examples

Let the set of training sample data be $\{(x_1, y_1) \ldots (x_i, y_i) \ldots (x_m, y_m)\}$ with labels $y_{j\in}\{\text{Normal, Attack}\}$, where x_i denotes i^{th} feature vector and m is the size of the dataset. Let be the number of iterations.

Initialize the weights $D_i(i) = 1/m$ for all i.

Repeat for t = 1, 2,…,T the following steps

    1. Call the weak classifier, and provide it with the instances of distribution D_t

    2. Calculate the error of each round of the hypothesis h_i: X ⊗ Y

$$\in_i = \Pr_{i \sim Dt}\left[h_t(x_i) \neq y_i\right] = \sum_{h_i(x_i \neq y_i)}\left(D_t(i)\right) \tag{1}$$

    If $\in_i > 0.5$, then set T = t-1 and abort loop.

    3. Calculate the reweight value by using the equation,

$$\beta_i = \in_i/1 - \in_i \tag{2}$$

    4. Update distribution D_t:

$$D_{t+1}(i) = \begin{cases} \beta_i \dfrac{D_t(i)}{Z_t} & (h_t(x_i) = y_i) \\ \dfrac{D_t(i)}{Z_t} & (\text{else}) \end{cases} \tag{3}$$

where Z_t is a normalization constant.

    Output: final hypothesis

$$hfin(x) = \sum_{y\in Y}^{\arg\max} h_t(x) = y \log\frac{1}{\beta} \tag{4}$$

    Let us write the error $\in_i$ of h_i as ½-γ_t. Then γ_t shows how much better of weak learner than random guessing. Freund and Schapire[18] have proven that the training error $\in$ of the final hypothesis is at most

$$\in = \prod\left[2\sqrt{\in t(1 - \in t)}\right]$$
$$= \prod_t \pi_t\sqrt{1 - 4\gamma 2} \leq \exp\left(\sum_t^{-2}\gamma 2\right) \tag{5}$$

From above equation (5), we can conclude that the training error of boosting algorithm drops exponentially fast.[18]

probability theory. Bayes Rule is applied here to calculate the posterior from the prior and the likelihood, because the later two is generally easier to be calculated from a probability model.

Consider X as a data sample consisting n features and C_i denotes a class to be predicted. Classification is determined by obtaining $P(C_i|X)$, probability for a class conditioned upon an observed data sample X, is equal to its likelihood $P(X|C_i)$ times it probability prior to any observed sample $P(C_i)$, normalized by dividing P(Xi).

$$P(C_i \mid X) = P(X \mid C_i)P(C_i) / P(X) \tag{6}$$

There are two types of Bayesian classifiers namely Naive Bayesian Classification and Bayes Net Classification. Consider a Naïve Bayesian Classification with n nodes, X_i to X_n. The features and classes are represented by nodes, labeled with X_n and C respectively. An assumption is made in Naïve Bayes Classification where features are conditionally independent from each other. Since P(X) is constant for all classes, only P(X|Ci) need to be maximized. Hence,

$$P(X \mid C_i) = \prod_{k=1}^{n} P(X_1 \mid C_i) * P(X_2 \mid C_i) * \ldots * P(X_n \mid C_i) \tag{7}$$

Naïve Bayes classifier is a popular classifier looking at its competitive performance in many research domains and its simplicity in computation that allows researchers to save a lot of computational costs. (Kok-Chin Khor et al., 2006, J.W.Han et al., 2006, N.Friedman et al., 1997].

A Bayes Net uses a graphical model to represent the relationship of features. An assumption is made in BayesNet where not every node is connected to each other. The structure of the graphical model and also a Conditional probability Table(CPT) of a BayesNet classifier could be built based on a training set.

The graphical model specifies a factorization of the join probability distributions, where a value of a node is conditioned onits parent nodes. Hence,

$$P(X_1, X_2, \ldots, X_n) = \prod_{i=1}^{n} P(X_i \mid Parents(C_i)) \tag{8}$$

A BayesNet can also be constructed manually by incorporating knowledge of a domain expert. The construction process is repetitive process which involves model verification and model revision .

2.3 Decision Tree Construction

The decision tree is one of the machine learning classifiers for generating classification models. Tin the decision tree, internal node denotes a test on an attribute and each branch represents an outcome of the test. The leaf node represents classes or the distribution of classes (Cheng Xiang et al., 2008). The pseudo code for decision tree construction is in Table 4.

3. PROPOSED WORK

As per the requirements of a Network Intrusion Detection system, the framework of our proposed system consists of the following four modules of AdaBoost Algorithm. Feature extraction, Instance labeling, design of weak classifiers and building of the strong classifier.

Process 1 - Feature extraction: For each network connection, the following three major groups of features for detecting intrusions are extracted.

Table 4. Decision tree construction algorithm

Step 1: Let S be the set of instances, select one instance at random from S and announce that it belongs to some class C_j. P_i is the probability that an arbitrary sample belongs to class Cj, which is estimated by,

$$Pi = freq(C_j, S) / |S| \tag{9}$$

where $|S| \in$ S. Here, $-\log_2 P_i$ bits of information is conveyed.

Step 2: Let P is the probability distribution, P = {$P_1,P_2,...,P_n$} then the information conveyed by this distribution is defined as,

$$Info(P) = \sum_{i=1}^{n} -P_i \log_2 P_i \tag{10}$$

Step 3: The weighted average of $Info(T_i)$ is calculated as given,

$$Info(X,T) = \sum_{i=1}^{m} \frac{|T_i|}{|T|} * Info(T_i) \tag{11}$$

Here T is a set of samples partitioned into sets $T_1, T_2,...T_m$ based on the non-categorical attribute X.
The Information gain, *Gain(X, T)* is calculated as,

$$Gain(X, T) = Info(T) - Infor(X, T) \tag{12}$$

The attribute with the highest information gain is chosen as the test attribute for the current node. This process continues until all the attributes are compared or when all the instances are all of the same class or there are no remaining attributes on which the instances may be further partitioned.

---

1. Basic Features: This category encapsulates all the attributes that can be extracted from a TCP/IP connection. Some of the basic features in the KDDCup99 dataset are protocol_type, service, src_bytes and dst_bytes.

2. Content Features: These features are purely based on the contents in the data portion of the data packet.

3. Traffic Features: This category includes features that are computed with respect to a two-second time window and it is divided into two groups: same host features and same service features. The same host features examine only the connections in the past 2 seconds that have the same destination host as the current connection. The same service features examine only the connections in the past 2 seconds that have the same service as the current connection. Some of the traffic features are count, rerror_rate, rerror_ratesrv_serror_rate and srv_diff_host_rate.

Process 2: Instance Labeling: After extracting KDDCup'99 features from each record, the instances are labeled as Normal or Attack.

Process 3: Selection of weak classifiers: The various weak classifiers used in our proposed system are Naïve Bayes, Bayes Net and Decision Tree. We have used the weak classifier along with the boosting algorithm to improve the classification accuracy.

Process 4: Building of strong classifier: A strong classifier is constructed by combining weak classifier and boosting algorithm. The strong classifier results higher attack detection rate and than single weak classifier.

Table 5. The experimental results of our approach using different weak classifiers

S.No	Name of the Weak Classifier with Adaboost algorithm	% of Detection Rate	% of false alarm rate	Time Taken (in sec)	Time Complexity
1	Bayes Net	91.12	2.78	170	$O(mn)$
2	Naïve Bayes	91.45	2.61	191	$O(mn^2)$
3	Decision Tree	92.12	2.85	121	$O(mn(logn))$

4. EXPERIMENTAL ANALYSIS

The major aim of the following experiment was to improve the attacks detection rate and to lower the false alarm rate. The experiment was conducted using Bayes Net, Naïve Bayes and Decision Tree weak classifiers. Weka 3.6 is a data mining software, contains a collection of machine learning program for classification tasks written in Java, is chosen to build the model.

4.1. Classification Using Weak Classifiers

The overall detection rates and the false alarm rates of the three weak classifiers in the boosting process are shown in Table 5.

Based on the attack detection rates and false alarm rates, the weak classifiers with adaboost seem to have comparable performances. Decision tree was able to give a high detection rate with low computational time as compared to other weak classifiers Bayes Net and Naïve Bayes.

4.2 Comparison of Performance of Weak Classifiers

Detection rate comparison: From Figure 1, it can be seen that, the detection rate increases to 92.12% when the weak classifier Decision Tree is combined with adaboost. It can also be seen that the Decision Tree with adaboost gives the better detection rate than other weak classifiers such as Bayes Net and Naïve Bayes.

False Alarm rate comparison: The false alarm rate of Naïve Bayes weak classifier with adaboost decreases to 2.61%, but it shows an increase in the case of Decision Tree as a weak classifier with adaboost algorithm as shown in Figure 2.

4.3. Comparisons of Detection Rate and False Alarm Rate with Different Algorithms

The detection rate and false alarm rate of our algorithm are compared with existing work, which are tested on the benchmark KDDCup'99 dataset. Their performances were comparable but the Decision Tree classifier with Adaboost performed well. Since the Decision Tree has comparable performance as weak classifier with Adaboost, it should be considered for the building of IDS (see Table 6).

Figure 1. Attack detection rate comparison of weak classifiers

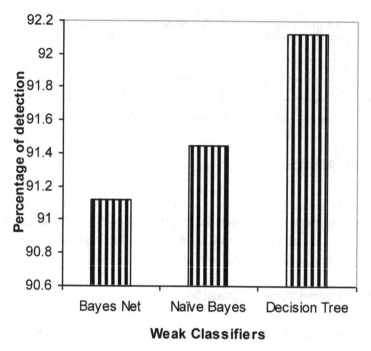

Figure 2. False alarm rate comparison of weak classifiers

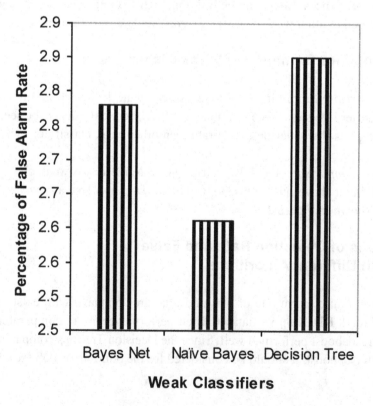

Table 6. Comparison of our algorithm with existing algorithms

Name of the Algorithm	% of Detection Rate	% of False Alarm Rate
Adaboost with Decision stump	90.73	3.14
Hierarchical SOM	90.04	2.19
IDS using SVM	91.20	6.12
Adaboost with Decision tree	92.12	3.26

5. CONCLUSION

We have proposed an Adaboost algorithm with weak classifiers. The weak classifiers such as Bayes Net, Naïve Bayes and Decision tree are used with adaboost algorithmto improve the classification accuracy. In this paper, we have addressed the dual problem of attack detection rate and false alarm rate for building robust, scalable and efficient intrusion detection system. It is important to have a low false alarm rate for an intrusion detection system. The experiment result shows that the Decision Tree with AdaBoost algorithm has a very low false-alarm rate with a high detection rate. We have focused mainly to obtain better classification though the time and computational complexities are theoretically high. But practically the time and computational complexities are reduced by processing speed of the computing device.

6. FUTURE RESEARCH DIRECTIONS

The areas for future research include the considering the other classifiers to seek the possibility of improving the classification performance and to combine two weak classifiers linearly with adaboost algorithm. We would like to further improve the Adaboost algorithm so that it can perform better in detecting the attacks.

REFERENCES

Maarof & Shasuddin. (2009). Ensemble classifiers for Network Intrusion Detection System. *Journal of Information Assurance and Security*, *4*, 217–225.

Eskin, E., Arnold, A., Prerau, M., Portnoy, L., & Stolfo, S. (2002). A geometric framework for unsupervised anomaly detection: Detecting intrusions in unlabeled data. In Applications of Data Mining in Computer Security. Norwell, MA: Kluwer.

Freund, Y., & Schapire, R. E. (1997). A Decision theoretic generalization of on-line learning and an application to boosting. *Journal of Computer and System Sciences*, *55*(1), 119–139. doi:10.1006/jcss.1997.1504

Friedman, N., Geiger, D., & Goldsmidt, M. (1997). Bayesian Network Classifiers. *Machine Learning*, *29*(Nov), 131–163. doi:10.1023/A:1007465528199

Giacinto, G., Roli, F., & Didaci, L. (2007). Fusion of multiple classifiers for Intrusion Detection in Computer Networks. In *Proc. IEEE Conference in Network security*.

Gudahe, Prasad, & Wankhade. (2010). *A New Data Mining Based Network Intrusion Detection Model.* International Conference on Computer & Communication Technology.

Gupta. (2010, January-April). Layered Approach Using Conditional Random Fields for Intrusion Detection. *IEEE Transactions on Dependable and Secure Computing, 7*(1).

Han, J. W., & Kamber, M. (2006). *Data Mining: Concepts and Techniques* (2nd ed.). Morgan Kaufmann.

Horng, Su, Chen, Kao, Chen, Lai, & Perkasa. (2011). A novel intrusion detection system based on hierarchical clustering and support vector machines. *Journal of Expert Systems with Applications, 38*, 306-313.

Hu, Hu, & Maybank. (2008). AdaBoost-Based Algorithm for Network Intrusion Detection. *IEEE Transactions on Systems, Man and Cybernetics, 38*, 577-583.

Kayacik, H. G., Zincir-Heywood & Heywood. (2003). On the capability of an SOM based intrusion detection systems. In *Proc. Int. Joint Conference in Neural Networks*.

KDDCup'99. (1999). *Dataset.* Retrieved from http://kdd.ics.uci.edu/databases/kddcup99/kddcup99.html

Khor. (2006). Comparing Single and Multiple Bayesian Classifiers Approaches for Network Intrusion Detection. Academic Press.

Liu, Y., Li, N., Shi, L., & Li, F. (2010). *An Intrusion Detection Method Based on Decision Tree.* In International Conference on E-Health Networking, Digital Ecosystems and Technologies.

Sarasamma, Zhu, & Huff. (2005). Hierarchical Kohonenen net for anomaly detection in network security. *IEEE Transactions on Systems, Man and Cybernetics, 35*(2), 302-312.

Xiang, C., Yong, P. C., & Meng, L. S. (2008). Design of multiple-level hybrid classifier for intrusion detection system using Bayesian clustering and decision trees. *Journal of Pattern Recognition Letters, 29*(7), 918–924. doi:10.1016/j.patrec.2008.01.008

Xin, Jinqiang, Junjie, Qinghaa, & Chongzhao. (2007). Article. *Journal of Electronics, 24*(3), 369-373.

Zhang, J., & Zulkernine, M. (2006). Anomaly Based Network Intrusion Detection with Unsupervised Outlier Detection. In *Proc. IEEE Communication Society*. doi:10.1109/ICC.2006.255127

KEY TERMS AND DEFINITIONS

Anomaly Detection: The system first learns normal system activities and then alerts all system events that deviate from the learned model.

Denial of Service (DoS): Denial of Service (DoS) attacks has the tactic of overloading the target system with Ping packets or SYN flood.

Misuse Detection: The misuse detection uses the signature of attacks to detect intrusions by modeling attacks.

Probe: Probe attack scans a range of IP addresses in the network to gather information in order to find known vulnerabilities.

Remote to Local (R2L): The Remote to Local (R2L) is an attack in which a remote user gains access of a local user account by sending packets to a machine over a network communication.

User to Root (U2R): User to Root (U2R) is an attack in which an intruder begins with the access of a normal user account and then becomes a root user by exploiting various vulnerabilities of the system.

Chapter 12

Countering RSA Vulnerabilities and Its Replacement by ECC:
Elliptic Curve Cryptographic Scheme for Key Generation

Behnam Rahnama
ScaleDB Inc., USA

Arif Sari
Girne American University, Cyprus

Marwan Yassin Ghafour
Sulaimani Polytechnic University, Iraq

ABSTRACT

Security is utilized to keep the information safe. Online resources, e-commerce, internet banking and a lot of similar services are protected by use of well-known protocols such as Secure Socket Layer (SSL). This protocol makes use of the RSA key exchange protocol for authentication. New innovations and boost ups in the computational power of supercomputers today makes it quite easier than before to break through RSA and consequently decrypt the payload transferred over SSL. In this research demonstrates the use of SSL; how to utilize it in the best shape? We also discuss reasons of why we need to improve its strength. The proposed solution is to replace the RSA key exchange mechanism utilized in SSL with Elliptic Curve Cryptography (ECC).

INTRODUCTION

In many life situations, we have private information that necessitates protection from illegal access. In order to give protection to our sensitive information and avoid any unauthorized access to it, the digital world offers us techniques using cryptography.

The aim of cryptography is to give protection to information while it is being transmitted between two parties, and avoiding access to any third illegitimate party who attempts to obtain a part of it through

DOI: 10.4018/978-1-4666-8761-5.ch012

prohibited means. Our aim is to improve current methods of combating such hackers aiming to obtain unauthorized access.

In the digital world, many applications and situations benefit from cryptography. Just a small selection includes but not limited to ATMs, SSL web based applications within browsers, authentication and authorization acceptance and server-client applications, military services, electronic commerce and satellite communication (Stallings, 2005; Cole, et al., 2008).

Problem Definition

The *Secure Sockets Layer* (SSL) protocol works alongside operations to perform the highly important task of transmitting our confidential data securely between authorized parties; the RSA algorithm is one of three components it uses to complete this task. Due to digital development and our growing use of the computing world to distribute our most sensitive information, such as banking details and even national security details, these days it has become highly important to provide a safeguard to protect these transmissions from attackers. A constant attempt to invade privacy with new techniques exists today, and therefore a primary aspiration should be to find a suitable algorithm to prevent attacks while neither slowing down a device not requiring extra resources.

Working Principles of SSL

SSL is a protocol, which was developed in 1994 by the Netscape Company, to establish a secure data transaction over a secure link between servers and their clients. Normally it is established on a trusted connection like TCP.

This protocol provides authentication by exchanging a key set of a public key algorithm like RSA, and a symmetric key algorithm like DES or RC4 for the encryption of transmitted messages (confidentiality), and one of MAC algorithms for preventing editing of a message by an attacker in the middle (integrity).

The function of this protocol is to encrypt sensitive, restricted or personal information, of which banking, military or governmental data constitute principal examples, where illegal interception of data by a third party could cause critical adverse. The protection of SSL being present is demonstrated on webpages by the letters https at the beginning of the URL with a small lock icon beside it declaring that any communication passing between web server and browser is encrypted, and therefore regarded as being secure.

The SSL can be used on any website that has a requirement to send and receive highly sensitive data which could incorporate credit card numbers or other such private information. Transmission of such data without use of SSL, can disclose the information to unauthorized parties and cause enormous damage. The procedure of an SSL connection would ensue in the following manner. At first instance, a client makes a connection to an SSL website, which is indicated by the letters https at the beginning of the address. The website then sends the client its public key; the client's browser confirms if key is valid and trustworthy by checking the site's digital certificate. Various checks are done to pursue this action. For example, the authentication of the issuer and the expiry date is checked accordingly. Client's browser verifies and confirms the server's public key. The server uses a unique hash for the encryption, which is encrypted using the client's public key and it is returned to the client for future use. The client's browser decrypts the message, and it enables the client to read sent messages. Finally, server and client can conduct an exchange of information with the assurance that the communication is totally secure.

Figure 1. SSL1 protocol architecture

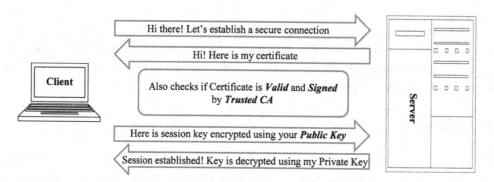

SSL protocol uses some cryptographic algorithms simultaneously. There are three methods used in recent cryptosystems, one algorithm is chosen for key exchange between both sender and receiver RSA cryptosystem is mostly used for this purpose as it provides highest level of security in compare with other ones. Therefore, we just focus on RSA and its imperfections. We aim to present solutions in how to improve it.

Additionally, DES or AES may be used as an encryption algorithm to encrypt the messages, and SHA or MD5 might be utilized as hash function for MAC (Lee, Hur, Won, & Kim, 2009; Huawei & Ruixia, 2009).

The Relationship between SSL, RSA Cryptosystem and Key Exchange

SSL uses a symmetric high speed and easily implementable algorithm to encrypt transmitted messages. The operation of encrypting messages is done by a set of keys called *pre-master secret keys* that is 48 bytes. This set of keys is sent to the server. RSA encrypts this set of keys by the server's public key to enable a secure link during transactions.

When the server receives an encrypted set of keys, it will decrypt it with its private key to understand the message, and then responds using another set of pre-master secret keys combined with *master secret keys*. All transmitted messages are encrypted using these keys (Huawei & Ruixia, 2009) (see Figure 1).

Types of Cryptography

Cryptography is categorized as symmetric and asymmetric cryptography based on the usage of the key for encryption and decryption purposes. Below we explain these two categories in detail.

Symmetric Key

Encryption and decryption of payload utilizes same key. An example is Playfair cipher shown in Figure 2 (Young).

Figure 2. Symmetric encryption2

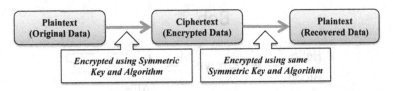

Figure 3. Asymmetric key encryption

Asymmetric Key

It is also known as public key encryption. Plain text is encrypted with a specific key called *public key*. Another key called private key that is obtained from the public key through mathematical rules is used for decrypting cipher text. In simpler words, a pair of related keys is used for encryption and decryption. The Figure 3 illustrates Asymmetric Key Encryption (Young).

Public Key Encryption

Public key encryption, is a big part of the Asymmetric encryption family. The plaintext is encrypted with a *public key* and can only be decrypted with the corresponding *private key*. Figure 4 illustrates a public key encryption (Cole, et al., 2008; Young).

Hybrid Cryptography

It is known that the asymmetric key is favorable for cryptography but it is computationally expensive. On the other hand, symmetric key cryptography is not so appropriate but yet it is computationally inexpensive. Both methods can be combined to form *Hybrid Cryptography*. Figure 5 illustrates Hybrid Cryptography. This improves security and efficiency. The reason is having more than one choice of algorithm for each specific task. A prime example of a modified algorithm would be RSA used for recognition (authentication), while within the same operation ECC used for the encryption of messages (confidentiality) and furthermore a hash function like SHA3 to protect the payload against the editing of transmitting messages from a third party (integrity). This produces a decent example of an enhancement to the SSL protocol (Dubai, Mahesh, & Ghosh, 2011; Huawei & Ruixia, 2009; Stallings, 2005).

Figure 4. Public key encryption

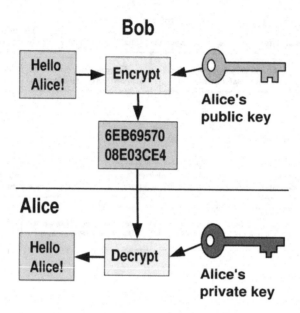

Relation between Encryption System and Key Size

When deciding on choosing algorithms for the cryptographic process, we need to pay attention to the key size as it has direct relation with effectiveness of an algorithm. Generally speaking, the bigger the key size, the more advantageous it is to the algorithms. For example using a public and private key in the same size only protects us from few attacks. To be favorable in size it should be at least [e, $d>n$].

Each algorithm presents a different level of security. A practical way is to use the same key size on various algorithms and evaluate their strength against attacks or by calculation of time elapsed for encryption, decryption and key generation.

For example in RSA 1024-bit it approximately provides the same security level with ECC 163-bit key size.

Finally, Vulnerabilities like small key size put our system at risk of hacking. We need constantly to research on preventing attacks and improving the protection in order to avoid leakage, as well as providing solutions to the common issues (Stallings, 2005; Cole, et al., 2008; Barenghi, Bertoni, Parrinello, & Pelosi, 2009; Rosen, 2007; Bou Nassif).

LITERATURE REVIEW

Ron Rivest, Adi Shamir and Leonard Adleman Diffie and Hellman, first introduced the RSA algorithm as a new symmetric method in cryptography in 1977 and it was first used in 1978. It is now widely used in the computing world as it is both simple to implement and simple to use. Some of the mathematical rules demonstrating how it works are given below (Stallings, 2005; Welschenbach, 2005).

Figure 5. Hybrid cryptography

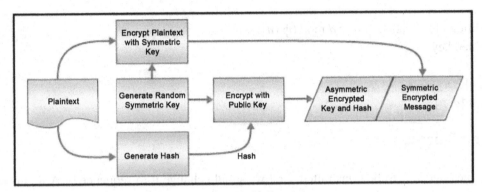

Encryption with a Hybrid Cryptosystem

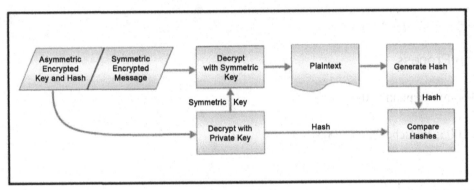

Decryption with a Hybrid Cryptosystem

RSA Principles

RSA is a public key cipher encryption (Asymmetric cipher) method that enables both encryption and decryption through to a range of mathematical rules and operations. RSA works with both public and private key systems. Choosing *p,* and *q* is done by selecting two integer primes and then multiplying them to obtain *n* and after that calculating ϕ *(n)* of *(p-1) (q-1)* continuing selecting *e* followed by this formula (Savari, Montazerolzohour, & Yeoh Eng, 2012):

Choose *p* and *q*

$$n = p*q \tag{1}$$

Calculate ϕ *(n):*

$$\varphi(n) = (p - 1)*(q - 1) \tag{2}$$

Choose e in condition: $(1<e<\varphi(n))$ and $(\gcd(e, \phi(n)) = 1)$ –gcd refers to the *Greatest Common Divisor* While we calculated e and ϕ **(n),** directly we can calculate d using this formula:

$[d = (\varphi(n) - 1)/e]$ or $d = e - 1 \pmod{\varphi(n)}$ (3)

With condition $(1 < d < \varphi(n))$ and $(e.d \bmod (\phi(n)) = 1)$
Both obtained key:

Public Key $[e, n]$
Private Key $[d, n]$

Encryption Process

Assuming message m is to be transmitted, first we should change it to sequence of ASCII codes to be manipulated in mathematical operation (Savari, Montazerolzohour, & Yeoh Eng, 2012)

$(m^\wedge e) \bmod n = c (c: cipher\ text)$ (4)

Decryption Process

$(c^\wedge d) \bmod n = m$ (m: plain text) (5)

(Stallings, 2005; Welschenbach, 2005).

Example

Encrypt plaintext 'a' and decrypt it

Solution:
Change 'a' to ASCII code=97
Choose $p=23$ and $q=41$

$n = p*q = 23*41 = 934$

$\theta(n) = (p - 1)*(q - 1) = 22*40 = 880$

Choose $e=31$
After calculation $d=511$
Public Key [31,934]
Private Key [511,934]
Encryption process:
$(97^{31}) \bmod 934 = 631$
Decryption process:
$(631^{511}) \bmod 934 = 97$
97 in ASCII code equal to 'a' as the original plain text

Figure 6. RSA operation description

Choose p,q   (p and q should be prime and $(gcd(p,q) = 1)$)

$n = p * q$

$\Phi(n) = (p - 1) * (q - 1)$

choose (e) $(1 < e <$

$\Phi(n))\ and\ (gcd(e,n) = 1)$

Calculate Φ(n):

$\Phi(n) = (p - 1) * (q - 1)$

getting d:

$\qquad (e.d \ mod \ (\Phi(n)) = 1) in\ condition\ (1 < d < \Phi(n))$

Public key [e,n]

Private key [d,n]

Encryption process:

$(m^\wedge e)\ mod\ n = c$

Decryption process:

$(c^\wedge d)\ mod\ n = m$

RSA Vulnerabilities

Despite RSA's wide usage, there have been some disadvantages noted in regards to security issues in the algorithm, for instance, the variety of successful attacks, were presented proving leakage of information. Decryption of messages has become possible due to several vulnerabilities and faults within RSA. Some of the general faults are discussed as follows (Shamir & Someren, 1998; Christensen, 2006; Cid, 2003).

Small Messages

The use of small messages can lead to information leakage. A short message can be easily captured over the network and decrypted by unauthorized parties through a low amount of possible keys in a short space of time, making an algorithm ineffective (Cid, 2003; Christensen, 2006).

Small Key

The use of a small key is another problem for system security because small keys can be decrypted in small mathematical operations (Kani).

Secure Link for Transmission

While sending and receiving encrypted messages, the most important issue is that enough security is in place stopping intruders having illegitimate access. This should be done by trying new ways to improve protection (Stallings, 2005).

RSA Main Vulnerabilities

RSA has three main vulnerabilities namely, Mathematical attack on RSA, Attacks on the RSA Function and finally, Implementation Attacks.

Mathematical Attack on RSA

The mathematical attacks on RSA includes Determination of n directly, Determination of d directly (Brute Force) and finally, Factorization (factoring n to find *p* and q

Determining (n) Directly

Here a cryptanalyst tries to calculate all possible n. To prevent this issue we must choose a long p and q to get a huge n. In addition, a large message is needed to increase the probability of guessing a real n for decryption (Fournaris, 2012; Cid, 2003; Stallings, 2005).

Determining d Directly (Brute Force)

The cryptanalyst tries all possible private keys d to reach the plain text. It is obvious that choosing a short n will also cause shortness in both public key e and private key d. Our message can be broken in a short amount of time especially in cases where n and d are small (Fournaris, 2012; Stallings, 2005; Salah, Darwish, & Oqeili, 2006).

Factorization

Factorization Means finding non-trivial factors for a composite integer. In other words it means finding two numbers that by multiplying them we get the original number. For example, n=p×q we try to find p × q, which is n. We are aware that numbers should be positive. This is done by multiplying two chosen big relatively prime numbers.

Remember that for calculating n we choose p, *and* q and then we multiplied them to get n. If a cryptanalyst factors n, it means that our public and private keys are known. Then all messages encrypted using these two known keys being transmitted is known.

We divide factorization into two parts *special* and *general* purposes. In special purpose factorization, we search for a special property of the number like trying to find the smallest factor p of n, but in the general type we focus only on n (Christensen, 2006; Sah, 2001).

Most Popular Ways of Factoring

There are several ways for factorization according to the literature. However, we list only the most widely used ones:

- Trial division
- Fermat Factorization
- Pollard P-1 algorithm
- Pollard RHO algorithm
- Pomerance Quadratic Sieve Algorithm QSA
- Number Field Sieve NFS
- Elliptic Curve Method ECM
- Schor's algorithm-Needs a quantum computer

Below we represent a Fermat factorization algorithm with examples as the most widely used factorization algorithm used in attacking RSA.

Fermat Factorization

Fermat factorization works on the procedure getting $k=\sqrt{r}$ (*r* is an integer number to be factored). This is the base of factorization. We continue calculation as follows:

$$k = \sqrt{r} + 1, \quad k = \sqrt{r} + 2, \quad k = \sqrt{r} + 3 \tag{6}$$

until we reach

$$\left(k^2 - \sqrt{r} = m^2 \right) \tag{7}$$

Then

$$r = (k - m)*(k + m) \tag{8}$$

Algorithm:

Step 1: Compute $\sqrt{r}$

Step 2: Calculate $n^2 - r$ (starting with n, n: should be first integer equal to $\sqrt{r}$ and continue with

$$\left(k = \sqrt{r} + 1, \quad k = \sqrt{r} + 2, \quad k = \sqrt{r} + 3 \right)$$

until you reach the square m^2

Figure 7. Fermat factorization algorithm

$$r = 26504551 \ so \ \sqrt[2]{r} \approx 5148.26 \ so, n = 5149$$

$(5149 + 1)^2 - 26504551 \ result \ is \ not \ equal \ to \ n^2 - r = m^2$

$(5149 + 2)^2 - 26504551 \ result \ is \ not \ equal \ to \ n^2 - r = m^2$

We will add more numbers to (5149) until we reach to (5840) then

$5840^2 - 26504551 = 2757^2 \ result \ is \ equal \ to \ n^2 - r = m^2$

Compute if its true:

$26504551 = 5840^2 - 2757^2 = (5840 + 2757) - (5840 + 2757)$

$= (8597 * 3083) \ and \ finaly \ we \ get \ (p * q)$

$k^2 - n^2 = (2589)^2 - (6699557)^2$

So

$6699557 = 2589 - 58 = (2589 + 58)(2589 - 58) = 2647 * 2531$

Step 3: Operation stops as soon as you reach $(n^2 - r = m^2)$. Then compute $[r = (n + m)*(n - m)]$

Finally the result of $[r = (n + m)*(n - m)]$ equals to $[r=p*q]$.
The corresponding Fermat factorization algorithm illustrated on Figure 7.
This algorithm works well if both n, **and** m are close to each other (Sah, 2001; Christensen, 2006).

Attacks on the RSA Function

Attacks on RSA function are categorized as follows:

- Small message
- Low Private Exponent Attack(small d)
- Partial Key Exposure Attack (small e)
- Short Pad Attack (bad padding: not a general case)

Small Messages

Using small messages and sending them to receiver may seem quite normal (i.e. transmitting a post or get method over an https page), but there is a definite disadvantage. A cryptanalyst in the middle (MITM) can easily capture it and decrypt it in a short time, no matter how strong your key is or how powerful your algorithm is, short messages can be easily intercepted. (Stallings, November 16, 2005) (Cid, 2003).

Low Private Exponent Attack (Relation between n and Small d)

While choosing d we should pay attention to its size, attackers are more likely to succeed in breaking RSA and finding *d* when *it* is small, especially when (*d*) is $< (1/3)*n^{(1/4)}$, and we know that $(1<d<\theta(n))$.

Then we should choose *d* almost as large as n value meaning that if the length of n is 1024 bits, then we should choose a value for d close to that size. On the contrary, choosing a d smaller than 256 bits makes *n* breakable in a short time (Cid, 2003).

Partial Key Exposure Attack (Relation between Small e, n and Small d)

As mentioned before, small keys are problematic because if the e is small, both n and d can be retrieved easily. Attackers try to find d in a variety of ways. If an attacker gets a fraction of the most significant bits (MSB) or a least significant bit (LSB) of the private exponent, d can be accessible by timing attack. An example of a small e is $(e<\sqrt{n})$ (Cid, 2003; Nita-Rotaru, 2003; Sarkar & Maitra, 2009; Ernst, Jochemsz, May, & Weger, 2005).

Partial key Exposure Attack (attacks of a small e)
By defining *e* and *d* we get the integer *k*

$$(ed)p - kp(n - p + 1) + kn = p(\text{mod } 2^{n/4}) \tag{9}$$

For each guessing of *k* we get some results of $p(\text{mod } 2^{n/4})$, that all results for one *k* calculation is $(e\log_2 e)$, While $(d<\theta(n))$, $(q = n/p)$, we get:

$$ed - k(n - p - q + 1) = 1 \tag{10}$$

We get *n* after completing all calculations (Boneh, 1999; Sarkar & Maitra, 2009).

Implementation Attacks (Side Channel Attack)

Implementation attacks include Timing Attack, Power Analysis Attack, Fault Analysis Attack, and Failure Analysis attack.

Timing Attack

In a timing attack, an adversary tries to crack the crypto system through analyzing the spent time of the running of a cryptographic algorithm. Every logical operation in a microprocessor of a computer takes a specific amount of time to execute. An opponent can find d through the relation between the private key and the execution time of cryptographic operations. By calculating the time of execution of a large amount of messages, the adversary can get bits of d starting from the least significant bit and continuing until finding d/*4*. Some countermeasures can be implemented however, to prevent hacking in this way, like padding or the use of blinding solution, This attack type gives a good reason for converting data by random values generated by the cryptographic system before encrypting it (Christensen, 2006) (Nita-Rotaru, 2003) (kocher, 1996).

Power Analysis

This is a physical attack against cryptosystem devices like ATMs or cryptographic devices, which use RSA. Fundamentally, it measures power consumption of the main processor of a computer using an Oscilloscope or any means of power measurement device that sketches different waves for each type of operation. Therefore measuring specific amounts of power spent in a microprocessor identifies when encryption cycles are happening.

For example, a multiplication operation needs more additional registers inside a Microprocessor in comparison to addition operation. Therefore, multiplication needs more power, and we can estimate when d is calculated and placed in the memory.

Three types of this attack are commonly used as follows. *Simple Power Analysis* (SPA) watches directly all power the cryptographic device consumes. *Differential Power Analysis* (DPA) method is more powerful, because it uses error correction and statistical analysis to find any relation to the private key. The other attack is *High Order Differential Power Analysis* (HO-DPA) is more difficult to be analyzed because it allows multiple data sources and different time offsets to be incorporated in the analysis. The Figure 8 illustrates the power analysis attack by oscilloscope device (Amiel, Villegas, Feix, & Marcel, 2007; Huiping & Zhigang, 2003).

Fault Analysis

This attack is based on working on fault Analysis of RSA based on the hardware features of physical implementation of the cryptographic devices, such as ATMs while the device tries to decrypt incoming

Figure 8. Power analysis attack by oscilloscope device (Kocher, Jaffe, & Jun, 2013)

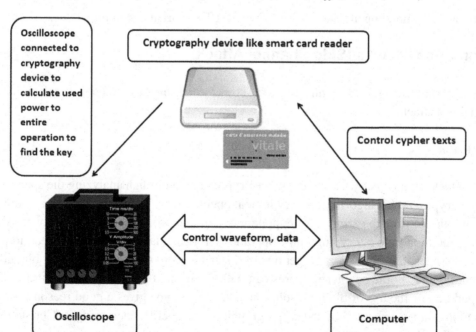

messages is a way to attack. The machine generates required interrupting signals such as watchdog for failure in operation.

Having the signal received by an exterior device and analyzing the input and output makes it possible to catch information on private key then finally it is theoretically possible to recover entire private key.

To prevent such an attack, another public key can be used in encryption of the output signals, without defecting speed of the target machine. Another solution is to apply random padding to the incoming message or putting blinding values to output signals from the cryptographic machine

A perfect protection against such an attack is using *Chinese Remainder Theorem* (CRT) for generating pairs of *n* p *and* q. CRT is used in generating both p and q before generating n (Cid, 2003; Fournaris & Koufopavlou, 2012; Barenghi, Bertoni, Parrinello, & Pelosi, 2009).

Failure Analysis

If a cryptographic machine fails to decrypt an incoming message, a failing feedback signal is generated, an adversary can catch this signal and try to work on it to recover the private key, but we can prevent this attack by using random padding to the message (Cid, 2003).

PROPOSED ALGORITHM

Elliptic Curve Cryptography (ECC) is a new algorithm to the public key cryptography family that depends on the algebraic structure of elliptic curves over finite fields. The use of elliptic curves in cryptography was first introduced by Victor Miller and N. Koblitz in 1985 as an alternative to designing and executing a new public-key system like RSA. Elliptic curve cryptography ECC demonstrates better security compared to all known public-key systems (Ha, Kim, Choi, Lee, & Kim, 2004; Kolheka & Jadhav, 2011). The Figure 9 illustrates graphical representation of ECC.

Elliptic curve cryptography defines a set of points for every point of (a,b) at (Weierstra equation), that described below

$$y^2 = [x^3 + ax + b] \bmod p \tag{11}$$

In condition of

$$4*a^3 + 27*b^2 \neq 0 \tag{12}$$

Figure 9. Graphical representation of ECC

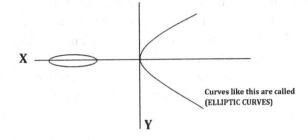

283

Two Types of ECC

These two types are different in basic ECC operations (addition) and (multiplication).

Elliptic Curves over Prime Finite Fields

That starts with $[F_p(p>3, \text{ which } (F_p) \neq 2, 3)]$, that we work on it to implement our algorithm.

Elliptic Curves over Binary Finite Fields

Such Elliptic Curves use Finite Field $F(2^m)$ to represent the values over the curve, considering each element has a multiplicative and additive inverse.

The main formula for $F(2^m)$ is:

$$y^2 + xy = x^3 + ax^2 + b (\text{in condition } b \neq 0) \tag{13}$$

In this type, each element of the finite field is integer in length at most **m** bits. In addition, all operations over finite fields like addition, subtraction, division, multiplication, and inversion can be done on it.

For example, we can construct it by polynomial basis representation, in this way the elements of the equation are binary polynomials that their coefficient is $\{0, 1\}$, and most highst degree of (m) should be $(m - 1)$

$$F2^m = \left\{ a_{m-1}z^{m-1} + a_{m-2}z^{m-2} + \cdots + a_2 z^2 + a_1 z + a_0 : a_i \in \{0, 1\} \right\}$$

To make our system more secure we should choose (m) in great value like ($113<m<571$) bits.

The geometrical graph for this formula is not a smooth curve. Hence the geometrical explanation of point addition and doubling as in real numbers that we described below, will not work here. However, the algebraic rules for point addition and point doubling can be adapted for elliptic curves over $F(2^m)$ (Ha, Kim, Choi, Lee, & Kim, 2004; Hankerson, Menezes, & Vanstone, 2004).

ECC Key Features

Here we propose the implementation of the ECC in protocols that are already using RSA such as SSL. ECC presents several better features as follows in comparison with RSA.

- **Functionality:** Working on ECC is easier than other public key cryptosystems.
- **Security:** ECC provides much higher security with the same key size. This is because ECC uses the elliptic curve discrete logarithm for EC systems for encryption and decryption. In this respect, attackers need to solve ECDLP for all pair points in ECC elements. Algorithms like RSA use factoring that is more vulnerable to attack.
- **Performance:** Research shows that ECC is better than other algorithms throughout the entire process using the same size of messages (Hankerson, Menezes, & Vanstone, 2004; Kumar, Rana, & Aggarwal, 2011).

Discrete Logarithm Problem for EC Systems

The security strength of ECC is built on the hardness of Elliptic Curve Discrete Logarithm Problem (ECDLP). The statement of ECDLP is calculated as below:

Suppose we have E as an elliptic curve and $P \in E$, k is an integer chosen calculate ($k*P = Q$) for each different value of k we get different Q, for example if $P = (2, 2)$ and (result of Q) equal to $Q = (153, 108)$. Here we choose ($k=5$) it mean ($Q = 5*p$), then the discrete logarithm of Q to the base P is 5.

Suppose if we have great (k), it makes the problem more difficult, getting Q is a small part of calculation, because we have (a), (b) in the main formula of elliptic curve and index of x then we make an attacker guessing too much, that is impossible to solve (Chen, 2004; Savari, Montazerolzohour, & Yeoh Eng, 2012; kumar, Rana, & Aggarwal, 2011).

Description of ECC Algorithm

An elliptic curve E takes the general form as:

$$E: y^2 = [x^3 + ax + b] \bmod p \tag{14}$$

While both (a), (b) are in the suitable set (rational numbers, real numbers, integers mod p, etc.) and (x, y) are elements of the finite field GF (p), providing $4a^3 + 27b^2 \neq 0 (\bmod p)$. In addition, p is introduced as integer modular prime making the elliptic curve finite field, there are two basic group operations on an elliptic curve, which are point addition and point doubling (Bhardwaj & Chaudhary, 2012; Hankerson, Menezes, & Vanstone, 2004; Savari, Montazerolzohour, & Yeoh Eng, 2012). The Figure 10 shows equation results with different values for (a) and (b).

Point Addition

The addition is one of main calculations inside ECC with two points (p), (q) and their matches given on elliptic curves and we try to find third point (Kumar, Rana, & Aggarwal, 2011). The point addition in ECC is also illustrated in Figure 11.

$P = (x_1, y_1)$ and $Q = (x_2, y_2)$ on $E(GF(p))$.

To compute the matches for third point R as below:

$(P + Q = R)$

$(x_1, y_1) + (x_2, y_2) = (x_3, y_3)$

This is the case where we compute

$$R = P + Q \text{ and in condition } P \neq Q \tag{15}$$

Figure 10. Equation result with different value for (a), (b)

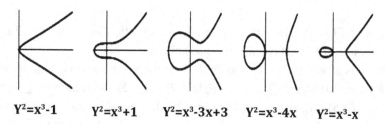

Y²=x³-1   Y²=x³+1   Y²=x³-3x+3   Y²=x³-4x   Y²=x³-x

Figure 11. Point addition in ECC

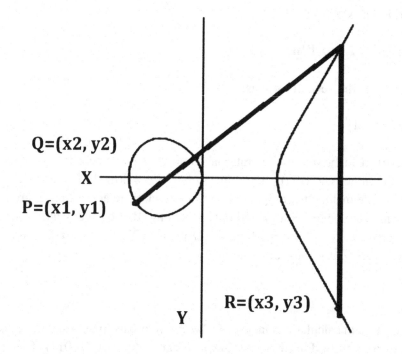

$$\lambda = (y_2 - y_1)/(x_2 - x_1) \tag{16}$$

Point R's matches are (x3, y3)

$$x_3 = [\lambda^2 - x_1 - x_2] \bmod p \tag{17}$$

$$y_3 = [-y_1 + \lambda^*(x_1 - x_3)] \bmod p \tag{18}$$

Example

The elliptic curve:

$y^2 = (x^3 + 3x + 2)\%5$

We get these points after calculation $(1, 1)$ $(1, 4)$ $(2, 1)$ $(2, 4)$
Add tow points $[p(1, 4), Q(2, 1)]$
Used rules in point addition

$R = P + Q$

$\lambda = (y_2 - y_1)/(x_2 - x_1)$

$x_3 = [\lambda^2 - x_1 - x_2]\%p$

$y_3 = [y_1 + \lambda*(x_1 - x_3)]\%p$

$\lambda = (4 - 1)/(2 - 1) = 3$

$x_3 = [9 - 1 - 2] = 6\%5 = 1$

$y_3 = [-4 + 3*(1 - 1)]\%5 = 1$

We get $(1, 1)$ also it's on the curve

Point Multiplication (Doubling)

Point multiplication is a series of point additions (repeated addition for same point) or we can say doubling, is the process of addition of a point P on the elliptic curve to itself to get to another point R. This is the case where we compute **P + Q** but **P = Q.** Then we can write **R = P + P = 2P,** if we write (**kp**) we mean (**p+p+p...k** times)

(λ) is calculated differently for addition and multiplication (Kumar, Rana, & Aggarwal, 2011; Liu, 2009).
Here we compute

$P + Q$ but $P = Q$ (19)

$$\lambda = \left(3 * x_1^2 + a\right) / \left(2 * y_1\right)$$ (20)

where (a) is coefficient of (x) in main ECC formula.

$x_3 = [\lambda^2 - 2x_1] \bmod p$ (21)

$y_3 = [-y_1 + \lambda*(x_1 - x_3)] \bmod p$ (22)

Figure 12. Point doubling in ECC

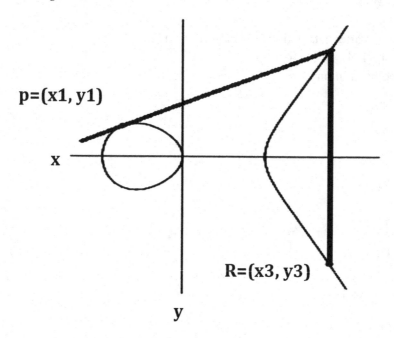

The Figure 12 illustrates the point doubling in ECC.

Both figures for point addition and multiplication are just for representation because we only discuss integer values to make it more clear and understandable. We also use negative and double values to make an operation for an adversary more difficult, for example, you can use two points as follows:

$R = P + Q$ while $P = (-2.35, -1.86)$,

$Q = (-0.1, 0.836)$ to get $R(3.89, -5.62)$.

With negative and double values, it makes guessing to find keys practically impossible because there are infinite numbers between two real integers, due to this reason using double values are better for cryptography.

Example

The elliptic curve:

$$y^2 = (x^3 + (3*x) + 2)\%5$$

We get these points after calculation

(1, 1) (1,(2, 1) (2, 4) 4)

Doubling point (1, 1)
Used rules in point doubling

$$R = P + P = 2P \tag{23}$$

$$\lambda = \left(3 * \left(x_1^2\right)\right) + a) / \left(2 * y_1\right)$$

where (a) is cofficient of (x) in main ECC formula here is (3).

$x_3 = [\lambda^2 - (2*x_1)] \, \%p$

$y_3 = [-y_1 + \lambda*(x_1 - x_3)] \, \%p$

$\lambda = (3*(1^2)+3)/(2*1) = 3$

$x_3 = [(3^2) - (2*1)] \, \%5 = 2$

$y_3 = [-1 + 3*(1 - 2)] \, \%5 = 1$

We get (2, 1), also it's on the curve

Menezes Vanstone Elliptic Curve Cryptosystem

ECC is described above; we aim to explain the new schema of ECC that is called (Menezes Vanstone elliptic curve cryptosystem) which works by using a point on an elliptic curve to "mask" a point in the plan. .Also it works over GF(*p*), in case (*p*) should be primed and at least (p>3),this algorithm is suitable too, it works on all major processes in ECC (point multiplication) and (point Dublin) it is nice to work with, fast and simple (Jarmoc, 2012).

Working Principles

Suppose we have (Alice) as a sender and (Bob) as receiver, and (Alice) wants to send (M) plaintext as a pair of points (x_1, x_2) To (Bob), (Alice) should use (Bob)'s public key to encrypt the message that can be decrypted by (Bob)'s private key, which is opposite to RSA. In ECC the private key is used to calculate the public key, and we know that public keys are distributed over the network, so we use the below rule to calculate the public key for (Bob):

A: random integer number selected by the (Bob) in the condition of (1<*a*<n) (private key for (Bob))
a: generator point that is an element inside the subset of elements and both sender and receiver should be agree on it.

We get public key (ß) in result of:

β = random integer selected (A)* generator point on curve (a) = (A*a) (ß) is disturbed over the network, sender select an integer (k) in a condition that (k) should ($1<K<n$) and she compute:

$$y_0 = k* \text{ generator point } (a) \tag{24}$$

After that, she (sender) computes:

$$(c_1, c_2) = k \bullet \beta \tag{25}$$

$$y_1 = c_1 * x_1 \bmod p \tag{26}$$

$$y_2 = c_2 * x_2 \bmod p \tag{27}$$

Then (Alice) will send Encrypted message

$$(y_0, y_1, y_2) \tag{28}$$

Bob will get the message and compute:

$$(c_1, c_2) = A \bullet y_0 \tag{29}$$

While (A) is the (Bob)'s private key that chosen above

$$M= (\text{``a'' plain text}) = \left(\left[y_1 * \left(\frac{1}{c_1} \right) mod \ p \right], \ \left[y_2 * \left(\frac{1}{c_2} \right) \right] mod \ p \right) \tag{30}$$

A list of variables inside the Menezes Vanstone elliptic curve cryptosystem makes it stronger and more difficult to crack, so an attacker would have to guess all variables,,,,(impossible).

E: An elliptic curve

P: A large prime number (should be least be larger than 3)

A: Private key (secret key for the receiver (Bob)) (random integer number selected)

a: For obtaining public key (should be on E) (called generator point) (chosen by the sender and receiver) (randomly selected from sub elements of elliptc curve)

ß: Public key obtained by ($A*a$)

K: Is randomly selected integer chosen by sender (private key of the sender) (Sagheer, 2012) (Allardyce & Goyal, April 15, 2004)

Key Generation

The receiver (B)chooses a random number that means (A), which starts from [1, n-1] and it is a private key. Also we should choose (a), which (a) is the generator point that may be any point on an elliptic curve which both sender and receiver agree on, and n is the order of α. Calculate (B)'s public key as follows:

(Bob(β)'s public key): $\beta = A \bullet a$

Encryption

When a sender wants to encrypt a message like ("a") letter it should use (B)'s public key that is calculated in a key generation step, then the sender will choose a random integer (k) which starts from [1, n-1], the sender will encrypt the message ("a" plaintext) [$x = (x_1, x_2)$] Then compute it.

$y_0 = k \bullet a$

$(c_1, c_2) = k \bullet \beta$

$y_1 = c_1 * x_1 \bmod p$

$y_2 = c_2 * x_2 \bmod p$

The encrypted message is ready to send

(y_0, y_1, y_2)

Decryption

$(c_1, c_2) = A \bullet y_0$

$$X = (\text{"a" plain text}) = \left(\left[y_1 * \left(\frac{1}{c_1} \right) \bmod p \right], \left[y_2 * \left(\frac{1}{c_2} \right) \right] \bmod p \right) \text{finally.}$$

COMPARISON AND EXPERIMENTAL RESULTS

SSL protocol has weaknesses. The RSA logarithm used for key exchange and authentication processes causes the disadvantage. Below we demonstrate some practical results in order to show a comparison between RSA and ECC.

Selection Criteria on RSA and ECC

According to certain measures, a decision is made on which algorithm is the better one to implement, depending on the resources and time complexity. Then the special complexity of both algorithms are taken into consideration (Bou Nassif; Hankerson, Menezes, & Vanstone, 2004).

- Time complexity
- Space complexity

Time Complexity

This is the total amount of time required for an algorithm to execute an operation. It describes the linkage between the size of input and run time of the algorithm. Several approaches for calculation of Tp is used including tabular form, formula expansion and time stamping. Performance of a machine should neither affect time complexity nor the language used for algorithm implementation, and the complete value of time complexity is taken from CPU (Bou Nassif; Stroppa, 2006; 2007; Liu, 2009).

Space Complexity

The size of working memory used for an algorithm execution given result, the value for the space complexity taken from RAM (Bou Nassif; Stroppa, 2006; 2007).

ECC vs. RSA

Here we aim to compare ECC and RSA in terms of execution and used space in memory, we implement these two algorithms in C++ language and executed them on Intel Core i5 2450M CPU at 2.50 GHz processor and 4GB 1066MHz DDR 3 RAM complied in Microsoft Visual Studio 2012 64 bit edition on Windows 7 x64.

The results of both algorithms were noted and analyzed. The conclusion we arrived at was that the results show that both of them have advantages and disadvantages, but ECC was the more superior in most properties such as the time to execute and its use of available resources.

To get very clear results we tried to use the smallest variables inside both algorithm programs to generate the smallest public key and private key, also we hid any unnecessary operation commands like (cout) and (cin) and we initialized all values manually to get clear time analysis and space complexity.

The RSA code contains a program for (brute force) attack also (trying all private keys(d)), and the ECC code contains preventative measures for an attack also on algorithms but we did not execute it.

All codes are shown in appendices; you can use any size for variables you wish.

RSA Analysis

The practical time complexity is calculated based on capturing timestamps in the program. RSA algorithm is discovered within three phases, namely, Initialization, Encryption and Decryption. The analytical time complexity is estimated as a linear function of $O(n)$. There are three loops sequentially that provide the key generation, encryption and decryption, which is indicated in Table 1.

Table 1. Consumed time for of RSA execution in msecs

Number of Tries	Initialization Time	Encryption Time	Decryption Time
1	2869	63	63
2	738	21	21
3	1668	19	19
4	2591	18	18
5	1394	14	14
6	1724	53	53
7	1555	18	18
8	1569	14	14
9	1445	25	25
10	1501	62	62
Average	1705.4	30.7	30.7

Table 2. Space Complexity for RSA

Types of Variables	No. of used Variables	Size of Variables	Total Bytes
Unsigned long long int	11 variables	11*8	88 bytes
Char	1 variable	1*1	1 bytes
Total	12 variables		89 bytes

Table 3. Consumed time for ECC execution in msecs

Number of Tries	Initialization Time	Encryption Time	Decryption Time
1	12	13	16
2	9	1	2
3	10	12	2
4	14	13	2
5	9	12	2
6	10	10	2
7	12	13	3
8	10	11	2
9	14	12	2
10	18	15	2
Average	11.8	11.2	3.5

Table 4. Space Complexity ECC execution

Used Variables	No. of used Variables	Size of Variables	Total Size
Int	63 variables	63*4	126 bytes
Unsigned int	1 variable	1*4	4 bytes
Char	1 variable	1*1	1 bytes
Float	2 variables	2*4	8 bytes
Total	67 variables		139 bytes

On the other hand, the space consumed by RSA is fixed to 89 bytes irrelevant to the input size. This is a key benefit for such security of an algorithm and it makes it possible to be used in embedded applications. The space complexity for RSA is shown in Table 2.

ECC Analysis

The ECC algorithm consists of more loops and theoretically, It is $O(m^2 + 7m) \equiv O(m^2)$. It seems to be more time consuming than RSA, however, the size of n is relatively small and therefore it utilizes much less time than RSA. The consumed time for ECC execution in milliseconds is shown on Table 3.

The Space used by the ECC is 144 bytes in general and it is fixed irrelative to the input size again. The Table 4 illustrates Space Complexity of ECC in execution.

SUMMARY

We compared two well-known asymmetric security algorithms namely, RSA and ECC. The literature review has covered information on cryptography and its application and properties, including the different parts of it. The symmetric and asymmetric cryptosystems, the public key cryptosystem and other relevant protocols were taken into consideration.

ECC provides higher security as the number of possible keys are theoretically infinite and practically too large to be feasibly broken. On the other side, RSA relies on relatively prime numbers and it limits the number of possible keys in a domain.

The space complexity of both algorithms are relatively small. ECC uses a few bytes overhead which is ignorable. On the other hand, theoretical Time Complexity of ECC is greater than the time complexity of RSA. However, utilizing very small loops in ECC makes it much faster than the RSA as the key size is much smaller than the one used in RSA for the same security level.

RSA is shown to be vulnerable to attacks. ECC is better than RSA in many ways. ECC consumes much less time than RSA in practice as the length of variables are much smaller than those used in RSA. There is a small extra memory usage in ECC that can be ignored from consideration.

Loops inside RSA calculate very big size values such as multiplication of very long integers (p),(q) to get (n). That makes RSA spend more time to initialize public and private keys.

$(ECC) \; O(m^2) \equiv O(n) \; (RSA)$

As presented earlier, RSA is vulnerable to mathematical and brute force attacks. ECC provides higher strength as prime numbers in a domain are limited however, ECC can rely on any real number in a domain and it makes it practically infeasible to be broken by brute force attack. RSA is shown to be less secure than ECC. It is the time now to implement the future SSL publicly used by people to utilize ECC instead of RSA.

REFERENCES

Allardyce, J., & Goyal, N. (2004). *Elliptic Curve Cryptography*. Texas A&M University.

Amiel, F., Villegas, K., Feix, B., & Marcel, L. (2007). Passive and Active Combined Attacks–Combining Fault Attacks and Side Channel Analysis. *Workshop on Fault Diagnosis and Tolerance in Cryptography*. doi:10.1109/FDTC.2007.12

Barenghi, A., Bertoni, G., Parrinello, E., & Pelosi, G. (2009). Low Voltage Fault Attacks on the RSA Cryptosystem. *Workshop on Fault Diagnosis and Tolerance in Cryptography*. doi:10.1109/FDTC.2009.30

Bhardwaj, K., & Chaudhary, S. (2012). Implementation of Elliptic Curve Cryptography in 'C'. *International Journal on Emerging Technologies*, *3*(2), 38–51.

Boneh, D. (1999). *Twenty Years of Attacks on the RSA Cryptosystem*. American Mathematical Society (AMS).

Bou Nassif, A. (n.d.). *Computer Science - Western University*. Retrieved from http://www.csd.uwo.ca/courses/CS1037a/

Chen, C.-C. (2004). RSA Scheme With MRF And ECC For Data Encryption. *2004 IEEE International Conference on Multimedia and Expo (ICME)*. doi:10.1109/ICME.2004.1394358

Christensen, C. (2006). *Mathematical attack on RSA*. Cambridge, MA: Cambridge Center-RSA Laboratories.

Cid, C. F. (2003). Cryptanalysis of RSA. In *GIAC Security Essentials Certification-A survey in RSA*. Academic Press.

Cole, E., Krutz, R. L., Conley, J. W., Reisman, B., Ruebush, M., & Gollmann, D. (2008). *Network Security Fundamentals*. Anne Smith.

Dubai, M., Mahesh, T., & Ghosh, P. (2011). Design Of New Security Algorithm Using Hybrid Cryptography Architecture. *Electronics Computer Technology (ICECT)-3rd International Conference*, *5*, 99-101.

Ernst, M., Jochemsz, E., May, A., & Weger, B. D. (2005). Partial Key Exposure Attacks on RSA Up to Full Size Exponents. International Association for Cryptologic Research.

Fournaris, A. P. (2012). CRT RSA Hardware Architecture with Fault and Simple Power Attack Countermeasures. *Digital System Design (DSD), 15th Euromicro Conference*.

Fournaris, A. P., & Koufopavlou, O. (2012). Protecting CRT RSA against Fault and Power Side Channel Attacks. *IEEE Computer Society Annual Symposium (ISVLSI)*. doi:10.1109/ISVLSI.2012.54

Ha, C.-S., Kim, J.-H., Choi, B.-Y., Lee, J.-H., & Kim, H.-W. (2004). *GF(2191) Elliptic Curve Processor using Montgomery Ladder and High Speed Finite Field Arithmetic Unit.* Information Security Basic Department, ETRI.

Hankerson, D., Menezes, A., & Vanstone, S. (2004). Guide to Elliptic Curve Cryptography. Springer-Verlag.

Huawei, Z., & Ruixia, L. (2009). A Scheme to Improve Security of SSL. *2009 Pacific-Asia Conference on Circuits, Communications and System.* doi:10.1109/PACCS.2009.148

Huiping, J., & Zhigang, M. (2003). Design of an RSA module Against power Analysis. *5th International Conference in ASCI.* doi:10.1109/ICASIC.2003.1277457

Jarmoc, J. (2012, March 21). *SSL/TLS Interception Proxies and Transitive Trust-Transitive Trust.* Retrieved July 21, 2013, from http://i.technet.microsoft.com/dyni

Kani, E. (n.d.). The State of the Art of Elliptic Curve Cryptography. Kingston, Ontario: Department of Mathematics and Statistics, Queen's University.

Kocher, P. C. (1996). *Timing Attacks on Implementations of Diffie-Hellman, RSA, DSS, and Other Systems.* San Francisco, CA: Cryptography Research, Inc. doi:10.1007/3-540-68697-5_9

Kolheka, M., & Jadhav, A. (2011). Implementation Of Elliptic Curve Cryptography On Text And Image. *International Journal of Enterprise Computing and Business Systems, 1*(2).

Kumar, A., Rana, M., & Aggarwal, N. (2011). A Comparative Study of Public Key Cryptosystem based on ECC and RSA. *International Journal on Computer Science and Engineering, 3*(5), 1904–1909.

Lee, Y., Hur, S., Won, D., & Kim, S. (2009). Cipher Suite Setting Problem of SSL Protocol and It's Solutions. *2009 International Conference on Advanced Information Networking and Applications Workshops.* doi:10.1109/WAINA.2009.76

Liu, F. (2009). *A Tutorial on Elliptic Curve Cryptography (ECC).* Brandenburg Technical University of Cottbus-omputer Networking Group.

Nita-Rotaru, C. (2003). *Cryptography CS 555.* Purdue University-Department of Computer Sciences.

Rosen, K. H. (2007). *An Introduction to Cryptography.* London: Taylor & Francis Group, LLC.

Sagheer, A. M. (2012). *Elliptic Curves Cryptographic Techniques.* Ramadi, Iraq: Department of Information System-College of Computer-University of Anbar. doi:10.1109/ICSPCS.2012.6507952

Sah, M. (2001). *Generalized Trial Division.* Ankara: Department of Mathematics, Tandogm.

Salah, I. K., Darwish, A., & Oqeili, S. (2006). Mathematical Attacks on RSA Cryptosystem. *Journal of Computer Science, 2*(8), 665–671. doi:10.3844/jcssp.2006.665.671

Sarkar, S., & Maitra, S. (2009). Partial Key Exposure Attacks On Rsa And Its Variant By Guessing A Few Bits Of One Of The Prime Factors. *Bull. Korean Math., 46*(4), 721–741. doi:10.4134/BKMS.2009.46.4.721

Savari, M., Montazerolzohour, M., & Yeoh Eng, T. (2012). Comparison of ECC and RSA Algorithm in Multipurpose Smart Card Application. *Cyber Warfare and Digital Forensic (CyberSec)*, 49-53.

Shamir, A., & Someren, N. V. (1998). *Playing hide and seek with stored keys.* Academic Press.

APPENDIX A

The following code is the RSA algorithm implementation. Tp calculation was performed in an alternative program.

```
#include<stdio.h>
#include<time.h>
#include<iostream>
#include<fstream>
#include<string>
#include<cmath>
#include <stdio.h>
using namespace std;
unsigned long long int M,n,e,d,p,q,gc, phi;
int gcd(unsigned long a, unsigned long b)
{
  if(b == 0)
  {
      return a;
  }
  else
  {
      return gcd(b, a % b);
  }
}
void main()
{

  unsigned long long int pti=0,ptext1=1,ptext=0,ctext=0,ctext1=0;
  char pt='a';
  clock_t ITime=clock();
  ///crack();
  //cout<<"inter p and q "<<endl;
  //cin>>p;
  //cin>>q;
  p=17,q=11;
  n=p*q;
  phi=(p-1)*(q-1);
  ////cout<<"n = "<<n<<endl;
  //cout<<"phi = "<<phi<<endl;
  //cout<<"inter e "<<endl;
  cin>>e;
```

```
/*
if(((gcd(e,n))==1) && (e<n))
{cout<<"true "<<endl;}
else
{cout<<"e should be less and GCD to n "<<endl;}
*/
//calculate d (d*e mod phi =1)
//cin>>d;
//d= (phi+1)/e;

for(int dco=1;dco<phi;dco=dco+2)
{
    if((e*dco)%phi==1)
    {
      d=dco;
      break;
    }
}
//cout<<"e  "<<e<<endl;
//e=7,d=23;
ITime=clock()-ITime;
clock_t ETime=clock();
//cout<<"e,d   "<<e<<","<<d<<endl;
for(int i=0;i<100;i++)
{


//cout<<"enter plain text "<<endl;
//cin>>pt;

pti= static_cast<char>(pt);
//cout<<pti<<endl;
//cout<<"your input in ascii code     "<<pti<<endl;
ptext1=pti;
for(int i=0;i<e-1;i++)
{
  ptext1=ptext1*pti;
  ptext1=ptext1%n;
  //cout<<ptext1;
}
ETime=clock()-ETime;
}
ETime=ETime/100;
```

```
/////////////////////////////////////
clock_t DTime = clock();
char new1;
for(int i=0;i<100;i++)
{
ctext1=ptext1;
for(int j=0;j<d-1;j++)
{
  ctext1=ctext1*ptext1;
  ctext1=ctext1%n;
  //cout<<ctext1;
}
/////////////////////////////////////
//cout<<"cipher text is   "<<ptext<<endl;
//cout<<"plain text is    "<<endl;


new1= static_cast<char>(ctext1);
DTime = clock()-DTime;
}
DTime=DTime/100;
cout<<"***********************************"<<endl;
cout<<"Init:"<<ITime<<"\tEncryption:"<<ETime<<"\tDecryption:"<<DTime<<endl;
cout<<new1;
getchar();
}
```

APPENDIX B

Help is taken from http://www.codeproject.com/ to implement (ECC Menezes Vanstone). Below is the ECC Menezes Vanstone Implementation.

```
#include <cstdlib>
#include <iostream>
#include <vector>
using namespace std;
#include <math.h>
#include "FiniteFieldElement.hpp"
namespace Cryptography
{
    template<int P>
```

```cpp
class   EllipticCurve
{
  public:
    typedef FiniteFieldElement<P> ffe_t;
    class   Point
    {
      friend  class   EllipticCurve<P>;
      typedef FiniteFieldElement<P> ffe_t;
      ffe_t   x_;
      ffe_t   y_;
      EllipticCurve       *ec_;
      void    addDouble(int m, Point& acc)
      {
        if (m > 0)
        {
          Point r = acc;
          for (int n=0; n < m; ++n)
          {
            r += r;  // doubling step
          }
          acc = r;
        }
      }
    Point scalarMultiply(int k, const Point& a)
    {
      Point acc = a;
      Point res = Point(0,0,*ec_);
      int i = 0, j = 0;
      int b = k;

      while(b)
      {
        if (b & 1)
        {
          // bit is set; acc = 2^(i-j)*acc
          addDouble(i-j,acc);
          res += acc;
          j = i;  // last bit set
        }
        b >>= 1;
        ++i;
      }
      return res;
    }
```

```
void  add(ffe_t x1, ffe_t y1, ffe_t x2, ffe_t y2, ffe_t & xR,
          ffe_t & yR) const
{
  // special cases involving the additive identity
  if (x1 == 0 && y1 == 0)
  {
    xR = x2;
    yR = y2;
    return;
  }
  if (x2 == 0 && y2 == 0)
  {
    xR = x1;
    yR = y1;
    return;
  }
  if (y1 == -y2)
  {
    xR = yR = 0;
    return;
  }
  ffe_t s;
  if (x1 == x2 && y1 == y2)
  {
    //2P
    s = (3*(x1.i()*x1.i()) + ec_->a()) / (2*y1);
    xR = ((s*s) - 2*x1);
  }
  else
  {
    //P+Q
    s = (y1 - y2) / (x1 - x2);
    xR = ((s*s) - x1 - x2);
  }

  if (s != 0)
  {
    yR = (-y1 + s*(x1 - xR));
  }
  else
  {
    xR = yR = 0;
  }
}
```

```
Point(int x, int y)
: x_(x),
  y_(y),
  ec_(0)
{}


Point(int x, int y, EllipticCurve<P> & EllipticCurve)
: x_(x),
  y_(y),
  ec_(&EllipticCurve)
{}


Point(const ffe_t& x, const ffe_t& y, EllipticCurve<P> & EllipticCurve)
: x_(x),
  y_(y),
  ec_(&EllipticCurve)
{}

public:
  static  Point   ONE;
  Point(const Point& rhs)
  {
    x_ = rhs.x_;
    y_ = rhs.y_;
    ec_ = rhs.ec_;
  }
  Point& operator=(const Point& rhs)
  {
    x_ = rhs.x_;
    y_ = rhs.y_;
    ec_ = rhs.ec_;
    return *this;
  }
  ffe_t x() const { return x_; }
  ffe_t y() const { return y_; }
  unsigned int  Order(unsigned int maxPeriod = ~0) const
  {
    Point r = *this;
    unsigned int n = 0;
    while(r.x_ != 0 && r.y_ != 0)
    {
      ++n;
      r += *this;
      if (n > maxPeriod) break;
    }
```

```
      return n;
    }
  Point  operator-()
  {
    return Point(x_,-y_);
  }
  // ==
  friend bool  operator==(const Point& lhs, const Point& rhs)
  {
    return (lhs.ec_ == rhs.ec_) && (lhs.x_ == rhs.x_) && (lhs.y_ == rhs.y_);
  }
  // !=
  friend bool  operator!=(const Point& lhs, const Point& rhs)
  {
    return (lhs.ec_ != rhs.ec_) || (lhs.x_ != rhs.x_) || (lhs.y_ != rhs.y_);
  }
  // a + b
  friend Point operator+(const Point& lhs, const Point& rhs)
  {
    ffe_t xR, yR;
    lhs.add(lhs.x_,lhs.y_,rhs.x_,rhs.y_,xR,yR);
    return Point(xR,yR,*lhs.ec_);
  }
  // a * int
  friend  Point operator*(int k, const Point& rhs)
  {
    return Point(rhs).operator*=(k);
  }
  // +=
  Point& operator+=(const Point& rhs)
  {
    add(x_,y_,rhs.x_,rhs.y_,x_,y_);
    return *this;
  }
  // a *= int
  Point& operator*=(int k)
  {
    return (*this = scalarMultiply(k,*this));
  }
  friend ostream& operator <<(ostream& os, const Point& p)
  {
    return (os << "(" << p.x_ << ", " << p.y_ << ")");
  }
};
```

```
typedef EllipticCurve<P> this_t;
typedef class EllipticCurve<P>::Point point_t;
EllipticCurve(int a, int b)
: a_(a),
  b_(b),
  m_table_(),
  table_filled_(false)
{
}
void  CalculatePoints()
{
  int x_val[P];
  int y_val[P];
  for (int n = 0; n < P; ++n)
  {
    int nsq = n*n;
    x_val[n] = ((n*nsq) + a_.i() * n + b_.i()) % P;
    y_val[n] = nsq % P;
  }

  for (int n = 0; n < P; ++n)
  {
    for (int m = 0; m < P; ++m)
    {
      if (x_val[n] == y_val[m])
      {
        m_table_.push_back(Point(n,m,*this));
      }
    }
  }

  table_filled_ = true;
}
Point  operator[](int n)
{
  if (!table_filled_)
  {
    CalculatePoints();
  }

  return m_table_[n];
}
size_t  Size() const { return m_table_.size(); }
```

```cpp
    // the degree P of this EC
    int  Degree() const { return P; }
    // the parameter a (as an element of Fp)
    FiniteFieldElement<P>  a() const { return a_; }
    // the paramter b (as an element of Fp)
    FiniteFieldElement<P>  b() const { return b_; }

    // ostream handler: print this curve in human readable form
    template<int T>
    friend ostream& operator <<(ostream& os, const EllipticCurve<T>&
                                EllipticCurve);
    // print all the elements of the EC group
    ostream&  PrintTable(ostream &os, int columns=4);

    private:
      typedef std::vector<Point>  m_table_t;

      m_table_t               m_table_;  // table of points
      FiniteFieldElement<P>  a_;         // paramter a of the EC equation
      FiniteFieldElement<P>  b_;         // parameter b of the EC equation
      bool          table_filled_;       // true if the table has been
                                         //      calculated
};

template<int T>
  typename EllipticCurve<T>::Point EllipticCurve<T>::Point::ONE(0,0);

template<int T>
ostream& operator <<(ostream& os, const EllipticCurve<T>& EllipticCurve)
{
  os << "y^2 mod " << T << " = (x^3" << showpos;
  if (EllipticCurve.a_ != 0)
  {
    os << EllipticCurve.a_ << "x";
  }

  if (EllipticCurve.b_.i() != 0)
  {
    os << EllipticCurve.b_;
  }

  os << noshowpos << ") mod " << T;
  return os;
}
```

```
        template<int P>
        ostream&  EllipticCurve<P>::PrintTable(ostream &os, int columns)
        {
          if (table_filled_)
          {
            int col = 0;
            typename EllipticCurve<P>::m_table_t::iterator iter = m_table_.begin();
            for (; iter!=m_table_.end(); ++iter)
            {
              os << "(" << (*iter).x_.i() << ", " << (*iter).y_.i() << ") ";
              if (++col > columns)
              {
                os << "\n";
                col = 0;
              }
            }
          }
          else
          {
            os << "EllipticCurve, F_" << P;
          }
          return os;
        }
}


namespace   utils
{
  float  frand()
  {
    static float norm = 1.0f / (float)RAND_MAX;
    return (float)rand()*norm;
  }

  int irand(int min, int max)
  {
    return min+(int)(frand()*(float)(max-min));
  }
}

using namespace Cryptography;
using namespace utils;

int main(int argc, char *argv[])
```

```cpp
{
  typedef EllipticCurve<263> ec_t;
  ec_t   myEllipticCurve(1,1);

  cout << "A little Elliptic Curve cryptography example\nby Jarl Ostensen, 2007\n\n";

  // print out a little info and test some properties
  cout << "The elliptic curve: " << myEllipticCurve << "\n";

  // calulate all the points for this curve. NOTE: in the real world this would not
  // be a very sensible thing to do. If the period is very large this is big and slow
  myEllipticCurve.CalculatePoints();

  cout << "\nPoints on the curve (i.e. the group elements):\n";
  myEllipticCurve.PrintTable(cout,5);
  cout << "\n\n";

  ec_t::Point P = myEllipticCurve[2];
  cout << "some point P  = " << P << ", 2P = " << (P+P) << "\n";
  ec_t::Point Q = myEllipticCurve[3];
  cout << "some point Q = " << Q << ", P+Q = " << (P+Q) << "\n";
  ec_t::Point R = P;
  R += Q;
  cout << "P += Q = " << R << "\n";
  R = P;
  R += R;
  cout << "P += P = 2P = " << R << "\n";

  cout << "\nEC message encryption example\n==============================\n\n";

  // Menes-Vanstone EC message encryption scheme

  // Public: the base point on the curve (i.e. base group element) used to generate keys
  // this is a REALLY slow way of picking a base point...
  ec_t::Point G = myEllipticCurve[0];
  while((G.y() == 0 || G.x() == 0) || (G.Order()<2))
  {
    int n = (int)(frand()*myEllipticCurve.Size());
    G = myEllipticCurve[n];
  }

  cout << "G = " << G << ", order(G) is " << G.Order() << "\n";
```

```
// Alice
int a = irand(1,myEllipticCurve.Degree()-1);
ec_t::Point Pa = a*G;   // public key
cout << "Alice' public key Pa = " << a << "*" << G << " = " << Pa << endl;

// Bob
int b = irand(1,myEllipticCurve.Degree()-1);;
ec_t::Point Pb = b*G;   // public key
cout << "Bob's public key Pb = " << b << "*" << G << " = " << Pb << endl;

// Jane, the eavesdropper
int j = irand(1,myEllipticCurve.Degree()-1);;
ec_t::Point Pj = j*G;
cout << "Jane's public key Pj = " << j << "*" << G << " = " << Pj << endl;

cout << "\n\n";
int m1 = 19;
int m2 = 72;

cout << "Plain text message from Alice to Bob: (" << m1 << ", " << m2 << ")\n";

// encrypt using Bob's key
ec_t::Point Pk = a*Pb;
ec_t::ffe_t c1(m1*Pk.x());
ec_t::ffe_t c2(m2*Pk.y());

// encrypted message is: Pa,c1,c2
cout << "Encrypted message from Alice to Bob = {Pa,c1,c2} = {" << Pa << ",
  " << c1 << ", " << c2 << "}\n\n";

// Bob now decrypts Alice's message, using her public key and his session
   integer "b" which was also used to generate his public key
 Pk = b*Pa;
 ec_t::ffe_t m1d = c1/Pk.x();
 ec_t::ffe_t m2d = c2/Pk.y();

cout << "\tBob's decrypted message from Alice = (" << m1d << ", " << m2d
     << ")" << endl;

// Jane intercepts the message and tries to decrypt it using her key
Pk = j*Pa;
m1d = c1/Pk.x();
m2d = c2/Pk.y();
```

```cpp
    cout << "\nJane's decrypted message from Alice = (" << m1d << ", " << m2d
        << ")" << endl;

  cout << endl;

  system("PAUSE");
  return EXIT_SUCCESS;
}


////////////////////////////////////////////////////////////////////////////

// helper functions
namespace Cryptography
{
    namespace  detail
    {
      int EGCD(int a, int b, int& u, int &v)
      {
        u = 1;
        v = 0;
        int g = a;
        int u1 = 0;
        int v1 = 1;
        int g1 = b;
        while (g1 != 0)
        {
          int q = g/g1; // Integer divide
          int t1 = u - q*u1;
          int t2 = v - q*v1;
          int t3 = g - q*g1;
          u = u1; v = v1; g = g1;
          u1 = t1; v1 = t2; g1 = t3;
        }

        return g;
      }

      int InvMod(int x, int n)
      {
        x = x % n;
        int u,v,g,z;
        g = EGCD(x, n, u,v);
        if (g != 1)
```

```
        {
          // x and n have to be relative prime for there to exist an x^-1 mod n
          z = 0;
        }
        else
        {
          z = u % n;
        }
        return z;
    }
}
template<int P>
class    FiniteFieldElement
{
  int  i_;

  void  assign(int i)
  {
    i_ = i;
    if (i<0)
    {
      i_ = (i%P) + 2*P;
    }

    i_ %= P;
  }

  public:
    // ctor
    FiniteFieldElement()
    : i_(0)
    {}
    explicit FiniteFieldElement(int i)
    {
      assign(i);
    }
    FiniteFieldElement(const FiniteFieldElement<P>& rhs)
    : i_(rhs.i_)
    {
    }
    int i() const { return i_; }
    FiniteFieldElement  operator-() const
    {
      return FiniteFieldElement(-i_);
    }
```

```cpp
  FiniteFieldElement& operator=(int i)
{
  assign(i);
  return *this;
}
// assign from field element
FiniteFieldElement<P>& operator=(const FiniteFieldElement<P>& rhs)
{
  i_ = rhs.i_;
  return *this;
}
// *=
FiniteFieldElement<P>& operator*=(const FiniteFieldElement<P>& rhs)
{
  i_ = (i_*rhs.i_) % P;
  return *this;
}
// ==
friend bool  operator==(const FiniteFieldElement<P>& lhs, const
FiniteFieldElement<P>& rhs)
{
  return (lhs.i_ == rhs.i_);
}
// == int
friend bool  operator==(const FiniteFieldElement<P>& lhs, int rhs)
{
  return (lhs.i_ == rhs);
}
// !=
friend bool  operator!=(const FiniteFieldElement<P>& lhs, int rhs)
{
  return (lhs.i_ != rhs);
}
// a / b
friend FiniteFieldElement<P> operator/(const FiniteFieldElement<P>& lhs,
  const FiniteFieldElement<P>& rhs)
{
  return FiniteFieldElement<P>(lhs.i_ * detail::InvMod(rhs.i_,P));
}
// a + b
friend FiniteFieldElement<P> operator+(const FiniteFieldElement<P>& lhs,
  const FiniteFieldElement<P>& rhs)
```

```
    {
      return FiniteFieldElement<P>(lhs.i_ + rhs.i_);
    }
    // a - b
    friend FiniteFieldElement<P> operator-(const FiniteFieldElement<P>& lhs,
      const FiniteFieldElement<P>& rhs)
    {
      return FiniteFieldElement<P>(lhs.i_ - rhs.i_);
    }
    // a + int
    friend FiniteFieldElement<P> operator+(const FiniteFieldElement<P>& lhs,
      int i)
    {
      return FiniteFieldElement<P>(lhs.i_+i);
    }
    // int + a
    friend FiniteFieldElement<P> operator+(int i, const
      FiniteFieldElement<P>& rhs)
    {
      return FiniteFieldElement<P>(rhs.i_+i);
    }
    // int * a
    friend FiniteFieldElement<P> operator*(int n, const
      FiniteFieldElement<P>& rhs)
    {
      return FiniteFieldElement<P>(n*rhs.i_);
    }
    // a * b
    friend FiniteFieldElement<P> operator*(const FiniteFieldElement<P>& lhs,
      const FiniteFieldElement<P>& rhs)
    {
      return FiniteFieldElement<P>(lhs.i_ * rhs.i_);
    }// ostream handler
    template<int T>
    friend ostream& operator<<(ostream& os, const FiniteFieldElement<T>& g)
    {
      return os << g.i_;
    }
  };
}
```

Chapter 13
Changing Dynamics of Network Security involving Hacking/Cracking with Next Generation Firewalls (NGFW)

Alok Vishwakarma
Sysbiz Technologies, India

Wafa Waheeda S
Qatar University, Qatar

ABSTRACT

With increasing number of users on the internet, risk of security and probability of vulnerable attacks are increasing day by day. For every user connected to network, security attacks like hacking and cracking are very frequent which leaves enormous amounts of sensitive data at the risk of being altered, lost or misused. This apparently leads to the need for security measures on ports and protocols also search for application security, VPN, IPS, and a firewall support. The hacking and cracking threats and attacks in a network are no longer in control with the existing methods and standard firewalls. The introduction of Next Generation Firewalls leads to improved security over network. This chapter deals with hacking and cracking attacks over network and their countermeasures, also focusing on the changing dynamics of network security with next generation firewalls.

INTRODUCTION

Network security has continuous growing necessitate for measures to prevent attacks, data loss and any kind of threat while hacking and cracking being the primary reasons (Negi, 2011). Internet being called the network of networks - empowers people, but also admonishes with restricted access in order to protect the network for having safe access with proper network security measures.

Hacking is unauthorised access to any network or a computer which leads to misuse of information and causes risk to the security of network (Negi, 2011). Whereas Cracking being similar to Hacking,

DOI: 10.4018/978-1-4666-8761-5.ch013

Figure 1. Hacking

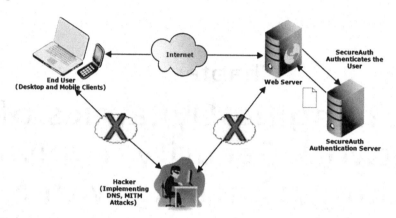

differing in the objective and methods. Both Hacking and Cracking cause intrusion and challenge the security of the individual system or systems in network. There are many ways to detect and prevent these intrusions from entering an individual system or systems in network.

Hacking and Cracking

Hacking is an intrusion in a computer or network which provides access to authorised or unauthorised data. This is a threat to the network security systems because of the risk factor (Simmonds, Sandilands, & Van Ekert, 2004, p. 317-323). The main objective of hacking is the serious attempts to find the flaws in a system or network, which leads to the risk factor involved.

Hackers break into a system with no intention to harm, rather to gain knowledge, have the interest of fulfilling their curiosity, to try creating different things or even to test their hacking capabilities (Negi, 2011). This might lead a hacker to face legal consequences, but mostly the hacker causes no harm to the system after they hack in. Generally, hacking is to try out new and different things from a system or software which is totally opposite to its usage or its purpose in the first place. But hacking can be ethical and unethical, as there are many types and groups of hackers present. The White Hat Hackers, Grey Hat Hackers and Black Hat Hackers etc. are the groups of hackers present.

Hackers try to attack a system or a server in a network with the many type of hacking attacks, like Denial of Service DOS, Man in the Middle MITM, E-mail Bombing, Spoofing, Phishing etc (Daya, 2013; Dwivedi, 2009; Kessler, Gary C., 2000). The hackers target a particular system by spamming or any kind of attack, and when a user - while clicking on a spammed file or link, a malicious code or program is installed and runs without the knowledge of user. In that way the hacker successfully hacks a user (victim) and controls the victim's system to hack the server or a network (see Figure 1).

Cracking is malicious as it deals with misuse of information present in the hacked system or network. The main objective of cracking is to steal and misuse the data for own personal reason. This is the most unethical and malicious form of hacking and intrusion, as it involves bad intensions and incorrect usage of hacked system or network's information (Negi, 2011).

Crackers perform certain type of attacks to exploit the system or network for their own benefit. This includes cracking of licensed software's and building keygens - key generators a software which helps crack a software licence and run for free. Crackers also crack bank security systems, network security systems etc. They deal with cracking the password with Brute force attack, Dictionary attack etc.

Differences in Hacking and Cracking

Hacking and cracking are two different forms of intrusion attacks in a network, which causes threat to network security. But hacking and cracking differ from each other in terms of objective, method and the type of attacks.

The main difference in terms of objective is that the hackers deplore from cracking. Even though hacking deals with stealing and modifying data without the owner's notice, the hackers are with a motive to learn and create new things. Whereas in cracking, the result is piracy as pirated software creation or cracking of systems and software for own personal benefit. Cracking is malicious as it deals with change of code, and functionality, which is highly illegal.

Difference in the method of attacks exists as in hacking, the hackers try to understand and apply their knowledge of programming to create something new out of the hacked source. Whereas in cracking, theflaws are targeted and complete exploitation occurs, which will be a illegal personal benefit.

Difference in the type of attacks - for hackers deal with type of attacks like phishing, spoofing and other web related hack attacks like SQL injection, brute force attacks, password lifting etc (Daya, 2013; Shema, 2012). Whereas in cracking, there is not much to do, as it deals with finding a flaw or back door to exploit, as crackers deal with creating key gens, cracking serial keys, passwords etc.

Common Methods of Hacking and Cracking in a Network

Hackers, while trying to learn about the system or software tend to find flaws in security and internal structure of the system. The common hacking methods are - hacking other systems present online, hacking servers via wireless attacks, Trojan, creating worms to attack other systems etc (Kwon, S. H., & Park, D. W., pp. 156-161 2012; Liu, V., 2007; Negi, Y., 2011; Zhang, Y., Chen, G., Weng, W., & Wang, Z., pp. 147-150, 2010). Email bombs or phishing techniques are used in hacking systems online, whereas Trojan horse is a malware that facilitates the hacker to enter a system and gain unauthorised access. Many such methods are deployed by a hacker while hacking.

In cracking, a cracker generally deals with malicious attacks to crack the system or software and pirate it i.e. generating key gens, password cracking, cracking a software's licence and exploit. Generally, for finding passwords which prevent unauthorised access, methods such as brute force attack, dictionary attacks and hybrid attacks are used to guess passwords and get inside the system. Many such attacks and techniques are also involved in cracking.

Prevention Methods

A system or network is always at risk of being attacked by hacking or cracking methods. In order to provide security from attacks, there are various types of prevention methods. There are a few types of general prevention methods for security, which are used for any kind of attack on the system. Such type of prevention methods will be discussed.

Firewalls act as one such effective prevention methods to stop these attacks. As web 2.0 and other latest technologies are evolved, the risk of security has increased. But the standard firewalls are no longer able to provide protection from various kind of attacks mainly because of different kind of complex rule sets involved in order to prevent attacks. The standard firewalls are no longer able to monitor the packets in TCP effectively, which gives rise to errors and increases risk of attacks. Thus, in this chapter we explore the features of Next Generation Firewalls (NGFW) and their capacity to adapt to the changing dynamics of network security (Patel, A., pp. 9-12, 2015; Simmonds, A., et.al, pp. 317-323, 2004). As the NGFWs were introduced in the first place as they ensure high prevention control of attacks than the other firewalls in their own way. Deep packet inspection, data inspection from packets with less complexity, detecting various kind of attacks, Intrusion prevention system IPS etc., are some of the utile features of NGFWs.

BACKGROUND

Types of Hackers

Hackers: Is a group term as the term hackers refers to groups in which hackers are classified as per their principles and objectives. Some groups or types of hackers are discussed below:

Phreak: A phreak is a group of hackers who are primarily interested in hacking phones and telephone systems. Generally the only difference between a traditional hacker and a phreak is the technology gap, as there was information communicated mostly over phones in early days. But now there has been many changes in information communication methods since the form of networks (Chirillo J., 2001). And phreak is no longer considered as an active group.

White Hat: The adept white hat hackers have a set of ethics to be followed with the flaws they find out by hacking. They do not cause harm to the system or network, in turn they try to fix the problem or report it to the appropriate owner. They are a group of hackers who like to experiment with their knowledge and not make money out of it for their own benefits by exploiting the vulnerabilities.

Grey Hat: Whereas the grey hat hackers are considered to be very adept in hacking and act according to the situation that they are present between the white hat and black hat hackers (Jordan, T., 2008). When a situation is present before the grey hackers, they react either ways as White Hat or a Black Hat hacker react. They use their knowledge and also test it by hacking other user's system and make proper or improper use of the information they get.

Black Hat: The black hat hackers are the ones to watch out for, as they are focused to put down the network security of a system or network (Patel, A., pp. 9-12, 2015; Simmonds, A., et.al, pp. 317-323, 2004). They exploit the vulnerabilities of a system, and get the unauthorised access to the confidential information. They do not make proper use of the data hacked, and use it for their own benefit too (Jordan, T., 2008). They do not follow any kind of ethics, as they consider themselves as masters and keep hacking the other systems to make them their slaves - i.e. control the other user systems.

Types of Hacking Attacks

There are many kinds of attacks imposed in a network and in order to protect your system from attacks, prevention methods should be taken (Negi, Y., 2011). The hacking attacks with which a network should remain protected are discussed in detail.

Denial-of-Service Attack: This attack takes place when a hacker tries to access data with some malicious code externally, i.e. without any internal access. The hacker creates a traffic flood so that the router does not respond and the data packets are affected. Not many tools are used by the hacker to plant a DoS attack, but the tools used are easily available. Also the hacker to do a DoS attack needs to know programming, as to operate those tools (Kessler, Gary C., 2000). A simple application - built be the hacker in some scenarios is used along with a router or network equipment. This would make the network unusable for some time and thus make the connections of the network easily hacked.

Phishing: This is when a hacker tries to get information such as user name and password to gain access to the user account and data from the trustworthy website or entity. In this attack, the hacker creates a basic webpage which resembles a trusted website and hosts it on a server, with similar URL (Liu, V., 2007). The Login form from the page of the website will be linked to a hacker's database. And when a normal user clicks on the link without paying much attention to the URL address, and logs in with the account details, the user's details will go to the hacker's database (Chirillo J., 2002; Daya, B., 2013; Jordan, T., 2008). And with those details, the hacker gets access to all the information from the user's account.

Spoofing: In this attack, the hacker forges an identity and pretends to be some other identity, in order to gain access to the information. Once the hacker identifies the target, the hacker tries to get connected to the same wireless network and gain access to the MAC or IP address of the target's computer (Daya, B., 2013; Dwivedi, H., 2009; Joel Snyder., 2012; Jordan, T., 2008; Kwon, S. H., & Park, D. W., pp. 156-161 2012; Liu, V., 2007; Zhang, Y., et.al., pp. 147-150, 2010). And using the target - who has become the victim of hacker, the hacker tries to hack the entire network from the victim - who is connected in the network's identity. These attacks can be hard to prevent.

Sniffing: Sniffing refers to the secret listening of some other channel or host which will allow the interception of TCP packets. This gives way to the secured information access to the hacker. Sniffing is also called as digital eavesdropping (Daya, B., 2013).

Trojans, Viruses and Worms: The virus and worms are self-multiplying malicious programs which destroy the security of a system. They flood the network router with a lot of traffic and this will allow the hacker to gain access to confidential information (Daya, B., 2013).

Man in the Middle Attack: This is an attack which deals with a person in the middle, communicating to the user with a trusted person's identity. And the user believes the man in middle and provides them with the user account information such as user name and password. This kind of attacks occurs easily and it becomes important for the users to crosscheck and be careful with these kinds of attacks.

SQL Injection/Database Access: Hacking websites through sql queries and logging into the website to gain access to the data. And this similar method can be used to enter into the registry of the database to get information access. For e.g.: 'OR 1=1; isasql query which can be used in place of username and passwords to login and get unauthorised access.

Email Bombing: The hacker firstly finds a way to install a program without the knowledge of a user by sending emails. Once the link is clicked or a file from email is opened, the attack occurs. And malicious software such as Key loggers helps get every single key information typed by the user. This type of information leakage occurs in a network which involves around and results to malicious file creation, adulterating the information, deleting files etc. (see Figure 2).

Spamming: Spamming refers to sending of irrelevant mails or messages to unknown email lists. The mails contain attacks hidden in them in form of link or files. When the user clicks on them, he becomes a target or a victim of the spamming attack.

Types of Cracking Attacks

Cracking is generally breaking into a system or network and exploit it for own personal benefit which is clearly illegal. Crackers generally create software using their own tools and programs to crack the license or generate a key gen for the particular software. The cracking is either for fun, which is a financial

Figure 2. Email bombing attack in hacking

crime or phreaking (Chirillo J., 2001) - i.e. cracking of software licenses and earning money. There are different types of attacks involved while cracking, they are discussed below:

Brute Force Attack: This is considered to be the most time consuming method for cracking passwords as the cracker will try every possible combination until a password is cracked.

Dictionary Attack: In this, the cracker runs a file, which consists of a set of words to run against the user account. The cracker finds out the password if it is a simple word not involving numbers and characters.

Hybrid Attack: This attack is similar to dictionary attack but it adds numbers and symbols at the end. The crackers use this method commonly to crack passwords.

Tools Used in Hacking and Cracking

Hacking in various forms requires tools and a fair amount of programming to cause attacks. There are many software tools available now a day for hacking. And the hackers need not be good at programming, as they only need to know basics of HTML for website hacking, and C Programming language. Hacking generally involves guessing of password, with the security questions, as it always helps the hacker if the hacker knows victim personally.

Scanning Tools are available for scanning ports which help the hackers to scan ports and discover the vulnerabilities. Once the TCP and UDP port are scanned, it becomes easier for the hacker to make the ports listen to his system and attack the user's system. There are Vulnerability Scanners which allow the hacker to connect to a target system and find out flaws. Nessus is one such open source vulnerability scanner used to help scan errors in security at a target computer.

Even in phishing attacks, the hacker needs to create fake login pages identical to a trusted website for which knowing html would suffice. There are many other ways in which phishing attacks can occur, like by link manipulation, desktop phishing can occur. Spam emails are also one way of phishing attack.

For sniffing attacks, the spoofing of MAC address is essential. Tools such as spoofed MAC, Iris Snort and also Ethereal are sued. For system hacking, keyloggers, Telnet, Snadboyetc. are used. For Google Hacking, i.e. hacking with Google, Google Cheat Sheet shows all kinds of cheats for smart hacks.

Keyloggers: Keyloggers are hardware or software, which help the hacker gain access to every key-stroke of the user. This will record the chat conversation, emails, etc. And also deliver a screenshot of the user's computer with the help of software or hardware. The important information can also be stored from a user's computer. Refog Keylogger, Actual Keylogger etc. are some types of software keyloggers. The keyloggers such as Winspy, Sniperspy keylogger can be installed in a remote location.

Cracking involves a lot of tools, which the crackers are capable of building it themselves to exploit the target. The password cracking tools for web such as Brutus - performs brute force and dictionary attacks, cracks multiple login authentications, HTTP, Telnet, POP3 - for Emails, FTPs etc. Web cracker is a simple tool used in cracking to involve a list of words as user account credentials to crack the password.

Detection of Hacking and Cracking Attacks

The most found scenario where attacks on a system or network occur in the following manner: Firstly, a target (which can be a victim system, software, website, server or a network etc) will be found by a hacker or cracker (Chirillo J., 2002). Then the method of attack will be figured based on trust relationships with the host server or most visited websites or even emails in some cases. Later the attack is imposed via the trusted source by forging, phishing or other types of attacks.

Generally, the attacks on a network are detected by a firewall or any other prevention mechanism employed for providing network security (Patel, A., pp. 9-12, 2015). The firewalls act as a scanner which scan every file for virus or threat. But since a lot of attacks happen online, with the change in technology and the introduction of web 2.0, there is a lot happening over the internet (Daya, B., 2013). It becomes highly complex for the traditional firewalls to scan every packet of data involved in the TCP (Chirillo J., 2002). As the web 2.0 also deals with multiple web applications running on web, there is a lot of data packets being transferred. So the traditional functioning of standard firewalls of scanning, blocking un-trusted websites, IP addresses and ports etc. with the data traffic existing on internet these days is not enough (see Figure 3).

The NGFWs will perform all kinds of security protection measures including deep packet inspection on the application layer of the network. The intrusion protection mechanism, intrusion prevention mechanism and gathering of all logs from a server are what a basic NGFW will do in combined (Chirillo J., 2002; Das, N., & Sarkar, T., 2014; Erdheim, S., pp. 8-12, 2013; Thomason, Steven, 2012). So that the data when passed through a NGFW will be safe and secured without no attack or threats detected.

Figure 3. Standard firewalls

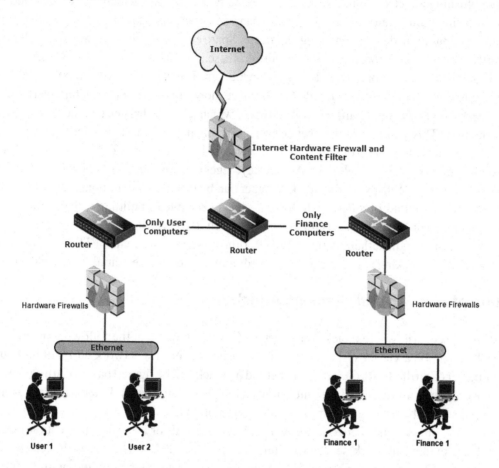

MAIN FOCUS OF THE CHAPTER

Protection Methodologies from Various Hack Attacks

In a network, the hacking attacks exploit the vulnerabilities of a system. It becomes mandatory for a system or a network to employ some kind of protection methods for detecting and preventing the attacks. The various kinds of hack attacks can have protection methodologies discussed below to avoid attacks and protect the security of a system or network.

Cryptographic systems are one kind of protection methodology widely being employed, as it provides secured access of information and prevents attacks. In this, the data or information is ciphered with a code or in short- encrypted, making the data illegible for any unauthorised person to understand. In this way, only the user gets access to encrypted information, as the original information is now transformed into unintelligible data. This kind of protection methodology can be used to protect the system or network from DOS Attack, Phishing Attacks, Spoofing Attacks etc. as these attacks involve around getting information access by finding out the password of the user's system. This cryptographic system will hence protect by leaving all the confidential information encrypted.

Intrusion Detection Systems IDS are generally used to scan data present in the network or system and detect any kind of intrusion in the system. They generally scan the entire data packets transferring over the network in a TCP for intrusions. The IDS systems can be both hardware and software and can be used to detect any kind of attack. They generally monitor connections and detect the presence of attacks in a system when connected to a network. But the major flaw with the IDS is that it does not work well when there is high traffic in networks, as the scanning of data from several data packets becomes tedious. This type of protection methodology can be used to overcome almost all kind of attacks. But with the changing dynamics of security in a network, the IDS does not comply with the required network security measures (Simmonds, A., et.al, pp. 317-323, 2004).

Intrusion Prevention System IPS is different from IDS in many ways. The major difference being that the IPS is compatible with the changing dynamics of technology. At present, as there is high traffic involved in networks due to the running of multiple applications on web, the IPS focuses on deep packet inspections. The IPS was primarily put forth to address the shortcoming of IDS. With deep packet inspections, the examining of inbound packets will occur at a faster rate, and the intrusions get identified, leaving the system or network secure from attacks. The IPS works for protecting a system or network from all kinds of attack.

Anti-Malware Scanners or software's are used to detect the Trojans and Worms or Virus presence in the system. When a simple file is sent over a network, it is likely to have virus. These scanners scan the system entirely for the malware attacks and detect their presence, thus leaving the system free from these attacks. These anti-malware scanner systems can also cure the virus or Trojan attacks on the system. This helps in protecting the system or network from Email Bombs, Spamming, Trojan attacks, Virus and Worms or any malicious code attack, DOS, Cookie poisoning etc.

Secure Socket Layer SSL is generally a set of rules or a protocol followed in order to maintain security between the network and website. Generally, any website will have to provide the network with a SSL to prove that it does not contain any malicious attacks and thereby helps create a secure tunnel between the web browser and website server, so that the information exchanged remains safe and secure. This provides clients the authentication to enter the server. Thus this method protects the system or network from all kinds of attack, except spamming and email bombing etc. as they can occur in any form and cannot be controlled by SSL.

Firewall can protect a system or network from all kinds of attacks. As the firewall acts as a wall or barrier between the user and the network and helps detect any attack. The firewall blocks traffic from outside so that the user's system remains secure. It blocks traffic from any untrusted server or from any private server. The firewall can be present as a software or hardware or as both. But the standard firewalls do not comply with the changing dynamics of technology and does not remain successful in providing network security (Patel, A., pp. 9-12, 2015).

Protection with NGFW

A basic firewall comes with the features such as application proxies, filters for data packets, state packet filters - for blocking ports and IP addresses etc. The other standard firewalls perform port inspection for the source/destination IP addresses in a network which send information and TCP/UDP port information, checking security certificates, along with other features of a basic firewall (Erdheim, S., pp. 8-12, 2013). On checking all these, it controls and decides whether the data should pass through or not. These firewalls inspect first few bytes alone and deep packet inspection is not performed by them. The port based firewalls are designed primarily to check for information security in ports, by allowing or disallowing the connection established through ports. Generally as the TCP/UDP protocols are the ones responsible for communication along with FTP, the port information of these help decide (Frahim, J., Santos, O., & Ossipov, A., 2014; Thomason, Steven, 2012). But with the introduction of Web 2.0 and the higher traffic on websites - because of running many web applications on website itself, is one among the major reasons for the failure of standard or basic firewalls.

Applications running on website bring a lot of traffic with them, as everyone focus on more powerful quick installing and easy usage applications. Some examples like Google Docs, Messengers, Web mails, other web 2.0 applications run alongside with the website on the server. The applications are evasive and are designed to communicate dynamically i.e. irrespective of the time and place. The applications involve shifting of ports over the session, use non-standard ports, tunnel within common services like Instant Messengers (P2P) Peer-to-peer communication or file sharing, with all these going around; the applications provide a host of opportunities for attackers to attack the system or network. Thus giving rise to more reasons for security threats and attacks. With the standard firewalls, which perform a check on data header packets of the information communicated via TCP, the deep packet inspection is not done. This allows the intrusions to occur and exploit vulnerabilities.

Other Protection Methods and NGFW

As the majority of the applications are open and cause traffic almost most of the time, the hacking and cracking attacks make use of the traffic caused in the website by using multiple web applications. For security, a protection mechanism was needed which could exert granular control and provide deep packet inspection i.e. protection in depth to the individual applications level. But the traditional security protection mechanisms like IDS, Anti-Malware Scanners and SSL etc (Dwivedi, H., 2009; Erdheim, S., pp. 8-12, 2013). are no longer able to provide the security access required. Even the standard firewalls were no longer found to be of help, as the dynamics of technology and so network security has changed everything (Simmonds, A., et.al, pp. 317-323, 2004). Most firewalls control traffic effectively and monitor all kind of traffic going inside and outside the network, thus providing security. But due to the changing dynamics, there was no regular behaviour in the accessing of standard ports by applications and traffic was beyond control, and so the traditional firewalls lost its compatibility. And it tends to allow connections from an untrusted server or private server, allows applications which should not be allowed in the network, tests or inspects everything on network which is irrelevant and not required. This all leads to the strain on a computer system or network because the unwanted applications not prevented by these firewalls consume the CPU space and decrease the performance efficiency in the system.

The traditional IPS is also not compatible to provide protection mechanism to the changing dynamics of network and its security measures, though it involves deep packet inspection and other mechanisms. The IPS generally provides control measures for security on ports and protocols involved in a network and to block attacks actively in them. But the IPS is not effective when it comes to preventing attacks from a network which involves controlling applications (Thomason, Steven, 2012). For the threats through applications, the applications have become a primary source of attack for attackers. They also send encrypted threads in the user-oriented application which contain attacks. Thus the traditional IPS cannot effectively provide security protection mechanism for networks.

Unified Threat Management UTM is another protection method to the changing dynamics of network security, but it does not seem to be effective and has flaws (Simmonds, A., et.al, pp. 317-323, 2004). The

UTM was a cost-effective methodology with an IPS and a built in add-on of stateful firewall. But the UTM is generally hard to manage and shows poor performance in terms of preventing security attacks on network. The UTM generally does a good job at addressing the threats, and instead of going for different types of threat identifiers, the UTM is a single package which can perform all kinds of counter measures for network security.

All these drawbacks are overcome and attacks are prevented with the help of Next Generation Firewalls NGFW, as the NGFWs help block the harmful activities which take place at high network traffic, that could also exploit the vulnerability of a network. The NGFWs combine the functionalities of many security attack prevention methods. The NGFWs should mainly include an Intrusion Prevention System and all other features of a standard firewall. As the elevations in technology keep arising, the NGFW should also meet the attack prevention mechanism to provide security. The NGFW monitors every single data packet even in tedious traffic rates for attacks. Thus results in making the networks safer with much authenticity.

NGFW and its Benefits

With the introduction of Web 2.0, the applications started to evolve, giving a challenge to the security measures with the high traffic - which would not allow deep packet inspection (Pescatore, J., & Young, G., 2009). Thus giving rise to security attacks. But the NGFW's are current and have a combination of standard traditional firewalls and a intrusion prevention system (IPS), which will focus on the stateful packet filtering mechanism as performed earlier by a firewall (Thomason, Steven, 2012). Thus the application layer - Layer 7 in a network will have a proper attack prevention mechanism with the NGFW, as they also include the IPS with traditional firewall features.

The NGFW provides many top benefits in comparison with the traditional firewall in terms of security. The NGFW has good speed in scanning data packets irrespective of the traffic and critical applications. It deals with port independent traffic, i.e. irrespective of the standard or non-standard port for applications, the NGFW does not sacrifice security. The NGFW identifies applications irrespective of ports, protocols, encryption for SSL, IPS etc., provide granular control over applications, policy controls, integrate the features of a traditional firewall and IPS and most importantly well adapted with the changing dynamics of network security (Patel, A., pp. 9-12, 2015; Simmonds, A., et.al, pp. 317-323, 2004) (see Figure 4).

NGFW will benefit a user or an organisation in many ways over the traditional firewalls, simply because of their compliance with the changing dynamics of network security. Simplification is one such major benefit of NGFW, as it keeps the security protection method procedure a lot less complex which could help in easy management and monitoring of network security. The visibility of attacks in NGFW and their control has made the NGFW system more appealing to thoroughly manage risks while providing an IPS (Thomason, Steven, 2012). The granularity control of the applications is only made available with a safe access in NGFW which helps the IT be aligned and stay protected through the threats and attacks.

Features of NGFW

NGFW features will help address and maintain the following in protection mechanism of a network:

The Application Identification feature of NGFW will identify the type of application to establish a port and protocol (Erdheim, S., pp. 8-12, 2013; Frahim, J. et.al., 2014). The fast and efficient identification of applications in a network will allow the NGFW to enable granular control of the flow of sessions. When

Figure 4. Next generation firewall

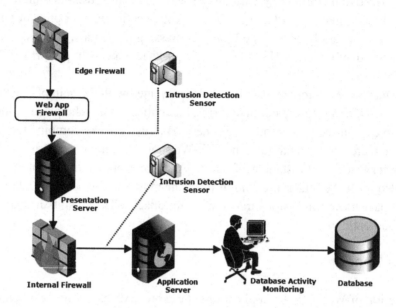

the application identified is clear without any attacks or threats, the application is allowed to enter the network. It first goes through Application protocol which detects and also decrypts - checking for SSL etc. and then the protocol decodes the information present, and finally the application protocol identifies the signatures present, instead of looking for the port or protocol - which keep changing dynamically (see Figure 5).

User Identification in a NGFW enables the use of user identity, also makes the troubleshooting and reporting easier and gets to know the particular application which was responsible for a particular kind of attack or traffic on a network (Thomason, Steven, 2012). The Content Identification feature of the NGFW helps scan the content with deep packet inspection and helps prevent threats - mainly because of an application decoder, inbuilt spyware scanner, IPS - providing protection for vulnerability attacks and having a uniform threat signature format which will help scan all types of threats, detect viruses, malware attacks in a single scan. URL filtering is also a part of content identification feature of NGFW (Frahim, J. et.al., 2014). The file and data is also filtered for viruses and other attacks.

The other protection mechanisms which perform similar functions as the NGFW but they differ in many ways from the NGFW and they are not successful in meeting the dynamics of network security like the NGFW does (Simmonds, A., et.al, pp. 317-323, 2004). The comparison of other protection mechanisms and their features with NGFW are listed below:

The UTM is similar to a combination of port firewall and a basic IPS system. The UTM is just a mere combination of all protection methods for detecting any kind of attack, but they are not build with high performance in mind and are focused to provide security only to a small network or environment.

Secure Web and Message Gateways provide solutions to the URL filtering, email filters, messenger attacks, and provide anti-spam and anti-malware protection. But they do not perform security checks in real time and are used for applications like emails in specific.

Figure 5. Next generation firewall mechanism

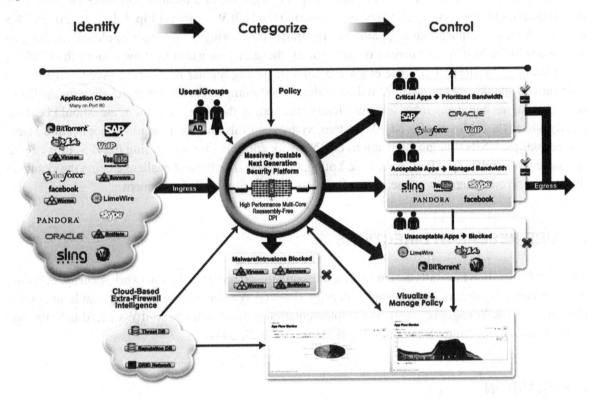

Vulnerability Management is used for scanning OS or software's for vulnerabilities and help prevent exploitation of the system or network. This is one such prevention feature which is not included in the NGFWs as they deal with internet security in real time (Chirillo J., 2002; Das, N., & Sarkar, T., 2014; Daya, B., 2013; Erdheim, S., pp. 8-12, 2013; Joel Snyder., 2012).

Web application firewall WAF is for scanning and preventing threats from the web applications, as there are many found due to the changing dynamics in technology such as web 2.0. The WAF focuses only on the applications unlike NGFW they do not protect networks.

Deployment of NGFW

The NGFW generally have a set of principles are set and followed while setting up. The User or system in a network who has NGFW should be able to allow or deny any application access or website access which might be blocked (Pescatore, J., & Young, G., 2009). Detection and alerting the user about the attacks and vulnerabilities is the primary role of a NGFW. Rest, the user should be given priority to decide on what he/she has to do with the following untrusted application or threat occurred in a file etc. The type of scan to be performed by a NGFW should also be given by the user, i.e. the user should be authorised to select between Scanning options for NGFW - scan for viruses, exploits, threats etc. Allowing particular application functions, decrypt and inspect a particular threat or application, apply traffic control etc. should be a few among many options to be present in the user's control. The NGFW has got high performance in times of high data traffic in a network too. It is important for a user to select a high performance NGFW for the organisation or network (Erdheim, S., pp. 8-12, 2013).

Deployment of a NGFW occurs through the policy control, in a business organisation, they give their requirements for security and they are enabled in the NGFW system (Filip, I. L. I. E., 2015). This includes the list of applications to be allowed, the traffic monitoring from certain applications, the scan for options in the NGFW for a certain type of attacks, the ability for a user to allow or deny the blocking of applications by firewall etc. The employee controls having regular monitoring over the list of bad applications and the ones allowed from them, informing the employees among themselves for the list of bad applications and many other features clearly mentioning the policy violation, etc. should be dealt clearly during the deployment of NGFW system. System controls - such as monitoring application access from desktops, USBs running applications etc. Network controls - for monitoring the IPS, Proxy Solutions, Network traffic etc. (Pescatore, J., & Young, G., 2009). The biggest challenge being the changing dynamics and compliance with the changes in network security while deployment.

FUTURE RESEARCH DIRECTIONS

The Next Generation Firewalls are currently addressing the growing need for network security. In future, with the changing dynamics of network security, the NGFWs may not be any longer able to comply (Pescatore, J., & Young, G., 2009). The implementation of biometrics in NGFWs could help provide network security in future (Simmonds, A., et.al, pp. 317-323, 2004).

CONCLUSION

The numbers of networks increasing day by day clearly signify that Network Security is a dynamic and highly critical field. The hacking and cracking attacks on the networks equally depict the importance of network security. Through the changing dynamics of network security, it became difficult for the prevention methodologies to keep up-to-date or comply with the growing standards. The Next Generation Firewalls designed to focus on complying with the growing standards and the changing dynamics of network security clearly addressed this problem.

REFERENCES

Chirillo, J. (2001). *Hack Attacks Encyclopedia: A Complete History of Hacks, Phreaks, and Spies over Time*. John Wiley & Sons, Inc.

Chirillo, J. (2002). *Hack attacks revealed: A complete reference with custom security hacking toolkit*. John Wiley & Sons.

Das, N., & Sarkar, T. (2014). Survey on Host and Network Based Intrusion Detection System. *Int. J. Advanced Networking and Applications*, 6(2), 2266–2269.

Daya, B. (2013). *Network security: History, importance, and future*. University of Florida Department of Electrical and Computer Engineering.

Dwivedi, H. (2009). *Hacking VoIP: protocols, attacks, and countermeasures*. No Starch Press.

Erdheim, S. (2013). Deployment and management with next-generation firewalls. *Network Security, 2013*(10), 8–12. doi:10.1016/S1353-4858(13)70113-2

Filip, I. L. I. E. (2015). Criteria of selecting and purchasing of the IT security solutions, used by retail companies. *Archives of Business Research, 3*(1).

Frahim, J., Santos, O., & Ossipov, A. (2014). *Cisco ASA: All-in-one Next-generation Firewall, IPS, and VPN Services*. Cisco Press.

Jordan, T. (2008). Hacking: Digital media and technological determinism. *Polity*.

Kessler, G. C. (2002). *Defenses against distributed denial of service attacks*. SANS Institute. (Original work published 2000)

Kwon, S. H., & Park, D. W. (2012). Hacking and security of encrypted access points in wireless network. *J Inf Commun Convergence Eng, 10*(2), 156–161. doi:10.6109/jicce.2012.10.2.156

Liu, V. (2007). *Hacking exposed wireless: Wireless security secrets and solutions*. McGraw-Hill Publishing.

Negi, Y. (2011). *Pragmatic Overview of Hacking & Its Counter Measures*. Academic Press.

Patel, A. (2015). Network performance without compromising security. *Network Security, 2015*(1), 9–12. doi:10.1016/S1353-4858(15)70008-5

Pescatore, J., & Young, G. (2009). *Defining the next-generation firewall*. Gartner RAS Core Research Note. Retrieved from http://www. ga1tner. com

Shema, M. (2012). *Hacking web apps: detecting and preventing web application security problems*. Newnes.

Simmonds, A., Sandilands, P., & Van Ekert, L. (2004). An ontology for network security attacks. In *Applied Computing* (pp. 317–323). Springer Berlin Heidelberg.

Snyder, J. (2012). Next-gen firewalls: Off to a good start. *Network World*. Retrieved from http://www. networkworld.com/article/2187980/network-security/next-gen-firewalls--off-to-a-good-start.html

Thomason, S. (2012). Improving Network Security: Next Generation Firewalls and Advanced Packet Inspection Devices. *Global Journal of Computer Science and Technology, 12*(13).

Zhang, Y., Chen, G., Weng, W., & Wang, Z. (2010, June). An overview of wireless intrusion prevention systems. In *Communication Systems, Networks and Applications (ICCSNA), 2010 Second International Conference on* (Vol. 1, pp. 147-150). IEEE.

KEY TERMS AND DEFINITIONS

Application Security: In Internet, there are multiple web applications running at the same time (Liu, V., 2007; Shema, M., 2012). The security provided to the applications running on website to prevent attacks is addressed as Application Security.

Firewall: A firewall is generally a wall or a barrier which protects or scans every connecting and data going in and outside the system or network.

Intrusion Detection System (IDS): A traditional method for providing internet security. It inspects data headers in the TCP, but only the first few bytes inspection is carried out. The IDS protection methodology is no longer of use for providing network security.

IPS: Intrusion Prevention System is a protection method for providing network security. This was introduced to overcome the shortcomings of IDS. It performs deep packet inspections to find intrusions in data packets transferred generally in a TCP for application layer in website applications (Liu, V., 2007; Shema, M., 2012).

SSL: Secure Socket Layer is a protection methodology which favours the security certificate policy to allow or disallow connections in a network, also refers to the method of encryption for providing protection from attacks in a network.

TCP: Transmission Control Protocol is present in networks to allow the data or information sharing between two user and systems in a network. It helps establish a connection and also help in data interchange. It deals with data transmitted over the connection established.

Virtual Private Network (VPN): Is used to establish connection to any private or public server virtually.

Compilation of References

Abraham, A. & Jain, R. (2007). Soft computing models for network intrusion detection systems. *Studies in Computational Intelligence*, 191–211.

Abraham, A. (2004). Evolutionary Computation in Intelligent Network Management. In Evolutionary Computing in Data Mining. Springer.

Agrawal, R., & Srikant, R. (1994). Fast algorithms for mining association rules. In *Proc. 20th int. conf. very large data bases, VLDB 1215*, 487-499.

Akyildiz, I. F. (2010). *Wireless Sensor Networks* (1st ed.). Wiley. doi:10.1002/9780470515181

Allardyce, J., & Goyal, N. (2004). *Elliptic Curve Cryptography*. Texas A&M University.

Al-Shurman & Yoo. (2004). *Black Hole Attack in Mobile Ad Hoc Networks*. ACMSE'04.

Al-Shurman, M., Yoo, S., & Park, S. (2004). Black Hole Attack in Mobile Ad Hoc Networks. In *Proceedings of 42nd Annual Southeast Regional Conference*. ACM. doi:10.1145/986537.986560

Amiel, F., Villegas, K., Feix, B., & Marcel, L. (2007). Passive and Active Combined Attacks–Combining Fault Attacks and Side Channel Analysis.*Workshop on Fault Diagnosis and Tolerance in Cryptography*. doi:10.1109/FDTC.2007.12

Andersen, D. G. (2003). *Mayday: Distributed Filtering for Internet Services*. In *4th USENIX Symposium on Internet Technologies and Systems (USITS)*, Seattle, WA.

Anderson, J. P. (1980). *Computer security threat monitoring and surveillance*. Anderson Co.

Anderson, T., Roscoe, T., & Wetherall, D. (2004). Preventing Internet Denial-of-Service with Capabilities. *Computer Communication Review*, *34*(1), 39–44. doi:10.1145/972374.972382

Ashland, R. E. (1985). B1 Security for Sperry 1100 Operating System. In *Proceedings of the 8th National Computer Security Conference* (pp. 105–7). Gaithersburg, MD: National Bureau of Standards.

Asokan, N., & Ginzboorg, P. (2000). Key Agreement in Ad-hoc networks. *Computer Communications*, *23*(17), 1627–1637. doi:10.1016/S0140-3664(00)00249-8

Awerbuch, B., Holmer, D., Nita Rotaru, C., & Rubens, . (2002). An On-Demand Secure Routing Protocol Resilient to Byzantine Failures.*Proceedings of the ACM Workshop on Wireless Security 2002*. doi:10.1145/570681.570684

BabuKaruppiah, A., Vidhya, G. S., & Rajaram, S. (2013). An Energy Efficient Wormhole Detection Technique by Traffic Analysis in Wireless Sensor Networks. *International Journal of Engineering and Computer Science*.

Bace, R.G. (2000). *Intrusion Detection*. Macmillan Technical Publishing.

Barbir, A., Murphy, S., & Yang, Y. (2004). *Generic Threats to Routing Protocols 2004, IETF Internet draft*. Available at: http://www.ietf.org/internet-drafts/draft-ietfrpsec-routing-threats-07.txt

Barenghi, A., Bertoni, G., Parrinello, E., & Pelosi, G. (2009). Low Voltage Fault Attacks on the RSA Cryptosystem. *Workshop on Fault Diagnosis and Tolerance in Cryptography*. doi:10.1109/FDTC.2009.30

Bellovin, S. M., & Merrit, M. (1992). Encrypted Key Exchange:*Password-Based Protocols Secure Against Dictionary Attacks. IEEE Symposium on Research in Security and Privacy.*

Bencsáth, B., & Vajda, I. (2004). *Protection Against DDoS Attacks Based On Traffic Level Measurements*. In *International Symposium on Collaborative Technologies and Systems,* San Diego, CA.

Berger, T. (2006). Analysis of current VPN technologies. In *Proceedings of the First IEEE International Conference on Availability, Reliability and Security*. IEEE. doi:10.1109/ARES.2006.30

Best Practices for Network Security in Emerging Businesses. (n.d.). Productive Corporation.

Bezdek, J. C. (1973). *Fuzzy mathematics in pattern classification*. Academic Press.

Bhalaji, N., & Shanmugam, A. (2011). A Trust Based Model to Mitigate Black Hole Attacks in DSR Based Manet. *European Journal of Scientific Research, 50*(1), 6–15.

Bhardwaj, K., & Chaudhary, S. (2012). Implementation of Elliptic Curve Cryptography in 'C'. *International Journal on Emerging Technologies, 3*(2), 38–51.

Binkley, J., & Trost, W. (2001). Authenticated Ad-hoc Routing at the Link Layer for Mobile Systems. *Wireless Networks, 7*(2), 139–145. doi:10.1023/A:1016633521987

Bishop, M. (2005). Malicious Logic. In Introduction to Computer Security. Addison Wesley.

Biswas & Ali. (2007). *Security Threats in Mobile Ad-Hoc Network*. (Master Thesis). Blekinge Institute of Technology Sweden.

Black Box Corp. (2003). *Network Security, A White Paper*. Available at: http://www.blackbox.com/Tech_Support/White-Papers/Network-Security2.pdf

Blake, S., Black, D., Carlson, M., Davies, E., Wang, Z., & Weiss, W. (1998). *An architecture for differentiated services*. Academic Press.

Blotcky, S., Lynch, K., & Lipner, S. (1986). SE/VMS: Implementing Mandatory Security in VAX/VMS. In *Proceedings of the 9th National Computer Security Conference* (pp. 47–54). Gaithersburg, MD: National Bureau of Standards.

Blum, J., & Eskandarian, A. (2004). The Threat of Intelligent Collisions. *IT Professional, 6*(1), 24–29. doi:10.1109/MITP.2004.1265539

Boneh, D. (1999). *Twenty Years of Attacks on the RSA Cryptosystem*. American Mathematical Society (AMS).

Bou Nassif, A. (n.d.). *Computer Science - Western University*. Retrieved from http://www.csd.uwo.ca/courses/CS1037a/

Brown, J., & Du, X. (2008). Detection of Selective Forwarding Attacks in Heterogeneous Sensor Networks.*2008 IEEE International Conference on Communications*. doi:10.1109/ICC.2008.306

Capkun, S., Buttyan, L., & Hubaux, J. P. (2003). Self Organized Public-Key Management for Mobile Ad Hoc Networks. *IEEE Transactions on Mobile Computing, 2*(1), 52–64. doi:10.1109/TMC.2003.1195151

Cardenas, A., Benammar, N., Papageorgiou, G., & Baras, J. (2004). Cross-Layered Security Analysis of Wireless Ad Hoc Networks. *Proc. of 24th Army Science Conference.*

CERT Coordination Center. (2003a). *Advisory CA-2003-04 MS-SQL Server Worm.* Retrieved from http://www.cert.org/advisories/CA-2003-04.html

CERT Coordination Center. (2003b). *Advisory CA-2003-20 W32/Blaster Worm.* Retrieved from http://www.cert.org/advisories/CA-2003-20.html

CERT. (1998). *Smurf Attack CERT Annual Report.* Available at CERT: http://www.cert.org/advisories/CA-1998-01.html

CERT. (2007). *CERT/CC Statistics 1988-2007.* CERTCoordination Center. Retrieved from http://www.cert.org/stats/

Chang, R. K. C. (2002). Defending against flooding-based, Distributed Denial of Service attacks: A tutorial. *IEEE Communications Magazine, 40*(10), 42–51. doi:10.1109/MCOM.2002.1039856

Charles, C. T. (2005). *Security Review of the Light-Weight Access Point Protocol. 2005.* IETF CAPWAP Working Group.

Chen, C., Song, M., & Hsieh, G. (2010). Intrusion detection of sinkhole attacks in large-scale wireless sensor networks. In *Wireless Communications, Networking and Information Security (WCNIS), 2010 IEEE International Conference on* (pp. 711-716). IEEE.

Chen, D., Deng, J., & Varshney, P. K. (2003). Protecting wireless networks against a denial of service attack based on virtual jamming. In *MOBICOM -Proceedings of the Ninth Annual International Conference on Mobile Computing and Networking.* ACM.

Chen, C.-C. (2004). RSA Scheme With MRF And ECC For Data Encryption. *2004 IEEE International Conference on Multimedia and Expo (ICME).* doi:10.1109/ICME.2004.1394358

Chien, E., & Szor, . (2002). *Blended Attacks Exploits, Vulnerabilities and Buffer-Overflow Techniques in Computer Viruses. Virus Bulletin Conference.*

Chirillo, J. (2001). *Hack Attacks Encyclopedia: A Complete History of Hacks, Phreaks, and Spies over Time.* John Wiley & Sons, Inc.

Chirillo, J. (2002). *Hack attacks revealed: A complete reference with custom security hacking toolkit.* John Wiley & Sons.

Choi, B. G., Cho, E. J., Kim, J. H., Hong, C. S., & Kim, J. H. (2009). *A sinkhole attack detection mechanism for LQI based mesh routing in WSN.* ICOIN.

Christensen, C. (2006). *Mathematical attack on RSA.* Cambridge, MA: Cambridge Center-RSA Laboratories.

Cid, C. F. (2003). Cryptanalysis of RSA. In *GIAC Security Essentials Certification-A survey in RSA.* Academic Press.

Cisco Security. (n.d.). Configuring AAA Servers and the Local Database. In *Cisco Security Appliance Command Line Configuration Guide.* Author.

Cisco. (2013, August). *Firewall and IPS, Technology Design Guide.* Cisco Networks Inc.

Cisco. (n.d.). Understanding Pseudowire. In *Cisco MWR 2941 Mobile Wireless Edge Router Software Configuration Guide, Release 15.0(1) MR.* Author.

Clure, M., Hart, R., Morgan, D., & Tran, H. (1999). An Introduction to Automated Intrusion Detection Approaches. *Information Management and Computer Security, 7*(1), 76-81.

Cohen, F. (1985). *Computer Viruses.* (PhD thesis). University of Southern California.

Cole, E., Krutz, R. L., Conley, J. W., Reisman, B., Ruebush, M., & Gollmann, D. (2008). *Network Security Fundamentals*. Anne Smith.

Computer and Network IDS. (2010). *Anomaly-Based IDStutorial.com*. Retrieved from http://idstutorial.com/anomaly-detection.php

Conti, M., Gregori, E., & Maselli, G. (2003). Towards Reliable Forwarding for Ad Hoc Networks. In *Personal Wireless Communications, IFIP-TC6 8th International Conference, PWC 2003*. Venice, Italy: Springer. doi:10.1007/978-3-540-39867-7_71

Convery, S., Miller, D., & Sundaralingam, S. (2003). *Cisco SAFE: Wireless LAN Security in Depth 2003*. CISCO Whitepaper.

Coppolino, L., D'Antonio, S., Romano, L., & Spagnuolo, G. (2010). An intrusion detection system for critical information infrastructures using wireless sensor network technologies. In *Critical Infrastructure (CRIS), 2010 5th International Conference on* (pp. 1-8). IEEE. doi:10.1109/CRIS.2010.5617547

Cormode, G., Korn, F., Muthukrishnan, S., & Srivastava, D. (2008). Finding hierarchical heavy hitters in streaming data. *ACM Transactions on Knowledge Discovery from Data, 1*(4), 2. doi:10.1145/1324172.1324174

Cramer, M. L., Cannady, J., & Harrell, J. (1996). New Methods of Intrusion Detection Using Control-loop Measurement. In *Fourth Technology for Information Security Conference*, Houston, TX.

Crepeau, C., Davis, C. R., & Maheswaran, M. (2007). *A secure MANET routing protocol with resilience against byzantine behaviors of malicious or selfish nodes*. 21st International Conference on Advanced Information Networking and Applications Workshops (AINAW'07).

Dallas, D., Leckie, C., & Ramamohanarao, K. (2007). Hop-Count Monitoring: Detecting Sinkhole Attacks in Wireless Sensor Networks. *2007 15th IEEE International Conference on Networks*. doi:10.1109/ICON.2007.4444082

Dallas, D., Leckie, C., & Ramamohanarao, K. (2007). Hop-count monitoring: Detecting sinkhole attacks in wireless sensor networks. In *Networks, 2007. ICON 2007. 15th IEEE International Conference on* (pp. 176-181). IEEE.

Dantzig, G. B. (1998). *Linear programming and extensions*. Princeton University Press.

Das, N., & Sarkar, T. (2014). Survey on Host and Network Based Intrusion Detection System. *Int. J. Advanced Networking and Applications, 6*(2), 2266–2269.

Daya, B. (2013). *Network security: History, importance, and future*. University of Florida Department of Electrical and Computer Engineering.

Deng, H., Li, W., & Agrawal, D. P. (2002). Routing Security in Wireless Ad hoc Networks. *IEEE Communications Magazine, 40*(10), 70–75. doi:10.1109/MCOM.2002.1039859

Denning, D. E. (1987). An Intrusion Detection Model. *IEEE Transactions on Software Engineering, SE-13*(2), 222–232. doi:10.1109/TSE.1987.232894

Department of Defense. (1985). DoD Trusted Computer System Evaluation Criteria. DOD 5200.28-STD. Washington, DC: Department of Defense. (U.S. Government Printing Office number 008-000-00461-7)

Desmedt, Y., & Frankel, Y. (1990). Threshold Cryptosystem. Springer Verlag. doi:10.1007/0-387-34805-0_28

Dialed Number Identification Service (DNIS). (n.d.). *Patton Tech Notes*.

Diffie, W., & Hellman, M. (1976). New Directions in Cryptography. *IEEE Transactions on Information Theory, IT*, *22*(6), 644–654. doi:10.1109/TIT.1976.1055638

Douligeris, & Kotzanikolaou. (n.d.). Network Security. *Telecommunication Systems and Technologies, 2*.

Douligeris, C., & Serpanos, D. (Eds.). (2006). Network Security: Current Status and Future Directions. Wiley–IEEE.

Doverspike, R. D., Ramakrishnan, K. K., & Chase, C. (n.d.). *Structural Overview of ISP Networks*. AT&T Labs Research.

Dowd, P. W., & McHenry, J. T. (1998). Network security: It's time to take it seriously.[Sep.]. *Computer*, *31*(9), 24–28. doi:10.1109/2.708446

Dubai, M., Mahesh, T., & Ghosh, P. (2011). Design Of New Security Algorithm Using Hybrid Cryptography Architecture. *Electronics Computer Technology (ICECT)-3rd International Conference, 5*, 99-101.

Dwivedi, H. (2009). *Hacking VoIP: protocols, attacks, and countermeasures*. No Starch Press.

El Kaissi, R. Z., Kayssi, A., Chehab, A., & Dawy, Z. (2005). *DAWWSEN: A defense mechanism against wormhole attacks in wireless sensor networks* (Doctoral dissertation). American University of Beirut, Department of Electrical and Computer Engineering.

Ensafi, R., Dehghanzadeh, S., Mohammad, R., & Akbarzadeh, T. (2008). Optimizing fuzzy k-means for network anomaly detection using pso. ACS/IEEE international conference on computer systems and applications, Doha, Qatar. doi:10.1109/AICCSA.2008.4493603

Erdheim, S. (2013). Deployment and management with next-generation firewalls. *Network Security*, *2013*(10), 8–12. doi:10.1016/S1353-4858(13)70113-2

Erman, J., Arlitt, M., & Mahanti, A. (2006). Traffic classification using clustering algorithms. In *Proceedings of the 2006 SIGCOMM workshop on Mining network data* (pp. 281-286). ACM. doi:10.1145/1162678.1162679

Ernst, M., Jochemsz, E., May, A., & Weger, B. D. (2005). Partial Key Exposure Attacks on RSA Up to Full Size Exponents. International Association for Cryptologic Research.

Eskin, E., Arnold, A., Prerau, M., Portnoy, L., & Stolfo, S. (2002). A geometric framework for unsupervised anomaly detection. In Applications of data mining in computer security (pp. 77-101). Springer US. doi:10.1007/978-1-4615-0953-0_4

Eskin, E., Arnold, A., Prerau, M., Portnoy, L., & Stolfo, S. (2002). A geometric framework for unsupervised anomaly detection: Detecting intrusions in unlabeled data. In Applications of Data Mining in Computer Security. Norwell, MA: Kluwer.

Ester, M., Kriegel, H. P., Sander, J., & Xu, X. (1996). A density-based algorithm for discovering clusters in large spatial databases with noise. In Kdd 96.

Fayyad, U., Piatetsky-Shapiro, G., & Smyth, P. (1996). From data mining to knowledge discovery in databases. *AI Magazine*, *17*(3), 37.

Ferguson, P., & Senie, D. (2000). *Network Ingress Filtering: Defeating Denial of Service Attacks Which Employ IP Source Address Spoofing*. Available on http://www.rfc-archive.org/getrfc.php?rfc=2827

Filip, I. L. I. E. (2015). Criteria of selecting and purchasing of the IT security solutions, used by retail companies. *Archives of Business Research*, *3*(1).

Fletcher, T., Richardson, H. W. K., Carlisle, M. C., & Hamilton, J. A. (2005). Simulation Experimentation with Secure Overlay Services. In *Summer Computer Simulation Conference*, Philadelphia, PA.

Fournaris, A. P. (2012). CRT RSA Hardware Architecture with Fault and Simple Power Attack Countermeasures. *Digital System Design (DSD), 15th Euromicro Conference.*

Fournaris, A. P., & Koufopavlou, O. (2012). Protecting CRT RSA against Fault and Power Side Channel Attacks.*IEEE Computer Society Annual Symposium (ISVLSI).* doi:10.1109/ISVLSI.2012.54

Frahim, J., Santos, O., & Ossipov, A. (2014). *Cisco ASA: All-in-one Next-generation Firewall, IPS, and VPN Services.* Cisco Press.

Fraim, L. J. (1983). SCOMP: A Solution to the Multilevel Security Problem. Computer, 16(7), 26–34.

Freund, Y., & Schapire, R. E. (1997). A Decision theoretic generalization of on-line learning and an application to boosting. *Journal of Computer and System Sciences, 55*(1), 119–139. doi:10.1006/jcss.1997.1504

Friedman, N., Geiger, D., & Goldsmidt, M. (1997). Bayesian Network Classifiers. *Machine Learning, 29*(Nov), 131–163. doi:10.1023/A:1007465528199

Furnell, S. M., Magklaras, G. B., Papadaki, M., & Dowland, P.S. (2001). A Generic system for Intrusion Specification and Response. *Proceedings of Euromedia 2001.*

Gasser, M., Goldstein, A., Kaufman, C., & Lampson, B. (1989). The Digital distributed system security architecture. In *Proceedings of the National Computer Security Conference.*

Gearhart, C., Herold, A., Self, B., Birdsong, C., & Slivovsky, L. (2009). *Use of Ultrasonic Sensors in the Development of an Electronic Travel Aid.* IEEE Sensors Applications Symposium, New Orleans, LA.

Gerhards-Padilla, E., Aschenbruck, N., & Martini, P. (2007). *Detecting Black Hole Attacks in Tactical MANETs using Topology Graphs Networks.* 32nd IEEE Conference on Local Computer Networks.

Ghosh, A. K., & Schwartzbard, A. (1999). A Study in using Neural Networks for Anomaly and Misuse Detection. In *Proc. th USENIX Security Symposium.*

Giacinto, G., Roli, F., & Didaci, L. (2007). Fusion of multiple classifiers for Intrusion Detection in Computer Networks. In *Proc. IEEE Conference in Network security.*

Glossary of Terms Used in Security and Intrusion Detection by SANS Institute. (n.d.). Accessed online at www.sans. org/resources/glossary.php

Government of the Hong Kong Special Administrative Region. (2008, February). *VPN Security.* Author.

Graf, K. (2005). *Addressing Challenges in Application Security.* Watchfire White Paper. Retrieved from http://www. watchfire.com

Gudahe, Prasad, & Wankhade. (2010). *A New Data Mining Based Network Intrusion Detection Model.* International Conference on Computer & Communication Technology.

Gupta. (2010, January-April). Layered Approach Using Conditional Random Fields for Intrusion Detection. *IEEE Transactions on Dependable and Secure Computing, 7*(1).

Gu, Y., McCallum, A., & Towsley, D. (2005). Detecting anomalies in network traffic using maximum entropy estimation. In *Proceedings of the 5th ACM SIGCOMM conference on Internet Measurement* (pp. 32-32). USENIX Association. doi:10.1145/1330107.1330148

Ha, C.-S., Kim, J.-H., Choi, B.-Y., Lee, J.-H., & Kim, H.-W. (2004). *GF(2191) Elliptic Curve Processor using Montgomery Ladder and High Speed Finite Field Arithmetic Unit.* Information Security Basic Department, ETRI.

Hai, T. H., & Huh, E.-N. (2008). Detecting Selective Forwarding Attacks in Wireless Sensor Networks Using Two-hops Neighbor Knowledge.*2008 Seventh IEEE International Symposium on Network Computing and Applications.* doi:10.1109/NCA.2008.13

Hamid, A. (2006). Defense against lap-top class attacker in wireless sensor network. *2006 8th International Conference Advanced Communication Technology.* doi:10.1109/ICACT.2006.205976

Han, J. W., & Kamber, M. (2006). *Data Mining: Concepts and Techniques* (2nd ed.). Morgan Kaufmann.

Hankerson, D., Menezes, A., & Vanstone, S. (2004). Guide to Elliptic Curve Cryptography. Springer-Verlag.

Hart, R., Morgan, D., & Tran, H. (1999). An introduction to automated Intrusion Detection Approach. *Information Management & Computer Security, 7*(1), 76–81. doi:10.1108/09685229910265501

Hastie, T., & Tibshirani, R. (1996). Discriminant adaptive nearest neighbor classification. *Pattern Analysis and Machine Intelligence. IEEE Transactions on, 18*(6), 607–616.

Hätönen, S., & Nyrhine, A., et al.. (n.d.). An Experimental Study of Home Gateway Characteristics. *University of Helsinki.*

Havinga, P. J. M. (2005). How to Secure a Wireless Sensor Network.*2005 International Conference on Intelligent Sensors, Sensor Networks and Information Processing.* doi:10.1109/ISSNIP.2005.1595561

Herringshaw, C. (1997). Detecting Attacks on Networks. *IEEE Computer, 30*(12), 16–17. doi:10.1109/2.642762

Hijazi, A., Inoue, H., Matrawy, A., Van Oorschot, P., & Somayaji, A. (2008). Discovering packet structure through lightweight hierarchical clustering. In *Communications, 2008. ICC'08. IEEE International Conference on* (pp. 33-39). IEEE. doi:10.1109/ICC.2008.15

Holland, J. H. (1975). *Adaptation in natural and artificial systems: An introductory analysis with applications to biology, control, and artificial intelligence.* U Michigan Press.

Hongfei, L., & Zhong, C. (2009). An Infusing Infrared-Sensor Simulator Design Based on USB2.0. *Computer Network and Multimedia Technology,2009. CNMT 2009. International Symposium on.* doi:10.1109/CNMT.2009.5374680

Horng, Su, Chen, Kao, Chen, Lai, & Perkasa. (2011). A novel intrusion detection system based on hierarchical clustering and support vector machines. *Journal of Expert Systems with Applications, 38,* 306-313.

Hossain, M. A., Islam, M. K., Das, S. K., & Nashiry, M. A. (n.d.). *Cryptanalyzing of Message Digest Algorithms MD4 AND MD5.* Department of Computer Science & Engineering, *Jessore Science & Technology University.*

Houle, K. J., & Weaver, G. M. (2001). *Trends in Denial of Service Attack Technology, CERT and CERT coordination center(CERT/CC).* Carnegie Mellon University. Available from http://www.cert.org/archive/pdf/DoS_trends.pdf

Hsieh, H., & Sivakumar, R. (2002). *Transport over Wireless Networks. Handbook of Wireless Networks and Mobile Computing* (I. Stojmenovic, Ed.). John Wiley and Sons, Inc.

Hu, Hu, & Maybank. (2008). AdaBoost-Based Algorithm for Network Intrusion Detection. *IEEE Transactions on Systems, Man and Cybernetics, 38,* 577-583.

Hu, Y-C., Perrig, A., & Johnson, D. B. (2003). Rushing Attacks and Defense in Wireless Ad Hoc Network Routing Protocols. In *2nd ACM Wireless Security* (WiSe'03).

Huawei, Z., & Ruixia, L. (2009). A Scheme to Improve Security of SSL.*2009 Pacific-Asia Conference on Circuits,Communications and System.* doi:10.1109/PACCS.2009.148

Hubaux, J. P., Gross, T., Boudec, J. Y., & Vetterli, M. (2001, January). Toward self-organized mobile ad hoc networks: The terminodes project. *IEEE Communications Magazine, 39*(1), 118–124. doi:10.1109/35.894385

Huiping, J., & Zhigang, M. (2003). Design of an RSA module Against power Analysis.*5th International Conference in ASCI*. doi:10.1109/ICASIC.2003.1277457

Humphries, J. W., & Carlisle, M. C. (2002). Introduction to Cryptography. *ACM Journal of Educational Resources in Computing, 2*(3), 2.

Hu, Y., Johnson, D., & Perrig, A. (2002). SEAD: Secure Efficient Distance Vector Routing in Mobile Wireless Ad-Hoc Networks.*Proc. of the 4th IEEE Workshop on Mobile Computing Systems and Applications (WMCSA'02)*.

Hu, Y., Perrig, A., & Johnson, D. B. (2003). Rushing Attacks and Defense in Wireless Ad Hoc Network Routing Protocols.*Proceedings of the ACM Workshop on Wireless Security 2003*. doi:10.1145/941311.941317

IMEX. (n.d.). *SAS, NAS, SAN Past, Present and Future*. IMEX Research White Paper.

Innell, P. (2010). *An Introduction to IDS*. Retrieved from http://www.symantec.com/connect/articles/introduction-ids

Intanagonwiwat, C., Govindan, R., & Estrin, D. (2000). Directed diffusion: a scalable and robust communication paradigm for sensor networks. In *Proceedings of the 6th annual international conference on Mobile computing and networking* (pp. 56-67). ACM. doi:10.1145/345910.345920

Internet History Timeline. (n.d.). Retrieved from www3.baylor.edu/~Sharon_P_Johnson/etg/inthistory.htm

Ioannidis, J., & Bellovin, S. M. (2002). *Implementing Pushback: Router-Based Defense Against DDoS Attacks*. In *Network and Distributed System Security Symposium*, San Diego, CA.

Ioannis, K., Dimitriou, T., & Freiling, F. C. (2007). Towards intrusion detection in wireless sensor networks. In *Proc. of the 13th European Wireless Conference*.

Iqbal, S., Srinivas, S. P. A., Sudarshan, G., & Kashyap, S. (2014). Comparison of Different Attacks on Leach Protocol In WSN. *International Journal of Electrical. Electronics and Data Communication, 2*, 16–19.

Iyengar, N. C. S., Banerjee, A., & Ganapathy, G. (2014). A Fuzzy Logic Based Defense Mechanism against Distributed Denial of Services Attack in Cloud Environment. *International Journal of Communication Networks and Information Security, 6*(3).

Jain, R. (n.d.). Secure Socket Layer (SSL) Secure Socket Layer (SSL) and Transport Layer and Transport Layer Security (TLS) Security (TLS). *Washington University*.

Jakobsson, M., Wetzel, S., & Yener, B. (2003). Stealth Attacks on Ad Hoc Wireless Networks.*Proc. of IEEE Vehicular Technology Conference (VTC)*. doi:10.1109/VETECF.2003.1285396

Jarmoc, J. (2012, March 21). *SSL/TLS Interception Proxies and Transitive Trust-Transitive Trust*. Retrieved July 21, 2013, from http://i.technet.microsoft.com/dyni

Jatav, V. K., Tripathi, M., Gaur, M. S., & Laxmi, V. (2012). Wireless sensor networks: Attack models and detection. In *Proceedings of the IACSIT Hong Kong conferences IPCSIT 30*, 144-149.

Jen, S.-M., Laih, C.-S., & Kuo, W.-C. (2009). A Hop-Count Analysis Scheme for Avoiding Wormhole Attacks in MANET. *Sensors (Basel, Switzerland), 9*(6), 5022–5039. doi:10.3390/s90605022 PMID:22408566

Johnson, D. B., & Maltz, D. A. (1996). Article. In T. Imielinski & H. Korth (Eds.), Dynamic source routing in ad hoc wireless networks, in mobile Computing (pp. 153–181). Kluwer Academic Publishers.

Jordan, T. (2008). Hacking: Digital media and technological determinism. *Polity*.

Just, M., Kranakis, E., & Wan, T. (2003). Resisting Malicious Packet Dropping in Wireless Ad Hoc Networks. In AD-HOCNOW'03, Montreal, Canada. doi:10.1007/978-3-540-39611-6_14

Kang, S. H., Park, K. Y., Yoo, S. G., & Kim, J. (2013). DDoS avoidance strategy for service availability. *Cluster Computing*, *16*(2), 241–248. doi:10.1007/s10586-011-0185-4

Kani, E. (n.d.). The State of the Art of Elliptic Curve Cryptography. Kingston, Ontario: Department of Mathematics and Statistics, Queen's University.

Kaplantzis, S., Shilton, A., Mani, N., & Sekercioglu, Y. A. (2007). Detecting Selective Forwarding Attacks in Wireless Sensor Networks using Support Vector Machines. *2007 3rd International Conference on Intelligent Sensors, Sensor Networks and Information*. doi:10.1109/ISSNIP.2007.4496866

Karlof, C., & Wagner, D. (2003). Secure routing in wireless sensor networks: Attacks and countermeasures. *Ad Hoc Networks*, *1*(2-3), 293–315. doi:10.1016/S1570-8705(03)00008-8

Karp, B., & Kung, H. T. (2000). *GPSR: Greedy Perimeter Stateless Routing for Wireless Networks*. Academic Press.

Kartalopoulos, S. V. (2008).Differentiating Data Security and Network Security. *Communications, ICC '08. IEEE International Conference on*. doi:10.1109/ICC.2008.284

Karygiannis, T., & Owens, L. (2002). *Wireless Network Security 802.11 Bluetooth and Handheld Devices*. National Institute of Standards and Technology Special Publication, 800-48. Available at: http://csrc.nist.gov/publications/nistpubs/800-48/NIST_SP_800-48.pdf

Katz, J. (2002). *Efficient Cryptographic Protocols Preventing "Man-in-the-Middle" Attacks*. (PhD Dissertation). Columbia University.

Kaufman, C., Perlman, R., & Speciner, M. (2002). *Network Security Private Communication in a Public World*. Prentice Hall PTR.

Kayacik, H. G., Zincir-Heywood & Heywood. (2003). On the capability of an SOM based intrusion detection systems. In *Proc. Int. Joint Conference in Neural Networks*.

KDDCup'99. (1999). *Dataset*. Retrieved from http://kdd.ics.uci.edu/databases/kddcup99/kddcup99.html

Keromytis, A. D., & Rubenstein, D. (2002). SOS: Secure Overlay Services. In ACM SIGCOMM'02, Pittsburgh, PA.

Keromytis, A. D., Misra, V., & Rubenstein, D. (2002). SOS: Secure overlay services. *Computer Communication Review*, *32*(4), 61–72. doi:10.1145/964725.633032

Kessler, G. C. (2002). *Defenses against distributed denial of service attacks*. SANS Institute. (Original work published 2000)

Khattab, S. M., Sangpachatanaruk, C., Melhem, R., Mossé, D., & Znati, T. (2003). Proactive server roaming for mitigating denial-of-service attacks. In *Information Technology: Research and Education, 2003. Proceedings. ITRE2003. International Conference on* (pp. 286-290). IEEE. doi:10.1109/ITRE.2003.1270623

Khor. (2006). Comparing Single and Multiple Bayesian Classifiers Approaches for Network Intrusion Detection. Academic Press.

Kibirige, G. W., & Sanga, C. A. (2015). A Survey on Detection of Sinkhole Attack in Wireless Sensor Network. *International Journal of Computer Science and Information Security*, *13*(5), 1–9.

Kilkki, K. (1999). *Differentiated services for the Internet*. Macmillan Publishing Co., Inc.

Kocher, P. C. (1996). *Timing Attacks on Implementations of Diffie-Hellman, RSA, DSS, and Other Systems*. San Francisco, CA: Cryptography Research, Inc. doi:10.1007/3-540-68697-5_9

Kolheka, M., & Jadhav, A. (2011). Implementation Of Elliptic Curve Cryptography On Text And Image. *International Journal of Enterprise Computing and Business Systems*, *1*(2).

Kong, J., Zerfos, P., Luo, H., Lu, S., & Zhang, L. (2001). Providing Robust and Ubiquitous Security Support for Mobile Adhoc Networks. In *Ninth International Conference on Network Protocols* (ICNP). Available at http://citeseer.nj.nec.com/kong01providing.html

Kong,, H., Yun, , & Lee, H. (2006). A Distributed Intrusion Detection. *Electrical Engineering*, 2–5.

Ko, Y.-B., & Vaidya, N. H. (1998). Location-aided routing (LAR) in mobile ad hoc networks.*Proceedings of the 4th Annual ACM/IEEE International Conference on Mobile Computing and Networking - MobiCom '98*. doi:10.1145/288235.288252

Krontiris, I., Giannetsos, T., & Dimitriou, T. (2008). Launching a sinkhole attack in wireless sensor networks; the intruder side. In *Networking and Communications, 2008. WIMOB'08.IEEE International Conference on Wireless and Mobile Computing*, (pp. 526-531). IEEE.

Krontiris, I., Dimitriou, T., Giannetsos, T., & Mpasoukos, M. (2008). Intrusion detection of sinkhole attacks in wireless sensor networks. In *Algorithmic Aspects of Wireless Sensor Networks* (pp. 150–161). Springer Berlin Heidelberg. doi:10.1007/978-3-540-77871-4_14

Krontiris, I., Giannetsos, T., & Dimitriou, T. (2008). Launching a Sinkhole Attack in Wireless Sensor Networks; The Intruder Side.*2008 IEEE International Conference on Wireless and Mobile Computing, Networking and Communications*. doi:10.1109/WiMob.2008.83

Kullback, S. (1997). *Information theory and statistics*. Courier Dover Publications.

Kumar, A., Rana, M., & Aggarwal, N. (2011). A Comparative Study of Public Key Cryptosystem based on ECC and RSA. *International Journal on Computer Science and Engineering*, *3*(5), 1904–1909.

Kwon, S. H., & Park, D. W. (2012). Hacking and security of encrypted access points in wireless network. *J Inf Commun Convergence Eng*, *10*(2), 156–161. doi:10.6109/jicce.2012.10.2.156

Lakhina, A., Crovella, M., & Diot, C. (2005). Mining anomalies using traffic feature distributions. *Computer Communication Review*, *35*(4), 217–228. doi:10.1145/1090191.1080118

Lakshminarayanan, K., Adkins, D., Perrig, A., & Stoica, I. (2003). Taming IP Packet Flooding Attacks. In *2nd ACM Workshop on Hot Topics in Networks*. Cambridge, MA: ACM Press. doi:10.1145/972374.972383

Lau, F., Rubin, S. H., Smith, M. H., & Trajkovic, L. (2000). Distributed denial of service attacks. In *Systems, Man, and Cybernetics, 2000 IEEE International Conference on*. IEEE. doi:10.1109/ICSMC.2000.886455

Lawson, L. (2005). *Session Hijacking Packet Analysis*. SecurityDocs.com Report.

Lazos, L., Poovendran, R., Meadows, C., Syverson, P., & Chang, L. W. (2005) Preventing Wormhole Attacks on Wireless Ad Hoc Networks: A Graph Theoretic Approach. In *IEEE Wireless Communications and Networking Conference*. doi:10.1109/WCNC.2005.1424678

Le Fessant, F., Papadimitriou, A., Viana, A. C., Sengul, C., & Palomar, E. (2012). A sinkhole resilient protocol for wireless sensor networks: Performance and security analysis. *Computer Communications*, *35*(2), 234–248. doi:10.1016/j.comcom.2011.09.005

Leduc, G. (n.d.). *Verification of two versions of the Challenge Handshake Authentication Protocol (CHAP)*. Research Unit in Networking (RUN), *Université de Liège*.

Lee, R. B. (2003). *Taxonomies of Distributed Denial of Service networks, attacks, tools and countermeasures*. Princeton University. Available: http://www.ee.princeton.edu/rblee

Lee, R. B., Karig, D. K., McGregor, J. P., & Shi, Z. (2004). Enlisting hardware architecture to thwart malicious code injection. In *Security in Pervasive Computing* (pp. 237–252). Springer Berlin Heidelberg. doi:10.1007/978-3-540-39881-3_21

Lee, Y., Hur, S., Won, D., & Kim, S. (2009). Cipher Suite Setting Problem of SSL Protocol and It's Solutions. *2009 International Conference on Advanced Information Networking and Applications Workshops*. doi:10.1109/WAINA.2009.76

Leiwo, J., Aura, T., & Nikander, P. (2000). *Towards Network Denial Of Service Resistant Protocols*. In 15th International Information Security Conference, Beijing, China. doi:10.1007/978-0-387-35515-3_31

Levijoki, S. (2000). *Authentication, Authorization and Accounting in Ad-hoc networks*. Department of Computer Science Helsinki University of Technology. Retrieved from http://www.hut.fi/~slevijok/aaa.htm

Li, J., Sung, M., Xu, J., & Li, L. E. (2004). *Large-Scale IP Traceback in High-Speed Internet: Practical Techniques and Theoretical Foundation*. In IEEE Symposium on Security and Privacy, Oakland, CA.

Li, J., Mirkovic, J., Wang, M., Reiher, P., & Zhang, L. (2002). SAVE: Source address validity enforcement protocol. *Proceedings of the IEEE, 3*, 1557–1566.

Li, M., & Li, M. (2010). An adaptive approach for defending against DDoS attacks. *Mathematical Problems in Engineering, 2010*.

Li, M., Li, M., & Jiang, X. (2008). DDoS attacks detection model and its application. *WSEAS Transactions on Computers, 7*(8), 1159–1168.

Lindqvist, U., & Jonsson, E. (2001). How to Systematically Classify Computer Security Intrusions. *IEEE Symposium on Security and Privacy*. Oakland, CA: IEEE Computer Society Press.

Lippmann, R. P., & Cunningham, R. K. (2000). Improving Intrusion Detection Performance using Keyword Selection and Neural Networks. *Computer Networks, 34*(4), 597–603. doi:10.1016/S1389-1286(00)00140-7

Liu, Y., Li, N., Shi, L., & Li, F. (2010). *An Intrusion Detection Method Based on Decision Tree*. In International Conference on E-Health Networking, Digital Ecosystems and Technologies.

Liu, F. (2009). *A Tutorial on Elliptic Curve Cryptography (ECC)*. Brandenburg Technical University of Cottbus-omputer Networking Group.

Liu, V. (2007). *Hacking exposed wireless: Wireless security secrets and solutions*. McGraw-Hill Publishing.

Luo, H., Kong, J., Zerfos, P., Lu, S., & Zhang, L. (2000). *Self Securing Ad-hoc Wireless Networks. IEEE Symposium on Computers and Communications (ISCC'02)*.

Luo, J., Fan, M., & Ye, D. (2008). *Black hole Attack Prevention based on Authentication Mechanism*. Science and Technology.

Maarof & Shasuddin. (2009). Ensemble classifiers for Network Intrusion Detection System. *Journal of Information Assurance and Security, 4*, 217–225.

Martins, D., & Guyennet, H. (2010). Wireless sensor network attacks and security mechanisms: A short survey. In *Network-Based Information Systems (NBiS), 2010 13th International Conference on* (pp. 313-320). IEEE. doi:10.1109/NBiS.2010.11

Marti, S., Giuli, T., Lai, K., & Baker, M. (2000). Mitigating Routing Misbehaviour in Mobile Ad-hoc Networks. In *Proceedings of the ACM International Conference on Mobile Computing and Networking MobiCom.*

Matrawy, A., van Oorschot, P. C., & Somayaji, A. (2005). Mitigating network denial-of-service through diversity-based traffic management. In *Applied Cryptography and Network Security* (pp. 104–121). Springer Berlin Heidelberg. doi:10.1007/11496137_8

Mc Hugh, J. (2001). Intrusion and Intrusion Detection. *International Journal of Information Security, 1*(1), 14–35. doi:10.1007/s102070100001

McGregor, A., Hall, M., Lorier, P., & Brunskill, J. (2004). Flow clustering using machine learning techniques. In *Passive and Active Network Measurement* (pp. 205–214). Springer Berlin Heidelberg. doi:10.1007/978-3-540-24668-8_21

Microsoft Corporation. (2014). *Point-to-Point Tunneling Protocol (PPTP) Profile.* Microsoft Corporation.

Miltchev, S., Ioannidis, S., & Keromytis, A. D. (n.d.). *A Study of the Relative Costs of Network Security Protocols.* University of Pennsylvania.

Min, S. (2004). *A Study on the Security of NTRUSign Digital Signature Scheme.* (Master Thesis). Information and Communications University, Korea.

Min, Z., & Jiliu, Z. (2009). *Cooperative Black Hole Attack Prevention for Mobile Ad Hoc Networks.International Symposium on Information Engineering and Electronic Commerce.* doi:10.1109/IEEC.2009.12

Mirkovic, & Reiher. (2004). A Taxonomy of DDoS Attack and DDoS defense Mechanisms. *ACM SIGCOMM Computer Communications Review, 34*(2), 39-53.

Mirkovic, J., Prier, G., & Reiher, P. (2002). Attacking DDoS at the Source. In *Proceedings of 10th IEEE International Conference on Network Protocols.* IEEE Computer Society.

Mirkovic, J., Hussain, A., Fahmy, S., Reiher, P., & Thomas, R. K. (2009). Accurately measuring denial of service in simulation and testbed experiments. *Dependable and Secure Computing. IEEE Transactions on, 6*(2), 81–95.

Mittal, A., Shrivastava, A. K., & Manoria, M. (2011). A Review of DDOS Attack and its Countermeasures in TCP Based Networks. *International Journal of Computer Science & Engineering Survey, 2,* 4.

Molva, R., & Michiardi, P. (2002). Security in Ad Hoc Networks. In *Personal Wireless Communications, IFIP-TC6 8th International Conference.* Venice, Italy: Springer. doi:10.1007/978-3-540-39867-7_69

Mosses, R. (2001). *Information Technology – Security Techniques.* ISO /IECJTC 1/SC 27 N 3011. Available at http://www.din.de/ni/sc27

Nagamalai, D., Dhinakaran, C., & Lee, J. K. (2007). Multi layer approach to defend DDoS attacks caused by spam. In *Multimedia and Ubiquitous Engineering, 2007. MUE'07. International Conference on* (pp. 97-102). IEEE. doi:10.1109/MUE.2007.157

Narayanan, A. E., & Vishwakarma, A. K. (2011). Cloud Automation: New Era of Electricity Bill Automation using GPRS and Web Interface. *International Journal of Computers and Applications, 11.*

National Computer Security Center. (1987). *Trusted Network Interpretation. NCSC-TG-005.* National Computer Security Center.

National Security Telecommunications and Information Systems Security. (1994). *National Training Standard for Information Systems Security (Infosec) Professionals*. Accessed 8 Feb 2007 from www.cnss.gov/Assets/pdf/nstissi_4011.pdf

Negi, Y. (2011). *Pragmatic Overview of Hacking & Its Counter Measures*. Academic Press.

Network. (n.d.). In *The New Lexicon Webster's Encyclopedic Dictionary of the English Language*. New York: Lexicon.

Newsome, J., Song, D., & Perrig, A. (2004). *The Sybil Attack in Sensor Networks : Analysis & Defenses*. Academic Press.

Next Generation Intrusion Detection Systems (IDS). (2010). *McAfee Network Protection Solutions*. Retrieved from http://www.mcafee.com/us/local_content/white_papers/wp_intruvertnextgenerationids.pdf

Ngai, E. C. H., Liu, J., & Lyu, M. R. (2006). *On the Intruder Detection for Sinkhole Attack in Wireless Sensor Networks*. Academic Press.

Ngai, E. C., Liu, J., & Lyu, M. R. (2006). On the intruder detection for sinkhole attack in wireless sensor networks. In *Communications, 2006. ICC'06. IEEE International Conference on*. IEEE.

Ngai, E. C., Liu, J., & Lyu, M. R. (2007). An efficient intruder detection algorithm against sinkhole attacks in wireless sensor networks. *Computer Communications*, *30*(11), 2353–2364. doi:10.1016/j.comcom.2007.04.025

Nguyan, D., Zhao, L., Uisawang, P., & Platt, J. (2000). Security Routing Analysis For Mobile Ad-hoc Networks. Interdisciplinary Telecommunications Program of Colorado University.

Nichols, R. K., & Lekkas, P. C. (2002). Wireless Security: Models, Threats, and Solutions. McGraw-Hill Professional.

Nita-Rotaru, C. (2003). *Cryptography CS 555*. Purdue University-Department of Computer Sciences.

Oldmeadow, J., Ravinutala, S., & Leckie, C. (2004). Adaptive clustering for network intrusion detection. In *Advances in Knowledge Discovery and Data Mining* (pp. 255–259). Springer Berlin Heidelberg. doi:10.1007/978-3-540-24775-3_33

Oliveira, R., Bhargava, B., Azarmi, M., Ferreira, E. W. T., Wang, W., & Lindermann, M. (2009). *Developing Attack Defense Ideas for Ad Hoc Wireless Networks*. Paper presented at the 2nd International Workshop on Dependable Network Computing and Mobile Systems (DNCMS 2009) (in Conjunction with IEEE SRDS 2009), New York, NY.

Organick, E. I. (1972). *The Multics System: An Examination of Its Structure*. Cambridge, MA: MIT Press.

Özdemir, S., Meghdadi, M., & Güler, Ý. (2008). A time and trust based wormhole detection algorithm for wireless sensor networks. In *3rd Information Security and Cryptology Conference (ISC'08)*.

Padmavathi, G. (2009). A Survey of Attacks. *Security Mechanisms and Challenges in Wireless Sensor Networks*, *4*(1), 1–9.

Pandey, A., & Tripathi, R. C. (2010). A survey on wireless sensor networks security. *International Journal of Computers and Applications*, *3*(2), 43–49. doi:10.5120/705-989

Papadimitratos, P., & Haas, Z. J. (2002). Secure Routing for Mobile Ad-hoc Networks. In *Proceedings of the SCS Communication Networks and Distributed Systems Modelling and Simulations Conference (CNDS 2002)*.

Papadimitriou, A., Le Fessant, F., Viana, A. C., & Sengul, C. (2009). Cryptographic protocols to fight sinkhole attacks on tree-based routing in wireless sensor networks. In *Secure Network Protocols, 2009. NPSec 2009. 5th IEEE Workshop on* (pp. 43-48). IEEE. doi:10.1109/NPSEC.2009.5342246

Patel, A. (2015). Network performance without compromising security. *Network Security*, *2015*(1), 9–12. doi:10.1016/S1353-4858(15)70008-5

Patel, K., & Manoranjitham, M. T. (2013). Detection of wormhole attack in wireless sensor network. *International Journal of Engineering Research and Technology, 2(5)*.

Pathan, A. S. K. (Ed.). (2010). Security of self-organizing networks: MANET, WSN, WMN, VANET. CRC Press. doi:10.1201/EBK1439819197

Patrikakis, C., Masikos, M., & Zouraraki, O. (2004). Distributed Denial of Service Attacks. *The Internet Protocol J., 7(4)*, 13–35.

Peltier, T. R. (2001). *Information security risk analysis*. Auerbach Publications.

Perkins, C. E., & Royer, E. M. (1999). Ad Hoc On-Demand Distance Vector Routing.*Proceedings of IEEE Workshop on Mobile Computing Systems and Applications*.

Pescatore, J., & Young, G. (2009). *Defining the next-generation firewall*. Gartner RAS Core Research Note. Retrieved from http://www. ga1tner. com

Petiz, I., Salvador, P., Nogueira, A., & Rocha, E. (2014, September). Detecting DDoS attacks at the source using multi-scaling analysis. In *Telecommunications Network Strategy and Planning Symposium (Networks), 2014 16th International* (pp. 1-5). IEEE. doi:10.1109/NETWKS.2014.6959267

Pirzada, A. A., & McDonald, C. (2005, May). Circumventing sinkholes and wormholes in wireless sensor networks. In *IWWAN'05: Proceedings of International Workshop on Wireless Ad-hoc Networks 71*.

Porras, P. A., & Neumann, P. G. (1997). *EMERALD: Event Monitoring Enabling Responses to Anomalous Live Disturbances*. Retrieved from http://www.sdi.sri.com/projects/emerald-niss97.html

Pradhan, M., Pradhan, S. K., & Sahu, S. K. (2012). Anomaly Detection Using Different Artificial Neural Network Training Functions. *IJCSET, 2(4)*, 1155–1159.

Price, K. (1997). *Intrusion Classification*. COAST Library. Available at http://www.cs.purdue.edu/coast/intrusion-detection

Puccinelli, D., & Haenggi, M. (2005). Wireless sensor networks: Applications and challenges of ubiquitous sensing. *IEEE Circuits and Systems Magazine, 5(3)*, 19–31. doi:10.1109/MCAS.2005.1507522

Rabin, T. (1998). A Simplified Approach to Threshold and Proactive RSA. In *Advances in Cryptology – Crypto 98 Proceedings*(LNCS), (Vol. 1462, pp. 89–104). Springer-Verlag. doi:10.1007/BFb0055722

Rafique, K. (2002). *A Survey of Mobile Ad Hoc Networks*. Available at: http://www.columbia.edu/itc/ee/e6951/2002spring/Projects/CVN/report13.pdf

Raghunandan, G. H., & Lakshmi, B. N. (2011). A comparative analysis of routing techniques for Wireless Sensor Networks. In *Innovations in Emerging Technology (NCOIET), 2011 National Conference on* (pp. 17-22). IEEE. doi:10.1109/NCOIET.2011.5738826

Rahman, A., & Gburzynski, P. (2006). *Hidden Problems with the Hidden Node Problem*. Available at: http://citeseerx.ist.psu.edu/viewdoc/download?doi=10.1.1.61.365&rep=rep1&type=pdf

Raj & Swades. (2009). DPRAODV: A Dynamic Learning System against Blackhole Attack in AODV based MANET. *International Journal of Computer Science Issues, 2*.

Ramaswamy, S., Fu, H., Sreekantaradhya, M., Dixon, J., & Nygard, K. (2003). Prevention of Cooperative Black Hole Attack in Wireless Ad Hoc Networks. In *Proceedings of International Conference on Wireless Networks*.

Rehman. (2010). *Analysis of Black Hole Attack on MANETs Using Different MANET Routing Protocols*. Academic Press.

RFC 2828–Internet Security Glossary from the Internet RFC/STD/FYI/BCP Archives. (n.d.). Accessed online at www.faqs.org/rfcs/rfc2828.html

Richtel, M. (2000). Yahoo Attributes a Lengthy Service Failure to an Attack. *NY Times*. Retrieved from http://www.nytimes.com/library/tech/00/02/biztech/articles/08yahoo.html

Rong, C. M., Eggen, S., & Cheng, H. B. (2011). A novel intrusion detection algorithm for wireless sensor networks. In *Wireless Communication, Vehicular Technology, Information Theory and Aerospace & Electronic Systems Technology (Wireless VITAE), 2011 2nd International Conference on* (pp. 1-7). IEEE. doi:10.1109/WIRELESSVITAE.2011.5940938

Ronghui, H., Guoqing, M., Chunlei, W., & Lan, F. (2009). Detecting and locating wormhole attacks in wireless sensor networks using beacon nodes. World Academy of Science, Engineering and Technology.

Rosen, K. H. (2007). *An Introduction to Cryptography*. London: Taylor & Francis Group, LLC.

Roy, S. D., Singh, S. A., Choudhury, S., & Debnath, N. C. (2008). Countering sinkhole and black hole attacks on sensor networks using dynamic trust management. In *Computers and Communications, 2008. ISCC 2008. IEEE Symposium on* (pp. 537-542). IEEE. doi:10.1109/ISCC.2008.4625768

Royer, E., & Toh, C. (1999). A Review of Current Routing Protocols for Ad Hoc Mobile Wireless Networks. *IEEE Personal Communications*, 6(2), 46–55. doi:10.1109/98.760423

Ryan, J., Lin, M. J., & Miikkulainen, R. (1998). Advances in Neural Information Processing Systems: Vol. 10. *Intrusion Detection with Neural Networks* (pp. 943–949). Cambridge, MA: MIT Press.

Sagheer, A. M. (2012). *Elliptic Curves Cryptographic Techniques*. Ramadi, Iraq: Department of Information System-College of Computer-University of Anbar. doi:10.1109/ICSPCS.2012.6507952

Sah, M. (2001). *Generalized Trial Division*. Ankara: Department of Mathematics, Tandogm.

Salah, I. K., Darwish, A., & Oqeili, S. (2006). Mathematical Attacks on RSA Cryptosystem. *Journal of Computer Science*, 2(8), 665–671. doi:10.3844/jcssp.2006.665.671

Samundiswary, P., Sathian, D., & Dananjayan, P. (2010). Secured greedy perimeter stateless routing for wireless sensor networks. *International Journal of Ad Hoc, Sensor & Ubiquitous Computing*, 1(2).

Sankarasubramaniam, Y., Akan, Ö. B., & Akyildiz, I. F. (2003). ESRT: event-to-sink reliable transport in wireless sensor networks. In *Proceedings of the 4th ACM international symposium on Mobile ad hoc networking & computing* (pp. 177-188). ACM. doi:10.1145/778415.778437

SANS Institute. (n.d.). *Global Information Assurance Certification Paper*. White Paper. SANS Institute.

Sans. (2000). *Egress Filtering v 0.2*. Available at: http://www.sans.org/y2k/egress.htm

Sanzgiri, K., Dahill, B., Levine, B. N., Shields, C., & Royer, E. M. B. (2002). A secure routing protocol for ad hoc networks. In *Network Protocols, 2002. Proceedings. 10th IEEE International Conference on* (pp. 78-87). IEEE. doi:10.1109/ICNP.2002.1181388

Sarasamma, Zhu, & Huff. (2005). Hierarchical Kohonen net for anomaly detection in network security. *IEEE Transactions on Systems, Man and Cybernetics*, 35(2), 302-312.

Sarkar, Basavaraju, & Puttamadappa. (n.d.). *Ad hoc Mobile Wireless Networks Principles, protocols and Applications*. Academic Press.

Sarkar, S., & Maitra, S. (2009). Partial Key Exposure Attacks On Rsa And Its Variant By Guessing A Few Bits Of One Of The Prime Factors. *Bull. Korean Math.*, *46*(4), 721–741. doi:10.4134/BKMS.2009.46.4.721

Sastry, N., Shankar, U., & Wagner, D. (2003). Secure verification of location claims. *Proceedings of the 2nd ACM Workshop*. Retrieved from http://dl.acm.org/citation.cfm?id=941313

Savage, S., Wetherall, D., Karlin, A., & Anderson, T. (2000). *Practical Network Support for IP Traceback*. In the 2000 ACM SIGCOMM Conference, Stockholm, Sweden.

Savari, M., Montazerolzohour, M., & Yeoh Eng, T. (2012). Comparison of ECC and RSA Algorithm in Multipurpose Smart Card Application. *Cyber Warfare and Digital Forensic (CyberSec)*, 49-53.

Schell, R. R., Tao, T. F., & Heckman, M. (1985). Designing the GEMSOS Security Kernel for Security and Performance. In *Proceedings of the 8th National Computer Security Conference* (pp. 108–19). Gaithersburg, MD: National Bureau of Standards.

Schnackenberg, D., Djahandari, K., & Sterne, D. (2000). Infrastructure for Intrusion Detection and Response. In DARPA Information Survivability Conference and Exposition.

Schneier, B., & Mudge. (n.d.). Cryptanalysis of Microsoft's Point-to-Point Tunneling Protocol (PPTP). *Counterpane Systems*.

Schuller, J. (2003). *Understanding Wireless LAN Technology and Its Security Risks*. Available at GIAC: http://www.giac.org/practical/GSEC/Julie_Schuller_GSEC.pdf

Schwingenschlögl, C., & Horn, M.-P. (2002). Building Blocks for Secure Communication in Ad-hoc Networks. In *Proceedings of the 4th European Wireless (EW'02)*.

Seada, K., & Helmy, A. (n.d.). Geographic Services for Wireless Networks. Electrical Engineering Department, *University of Southern California*.

Security Department of Homeland Cyber Security Research and Development. (2007). Department of Homeland Security, Science and Technologies Division.

Security Overview. (n.d.). Retrieved from www.redhat.com/docs/manuals/enterprise/RHEL-4-Manual/security-guide / ch-sgs-ov.html

Security Overview. (n.d.). Retrieved from www.redhat.com/docs/manuals/enterprise/RHEL-4-Manual/security-guide/ ch-sgs-ov.html

Security. (n.d.). In *Merriam-Webster Online*. Accessed 8 February 2007 from www.m-w.com/dictionary/security

Sen, J. (2010). A survey on wireless sensor network security. *International Journal of Communication Networks and Information Security*, *1*(2), 55–78.

Shamir, A., & Someren, N. V. (1998). *Playing hide and seek with stored keys*. Academic Press.

Sharif, L., & Ahmed, M. (2010). The Wormhole Routing Attack in Wireless Sensor Networks (WSN). *Journal of Information Processing Systems*, *6*(2), 177–184. doi:10.3745/JIPS.2010.6.2.177

Sharma, K., & Ghose, M. K. (2010). Wireless sensor networks: An overview on its security threats. *IJCA*, 42-45.

Sharmila, S., & Umamaheswari, G. (2011). Detection of sinkhole attack in wireless sensor networks using message digest algorithms. In *Process Automation, Control and Computing (PACC), 2011 International Conference on* (pp. 1-6). IEEE. doi:10.1109/PACC.2011.5978973

Sheela, D. (2011). A non cryptographic method of sink hole attack detection in wireless sensor networks. *IEEE-International Conference on Recent Trends in Information Technology.*

Sheela, D., Naveen, K. C., & Mahadevan, G. (2011). A non cryptographic method of sink hole attack detection in wireless sensor networks. In *Recent Trends in Information Technology (ICRTIT), 2011 International Conference on* (pp. 527-532). IEEE. doi:10.1109/ICRTIT.2011.5972397

Shema, M. (2012). *Hacking web apps: detecting and preventing web application security problems.* Newnes.

Shoup, V. (2000). Practical Threshold Signatures. In *Advances in Cryptology-Eurocrypt 2000 proceedings (LNCS),* (Vol. 1807, pp. 207–221). Springer Verlag. doi:10.1007/3-540-45539-6_15

Shue, C. A. (2007). *IPSec: Performance Analysis and Enhancements.* IEEE.

Shu-Jun, L., Cun-Hu, Z., You-Song, Y., & Jia, X-M. (2011). Design research on the temperature sensor in hot iron based on ANSYS emulation. *Mechanic Automation and Control Engineering (MACE), 2011 Second International Conference on.*

Simmonds, A., Sandilands, P., & van Ekert, L. (2004). An Ontology for Network Security Attacks. Lecture Notes in Computer Science, 3285, 317–323. Doi:10.1007/978-3-540-30176-9_41

Simmonds, A., Sandilands, P., & Van Ekert, L. (2004). An ontology for network security attacks. In *Applied Computing* (pp. 317–323). Springer Berlin Heidelberg.

Singh, V. P., Jain, S., & Singhai, J. (2010). *Hello Flood Attack and its Countermeasures in Wireless Sensor Networks.* Academic Press.

Singh, G., & Singh, J. (2013). Prevention of Blackhole Attack in Wireless Sensor Network using IPSec Protocol. *International Journal of Advanced Research in Computer Science, 4*(11), 45–49.

Singh, S., & Verma, H. K. (2011). Security for Wireless Sensor Network. *International Journal on Computer Science and Engineering, 3*(6), 2393–2399.

Snyder, J. (2012). Next-gen firewalls: Off to a good start. *Network World.* Retrieved from http://www.networkworld.com/article/2187980/network-security/next-gen-firewalls--off-to-a-good-start.html

Sonal. (2013). Black hole Attack Detection using Fuzzy Logic. *International Journal of Science and Research, 2*(8).

Song, M., & Hsieh, G. (2010). Intrusion detection of sinkhole attacks in large-scale wireless sensor networks. *2010 IEEE International Conference on Wireless Communications, Networking and Information Security.* doi:10.1109/WCINS.2010.5541872

Soni, V., Modi, P., & Chaudhri, V. (2013). *Detecting Sinkhole Attack in Wireless Sensor Network.* Academic Press.

Spafford, E. (1988). *The Internet Worm Program: An Analysis. Technical report.* Department of Computer Sciences, Purdue University.

Spatscheck, O., & Peterson, L. L. (1999). Defending against denial of service attacks in Scout. In OSDI.

Spitzner, L. (2003). *Honeypots: tracking hackers* (Vol. 1). Reading: Addison-Wesley.

Stajano, F., & Anderson, R. (1999). The Resurrecting Duckling: Security Issues for Ad-Hoc Wireless networks. In *Proceedings of the 7th International Workshop on Security Protocols.*

Stallings, W. (2005). *Cryptography and Network Security Principles and Practices.* Prentice Hall.

Stoecklin, M. (2006). Anomaly detection by finding feature distribution outliers. In *Proceedings of the 2006 ACM CoNEXT conference* (p. 32). ACM. doi:10.1145/1368436.1368476

Stoica, I., Adkins, D., Zhuang, S., Shenker, S., & Surana, S. (2002). *Internet Indirection Infrastructure*. In ACM SIGCOMM Conference, Pittsburgh, PA.

Stroppa, N. (2006-2007). *Algorithms & Complexity-Space Complexity*. Dublin, Ireland: Dublin City University.

Stubblefield, A., Ioannidis, J., & Rubin, A. D. (2002). *Using the Fluhrer, Mantin, and Shamir attack to break WEP*. In Symposium on Network and Distributed System Security. Available at http://www.isoc.org/isoc/conferences/ndss/02/proceedings/papers/stubbl.pdf

Su, M. Y. (2011). Real-time anomaly detection systems for Denial-of-Service attacks by weighted k-nearest-neighbor classifiers. *Expert Systems with Applications, 38*(4), 3492–3498. doi:10.1016/j.eswa.2010.08.137

Sun, H., Chen, C., & Hsiao, Y. (2007). An efficient countermeasure to the selective forwarding attack in wireless sensor networks. *TENCON 2007 - 2007 IEEE Region 10 Conference*. doi:10.1109/TENCON.2007.4428866

Sundaram, A. (1996). *An Introduction to Intrusion Detection*. ACM. Available from http://www.acm.org/crossroads/xrds2-4/intrus.html

Symantec. (2003a). *Symantec Internet Security Threat Report Volume III*. Retrieved from http://enterprisesecurity.symantec.com/content.cfm?articleid=1539&EID=0%

Symantec. (2003b). *Symantec Internet Security Threat Report Volume IV*. Retrieved from http://enterprisesecurity.symantec.com/content.cfm?articleid=1539&EID=0%

Tamilselvan & Sankaranarayanan. (2007). *Prevention of Blackhole Attack in MANET*. The 2nd International Conference on Wireless Broadband and Ultra Wideband Communications (AusWireless).

Tangpong, Kesidis, Yuan, & Hurson. (2007). *Robust Sybil Detection for MANETs*. IEEE.

Teng, L., & Zhang, Y. (2010). SeRA: a secure routing algorithm against sinkhole attacks for mobile wireless sensor networks. In *Computer Modeling and Simulation, 2010. ICCMS'10. Second International Conference on*. IEEE. doi:10.1109/ICCMS.2010.95

Thangadurai, K., & Anchugam, C. V. (2013). *Survey of routing Protocols in Mobile Ad hoc Network. ICIESMS*. Enathi, Madurai: Vickram Engineering College.

Thomason, S. (2012). Improving Network Security: Next Generation Firewalls and Advanced Packet Inspection Devices. *Global Journal of Computer Science and Technology, 12*(13).

Thuente, D., & Acharya, M. (2006). Intelligent jamming in wireless networks with applications to 802.11b and other networks. In *Proceedings of the 25th IEEE Communications Society Military Communications Conference (MILCOM)*.

Torgerson, M. & Leeuwen, B.V. (2001). *Routing Data in Wireless Ad-hoc Networks*. Sandia laboratories report SAND2001-3119 October 2001.

Treytl, A. (2010). *Securing IEEE 1588 by IPsec tunnels - An analysis*. IEEE. doi:10.1109/ISPCS.2010.5609765

Tumrongwittayapak, C., & Varakulsiripunth, R. (2009). Detecting sinkhole attack and selective forwarding attack in wireless sensor networks. In *Information, Communications and Signal Processing, 2009. ICICS 2009. 7th International Conference on* (pp. 1-5). IEEE. doi:10.1109/ICICS.2009.5397594

Tumrongwittayapak, C., & Varakulsiripunth, R. (2009). Detecting Sinkhole attacks in wireless sensor networks. *ICCAS-SICE, 2009*. Retrieved from http://ieeexplore.ieee.org/xpls/abs_all.jsp?arnumber=5334764

Tumrongwittayapak, C., & Varakulsiripunth, R. (2009). Detecting Sinkhole attacks in wireless sensor networks. In ICCAS-SICE, 2009 (pp. 1966-1971). IEEE.

Ulanoff, L. (2010, November). Computer Trouble Isn`t Always What You Think It Is. *PC Magazine*.

Vaithiyanathan, G. S. R., Edna, E. N., & Radha, S. (2010). *A Novel method for Detection and Elimination of Modification Attack and TTL attack in NTP based routing algorithm*. 2010 International Conference on Recent Trends in Information, Telecommunication and Computing. doi:10.1109/ITC.2010.23

Valencia, A., Littlewood, M., & Kolar, T. (1998, May). *Cisco Layer Two Forwarding (Protocol) "L2F"*. Cisco Systems.

Vanguard Managed Solutions. (n.d.). *Vanguard Applications Ware Basic Protocols, Serial Line IP*. Author.

Venkatraman, L., & Agrawal, D. P. (2001). An Optimized Inter-Router Authentication Scheme for Ad-hoc networks. In *Proceedings of the 13th International Conference on Wireless Communications*.

Vigna, G., Gwalani, S., Srinivasan, K., Elizabeth, M., Royer, B., & Kemmerer, R. (2004). An Intrusion Detection Tool for AODV-based Ad hoc Wireless Networks. In *Proceedings of 20th Annual Computer Security Applications Conference (ACSAC'04)*. IEEE Computer Society.

Wan, C. Y., Campbell, A. T., & Krishnamurthy, L. (2002). PSFQ: a reliable transport protocol for wireless sensor networks. In *Proceedings of the 1st ACM international workshop on Wireless sensor networks and applications* (pp. 1-11). ACM. doi:10.1145/570738.570740

Wang, X., Feng, D., Lai, X. & H. Yu (2004). *Collisions for Hash Functions MD4, MD5, HAVAL-128 and RIPEMD*. Cryptology ePrint Archive.

Weaver, N., Paxson, V., Staniford, S., & Cunningham, R. (2003). *A taxonomy of Computer Worms.First Workshop on Rapid Malcode (WORM)*.

Web ProForum Tutorials. (n.d.). *Intelligent Network*. Paper presented at the International Engineering Consortium.

Wei, Lan, Xiao, Han, & Tsai. (2011). Optical fiber sensors for high temperature harsh environment sensing. *Instrumentation and Measurement Technology Conference (I2MTC)*. IEEE.

Weimerskirch, A., & Thonet, G. (2001). A Distributed Lightweight Authentication Model for Ad-hoc Networks. In *Proceedings of the 4th International Conference on Information Security and Cryptology* (ICICS 2001).

Welschenbach, M. (2005). *Cryptography in C and C++*. Grace Wong.

Whitmore, J., Bensoussan, A., Green, P., Hunt, D., Kobziar, A., & Stern, J. (1973). Design for Multics Security Enhancements. ESD-TR-74-176. Hanscom AFB, MA: Air Force Electronic Systems Division.

Wilson, J. (2005). *Sensor Technology – Handbook*. Academic Press.

Wood, A. D., & Stankovic, J. A. (2002). Denial of Service in Sensor Networks. *Computer*, *35*(10), 54–62. doi:10.1109/MC.2002.1039518

Wu, S-Y. & Yen, E. (2009). Data mining-based intrusion detectors. *Expert Systems with Application, 36*, 5605-5612.

Xerox Palo Alto Research Center. (2003). *Parc history*. Retrieved from http://www.parc.xerox.com/about/history/default.html

Xiang, C., Yong, P. C., & Meng, L. S. (2008). Design of multiple-level hybrid classifier for intrusion detection system using Bayesian clustering and decision trees. *Journal of Pattern Recognition Letters, 29*(7), 918–924. doi:10.1016/j.patrec.2008.01.008

Xiaopeng & Wei. (2007). *A Novel Gray Hole Attack Detection Scheme for Mobile Ad-Hoc Networks.* 2007 IFIP International Conference on Network and Parallel Computing – Workshops.

Xin, Jinqiang, Junjie, Qinghaa, & Chongzhao. (2007). Article. *Journal of Electronics, 24*(3), 369-373.

Xin-sheng, W., Yong-zhao, Z., Shu-ming, X., & Liang-min, W. (2009). Lightweight defense scheme against selective forwarding attacks in wireless sensor networks.*2009 International Conference on Cyber-Enabled Distributed Computing and Knowledge Discovery.* doi:10.1109/CYBERC.2009.5342206

Xu, W., Trappe, W., Zhang, Y., & Wood, T. (2005). The feasibility of launching and detecting jamming attacks in wireless networks. In *Proceedings of the 6th ACM international symposium on Mobile ad hoc networking and computing.*

Xu, W., Wade, T., Yanyong, Z., & Timothy, W. (2005). The Feasibility of Launching and Detecting Jamming Attacks in Wireless Networks. In *Proceedings of 6th ACM International Symposium on Mobile Ad Hoc Networking and Computing 2005.* Urbana-Champaign, IL: ACM Press.

Xu, Y., Chen, G., Ford, J., & Makedon, F. (2008). Detecting wormhole attacks in wireless sensor networks. In Critical infrastructure protection (pp. 267-279). Springer US.

Yaar, A., Perrig, A., & Song, D. (2003). Pi: A path identification mechanism to defend against DDoS attacks. In *Security and Privacy, 2003. Proceedings. 2003 Symposium on* (pp. 93-107). IEEE. doi:10.1109/SECPRI.2003.1199330

Yaar, A., Perrig, A., & Song, D. (2004). SIFF: A Stateless Internet Flow Filter to Mitigate DDoS Flooding Attacks. In *Proceedings of the IEEE Security and Privacy Symposium.* Philadelphia, PA: ACM Press. doi:10.1109/SECPRI.2004.1301320

Yau, S. S., Wang, Y., & Karim, F. (2002). Development of Situation-Aware Application Software for Ubiquitous Computing Environment. In *Proceedings of 26th International Computer Software and Applications Conference on Prolonging Software Life: Development and Redevelopment.* IEEE Computer Society. doi:10.1109/CMPSAC.2002.1044557

Yi, P., Dai, Z., Zhong, Y., & Zhang, S. (2005). Resisting Flooding Attacks in Ad Hoc Networks. In *Proceedings of the International Conference on Information Technology: Coding and Computing* (ITCC'05).

Yocom, B., Brown, K., & Van Der Veer, D. (2001). Review: Intrusion-Detection Products Grow Up. *Network World.* Retrieved 27 May 2002 from http://www.nwfusion.com/reviews/2001/1008rev.html

Young, B. (n.d.). *Foundations of Computer Security-Symmetric vs. Asymmetric Encryption. Department of Computer Sciences, University of Texas.*

Yu, B. (2006). Detecting selective forwarding attacks in wireless sensor networks.*Proceedings 20th IEEE International Parallel & Distributed Processing Symposium.* doi:10.1109/IPDPS.2006.1639675

Yu, B., & Xiao, B. (2006). Detecting selective forwarding attacks in wireless sensor networks. In *Parallel and Distributed Processing Symposium, 2006. IPDPS 2006. 20th International.* IEEE.

Zaroo. (2003). *A Survey of DDoS attacks and some DDoS defense mechanisms.* Advanced Information Assurance (CS 626).

Zhang, Y., & Lee, W. (2000). Intrusion detection in wireless ad-hoc networks. In *Proceedings of the 6th Annual International Conference on Mobile Computing and Networking.*

Zhang, Y., Chen, G., Weng, W., & Wang, Z. (2010, June). An overview of wireless intrusion prevention systems. In *Communication Systems, Networks and Applications (ICCSNA), 2010 Second International Conference on* (Vol. 1, pp. 147-150). IEEE.

Zhang, J., & Zulkernine, M. (2006). Anomaly Based Network Intrusion Detection with Unsupervised Outlier Detection. In *Proc. IEEE Communication Society*. doi:10.1109/ICC.2006.255127

Zhong, R., & Yue, G. (2010). DDoS detection system based on data mining. In *Proceedings of the Second International Symposium on Networking and Network Security*.

Zhou, L., & Haas, Z. J. (1999, November/December). *Securing Ad-hoc Networks. IEEE Networks,* 24–30.

Zhou, L., Schneider, F. B., & Renesse, R. V. (2002). COCA: A Secure Distributed On-line Certification Authority. *ACM Transactions on Computer Systems, 20*(4), 329–368. doi:10.1145/571637.571638

Znaidi, , & Minier, . (2008). An Ontology for Attacks in Wireless Sensor Networks. *Society of General Physiologists Series, 32*, 1–13.

About the Contributors

Dileep Kumar G was born at 1982, in India. He has got B.Tech in Computer Science & Engineering and M.Tech in Software Engineering degrees from Jawaharlal Nehru Technology University, Hyderabad, India, in 2000 and in 2009. He is pursuing PhD degree in Computer Science from Jawaharlal Nehru Technology University, Hyderabad, India. Currently he is an Assistant Professor in the Department of Computing, Adama Science and Technology University, Adama, Ethiopia. He has authored more than 20 publications in international journals, books chapters, and refereed international conference proceedings. He has also authored the book Data structures Through C++(ISBN: 978-81-8487-488-4, Narosa Publications,2015). His research interests include Network Security, Data Mining, Mobile Adhoc Networks, Grid Computing and Big Data. He is a Member of ACM and Life Member of ISTE and Senior Member of IEEE.

Manoj Kumar Singh is an Assistant Professor at the Department of Computing, School of Engineering, Adama Science & Technology, Adama, Ethiopia. His research areas are network security, data mining, data science, human-computer interaction, computing education, and software engineering. His research specifically focuses on software defects and how people and society discover, diagnose, repair and recover from them, spanning everyone from the people use software to the people who develop it. Dr. Manoj Kumar Singh holds an M.Tech. and a Ph.D. in Computer Science & Engineering from India. He is the author of over 6 books, 52 peer-reviewed publications, and 8 receiving best paper awards.

M. K. Jayanthi is working as University Professor in Dept. of Computer Science in King Khalid University, Abha, Kingdom of Saudi Arabia and Quality Coordinator for both the Departments (CS & IS) – NCAAA – ABET Accreditation Process from Accreditation Board for Engineering and Technology (ABET), USA. She did B.E.,(Computer Science and Engineering) in Adhiyamaan College of Engineering, Hosur, M.E.,(Computer Science and Engineering) from Anna University, Chennai, M.S.,(Software Systems) from Birla Institute of Technology and Science, BITS, Pilani, Rajasthan, Ph.D., in Computer Science and Engineering, form SCSVMV University, Kancheepuram and M.B.A.,(Operations Management) from IGNOU., M.Phil. (Computer Science) from Madurai Kamaraj University & PGDPMIR., from Annamalai University. She has 18 years Teaching Experience in Computer Science and Engineering Dept. in University level and guiding research scholars at Doctoral Level. Produced 2 Ph.D., Doctorates in Computer Science and Information Technology under her Guidance. She Received VIT Research Award 2012-13 for Publishing 5 papers during the year 2012 in Scopus Indexed Research Journals. She guided 4 M.Phil., & 5 M.S., students. I have published more than 32 high quality research papers in refereed International Journals like World Scientific, IEEE Explore, and World Applied Sciences. She is

JNTU - Annathapur ratified Principal of Engineering College and JNTU – Hyderabad ratified Professor of Computer Science and Engineering. She has Submitted an R&D PROJECT PROPOSAL Titled " e-Learning System Design using Mobile Agent based Learning Objects" to Ministry of Communications & Information Technology, Department of Information Technology.

* * *

C. V. Anchugam is presently doing Ph.D in P.G. and Research Department of Computer Science, at Government Arts College (Autonomous), Karur, Tamil Nadu, India. She has received her B.Sc (Computer Science) degree from Sri Saradha College of Arts and Science, Karur, TamilNadu, India in 2002. She has received her MCA degree from M.Kumarasamy College of Engineering, Karur, TamilNadu, India in 2005.She has published number of papers in esteemed National/International Conferences and Journals. Her interests are in Cryptography, Network security and Ad hoc networks.

Mamta Bachani is a Graduate of Computer Science Department MUET, Jamshoro, and Lecturer (Visiting) Szabist Hyderabad.

Mohammad Jabed Morshed Chowdhury is currently working as a Senior Lecturer at Daffodil International University, Bangladesh. He earned his double Master's in Security and Mobile Computing from Norwegian University of Science and Technology (NTNU) and University of Tartu, Estonia. He has worked with different security related issues which include security modeling languages, cryptography and security in real time system. Previously, he served as e-Service Programmer in United Nations Development Programme which was hosted in Prime Minister's Office of Bangladesh Government. His research interest includes network security, privacy and trust in web application. He is the author of several conference paper which has been published from IEEE, Springer sponsored conferences in Europe and Asia.

Marwan Yassin Ghafour is a computer engineer. He completed his BSc a Koya University. After that he completed his master in European University of Lefke. He did his thesis on security by solving SSL problem to make HTTPS more secure. He is a lecturer at Sulaimania Polytechnic University Kurdistan Region, Iraq.

George W. Kibirige was born in Tanzania. He received B.Sc. of Information Communication and Technology Management from Mzumbe University and M.Sc. of Computer Science (Information Security) from University of Technology Malaysia in 2007 and 2012 respectively. He joined Africa Online LTD Dar es Salaam at 2007; he was working as Services Delivery Engineer up to July 2008. In August 2008 he was employed by Sokoine University of Agriculture. He has been working as Assistant Lecturer at the Faculty of Science, Department of Informatics at Solomon Mahlangu Campus. His main areas of research interest are Information Security and application of ICT. Also, Mr. George is a member of EC-Council since 2011(CEH with ID ECC956297).

Ahsan Memon is a graduate of Telecommunication Engineering from Mehran University of Engineering & Technology, Jamshoro and now working as a faculty member at SZABIST Hyderabad. He has participated actively in research regarding Wireless Sensor Networks whilst in Pakistan and during his time at Wroclaw University of Technology, Poland. He has also conducted research in the field of Antenna Design during his undergraduate in Mehran University. He has an international publication, a book chapter and is currently working on research that aims to conjunct augmented reality and wireless sensor networks. He is also one of the founding members of DEWSNeT: Dependable Wireless Sensor Networks, a research group established to commercialize and advance Wireless Sensor Networks for personal and industrial use.

P. Natesan has completed his M.E (Computer Science & Engineering) in Anna University, Tamilnadu, India in 2005 and Ph.D in the year 2013 in Anna University . Currently, he is working as Associate Professor in the Department of Computer Science & Engineering, Kongu Engineering College, Tamil Nadu, India. He has completed 18 years of teaching service. He has published 10 articles in International / National journals.

Chinmaya Kumar Nayak is an Assistant Professor in the Department of Computer Science & Engineering, Gandhi Institute for Technological Advancement (GITA), Bhubaneswar, Odisha, India. He is an author of the book "Data Structure Using C". He published many papers in national seminars and international journals. His research area includes image processing, adhoc networks, etc.

Bijaya Kumar Panda is an Assistant Professor in the Department of Computer Science & Engineering, Gandhi Institute for Technological Advancement (GITA), Bhubaneswar, Odisha, India. He is having 13 years of teaching experiences and currently persuing Ph.D in computer science in S'O'A University. He has published many papers in national seminars and international journals. His research areas include Computer security, Soft computing and IDS.

Manoranjan Pradhan holds a Ph.D degree in Computer Science from Sambalpur University. He obtained his M.Tech in Computer Science from Utkal University in 2004, MCA from Utkal University in 1999 and M.Sc from Berhampur University in 1996. He is having 14 years of teaching and research experience. He is presently working as Professor and Head, department of CSE, Gandhi Institute for technological advancement (GITA), Bhubaneswar, Odisha, India. He is a member of CSI(I), ISTE(I) and OIS(I). He has published about 15 papers in International and national journals and conferences. He has also published 2 books to his credit. He is a program committee member of various international conferences. He is acting as a member of various international journals. His active area of research includes Computer Security, Intrusion Detection System, Computational Intelligence, Mobile Adhoc Network, Cloud Computing, Social Networks, etc.

Sateesh Kumar Pradhan obtained his Ph.D. Degree in Computer Science from Berhampur University, India during the year 1999. He joined Berhampur University, as Lecturer in the year 1987 and promoted to Reader in 1999. He was Head, Post Graduate Department of Computer Science, Utkal University, India during 2001-2003. He was the Organizing Chair of the International Conference on Information Technology-2005. He served as a senior faculty in the Computer Engineering Department of King Khalid University, Ministry of Higher Education, Saudi Arab from September 2006 to July 2011. At present he is the Head, Post Graduate Department of Computer Science, Utkal University, Bhubaneswar, India. His research interest includes Neural Computing, Computer Architecture, Adhoc Networks, Computer Forensic.

Behnam Rahnama received PhD (2009) and MSc (2005) in Computer Engineering at Eastern Mediterranean University and his BSc degree - in Computer Software Engineering - (2003) at Shiraz Azad University of Iran. He has published various papers, book chapters and couple of books in the fields of Intelligent Systems, Robotics, Semantic Web Services, Data Structure, and Security (more than 55 publications). His research interests include Distributed Collaborative Autonomous Semantic Robotic Systems, Semantic Reasoning, and Semantic Intelligence, Efficient Hierarchical Schemas for RDBMS, Security and Cryptography, Embedded OS/Hardware for Robotics and partially solving and parallelization of ultra dense linear matrices on GPGPU based supercomputers. He is reviewer of many international journals and refereed conferences in addition to co-chairing COMPSAC-MEDIS, SINCONF, IJRCS, and biannual EEECS symposiums.

Camilius A. Sanga is Associate Professor of Informatics at the Department of Informatics, Sokoine University of Agriculture, Tanzania. Currently, he is head of the Department of Informatics. He holds BSc in Computer Science from University of Dar es Salaam and MSc. Computer Science from Osmania University, India. Also, he has PhD in Computer Science from the University of the Western Cape, South Africa. His research interest is in the area of Information and Communication Technology for Development (ICT4D). He has published papers in proceedings of International conferences in ICT. He has also published journal papers in many peer reviewed International Journals (http://scholar.google.com/citations?user=vuJQthUAAAAJ&hl=en). Furthermore, he has co-authored two books as well as co-authored book chapters in the following books: Information and Communication Technology: Changing Education published by ICFAI University Press (India) and Technology-Mediated Open and Distance Education for Agricultural Education and Improved Livelihood in Sub-Saharan Africa published by Commonwealth of Learning (Canada). In addition, he had co-authored a book chapter in the book titled, "Technology Development and Platform Enhancements for Successful Global E-Government Design" published by IGI-Global (USA).

Arif Sari is a full time Assistant Professor of the department of Management Information Systems at the Girne American University, North Cyprus. He received his BS degree - in Computer Information Systems and MBA degree - (2008 and 2010) at European University of Lefke, and Ph.D. degree (2013) in Management Information Systems at The Girne American University. He has been granted as Visiting Scholar of Sapienza University of Rome in Italy (2012). He is an IEEE, ACM, and IEICE Member since Sept. 2012 and has published various papers, book chapters, participated in variety of conferences in the fields of Network Security, Network Simulation, Computer Applications, Mobile Networks, Information Communication Technologies, Mobile Network Security and Mobile Security Systems.

Faisal K. Shaikh is currently doing post doctorate at University of Umm Al-Qura, Makkah, Kingdom of Saudi Arabia. He did his PhD from TU Darmstadt, Germany and working as Associate Professor at Mehran University of Engineering and Technology, Pakistan. He served as Technical Program Committee (TPC) chair and TPC member for several National and International conferences. His research interests include dependable WSNs, MANETs, VANETs, and WBANs.

Alok Kumar Vishwakarma is an Software Engineer by profession, an Artist & Photographer by hobby with Rich Experience in broad spectrum of areas in IT (Research & Development), Software Development, Project Operations and Client Support and currently working as Software Engineer at Sysbiz

Technologies Pvt.Ltd, Chennai (A subsidiary of BPI Technologies, USA). He Worked on multiple skills ranging from Java/J2EE,Struts,Spring,Hibernate,Liferay,Vaadin,Cloud,Networking,Weblogic Server Administration, Jboss Server Configuration and Security Implementation etc. As a whole involved with GTN (Gross to Net), Revenue Recognition (R2) and Revenue Management (RM) Product Development for world's top Life-sciences & Pharmaceutical Companies listed in fortune 500. He Published 10 Research papers during his UG, both International & National in various reputed journals such as IEEE, IJCA in the field of Cloud Computing, Distributed Systems and Computer Networks. He is Associate Member of UACEE (Universal Association of Computer and Electronics Engineers) and also the member of IEEE, IACSIT, IEEE Communication Society and Intel's Software Network. He delivered various oral presentations at IEEE International Conferences & Guest Lectures at various Engineering colleges. He also been Reviewer and Technical Program Committee Member at various National Symposiums/Conferences and International Symposiums/Conferences. His Research area includes Cloud Computing, Distributed Systems & Computer Networks.

Wafa Waheeda Syed is a Research Assistant & Graduate Student in Computer Science at Qatar University. She is also a Computer Science Engineer, Developer and a Tech Enthusiast with love for Data. Her areas of interest are Data Science, Social Computing, Data Analysis and Visualization and is actively looking for research opportunities, to work on projects. Wafa has been associated with organizations like Qatar Computing Research Institute and Almana Networks for internship and freelance work. She is a member and volunteer of communities like IEEE, Women In Engineering and ArabWIC.

Index

Become an IRMA Member

Members of the **Information Resources Management Association (IRMA)** understand the importance of community within their field of study. The Information Resources Management Association is an ideal venue through which professionals, students, and academicians can convene and share the latest industry innovations and scholarly research that is changing the field of information science and technology. Become a member today and enjoy the benefits of membership as well as the opportunity to collaborate and network with fellow experts in the field.

IRMA Membership Benefits:

- **One FREE Journal Subscription**

- **30% Off Additional Journal Subscriptions**

- **20% Off Book Purchases**

- Updates on the latest events and research on Information Resources Management through the IRMA-L listserv.

- Updates on new open access and downloadable content added to Research IRM.

- A copy of the Information Technology Management Newsletter twice a year.

- A certificate of membership.

IRMA Membership $195

Scan code to visit irma-international.org and begin by selecting your free journal subscription.

Membership is good for one full year.